New England
Gardener's Guide

Published by Cool Springs Press, a Division of Thomas Nelson, Inc., P.O. Box 141000, Nashville, Tennessee 37214.

Hériteau, Jacqueline.
    New England gardener's guide / Jacqueline Hériteau and Holly Hunter Stonehill.
        p. cm.
    Includes bibliographical references and index.
    ISBN 1-930604-49-1 (pbk. : alk. paper)
    1. Landscape plants—New England. 2. Landscape gardening—New England.
    I. Stonehill, Holly Hunter. II. Title.
SB407 .H4932 2003
635.9'0974--dc21

                                        2002151414

First Printing 2003
Printed in the United States of America
10 9 8 7 6 5 4 3 2

Managing Editor: Jenny Andrews
Horticulture Editor: Michael Wenzel
Copyeditor: Julie Pinkerton
Cover Design: Sheri Ferguson
Production Artist: S.E. Anderson

On the cover: 'Connecticut King' Asiatic Lily, photographed by Thomas Eltzroth

Visit the Thomas Nelson website at www.ThomasNelson.com

New England
Gardener's Guide

Jacqueline Hériteau
Holly Hunter Stonehill

COOL
SPRINGS
PRESS

Nashville, Tennessee
A Division of Thomas Nelson, Inc.
www.ThomasNelson.com

Dedication

With thanks to Grandpere Marcel Hériteau who taught our family to love food and gardens, this is for our children and grandchildren whose enthusiasm for our family projects gives us so much joy...William Ian and Alexa Littledale, Marcel, Colton, and Kristen Stonehill, and the weensies, MacKenzie Rose and Cameron Sutherland Hunter.

—Jacqueline Hériteau and Holly Hunter Stonehill

Acknowledgments

We believe that the right plant in the right place makes a garden beautiful and a lazy gardener (us) happy. By the "right plant" we mean one that has lasting beauty, high resistance to pests and diseases, and which will thrive in our climate. So, making plant choices was the most important and difficult aspect of this work. For major help with plant choices and for a garden philosophy we believe in, we are very indebted to friend and sometime co-author, André Viette. Second generation nurseryman, graduate of the Floriculture School of Cornell University, New York, instructor in horticulture, distinguished lecturer, noted breeder of daylilies, and Past President of the Perennial Plant Association of America, André's outstanding contribution to horticulture has won him many honors, including the 2001 PPA Award of Merit and the 1999 Garden Club of America Medal of Honor.

For additional help with our plant lists we thank Connie Waller, Nina Daniels, Emma Lou Craig, Sarah Adams, and we are very, very grateful to the following outstanding New England horticulturists and gardeners:

Pierre Bennerup
Comstock, Ferre and Co.
263 Main Street
Wethersfield, CT 06109
Phone: 860-571-6590

Lynette Courtney
New Leaf Designs
P.O. Box 66
Greensboro Bend, VT 05842

Chris Donnelly
Connecticut Department of
    Environmental Protection
Division of Forestry
79 Elm Street
Hartford, CT 06106-5127

Donna Fuss
Consulting Rosarian for the
    American Rose Society
10 Hampton Lane
Bloomfield, CT 06002

Nancy Hulett, Coordinator
Vermont Master Gardener
    Program
University of Vermont
South Burlington Extension
655 Spear Street
Burlington, VT 05405-0107
Master Gardener Helpline
Phone: 800-639-2230;
802-656-5421

Judith Irven
Outdoor Spaces Landscape
    Designs
423 Goshen Ripton Road
Goshen, VT 05733

Judy Murphy
Old Farm Nursery
158 Lime Rock Road
Lakeville, CT 06039
Phone: 860-435-2272

Marijke Niles
1299 Robert Young Road
South Starksboro, VT
05487-7156

Lois Berg Stack, Extension
    Specialist,
Ornamental Horticulture
University of Maine Cooperative
    Extension
495 College Avenue
Orono, ME 04473

Carol Schminke
Down to Earth Gardens
432 Sprout Brook Road
Garrison, New York 10524
Phone: 845-737-0061
downtoearthgrdns@aol.com

Rosanne Sherry, Coordinator
Cooperative Extension Master
    Gardeners
CE Education Center
3 East Alumni Avenue
Kingston, RI 02881-0804

Leslie Van Berkum
Van Berkum Nurseries
4 James Road
Deerfield NH 03037
603-462-7663

Table of Contents

Featured Plants *for New England*

Annuals

Ageratum, 26
Bedding Begonia, 27
Celosia, 28
Coleus, 29
Cosmos, 30
Edging Lobelia, 31
Foxglove, 32
Geranium, 33
Impatiens, 34
Marigold, 35
Nasturtium, 36
Pansy, 37
Petunia, 38
Pot Marigold, 39
Salvia, 40
Snapdragon, 41
Spider Flower, 42
Sunflower, 43
Sweet Alyssum, 44
Zinnia, 45

Bulbs, Corms, and Tubers

Bearded Iris, 50
Crocosmia, 51
Crocus, 52
Daffodil, 53
Dahlia, 54
Fancy-Leaved Caladium, 55
Flowering Onion, 56
Gladiola, 57
Grape Hyacinth, 58
Hyacinth, 59
Lily, 60
Tulip, 61

Conifers

Arborvitae, 64
Blue Atlas Cedar, 65
Canadian Hemlock, 66
Colorado Blue Spruce, 67
Douglas Fir, 68
Dwarf Hinoki Cypress, 69
Eastern White Pine, 70
Juniper, 71
Leyland Cypress, 72
Umbrella Pine, 73
White Fir, 74
Yew, 75

Ground Covers

Barrenwort, 78
Bearberry, 79
Blue Lily-Turf, 80
Bugleweed, 81
Christmas Fern, 82
Creeping Juniper, 83
Dead Nettle, 84
English Ivy, 85
Foamflower, 86
Golden Moneywort, 87
Japanese Painted Fern, 88
Japanese Spurge, 89
Leadwort, 90
Lenten Rose, 91
Lily-of-the-Valley, 92
Periwinkle, 93

Herbs

Basil, 96
Chives, 97
Dill, 98
Italian Oregano, 99
Lavender, 100
Mint, 101
Parsley, 102
Rosemary, 103
Sage, 104
Tarragon, 105
Thyme, 106
Winter Savory, 107

Ornamental Grasses

American Beach Grass, 110
Blue Fescue, 111
Blue Oat Grass, 112
Chinese Silver Grass, 113
Feather Reed Grass, 114
Northern Sea Oats, 115
Switch Grass, 116
Tufted Hair Grass, 117

Perennials

Aster, 122
Astilbe, 123
Bellflower, 124
Bleeding Heart, 125
Blue False Indigo, 126
Catmint, 127
Chrysanthemum, 128
Columbine, 129
Coneflower, 130
Coral Bells, 131
Daylily, 132
Globe Thistle, 133
Hosta, 134
Japanese Anemone, 135
Lady's Mantle, 136
Lamb's Ears, 137
Marsh Rose Mallow, 138
Monarda, 139
Oriental Poppy, 140
Peony, 141
Phlox, 142
Pinks, 143
Purple Coneflower, 144
Russian Sage, 145
Salvia 'May Night', 146
Scabiosa, 147

Gardening
in New England

Our very first real garden was in Vermont, close to Montpelier. That's not far from the Canadian border, Zone 3. In winter the fields were knee-deep in snow and temperatures now and then went to 30 below zero. As far as knowing anything about gardens or plants, we were "buck naked" at the time. So when the bulblike things we had transplanted from the previous owner's garden sent up single stems topped with clusters of small dainty white flowers with an unforgettable perfume, we decided they were tuberoses—it was the only heavily perfumed bulb flower we knew by name. Our gardening friends laughed, of course. They knew what we didn't—that tuberoses, *Polianthes tuberosa*, came originally from Mexico, and no way could they winter in the ground north of Zone 8 or 9. Someone suggested our perfumed posies must be narcissus, the very perfumed Poetaz or Polyanthus types. A fine suggestion—except those can't survive Zone 3 winters either, nothing north of Zone 5.

Yes, well, whether or not they could, one or the other did make it in our garden in hilly northern Vermont. The moral of this story is, the weather that governs our gardens, is, like much else in New England, idiosyncratic. Its outrageous eccentricities are our favorite small talk. So seize the moment. Take a chance. If the butterfly bush you must have dies over the winter in your garden, grow it as an annual, like a geranium. If it survives, cheer. If not, replant next year.

To help gardeners choose plants that will survive winters in their gardens, the USDA has created a climate zone map that identifies regions according to their average lowest winter temperature. Zone 1 has the coldest climate, Zone 11 the warmest. But New England topography requires that you use your noggin. The plains and the coasts are one or two zones warmer than the hills—and we have lots of hills. Can you count on lots of snow? Under a protective blanket of snow, plants can survive more cold than where the earth is bare and frigid. High hills are colder than their respective zones. For every additional 1,000 feet of elevation, you are one zone colder. The authors' gardens are about ten minutes apart as the crow flies, but Jacqui lives in a narrow valley that follows the Housatonic River, while Holly lives on the tip-top of a hill at least 1,000 feet higher up: Jacqui's in Zone 5, Holly's in Zone 4.

The dynamic of mountainous areas versus valley areas can be baffling: mountaintops hold the extremes of temperatures while valleys hold the best of circumstances. When the weather is hot, the mountaintops are hotter than the valleys because the valleys hold the cool evening air longer. Conversely, when the weather is cold, the mountains are colder than the valleys because the valleys hold the heat from the previous day's sun. Mountaintops = extremes: valleys = insulated havens. The north side of a hill is subject to more cold than the south-facing slope below the crest. Cities are 5 to 10 degrees warmer than

Mountain Laurels

the suburbs and the countryside. Large bodies of water modify temperatures. In winter the coast and 10 to 20 miles inland is warmer than the landmass behind. But as spring warms the air, the shore and 10 to 20 miles inland is colder by 10 degrees or more than farther inland because the ocean holds winter cold. In summer the shore is cooler because the ocean is cooler than the air.

That said, it's our experience that putting the right plant in the right place is the key to having a garden that will give you joy for years. Knowing your own backyard and its potentially unconventional reaction to the weather has to dictate most of your plant choices, especially long-lived trees and shrubs. This is why New England gardeners have so much fun! There is ALWAYS room for experimental zone choices. No one ever has the "final word."

Outwitting Your Climate

Since the zone the USDA map assigns to you isn't the last word on plant survival, good or bad, if a plant you really want seems successful just outside your climate zone, give it a try. Large trees need open space all around, so they are vulnerable to whatever the zone tag on the plant and the USDA map says about your area. But plants that can be protected, or are small enough to inhabit a microclimate—small flowering trees, shrubs, perennials—often will make it. Within every garden there are microclimates hospitable to plants normally a bit outside your zone. A south-facing wall can warm a corner, and shade can cool it. You can even create microclimates: a wall painted white, a reflective surface, increases light and heat. A vine-covered pergola, a trellis, a tree, or a high hedge can provide protection from early and late frost. Walls and windbreaks—and a position below the crest of a south-facing slope—protect plants from sweeping winds that intensify cold. A burlap wrap and an anti-dessicant spray can save evergreens from the wind, and also deer. Mulch protects roots from extremes of cold and from heat as well.

If you live in a borderline area—almost in cooler Zone 4, but not quite, for example—the safest choices are species that are well within their cold hardiness range in your garden. Borderline plants may live but not always bloom in a satisfying way. Forsythia will leaf out in northern Vermont, but generally blooms only on the portion of the plant below the snow line. Late frosts can devastate the flower buds on a hardy magnolia though the plant itself may do well year after year. Many plants are offered in varieties described as blooming early, midseason, or late. Where the growing season is short, choose varieties that will bloom early. If you wish to enjoy a very long season of bloom of any particular plant, plant varieties of all three types, early, midseason, and late.

We also outwit the climate by covering plants to protect them from late spring and early fall frosts, and by starting seeds indoors weeks before they can be sown in the open garden. Seed starting is detailed in the Appendix. Garden centers and catalogs offer seed starting equipment, as well as protective covers of all sorts. To protect individual plants, we use plastic cones called "hot caps;" and we add, for elegance, a Victorian glass cloche or two. To protect whole rows of seedlings, we use filmy tenting, the Remay type. Hot beds and cold frames, though simple enough to make, are projects beyond the scope of this book.

Plants That Succeed

The plants we recommend are the best of the best for New England. There are 180 featured plants, and information on another 500 species and cultivars we recommend. We chose them for their lasting beauty, ease of maintenance, and immunity or strong resistance to pests and diseases. We're not recommending pesticides and other deterrents—they come and go too frequently. But more important to us is that we have learned from decades of experience that the best protection you can give your garden is 1) to choose pest- and disease-resistant plants that thrive in New England, and 2) to give them the light, nutrients, and moisture they need. We do everything possible at the start to provide the right growing environment: after that, either it grows, or it's gotta go!

Light

After climate, the next most important element for success in a garden is the light. On each plant page we tell you the light in which that plant thrives. When a flowering species fails to flower, check the hours of direct sun it receives: unless we say a plant flowers in part or full shade, it requires at least six hours of direct sun to bloom well. Full sun occurs between 10 A.M. and 6 P.M. through mid-August. Plants receiving full sunlight are often the most cold hardy. Plants that flop forward are telling you they need more light. You can increase the amount of light the plants receive by planting them near a wall painted white, or a reflective surface. Plants that do best in partial sun or shade, New Guinea impatiens, hostas, and daphnes for example, can be grown in full sun, if you provide an overhead trellis, a pergola, something to shade them from the hottest sun of the day—noonday and late afternoon sun.

Quaint arbor with old-fashioned *Nicotiana sylvestris*, Roses, and hanging baskets of Begonias.

Soil Preparation and Improvement

Soil is your plant's support system, its drinking fountain, and its larder. In New England acid soils prevail. Then the soil becomes sandy as you approach the coast. And there's often a layer of hardpan under thin topsoil in new housing developments. Sandy soils are easy to dig and drain well, which is essential for a great many plants. On the other hand they don't retain water, or the nutrients dissolved in it. Whichever your soil type, the way to make it right is to mix it with humusy organic materials—such as compost, leaf mold (rotted leaves), or peat—and slow-release fertilizers.

The ideal garden soil has good drainage, lots of water-holding humus, and is loose enough so you can dig in it with your fingers. We evaluate garden soil in terms of its structure or composition, its pH, and its fertility. Structure governs the soil's ability to absorb and maintain moisture. Gritty particles create air spaces, allowing tender rootlets to seek oxygen, moisture, and the nutrients dissolved in it. They also allow water to drain. Soil containing humus retains enough moisture to keep the rootlets from drying out and starving: roots "drink" nutrients dissolved in water. We add lots of humusy organic amendments to new planting beds to improve the soil's structure.

A plant's access to nutrients also depends on the soil's pH (potential of hydrogen), its relative acidity or alkalinity. A pH of 7.0 is neutral; a pH of 4.0 is very, very acid; a pH of 8.0 is very alkaline. Most garden ornamentals do best in soil whose pH is between 5.5 and 6.5. Trees and shrubs are apt to be more finicky about pH than herbaceous plants. You can use relatively inexpensive testing kits to determine the pH of your soil. If it's above pH 6.5, and you are preparing a bed for plants that do not do well in alkaline ("sweet") soil, apply water soluble sulfur or iron sulfate. If the soil is below pH 5.5, and the plants

Meadow garden with pink and white Cosmos and purple South American Vervain.

13

Climbing Roses frame an entrance to the garden of a Cape Cod house.

need "sweeter" soil, spread finely ground limestone or hydrated lime. Ask your garden center or nursery for recommendations.

Plants empty their larder of nutrients every season. If you want plants to be all they can be, you must fertilize a new bed before planting, and all beds every year. The fertilizers we use are organic and release their nutrients slowly during the season, so we get solid stocky plants with loads of gorgeous foliage and flowers.

We mostly plant in raised beds of improved soil. When we're digging a planting hole we add the same soil amendments and fertilizers in the same proportions. The best times to prepare a new bed are fall, and spring as soon as cold and moisture are out of the ground. Here's how:

1) Use a garden hose to outline the bed. A bed beside a fence, a wall, or a path can be formal or informal. For an informal look, lay out long, slow, gentle curves rather than scallops or straight lines. For a formal look, make the bed symmetrical—a half circle, oval, square, or rectangle. An island bed can be a large oval, an elongated S, or kidney shaped. Island beds are the easiest to work since you can get at the middle from either side.

2) Thoroughly water the turf covering the area to get the grass roots activated.

3) Spray the entire area with a weed killer, following the instructions on the label. It takes about two weeks to completely die. Alternately, you can remove the turf—the top layer of growth and its roots—but that's pretty hard work.

4) Cover the area with enough of the most weed-free garden soil you can find to raise the soil level about 12 to 16 inches above ground.

5) Cover the bed with 3 to 4 inches of humus, enough so that one quarter of the content of the soil is organic matter. The humus can be decomposed bark, compost, partially decomposed leaves or seaweed, sphagnum peat moss, black peat humus, decomposed animal manures, or other decomposed organic material.

6) Next, with a rear-tine rototiller, which you can rent from a garden center, mix all this deeply and thoroughly. The bed should now be so soft you can dig in it with your bare hands.

7) The next step is to determine the pH reaction of the soil and amend it as needed to reach a pH between 5.5 and 6.5 following the steps described under Soil Preparation and Improvement.

8) Next, for each 10 by 10 foot area (100 square feet), mix in the following and rototill or fork into the improved soil:

For a new garden in full sun:
Organic fertilizer 5-3-3: 5 to 10 pounds
Rock phosphate: 5 to 10 pounds
Greensand: 5 to 10 pounds
Clay soils only: gypsum 5 to 10 pounds
Slow-release fertilizer that lasts eight
    months: 2 pounds

For a new garden in shade:
Organic fertilizer for acid-loving plants
    4-6-4: 4 to 7 pounds
Superphosphate: 3 to 5 pounds
Greensand: 5 to 10 pounds
Clay soils only: gypsum 5 to 10 pounds
Slow-release fertilizer that lasts eight months:
    2 pounds

For a new bed for bulbs:
Organic bulb food: 5 to 10 pounds

9) When you are ready to plant, rake the bed smooth and discard rocks, lumps, and bumps.

10) Finally, tamp the edge of the bed into a long, gradual slope and cover it with mulch to keep the soil from eroding. Or, frame the bed with low retaining walls of stone or painted cement blocks, 2 × 2 red cedar or pressure treated wood, or railroad ties.

Planting

When you are planting in a new raised bed with improved, fluffed up soil, digging a generous planting hole is easy. Digging a big hole in an unimproved spot, even in an old established garden, is tough. But the plant still needs a big planting hole, and soil mixed with 3 to 4 inches of humus (Step 5 above), enough so that one quarter of the content of the soil is organic matter mixed with slow-release organic fertilizers. Each chapter introduction has directions for planting the type of plants in that chapter. Whether the plants are large or small our basic approach is this:

1) Make the planting hole BIG. For trees and shrubs, make it three times as wide and two times as deep as the rootball. For perennials and annuals, dig a hole two times as wide and two times as deep as the rootball.

2) For perennials, annuals, and bulbs provide a base of improved soil for the rootball to rest on by half filling the planting hole with improved soil before setting the plant in it. For shrubs and trees half fill the hole with improved soil, and tamp it down very firmly before setting the plant into the hole.

3) Free the plant from matted roots. When it's possible, unwind roots that may be circling the rootball. If you can't untangle them, make four shallow vertical slashes in the mass. Cut off about a half inch of the matted roots on the bottom. Soak the rootball in a bucket containing starter solution.

4) Set the plant in the hole. Half fill the hole with soil, tamp it down firmly; fill the hole all the way to the top with soil, tamp it firmly again. Shape the soil around the stem or the crown into a wide saucer. The saucer is really important for shrubs and trees, less so for perennials and annuals.

'Whitespire' Birches, Dwarf Barberries, Shore Junipers, and Hay-Scented Ferns in the afternoon sun.

A snowy retreat, with a Crabapplee and Hydrangeas outlined in white.

Watering

Deep, slow, gentle watering is what keeps plants growing well. After planting, water the bed deeply, gently and slowly. Ideal for a new bed is to put down $1^1/2$ inches of water after planting. Set an empty coffee tin, regular size, to catch the water and record how long it takes your sprinkler to deliver $1^1/2$ inches. Water a newly planted shrub or tree by slowly pouring 10 to 15 gallons of water into the saucer around the plant. For a tree or a shrub's first season, unless there's a soaking rain, in spring and fall slowly and gently pour two to three bucketsful of water around the roots every two weeks, in summer every week or ten days. Flower beds thrive with two to three hours of gentle rain every ten days to two weeks. If the sky fails you, water long enough to lay down $1^1/2$ inches of water gently over a long period of time, at least six to eight hours, every ten days to two weeks. And, of course, water any time the plants show signs of wilting.

Overhead watering is fine as long as you water deeply. There's less waste if you water before the sun reaches the garden in the early morning, or late afternoon or evening. In hot dry periods you need to water during the day. Daytime watering lowers leaf temperatures and reduces stress in very hot dry periods. Evening watering is fine—dew does it and plants like it. We do not recommend electrically timed mechanical watering systems that ignore the weather and water too often and shallowly. However, they can do a good job if they are set up with the correct nozzles, and timed to run long enough to water deeply every week or ten days. Windy, hot times, such as occur in summer require more water and the cool spring and fall days less.

Staking and Stem Protection

Growing in improved soil and fertilized with slow-release organic fertilizers, only a few of the tallest flowers should need staking. Tall, weak growth is often caused by force-feeding with non-organic fertilizers. Wide spacing improves air circulation, and reduces the risk of disease and mildew. Staking is easy: set a wood, bamboo, or metal stake close to the plant stem while it is still young. As it leafs out, it will hide the stake. Use soft green wool, raffia, or cotton string and tie the main stem loosely to the stake. Staking a tree isn't necessary unless the stem or trunk shows a tendency to lean over or to grow at an angle—and it should not need the stake for more than a year. In cold regions a burlap windbreak is helpful to young shrubs and trees for their first winter. You may need to protect a young tree trunk from rubbing or nibbling by deer: you can surround it with stakes wrapped with mesh, or attach a rubber or plastic stem guard. Remove the wrap in spring when growth starts. To protect the tender bark of a young tree from sunscald, paint it with a wash of calcium carbonate.

Mulches

If you love your plants, maintain a 2- to 3-inch layer of organic mulch over the roots from early spring through fall and winter. Start the mulch about 3 inches from the main stem or stems. We mulch in part to buffer soil temperatures and maintain soil moisture, to prevent erosion and control weeds. An organic mulch does more: as it decomposes on the underside it replenishes the soil's supply of humus, which is dissipated during the growing season. The mulches we use suit all plants equally well. Tests have shown that an acid mulch, such as pine needles, has no lasting impact on the pH of the soil beneath. You can mulch with almost any healthy organic material available—seaweed or chopped leaves for example—as long as it is at least partially decomposed. The commercial mulches we recommend include: cypress mulch, pine needles, fir, hardwood, pine bark, and cocoa mulch.

Maintaining Fertility

We fertilize planting beds, not individual plants. The rule of thumb is to apply a slow- release organic fertilizer to the bed before growth begins in early spring; for some plants you'll see we recommend fertilizing again in the fall. The fertilizer we recommend for general garden use is a complete organic fertilizer, not one for acid-loving plants—that tends to balance out New England's generally acid pH. For plants that do best in quite acid soil, we apply a complete organic fertilizer for acid-loving plants. For bulbs we use a complete organic fertilizer for bulbs. If plants need a boost in midseason we apply a water-soluble organic fertilizer such as fish emulsion. In high heat we don't try to force plant growth by feeding, and we avoid pruning at that time, which stimulates growth. The plants will naturally slow their growth in extremes of weather.

Grooming and Weeding

To realize their potential, plants need grooming. In early spring gardens must be cleared of last year's dead foliage. In summer we dead-head and shear spent blooms to encourage flowering this year or next. We prune woody plants to keep them shapely and healthy. We weed, eliminating the competition. Weeds can even be volunteers from last year's cosmos or phlox. They start up in spring and come into their own in midsummer, along with drought and high heat. Although a permanent mulch dis-

Lush water garden with Yellow Flag Irises and Water Lilies.

courages weeds, you can easily rake up the little green heads if you do it before they're 1 inch high. When they're 8 inches high, you'll need a hoe. After that you'll just be sorry you didn't get to it earlier. Let weeds flourish in or near a newly established garden and go to seed, and they'll haunt you for years. If some get away from you, don't pull big weeds from bone-dry soil during a drought—they are made difficult to dig out, and the upheaval of soil can cost precious moisture. Water the garden first, then gently free the weeds and their roots.

Looking back on years of gardening, the moments that stand out in memory are those spent grooming the garden. Grooming is a quiet time. Pruning boxwoods in the cool early morning, birds a-twitter, strolling the flowers beds at sunset checking for spent blooms that need deadheading, weeding in summer, raking leaves in autumn. These homely chores lift us out of our everyday lives and into the life of the garden and a potential for beauty that nourishes the soul.

How to Use the *New England Gardener's Guide*

Each entry in this guide provides information about a plant's characteristics, habits and requirements for growth, as well as our personal experience and knowledge of the plant. Use this information to realize each plant's potential. You will find such pertinent information as mature height and spread, bloom period and seasonal colors, sun and soil preferences, water requirements, fertilizing needs, pruning and care tips, and pest information. Each section is clearly marked for easy reference.

Sun Preferences

Symbols represent the range of sunlight suitable for each plant. The symbol representing "Full Sun" means the plant needs 6 or more hours of sun daily. A ranking of "Part Sun" means the plant can thrive in 4 to 6 hours of sun a day. "Part Shade" designates plants for sites with fewer than 4 hours of sun a day, including dappled or high shade. "Full Shade" means the plant needs protection from direct sunlight. Some plants can be grown successfully in more than one exposure, so you will sometimes see more than one light symbol with an entry.

Full Sun　　**Part Sun**　　**Part Shade**　　**Full Shade**

Additional Benefits

Many plants offer benefits that further enhance their appeal. These symbols indicate some of these benefits:

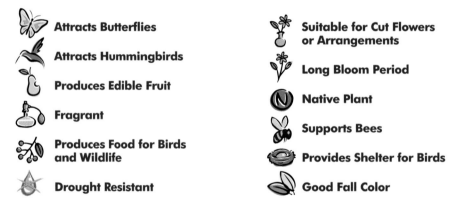

Attracts Butterflies

Attracts Hummingbirds

Produces Edible Fruit

Fragrant

Produces Food for Birds and Wildlife

Drought Resistant

Suitable for Cut Flowers or Arrangements

Long Bloom Period

Native Plant

Supports Bees

Provides Shelter for Birds

Good Fall Color

Companion Planting and Design

For most of the entries, we provide landscape design ideas as well as suggestions for companion plants to help you achieve striking and personal results from your garden.

Our Personal Recommendations

This section describes cultivars or varieties we have found particularly noteworthy, as well as interesting related plants and other relevant information.

USDA Cold Hardiness Zones

Connecticut, Maine, Massachusetts, New Hampshire, Rhode Island, and Vermont

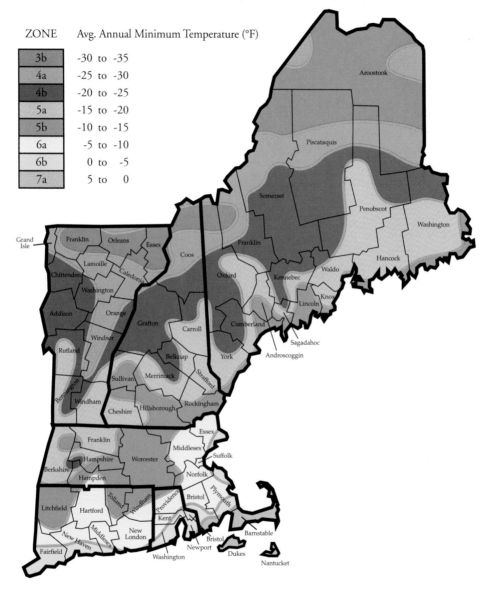

ZONE	Avg. Annual Minimum Temperature (°F)
3b	-30 to -35
4a	-25 to -30
4b	-20 to -25
5a	-15 to -20
5b	-10 to -15
6a	-5 to -10
6b	0 to -5
7a	5 to 0

Hardiness Zones

Cold-hardiness zone designations were developed by the United States Department of Agriculture (USDA) to indicate the minimum average temperature for an area. A zone assigned to an individual plant indicates the lowest temperature at which the plant can be expected to survive over the winter. New England has zones ranging from 3b to 7a. Though a plant may grow (and grow well) in zones other than its recommended cold-hardiness zone, it is a good indication of which plants to consider for your landscape.

Annuals *for New England*

Foxglove

Annuals and tender perennials last just one season but they're a delight to grow and dear to every gardener's heart. Just weeks after planting, annuals carpet empty spaces with lasting color and soon grow big enough to screen out the ripening of spring bulb foliage. The vivid zinnias and marigolds are so easy and so satisfying they're ideal for a child's garden. In dappled light, impatiens and coleus color well and grow more beautiful as summer advances: planted in complementary colors, they're stunning. Petunias, geraniums, and other tender (not winter hardy) perennials keep window boxes and patio planters blooming all summer long. Some annuals self-sow and may spare you the trouble of replanting the next year. Rogue out those you don't want and transplant others for a late show.

Many annuals have a rewarding cut-and-come again habit: the more flowers you harvest, the more the plant produces. Many of the best cutting flowers are annuals. Knowing how to harvest— where to cut the stems—is the key to keeping them blooming. We've described the process below, and, where relevant, with each plant in this chapter. For a continuous supply of vivid zinnias, giant golden marigolds, and late summer bouquets of pastel cosmos scented with basil, establish a cutting garden where your pleasure in harvesting won't spoil the view. Or, plant cutting flowers in a kitchen garden with vegetables, herbs, and dwarf fruit trees.

Planting and Fertilizing

Annuals have modest root systems. To be all they can be, like vegetables, they require sustained moisture and plenty of nutrients. The Introduction explains how to prepare beds for annuals in order to bring the soil to pH 5.5 to 7.0, the ideal range for most. The organic fertilizers release their nutrients slowly so the plants should do well the first season without further fertilization. Then every year, in late winter or early spring, fertilize beds for annuals with applications of these same slow-release, long-feeding organic fertilizers. If your annuals seem to slow after periods of intense bloom, they may benefit from fertilization with one of the water-soluble organic fertilizers, such as seaweed or fish emulsion.

Nursery-grown seedlings of annuals are very tempting in mid-spring when you're looking for instant flowers. Those available at garden centers in spring are beautiful, already in bloom, healthy—and in everybody else's garden. Eventually you will want to try the alluring other varieties you see in garden magazines and catalogs. Then you will have to sow seeds—in the garden or, for a head start, indoors. See Starting Seeds Indoors in the Appendix. The time to sow seeds outdoors for annuals is well after the last frost for your area. Please don't rush the season! Most annuals just won't take off until the ground and the air warm up—seeds and seedlings set out too early sulk. Flowers whose seed packets say they are "cold hardy" you can sow outdoors somewhat earlier than the others. Most annuals sown outdoors will come into bloom soonest when they are planted where they are to stay and flower.

Sow smaller seeds by "broadcasting," that is, sprinkling them thinly over the area. Larger seeds you can sow in "hills," groups of four to six, or three to five, equidistant from each other. Flowers for edging beds can be sown in "drills," that is, dribbled at spaced intervals along a shallow furrow, which is drilled in the soil by dragging the edge of a rake or hoe handle along the planting line. For planting depth, follow the instructions on the seed packet, or sow seeds at a depth that is about three times the seed's diameter, not its length. Seed packets usually suggest how much to thin seedlings to give the mature plants space to develop.

After sowing your seeds, give the planting bed a slow, thorough overhead soaking. See Watering in the Introduction. Water often enough during the next two or three weeks to maintain soil moisture. Thin

Creeping Zinnia

the seedlings to 3 to 5 inches apart and apply a 2-inch layer of mulch. In periods of drought, water gently and deeply every week or ten days, or when you see signs of wilting.

For window box, basket, and container plantings we recommend using a commercial potting mix. If you mix into the soil a polymer such as Soil Moist™ you'll find maintaining moisture much easier. It holds twenty times its weight in water, and releases the water (and dissolved soil nutrients) slowly.

Annuals Can Take a Lot of Pinching

To be all they can be, some annuals need pinching at several junctures in the season. The pinching begins right at planting time. It's a fact that once an annual gets into flower production, the plant puts less strength into growing its root system. But the plant needs a big, healthy root system to get through hot summer days. The way to encourage the plant to grow its root system is to pinch out the flowering tips at planting time. If you are using the color of budded or opening flowers to decide where the plant goes, wait until it is in the ground to pinch out the flowers and buds. Then, at planting time, or very early in their careers, the branching tips of many, even most, annuals should be pinched out to encourage the production of side branches where flowers will develop. Again, at midseason, when the plants are fully matured, you can encourage new branching and more flowering in some long-branching annuals, such as petunias, by shearing all the stems back by a third or half. And some annuals bloom more fully and over a longer period if you deadhead them consistently and persistently. Pinch out the spent flowers between your thumb and forefinger— it's fast and easy. Frequent harvesting of most annuals has the same beneficial effect. Cut the stems for bouquets just above the next set of leaves: that's where the new flowering stems will arise.

Coleus 'Rusty'

To Encourage Self-Sowers

Annual flowers that sow their own seeds will naturalize—come back year after year—under favorable conditions. Volunteers self-sown by petunias, snapdragons, and little French marigolds

Viola

pop up every year in our gardens. They'll come into bloom late, and for Zones 3 and 4—even 5—can't be counted on for late summer and fall bloom. But we often transplant them for the fun of seeing what will happen. Other self-sowers are so productive they become weeds—morning glory comes to mind—and should be rogued out as soon as you identify them.

You can encourage self-sowing by spreading a 1- or 2-inch layer of humusy soil around the crowns of the parent plants and allowing flowers to ripen seedheads toward the end of the growing season. Keep the soil damp, and gather the seeds as they ripen and scatter them over the soil. Or, wait until the seeds are dry and loose in their casings, then shake the seedheads vigorously over the soil.

Other Good Options

The annuals on the following pages are some of the best. But there are others that are "good doers" in New England:

Bachelor's-Button, Cornflower,
    Centaurea cyanus
Browallia, Bush Violet, *Browallia speciosa*
Butter Daisy, *Melampodium paludosum*
Flowering Tobacco, *Nicotiana* spp. and
    hybrids, *N. sylvestris*
Four O'Clock, *Mirabilis jalapa*
Garden Heliotrope, *Heliotropium arborescens*

Globe Amaranth, *Gomphrena globosa*
Larkspur, *Consolida ajacis*
    (syn. *Delphinium ajacis*)
Moss Rose, *Portulaca grandiflora*
Ornamental Kale and Cabbage,
    Brassica oleracea Acephala Group
Wishbone Plant, Bluewings,
    Torenia fournieri

Ageratum
Ageratum houstonianum

Ageratum is the annual flower we rely on for mid-height summer-long drifts of blue in flower borders. The blossoms are rounded clusters of tiny powder puffs held in nosegays of pointed fresh green foliage. The varieties offered as seedlings by most garden centers now are dwarfish, 6 to 12 in. high. Seeds of old-fashioned varieties 18 in. high are out there but hard to find. The taller sorts are suitable for planting farther back in the garden and they make fairly lasting cut flowers. Deadheading keeps ageratum blooming, and while it may brown in the high heat of midsummer, ageratum comes back in our garden with the September rains. The plant known as the hardy ageratum, Eupatorium coelestinum, *winters over in warm coastal Maine and in areas that have good snow cover.*

Other Name
Flossflower

Bloom Period and Seasonal Color
Late spring to mid-autumn; blue, lavender-blue, pink, white.

Mature Height × Spread
6 to 12 in. × 6 to 12 in.

When, Where, and How to Plant
You can start ageratum seeds indoors in flats six to eight weeks before planting time. See Starting Seeds Indoors in the Appendix. Ageratum seeds need light to germinate, so do not cover the seeds with soil. In mid-spring after the weather has become reliably warm, you can sow seeds or plant seedlings directly in the garden. Sow ageratum seeds where the plants are to bloom. For a quick show of their lovely soft blue color we plant seedlings already blooming in sets of three. Ageratum does best in full or partial sun, in well-drained, humusy soil whose pH is 5.5 to 7.0. See Soil Preparation and Planting in the Introduction. For seedlings, provide holes 8 to 12 in. deep. For smaller varieties, allow 6 in. between plants; for larger varieties, allow 12 in. Provide a 2-in. mulch starting 3 in. from the plant.

Growing Tips
The plants will be fuller if you pinch out the first sets of flowering tips. For the first several weeks, keep the soil around the plants well watered.

Care
During the flowering season, shear spent blooms often to keep the plants producing. If the tips brown out in heat, cut off the darkened portions and water the plants often enough to make sure they don't go dry. They will freshen in late summer with cooler weather and rain, and go on blooming until the real cold comes.

Companion Planting and Design
Ageratum is lovely with silver artemisia and mid-size pink-and-white snapdragons. It makes a pretty edging for a flower border when it is interplanted with white sweet alyssum and large-flowered pink wax begonias.

Our Personal Recommendations
Our favorites are compact, lavishly blooming, lavender-blue 'Blue Danube' ('Blue Puff'); extra-early bright blue 'Adriatic'; and 'Blue Surf', which grows to 9 in. tall.

Bedding Begonia

Begonia Semperflorens-Cultorum Hybrids

When, Where, and How to Plant

You can start wax begonias indoors from seed in early January—and you will find lots of seedlings at the market gardens in April and May. We find they grow strong root systems and flower fully when they are set out rather early, a few weeks after the last frost date. Wax begonias growing in bright dappled light bloom all season long. In cool regions, they can take full sun. In shade, begonias keep their lovely leaves but they do not bloom very well. Wax begonias do best in soil with a pH of 5.5 to 7.0. See Soil Preparation and Planting in the Introduction. Work the soil 8 to 12 in. deep. Set the seedlings high, and 6 to 8 in. apart. Apply a 2-in. layer of mulch.

Growing Tip

To promote rapid, unchecked growth, for two or three weeks after planting, water often enough to maintain soil moisture.

Care

After that, water deeply when other flowers show signs of wilting. Wax begonias are able to remain crisp even in the first stages of water deprivation.

Companion Planting and Design

Wax begonias are perfect edgers for semi-shaded flower borders, and look just great planted in clumps of three behind a ribbon of sweet alyssum. They're attractive in containers, and thrive in window boxes.

Our Personal Recommendations

The prettiest wax begonias are the green-leaved Wing F_1 hybrids that are 10 to 12 in. tall and have 3-in. flowers. 'Picotee Wings' is a treasure, a soft white rimmed in rose. For edging, choose dwarf Semperflorens-Cultorum forms. For hanging baskets, choose hybrids with cascading branches. The attractive 24-in. perennial begonia is *Begonia grandis*, also known as Evans begonia (formerly *B. evansiana*). It survives winters in Zone 7, along the warm southern coasts of New England. In cooler regions it is sometimes used in containers and performs quite well. There are white and pink flowered varieties.

In dappled light the carefree Semperflorens-Cultorum hybrids produce small colorful flowers nestled in neat mounds of crisp, waxy, rounded leaves that stay fresh-looking all season. Some strains have maroon-bronze leaves, others are bright green, and there are forms whose leaves are variegated with dabs of white. Bedding begonias are a maintenance-free delight, our favorite edgers for partly shaded flower borders. These wonderfully carefree little plants need no deadheading to keep blooming. They are tender perennials that can take a lot of cold at the end of the season, but no frost. Potted up and brought indoors in September, they bloom all winter on a sunny sill. The wax begonia's gorgeous cousin, the tuberous begonia, is a superb but challenging bedding and basket plant that does best in cool areas and thrives in the cool nights of coastal gardens.

Other Names

Wax Begonia, Fibrous-Rooted Begonia

Bloom Period and Seasonal Color

Mid-spring to September; white, pale pink, rose, coral, deep pink, red, and bi-colors.

Mature Height × Spread

6 to 9 in. × 12 to 18 in.

Celosia

Celosia argentea var. *cristata*

Celosia is one of the most colorful and enduring of the annuals. The "blooms" are either fanciful velvety crests, much like a cockscomb (Cristata group), or feathered plumes (Plumosa group, called feathered amaranth), that bloom from summer until frost touches them. The foliage is an asset and may be green or bronze, depending on the color of the blossom. There are dwarfs, and also taller types whose plumes may need staking. The feathery celosias provide strong color and graceful accents for bouquets of cut flowers. Celosia blooms are dryish to start with, so they are ideal subjects for drying: to make them into keepers, remove the lower foliage from stems 8 to 12 in. long, bundle the stems loosely, and hang them up to dry in an airy place out of bright sun. Maine summers aren't hot enough to grow celosia really well.

Other Names
Cockscomb, Feathered Amaranth

Bloom Period and Seasonal Color
Summer; red, pink, yellow, apricot, burgundy-red, gold, or cream.

Mature Height × Spread
4 to 24 in. × 8 to 12 in.

When, Where, and How to Plant
Start seeds indoors in late winter. See Starting Seeds Indoors in the Appendix. Or, as soon as the soil has warmed, sow the seeds directly in full sun in fertile, well-drained soil worked to a depth of 8 to 12 in. The celosias do well in almost any soil. See Soil Preparation in the Introduction, and Planting in the beginning of this chapter. Transplant seedlings, or thin garden-grown seedlings, to stand 12 in. apart. The plants start well but sulk if the roots are disturbed. Provide a 2-in. mulch starting 3 in. from the plant.

Growing Tips
Water the bed well after planting and maintain the moisture the first few weeks after planting.

Care
During the summer growing season provide enough water so the plants do not dry out. But don't overwater, as the celosias are susceptible to fungus. Once established, the plants withstand some drought.

Companion Planting and Design
Groups of celosia create solid splashes of vibrant color anywhere you plant them. A row of the cockscomb varieties makes a big color statement in the kitchen garden, and the feathery varieties are graceful wherever situated.

Our Personal Recommendations
The dwarf Fairy Fountains group has 4- to 6-in. plumes on 12-in. plants, and are charming edgers. The larger Century celosias are most effective massed in beds. The scarlet-plumed 'New Look' celosia endures hot summers.

Coleus

Solenostemon scutellarioides

When, Where, and How to Plant

Coleus grows quickly from seed sown in flats indoors anytime. See Starting Seeds Indoors in the Appendix. Garden centers offer flats of seedlings of mixed foliage color combinations when the weather warms in mid-May, just in time to plant. The leaf colors are more intense when grown in part shade. Grow coleus on a shaded terrace, or in the bright shade of tall shrubs or trees, or in dappled light. In cool, hilly regions, coleus takes full sun: the more red there is in the foliage, the more direct sun the plant can take. Plant coleus in moderately rich, humusy soil. See Soil Preparation in the Introduction, and Planting in the beginning of this chapter. Make the planting holes 6 to 8 in. deep. Allow 12 to 14 in. between plants. Apply a 2-in. layer of mulch.

Growing Tips

To promote rapid, unchecked growth, for the first two or three weeks water to maintain soil moisture. When the plants show signs of new growth, encourage branching and full stocky growth by pinching out the top 3 to 4 in. of the lead stems.

Care

Maintain moderate soil moisture. Encourage fuller growth by removing flower spikes as they start up, and pinch out the leggy tips of branches.

Companion Planting and Design

A container full of coleus in mixed colors is breathtaking. In flower boxes we like coleus combined with impatiens in matching or contrasting colors—scarlet-variegated coleus with scarlet impatiens, for example, and lime-green coleus with white impatiens. Sunny green and gold varieties planted with hosta lighten shaded shrub beds. Trailing varieties, like red and gold 'Scarlet Poncho', are great in hanging baskets.

Our Personal Recommendations

The new coleus hybrids are better branching and more successful in full sun gardens than earlier varieties. A pretty coleus is 'Salmon Lace', which is green and cream-white edged with salmon. Yellow and green 'Highland Fling' pairs well with 'Molten Lava', whose red leaves have red margins. The Stained Glassworks™ varieties have lacy leaves and speckled and whorled foliage in sophisticated color variegations.

Coleus's gift to the garden is its brightly patterned, mid-height foliage that brings eye-catching color to shaded areas. The large heart-shaped leaves emerge from lush, pale green stems that are squarish, a characteristic of the mint family. And coleus is as wonderfully (or terribly) generous as mint. If you keep the leaf tips and the untidy flower spikes pinched out, the plants grow bigger and more beautiful until killed by early frosts. This is a great container plant. The color combinations get wilder every year. Coleus cuttings root quickly in water and thrive indoors in a semi-sunny window. You can plant them in potting soil and grow them as houseplants and a source for next year's outdoor bedding plants.

Other Name

Painted Nettle

Bloom Period and Seasonal Color

Colorful foliage all season; foliage colors in combinations of red, mahogany, chartreuse, yellow, white, rose, near-black.

Mature Height × Spread

14 to 24 in. × 12 to 18 in.

Cosmos
Cosmos bipinnatus

Willowy, drought-tolerant, no-problems cosmos brings to the late summer garden airy, fresh green foliage and bright, open-faced pastel flowers that bloom until early frosts. As the plant grows, lacy foliage fills in around the other flowers in the border so it makes a great filler. As the plants mature, the graceful 3- to 4-ft. branches are spangled with 2- to 4-in. flowers that have crested or tufted centers. Harvest the flowers, and the plants keep on producing. The flowers last well in arrangements and add lovely pastels to late summer bouquets of dahlias, blue salvia, mint, and basil. Cosmos is delicate, but tough. We transplant volunteers to places left empty by the passing of spring flowers.

Bloom Period and Seasonal Color
Late summer to frost; crimson, orange, rose, yellow, white, pink, burgundy-red, and bi-colors.

Mature Height × Spread
2 to 6 ft. × 2 ft. and more

When, Where, and How to Plant
Sow seeds indoors and transplant the seedlings outdoors after the ground has warmed. See Starting Seeds Indoors in the Appendix. In the garden sow seeds where the plants are to bloom. Early-flowering strains bloom in eight to ten weeks from seeds sown outdoors. Cosmos does best in full sun but makes do with four to six hours a day. It withstands drying winds but may need staking in an exposed location. Cosmos does well in well-drained soil of only average fertility. Overfeeding and rich soil result in plants that need staking. See Soil Preparation in the Introduction, and Planting in the beginning of this chapter. Dig the bed 6 to 8 in. deep. Space seedlings of the tall varieties at least 12 in. apart. Apply a 2-in. layer of mulch.

Growing Tips
For the first two or three weeks, water often enough to sustain soil moisture, but grow the plants "hard"—no pampering. If the seedlings tilt, stake the central stem. When they reach 24 in., encourage branching by pinching out the top 3 to 4 in. of the lead stem. Repeat as the next set of branches develops.

Care
Once established, water cosmos only if it shows signs of wilting. Cosmos blooms lavishly even without deadheading. When harvesting the flowers, cut the stems to just above a branching node to encourage new growth.

Companion Planting and Design
Cosmos is essential in a cottage garden, great in a meadow garden, and makes a good follow-on plant for spring bulbs. Use tall varieties as fillers for the back of the flower border. Cosmos combines especially well with snapdragons, blue salvia, and shasta daisies.

Our Personal Recommendations
For cutting, plant 'Sea Shells', which bears flowers that have creamy-white, shell-pink, or crimson and pink interiors; 'Psyche Mixed', for its semi-double and single flowers; and the bi-colored white and pink 'Candy Stripe'. For fresh color, plant orange-juice colored *C. sulphureus*.

When, Where, and How to Plant

Plant seedlings two to four weeks after the last frost date in part sun or semi-shade; in cool regions, lobelia succeeds in full sun. See Soil Preparation in the Introduction, and Planting in the beginning of this chapter. Prepare a well-drained, humusy bed worked to a depth of 6 or 8 in. Set the seedlings 10 to 12 in. apart. Water well and apply a 2-in. mulch between plants.

Growing Tip

To promote rapid, unchecked growth, for the first two or three weeks water often enough to sustain the moisture in the soil.

Care

Maintain soil moisture throughout the growing season, especially when the weather heats up and in sandy coastal soils. After every flush of bloom, shear played-out stems to encourage a new round of flowering.

Companion Planting and Design

We use edging lobelia to carpet empty spaces between fading early spring flowers. It is most beautiful drooping from a basket or an urn. For hanging baskets, choose the trailing Cascade or Fountain series, which bloom profusely. 'Crystal Palace' combines beautifully with zonal geraniums.

Our Personal Recommendations

A favorite edging lobelia is deep blue 'Crystal Palace'. The Moon series is especially heat-resistant: 'Paper Moon' is an exquisite white that covers itself with moon-shaped flowers. The blue cardinal flower, upright *L. siphilitica* is a perennial that naturalizes and is a long-lasting cutting flower.

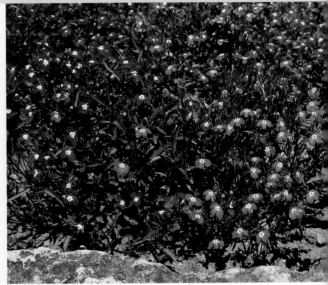

In semi-shade these dainty little plants produce clouds of thin, fragile stems spangled with tiny florets in luminous, intense shades (there's a glorious peacock blue), often with a white eye. In the garden the stems spread to carpet nearby plantings; growing in a basket or an urn, they cascade. Some varieties have fresh green foliage, and some have decorative bronze leaves. Edging lobelia is especially popular in Maine and other regions where it blooms all season long because summers tend to stay cool. In warmer regions it's gorgeous in spring, but tends to die out with the coming of high heat. If you love lobelia's intense colors, investigate the large, upright perennial blue and red lobelias, Lobelia siphilitica and L. cardinalis.

Other Name
Lobelia

Bloom Period and Seasonal Color
Spring into summer; light blue or intense deep blue, wine-red spotted white, and pure white varieties.

Mature Height × Spread
4 to 6 in. × 8 to 12 in.

Foxglove

Digitalis spp. and hybrids

This spring to early summer bloomer is as tall and stately as a hollyhock and makes a dramatic upright element in the garden. Two to 5 ft. tall, the straight-up stems are hung with pendulous, thimble-shaped blooms in pink, red, purple, yellow, or white with dark spots. Among the foxglove species there are annuals, biennials, and perennials. The dwarfish Foxy strain, beautiful hybrids of the biennial Digitalis purpurea, are favorites that we grow as annuals since they flower in early summer from seedlings planted in spring. They're a good size for containers. 'Alba' is taller, an extraordinarily beautiful pure white that makes a fabulous cutting flower.

Other Name
Common Foxglove

Bloom Period and Seasonal Color
Mid-spring to early summer; assorted colors.

Mature Height × Spread
30 in. or more × 30 in. or more

When, Where, and How to Plant
Sow seeds in the garden where the plants are to bloom in early fall, or in early spring. Spring-sown digitalis may be grown over the summer in a starter bed and moved in early fall to their place in the garden, for quick-blooming annual strains. Or, set out seedlings as soon as the soil becomes workable. Plant in sun in cooler regions, in part shade where summers are warm. Foxgloves cannot stand excessive heat, so avoid planting them in hot, windless pockets. 'Foxy' withstands some wind, but taller cultivars may need staking unless sheltered by a wall or other plantings. See Soil Preparation in the Introduction, and Planting in the beginning of this chapter. Provide planting holes for seedlings 12 to 15 in. apart. Apply mulch 3 in. deep starting 3 in. from the stems.

Growing Tips
To promote rapid, unchecked growth, for the first two or three weeks water often enough to sustain the moisture in the soil. After that, water deeply every week unless you have a soaking rain. Thin the seedlings if they become crowded.

Care
Foxgloves require sustained moisture. When flowering is finished, cut common foxglove back to the basal foliage (foliage at the base of the stem) to encourage the plant to bloom again next year. To encourage self-sowing, allow the last stalks of blooms to go to seed, look for seedlings to develop, and warn whoever does the weeding.

Companion Planting and Design
Foxglove is essential to the cottage garden's romantic tangle, absolutely striking planted in clumps of three to five with columbines, poppies, and zinnias, and gorgeous by itself in a container dripping with small-leaved ivy.

Our Personal Recommendations
'Foxy' is our favorite but there are other striking forms. 'Pam's Choice' bears 3- to 4-ft. spikes whose flowers have maroon interiors. Rusty foxglove, *D. ferruginea*, is a striking, lanky, 6-ft. biennial with coppery yellow flowers that have a furry lower lip. *D. grandiflora* (syn. *D. ambigua*), yellow foxglove, which is 24 to 36 in. tall, is a refined, creamy yellow perennial that will live for years.

When, Where, and How to Plant

Geraniums take cold well at the end of the season, but are not safe outdoors in spring until the air begins to warm. Good morning light or a western exposure is ideal. Geraniums maintain themselves in hot, dry, windy exposures but do best where nights are cool. Plant zonal geraniums in well-drained potting or garden soil. Ivy-leaved and scented geraniums do best in a fertile, humusy soil. All prefer soil with a pH of 5.5 to 6.5, neutral to slightly acid. See Soil Preparation in the Introduction, and Planting in the beginning of this chapter. Plant the small bedding geraniums 8 in. apart. Do not mulch.

Growing Tips

When there are signs of new growth, encourage branching by pinching out the end 3 to 4 in. of the lead stem and the side branches. Repeat once more during the growing season.

Care

Allow the soil surface to dry between deep waterings. Deadhead consistently to encourage flowering. In late September pot up a few geraniums and bring them indoors for the winter: in a sunny window they will bloom for weeks to come. Softwood cuttings taken in January root easily in water.

Companion Planting and Design

Geraniums are great container plants. Bright red zonal geraniums combine well in a window box with silvery dusty miller, petunias, and variegated vinca. A handsome combination for a big container is pink zonal geraniums, blue ageratum, white sweet alyssum, and the cascading branches of ivy-leaved geranium. For bedding, use compact varieties like the Tango series; for landscaping, use the larger Rocky Mountain group. Scented geraniums grow tall in a flower bed, and must be brought indoors for the winter.

Our Personal Recommendations

Bedding geraniums are increasingly popular. Variegated zonal geranium 'Ben Franklin' has semi-double, rosy pink flowers, and leaves splashed with beautiful crisp white markings. The Orbit series is known for its ease of growth, compact form, and large flowers in a range of colors, including 'Apple Blossom', a favorite.

The showy geranium's special appeal is that it blooms all summer and has handsome foliage. There are many forms. The old-fashioned geranium with big, rounded flower heads and green horseshoe-shaped leaves banded maroon or bronze is called a zonal geranium, Pelargonium × hortorum. White-splashed variegated forms are perfect to feature in a container. The airy Balcon, or Alpine ivy geranium, P. peltatum, covers itself and its deeply cut foliage with florets that stand out on slender stems: it is perfect in urns and lofty planters. Other ivy-leaved geraniums have fewer flowers but produce cascades of thick waxy foliage on drooping stems, and make beautiful basket plants; there are variegated forms. Martha Washington geraniums, P. × domesticum, have exceptionally showy flowers and are used as pot plants. The several species of scent-leaved geraniums have crinkly leaves that give off a strong aroma when brushed; they are grown for their foliage and scent. The geranium is a tender perennial: we bring our favorites indoors for the winter.

Bloom Period and Seasonal Color

Spring, summer, fall, some blooms in winter; shades of red, salmon, fuchsia, pink, white, and bi-colors.

Mature Height × Spread

Zonal and Balcon Geraniums: 1 to 2 ft. × 1 to 2 ft. (zonal geraniums can be trained to tree form)
Scent-Leaved Geraniums: 8 to 36 in. × 8 to 12 in.

Impatiens

Impatiens walleriana

Impatiens has the rare ability to flower generously in partial or full shade and that has made a place for it in gardens and woodlands from coast to coast. It's a care-free plant that blooms early and more and more lavishly until the first frosts. By early September a mass planting looks like a low hedge. The foliage may be either dark green or bronzed, and there are white variegated forms. The blossoms of double-flowered impatiens are as pretty as miniature roses, but flower more sparsely than ordinary impatiens. The beautiful hybrid called New Guinea impatiens, from the species Impatiens hawkeri, is a superb bedding plant and tolerates more sun: it is showier, more substantial, grows upright, and has large blossoms and colorful foliage, especially in the Painted Paradise series.

Other Names
Busy Lizzie, Sultana

Bloom Period and Seasonal Color
Late spring till frost; white, red, orange, salmon, melon, lavender, orchid, spotted forms, and bi-colors.

Mature Height × Spread
6 to 36 in. × 8 to 24 in.

When, Where, and How to Plant
We start with seedlings and set them out when night temperatures are in the high 50s and low 60s. Blooming starts when night temperatures are 60 to 65 degrees Fahrenheit. High and filtered shade are best, though modern cultivars tolerate four or five hours of direct sun, especially morning sun, when mulched and growing in humusy, moist soil. Impatiens needs well-drained soil rich in humus. In sandy areas, plant impatiens in containers or potting soil that contains humus, peat moss, and other moisture-holding organic materials. Work the soil for impatiens 8 to 10 in. deep. See Soil Preparation in the Introduction, and Planting in the beginning of this chapter. Set the seedlings 8 to 10 in. apart. After planting, apply a fine mulch 2 in. deep.

Growing Tips
Keep impatiens seedlings nicely watered the first few weeks after planting. In high heat flowering may slow: a light shower to cool them off can be a help.

Care
To keep the plants compact, in summer water impatiens only enough to keep it from wilting. Water early in the day or after the sun has gone by. Once flower buds have formed, fertilize rarely, if at all, and only very lightly with an organic, water-soluble fertilizer such as seaweed or fish emulsion.

Companion Planting and Design
Impatiens and coleus or caladiums in similar colors are beautiful together. Combinations we like are gray-white artemisia with light and dark pink and white impatiens, and white impatiens carpeting under miniature white cushion mums. Impatiens is lovely with variegated hostas. New Guinea impatiens is a great follow-on plant for bulbs growing under deciduous trees. Plants of the compact Sonic series are suited to small containers. The larger Super Sonics are meant for landscaping.

Our Personal Recommendations
The Victorian Rose double impatiens series has won impressive prizes. For containers and hanging baskets we like the Super Elfin® series. Under 10 in., they branch freely, and spread to 12 in. or more. For the front of the border, choose colors in the Accent series, 2^1/$_2$-in. flowers on plants 10 to 12 in. tall. For bedding, choose the tall Blitz series, 14 to 16 in. high, and New Guinea impatiens.

When, Where, and How to Plant

Indoors or in the garden, marigolds are easy to grow from seed. Sow seeds in the garden after the soil warms, or get a head start by sowing seeds indoors four to six weeks earlier. See Starting Seeds Indoors in the Appendix. Small early marigolds bloom in as little as six to seven weeks from seed sown where they are to grow. The larger types need twelve or thirteen weeks to bloom. Marigolds need full sun to develop fully, except for the white varieties, which prefer a little shade. They all do best in well-drained, moderately fertile soil enriched with humus. See Soil Preparation in the Introduction, and Planting in the beginning of this chapter. Space small marigolds 6 to 8 in. apart; allow 15 to 24 in. between tall marigolds. Apply a 2-in. layer of mulch.

Growing Tips

Keep the bed watered until the plants are a few inches high. To encourage branching in big marigolds, as the plants develop, pinch out the lead stems and branch tips.

Care

Deadhead, or shear, marigolds to keep blooms coming. The big-flowered marigolds are handsome in a vase, and last well if you strip the leaves from the part of the stem that will be immersed. The little French marigolds often self-sow, even in window boxes. Gather seed for next year's garden.

Companion Planting and Design

You can use marigolds large and small to ornament dry, neglected corners. They're also great follow-on flowers for spring bulbs. When marigolds are touched by frost, replace them with ornamental cabbages, kales, or potted mums in bloom. The little French marigolds are believed to protect other plants from soil nematodes, and repel mosquitoes and some insects that attack vegetables. Rototilling the big orange African marigolds into the soil seems to protect flowers planted later in the same ground from nematodes; and rows of them planted between rows of nematode-susceptible vegetables and flowers reduces nematode infestations.

Our Personal Recommendation

Our favorites are the big Climax marigolds whose dramatic blooms are 4 in. or more across on plants that grow 3 to 4 ft. tall. You can use them to create a fast-growing, bushy, eye-catching annual hedge.

Marigolds fill the garden with bursts of sunny colors, from yellow-white to gold to burnt orange. They bloom non-stop until frosts and have lacy foliage and a sharp, if not universally popular, aroma. They grow quickly from seed and tolerate drought, heat, and neglect. There are two major groups. The small French marigolds are varieties of Tagetes patula. *The big, round, fluffy, African or Aztec marigolds are varieties of* T. erecta. *Near-white and "odorless" marigolds belong to this group. The big-flowered varieties come in sizes from semi-dwarf to 4-ft. hedge forms. Triploid marigolds are crosses between these species: they bloom early, are as durable as the French marigolds, and they are also as full as the African marigolds—and almost indestructible.*

Bloom Period and Seasonal Color
Summer until frost; off-white, shades of gold, orange, yellow, mahogany, and bi-colors.

Mature Height × Spread
8 in. to 4 ft. × 10 in. to 3 ft.

Nasturtium

Tropaeolum majus

We love nasturtiums! These trumpet-shaped, spurred, vibrant red-orange, orange-red, and deep yellow flowers shine out from mounds of fresh, round, green leaves. In our gardens they are in bloom from early summer until frosts get them in September. They flourish in cool climates and are choice for a child's garden because they will bloom all summer in spite of neglect where the soil is poor, and in places where nothing much does well. Sown as seed, in fifty or sixty days the plants will be covered with bright blooms that have a nice sharp smell. Furthermore, the blooms are edible, as is the foliage. The flavor is citrusy and mildly sharp. Nasturtium blossoms are gorgeous on appetizer platters, in sandwiches and salads, and floating on cool creamy summer soups. Children enjoy stringing the flowers on a fishing line to make necklaces and crowns. There are vining forms.

Other Name
Indian Cress

Bloom Period and Seasonal Color
Summer; orange, yellow, red, and bi-colors.

Mature Height × Spread
12 to 15 in. × 20 to 24 in.

When, Where, and How to Plant

As soon as the weather warms, sow seeds in full sun where the plants are to bloom. Soak the big seeds in water all night before you plant them. You can also start nasturtium seeds indoors four weeks or so before planting time, which is about mid-May. See Starting Seeds Indoors in the Appendix. Nasturtiums do best in full sun, but in warmer areas they can succeed in part sun. This is a plant that likes poor soil. So provide a well-drained bed and work the soil 8 to 12 in. deep, but don't fertilize. In well-drained inhospitable soils, including gravely banks, the plants flower lavishly. High fertility produces abundant foliage and few flowers. See Soil Preparation and Planting in the Introduction. For seedlings provide holes 8 to 12 in. deep. Provide a mulch 2-in. deep starting 3 in. from the plant.

Growing Tip

Keep the bed watered until the plants are a few inches high.

Care

Deadhead consistently.

Companion Planting and Design

We plant nasturtiums for their shining colors, and because we harvest them often, among the herbs fronting our kitchen garden, and in the kitchen garden itself at the ends of the vegetable rows. Wrapped in a damp paper towel and stored in the fridge, nasturtium blooms stay fresh a day or two.

Our Personal Recommendations

There are bush nasturtiums, and vining nasturtiums that climb by twisting leaf stems around slender supports such as string or mesh. 'Fordhook Favorite' is a vigorous climbing type with single flowers that mix yellow and orange. 'Alaska' is a beautiful variety with variegated leaves.

Pansy

Viola × wittrockiana

When, Where, and How to Plant

Pansies here are planted in early spring. They live longest where the light will become dappled when the trees leaf out. In cool regions, pansies can take more sun and may live through the summer. The ideal soil for pansies is well drained and humusy. See Soil Preparation in the Introduction, and Planting in the beginning of this chapter. Make the planting holes 8 to 10 in. deep. Plant seedlings with about 3 in. between plants. Apply a 2-in. layer of mulch.

Growing Tips

As spring advances pansies become leggy. If you keep the soil well moistened, and deadhead consistently—a killer job when done correctly—some bloom into summer.

Care

When the weather begins to warm in the spring, fertilize the bed with a liquid, organic fertilizer. When the plants show vigorous growth start deadheading.

Companion Planting and Design

For a showy spring display, plant mixed colors of large-flowered pansies, including lots of yellows, and interplant with early tulips. For loads of blooms, plant mixed varieties of the solid-colored hybrids. Pansies make handsome window box and container plants, and are delightful as accent plants and edgers for moist places in rock gardens, wild gardens, and woodsy places. Replace fading pansies with shade-loving edging lobelia, forget-me-not 'Victoria Blue', wax begonias, or impatiens. For a lovely spring show, carpet under daffodils with 'Sorbet Blueberry Cream' Johnny-jump-ups.

Our Personal Recommendations

'Maxim Marina', an All-America Selections winner, bears 2-in., pansy-faced, lavender-blue blossoms on 4-in. stems. 'Sorbet Blueberry Cream' Johnny-jump-ups carpet a semi-sunny corner of our front entrance garden all summer long. Icicle™ pansies show great promise.

The pansy is a strange breed—seedlings planted in the fall in Zone 7, our warmest coastal region, bloom some in winter, and withstand snow and ice. Here in Zones 4 and 5 we set them out in early spring as bedding plants. We've had modern strains of pansies bloom (sparsely but still) through snow and ice storms in Zone 7. The pansies trademarked with the name Icicle™ were tested and lived through much colder winters in Zone 4. The pansy is a hybrid violet beloved at least since the Elizabethan era. Over the centuries this lovely little flower has acquired a string of delightful common names—heartsease, ladies-delight, and stepmother's flower. Old-fashioned pansies with painted faces in combinations of white, yellow, pink, blue, purple, black, and mahogany-red have the biggest blooms and are the showiest. Modern pansy strains are smaller flowered and come in solid colors and tender shades. Massed, some pansies have a faint, sweet perfume. The pansy-faced little Johnny-jump-ups are true violas: they do jump everywhere, even into next year. In ideal conditions they can become a weed problem.

Other Names

Viola, Heartsease

Bloom Period and Seasonal Color

Spring through cool summers; shades and combinations of yellow, blue, white, orange, pink, rose, purple, black.

Mature Height × Spread

8 to 10 in. × 8 to 18 in.

Petunia

Petunia × hybrida

The old-fashioned petunia with its single or double trumpet-shaped blooms comes in colors to match every dream. Cascade varieties tumble from window boxes and hanging baskets, growing fuller as summer advances. Upright forms make superb full-flowered bedding plants. Some purple and white varieties spread a sweet cinnamon scent over the evening air: those include in their genetic makeup the night-scented Petunia axillaris, the large white petunia. Newer varieties don't set seed, so they last longer. The F1 hybrid single multifloras seem better able to stand high heat. Supertunia™ and Surfinia® petunias are stronger, fuller plants. The new Wave™ petunias are low, dense, wide-spreading, hold their flowers up, need no deadheading, pinching, or pruning to flower all season, and can be used as a ground cover or as basket plants. Common petunias are perennials that can't stand our winters, but the scented, full-flowering, hot magenta species P. integrifolia is quite hardy.

Bloom Period and Seasonal Color
Summer; white, yellow, orange, pink, red, blue, lavender, magenta, purple, and showy bi-colors.

Mature Height × Spread
1/2 to 2 ft. × 3 to 4 ft.

When, Where, and How to Plant
You can start petunia seeds indoors ten to twelve weeks before the weather warms. See Starting Seeds Indoors in the Appendix. We prefer to choose from the many varieties of seedlings available at garden markets. Plant petunias when temperatures reach 60 to 65 degrees Fahrenheit. In midsummer we add fresh seedlings to containers to keep the displays going longer. For the fullest bloom, grow petunias where they will receive at least six hours of direct sun daily. Provide well-drained, humusy soil, pH 6.0 to 7.0, worked to a depth of 8 to 10 in. See Soil Preparation in the Introduction, and Planting in the beginning of this chapter. Allow 4 to 6 in. between plants. Spread a 2-in. mulch around bedding petunias.

Growing Tips
Pinch out the tips of young petunias to encourage branching. Keep the soil evenly moist.

Care
You must deadhead most petunias to keep them in full bloom. Midsummer, trim the stems back by a third to encourage late blooming, and repeat as blooms become sparse. Surprisingly, petunias last well as cut flowers: individual blossoms fade but others on the stem open. Wave™ petunias need no deadheading, pinching, or pruning, but they are heavy feeders: add the slow-release, organic fertilizer recommended at planting time, and add more to Wave™ petunias in July and August.

Companion Planting and Design
Bedding petunias make good follow-on plants for spring flowers. The sparkling whites of the cascade varieties harmonize mixed colors in baskets and planters. The grandiflora (big-flowered) forms and doubles produce fewer flowers, but they are magnificent. The multifloras (many flowered) cover themselves with smaller, single blossoms that froth into summer's prettiest multicolor display.

Our Personal Recommendations
The charming Fantasy series miniatures bloom all winter indoors in a sunny window. For cascading window box flowers we plant Surfinia® and Supertunia™ hybrids; for mixed baskets we like Million Bells® petunias; for bedding, we use Wave™ and Tidal Wave™ hybrids. We love the new 'Blue Wave'™ for its velvety, dark blue, 2-in. blooms.

When, Where, and How to Plant

Calendula is a hardy annual whose seeds can be sown in the garden in spring as soon as the garden can be worked. You can also start seeds indoors six to eight weeks before the spring planting season begins. See Starting Seeds Indoors in the Appendix. Calendulas need full sun or very bright shade and rich, well-drained soil that contains enough humus to sustain moisture. See Soil Preparation in the Introduction, and Planting in the beginning of this chapter. Work the planting holes to a depth of 8 to 10 in. Space the seedlings 12 to 15 in. apart. Apply a 2-in. layer of mulch.

Growing Tips

Calendula needs moisture in the soil, both during germination and as the seedlings grow. But it doesn't like to be soggy wet.

Care

Deadhead to prolong flowering. During the hottest weeks of summer the plants may slow blooming: deadhead and be patient. The blooms will return when the weather freshens.

Companion Planting and Design

These are great bedding plants. In a flower bed, we group the plants in minimums of six. They are handsome in big tubs.

Our Personal Recommendations

Recommended for the front of the border is the Bon Bon series, compact 12-in. plants with $2^1/_2$- to 3-in. blooms in clear bright colors. The Kablouna series, 12 to 24 in. tall, has elegant crested flowers. 'Pacific Beauty' is double-flowered and excellent for cutting.

This is the plant referred to as a "marigold" in Shakespearian plays and in ancient herbals. An old-fashioned, bushy favorite about 24 in. tall, we love it for the lush fresh green of the foliage, the brilliance of the daisy-like flowers, and for their tangy aroma. There are singles and fluffy doubles. The flowers look wonderful in bouquets and they will last a week and more in vase water. The petals impart color and are so aromatic they once were used to flavor as well as to color desserts. One tablespoon of minced petals transforms cream cheese dips and desserts. In cool regions, pot marigolds bloom from early summer to fall. The plant actually does best in cool weather and even withstands light frosts.

Bloom Period and Seasonal Color
Early summer to fall; shades of orange, gold, lemon, apricot, and white.

Mature Height × Spread
12 to 30 in. × 12 to 15 in.

Salvia
Salvia splendens

Scarlet sage, the reddest of the summer flowers, is the parent of today's short, spiky cultivars in designer shades, aubergine to purple, gold to salmon, and, of course, red. The plant, a perennial subshrub we grow here as an annual, has glossy green foliage and small tubular red flowers clustered at the tops of leafy stems in thick, showy spikes. Massed in the sun, scarlet sage makes a striking display! Scarlet sage is a cousin of the lovely blue sages, varieties of Salvia farinacea, which are less showy but wonderful filler plants for borders and bouquets. The blue sages bush out and produce masses of slender, lavender-blue flower spikes that are beautiful in the garden, in late summer bouquets, and in dried arrangements.

Other Names
Sage, Scarlet Sage, Blue Sage

Bloom Period and Seasonal Color
Midsummer till frosts; many colors, and lavender blue.

Mature Height × Spread
1 to 3 ft. × 1 to 1¹/₂ ft.

When, Where, and How to Plant
You can start salvia seeds indoors ten to twelve weeks before mid-spring: grow the seedlings at about 55 degrees Fahrenheit. See Starting Seeds Indoors in the Appendix. Or, sow seeds in the garden in mid-spring. Full sun is best for scarlet sage, but blue sages flower moderately well with morning sun. Any well-drained, humusy soil is suitable. See Soil Preparation in the Introduction, and Planting in the beginning of this chapter. Work the planting holes to a depth of 8 to 10 in. Space the seedlings 6 to 8 in. apart. Apply a 2-in. layer of mulch.

Growing Tips
To promote rapid, unchecked growth, for the first two or three weeks water often enough to maintain the soil moisture. To encourage branching, pinch out the top 3 to 4 in. of the lead stem.

Care
After every flush of bloom, remove spent flower stems to promote flowering. The sages are drought-tolerant but need watering during prolonged dry spells.

Companion Planting and Design
Aubergine scarlet sage planted with coral New Guinea impatiens makes a striking show. The blue salvias are beautiful filler plants for shrub roses, and lovely with snapdragons or cosmos in complementary colors.

Our Personal Recommendations
Heat- and drought-tolerant *S. farinacea* 'Victoria', which is 18 to 20 in. tall, and the slightly taller Wedgewood blue 'Blue Bedder', are among the best blue salvias. 'Rhea' is a 14-in. blue salvia recommended for planters and small gardens. 'Sighum Blue' is a favorite of Carol Schminke, owner of Down to Earth Garden in New York State.

Snapdragon
Antirrhinum majus

When, Where, and How to Plant
Planting time for snapdragon seeds and seedlings is mid-spring, after the soil and the air have warmed. For a head start, sow seeds indoors ten to twelve weeks earlier. They're very easy to start. See Starting Seeds Indoors in the Appendix. Seedlings of every variety are offered at garden centers at planting time. Plant snapdragons in full sun. The ideal soil pH for snapdragons is 5.5 to 7.0. See Soil Preparation in the Introduction, and Planting in the beginning of this chapter. For seedlings make the planting holes 8 to 12 in. deep, and space them 6 to 10 in. apart. Apply mulch 3 in. deep starting 3 in. from the stems.

Growing Tips
For the first several weeks after planting, water often enough to keep the soil damp. When the seedlings are 4 in. high, pinch out the tips of the lead stems, and repeat for the next two sets of branches. Deadhead or harvest consistently. When the tall varieties are 18 in. high, stake the lead stem. Where rust is a problem, plant only rust-resistant strains.

Care
In midsummer, water deeply every week to ten days unless you have a soaking rain. When harvesting or deadheading snapdragons, cut the stem just above the next branching node to encourage continued blooming. Shear dwarf snapdragons after every flush of bloom.

Companion Planting and Design
The tall pastel snaps in rosy colors are beautiful with tall ageratum and silver artemisia. For windy places, choose large-flowered tetraploids like 'Ruffled Super Tetra' for their strong stems.

Our Personal Recommendations
For big bouquets and a back of the border show, plant Double Supreme hybrids that reach to 36 in. tall and bloom in clear, solid shades of red, pink, rose, and yellow. White Flower Farm is offering a new perennial snapdragon, 'Debutante', which is hardy in Zones 5 to 8. The flowering spikes bear raspberry pink flowers touched with yellow, and they will bloom June to September. The height is 18 to 24 in.

Spring through fall, snapdragons fill cutting gardens and flower borders with an abundance of soaring spires covered with colorful flowers in many colors and bi-colors. Press the flower at the throat, and the blossoms will open and close, like a snapping dragon. There's a snap variety for every garden purpose. As long as they are either harvested or deadheaded, snapdragons will bloom from early summer until frost. Very tall snapdragons are perfect for cutting and for color at the back of a flower bed. The Princess strain's luscious bi-colors are mid-height and also good cutting flowers. Mid-height, open-faced Monarch and "butterfly" hybrids are excellent border flowers. Dwarf snapdragons like 'Tahiti' make full, fluffy edgers.

Other Name
Snaps

Bloom Period and Seasonal Color
Spring through early fall; clear solid shades of red, pink, rose, yellow, and bi-colors.

Mature Height × Spread
7 to 30 in. × 8 to 15 in.

Spider Flower
Cleome hassleriana

Spider flower is an airy, wonderfully useful back-of-the-border filler flower that develops a big, rangy, multi-branched, and interesting structure. It produces masses of big, open, globe-shaped white, pink, or purple flowers, and has elegant divided leaves. The flowers are somewhat scented and are followed by attractive seedpods. Spider flower seedlings, and even seeds planted in the open garden, fairly leap to full maturity by midsummer and they stay beautiful well into early fall. The plant handles high heat and drought and is absolutely trouble free, but often gets to be so big it need staking. It self-sows lavishly (unless you deadhead) and will save you the trouble of replanting next year.

Bloom Period and Seasonal Color
Midsummer till frosts; white and shades of pink, rose, lilac, purple.

Mature Height × Spread
3 to 5 ft. × 1¹/₂ to 2 ft.

When, Where, and How to Plant
You can start seeds for spider flower indoors eight to ten weeks before the last local frost date: they grow well where temperatures are about 64 degrees Fahrenheit. See Starting Seeds Indoors in the Appendix. Cleome also flowers readily from seed sown in spring in the open garden in full sun. Not all garden markets offer spider flower seedlings, but the plants self-sow so generously, once you have planted cleome it probably will maintain itself in your garden. Almost any well-worked, well-drained, light soil suits the spider flower, and it does well even in sandy soil. See Soil Preparation in the Introduction, and Planting in the beginning of this chapter. Space seedlings 15 to 20 in. apart and mulch 2 in. deep.

Growing Tips
Maintain soil moisture until the seedlings are growing well. If you have sown seeds outdoors in the open garden, once the seedlings are up, water them weekly.

Care
Water deeply if the plants show signs of wilting in a drought. If the plants take off and begin to look like they're headed for shrub size, tie the lead stem to a sturdy stake. Since cleome self-sows lavishly, deadhead now and then to minimize the thinning you will have to do next year.

Companion Planting and Design
A mass planting of spider flowers is handsome growing against a stone wall, and it is an excellent background plant for the flower border, and a lovely addition to a meadow garden.

Our Personal Recommendations
'Rose Queen', with its deep pink buds and pale pink flowers is a favorite, along with 'Purple Queen' and 'Helen Campbell', a beautiful white spider flower. New dwarf varieties such as 'Linde Armstrong' and 'Sparkler Blush' are excellent fillers for the middle of the flowering border.

Sunflower

Helianthus annuus

When, Where, and How to Plant

Sunflowers pop up and grow so quickly, you can sow the seeds directly in the garden once the soil is warm. Thin, or plant, the seedlings to stand about 18 in. apart. Sow seeds where the plants are to grow. We have started sunflowers successfully indoors about four weeks before planting season, which is mid-spring; however, they quickly become leggy, so don't start them too early. See Starting Seeds Indoors in the Appendix. Sunflowers bloom most fully in full sun, thrive in ordinary even poor soil, and tolerate drought. See Soil Preparation in the Introduction, and Planting in the beginning of this chapter. The very tall varieties may need staking as the seedheads become very heavy. Mulch 2 in. deep between plants. When deer chomped the tops off a row of tall sunflowers, we learned that the plants will branch if topped, so now we shorten the sunflowers at the front of the row to about 2 to 3 ft., which makes a pretty picture.

Growing Tip

Keep the soil moist until the sunflowers are growing lustily.

Care

To save the seedheads from the birds, wrap the heads in gauze before the seeds ripen—then you can harvest the seeds for winter use.

Companion Planting and Design

The tall sunflowers belong in a row of their own in the kitchen garden, or lining a fence or a blank wall. The new dwarfish forms look well in a flowering border, and we plant them with the vegetables and herbs in our kitchen gardens.

Our Personal Recommendations

Holly's favorite sunflower is 'Golden Pheasant': instead of ray petals around a disc of seeds, the whole flower head is a mass of glorious golden yellow petals. Another favorite for cutting is 'Sunburst Mixed', which bears 4-in. flowers in deep crimson, lemon, bronze, and gold on strong branching stems to 4 ft. high.

The sunflower is neither the most beautiful, nor the most exotic, nor the most colorful flower we have, but it's a real charmer where children are concerned, and newer branching varieties provide masses of huge, glorious cut flowers. The annual species, planted in spring, sends thick stalks soaring as high as 12 ft. and the flower heads often are 12 in. across with a central disk surrounded by yellow ray petals. The flowers are best picked in evening or early morning. Remove the leaves and plunge the stems into boiling water for one and a half to two minutes, then condition the stems in water in a tall container overnight. Once hardened, the stems can usually be re-cut and used without further treatment. Birds love the seeds and deer relish both leaves and flowers, alas!

Bloom Period and Seasonal Color

Summer to fall; yellow, orange, maroon, creamy white, bi-colors; some with green centers, some with maroon or black centers.

Mature Height × Spread

2 to 12 ft. × 2 to 2¹/₂ ft.

Sweet Alyssum

Lobularia maritima

Sweet alyssum is a fragrant, frothy little edging plant that from summer through fall just covers itself with tiny, scented florets in sparkling white, rosy-violet, or purple. The plant has a dainty appearance and spreads outward, becoming a low sprawling mound by the end of the season. In extreme heat in midsummer, a slump in flower production can occur, but the blossoms return when cooler weather arrives. However you use alyssum, be sure to set at least a few plants by the porch or patio where you can enjoy its sweet scent in late summer. Alyssum is one of the plants that does exceptionally well near the sea and it can be set out around taller plants as a living mulch to keep the ground cool.

Bloom Period and Seasonal Color
June until frosts; white, rosy-violet, purple.

Mature Height × Spread
4 to 8 in. × 1 to 1¹/₂ ft.

When, Where, and How to Plant
If you want to grow your own alyssum, start the seeds indoors between February 1 and 15—but alyssum is slow to germinate. See Starting Seeds Indoors in the Appendix. Plant the seedlings when the soil has warmed. Sweet alyssum can do with a little less than direct sun all day, but it needs at least four to six hours of direct sun to flower well. The ideal for sweet alyssum is well-drained, humusy soil with a pH between 6.0 and 7.0. Dig the bed, or generous planting holes, 6 in. deep. See Soil Preparation in the Introduction, and Planting in the beginning of this chapter. Set the seedlings 6 to 8 in. apart. Apply mulch 2-in. thick starting 3 in. from the stems.

Growing Tip
To promote rapid, unchecked growth, for the first two or three weeks water often enough to sustain the soil moisture.

Care
In midsummer, water deeply when you water the flower garden. Sweet alyssum readily self-sows. Discard volunteers, because chances are these will turn out to be plants that have reverted to the original, less-interesting species, not the beautiful cultivar you planted.

Companion Planting and Design
Sweet alyssum makes a neat, fragrant edger for flowering borders and walks. We add sweet alyssum to hanging baskets, planters, and tubs, set so the stems will drip over the container edges as the plant fills out. It thrives tucked into moist planting pockets in a dry stone wall and is very pretty with purplish ornamental peppers.

Our Personal Recommendations
Some of our favorite varieties are 'Little Dorrit', 'Noel Sutton', 'Elizabeth Taylor', 'Royal Wedding', 'Creme Beauty', and 'Geranium Pink'. 'Snowcloth' is a really small form. 'Carpet of Snow' is a favorite among our consultants for its evening fragrance.

Zinnia

Zinnia elegans and hybrids

When, Where, and How to Plant

You can sow seeds indoors about four weeks before planting time, which is when the soil has warmed. See Starting Seeds Indoors in the Appendix. The smaller varieties bloom in four to five weeks from sowing. Zinnias do best with full sun, but bloom with four to six hours of sun. Dig the soil 8 to 12 in. deep. See Soil Preparation in the Introduction, and Planting in the beginning of this chapter. Set seedlings of miniatures 6 in. apart, and the larger zinnias 18 in. apart. We can't do without zinnias, but they are subject to leaf spot and mildew, so avoid mulch and crowding, which encourages mildew.

Growing Tips

When the seedlings are 6 in. high, pinch out the tips of the lead stems to encourage branching. Deadhead consistently, and harvest flowers at will. Cut the stem just above the next branching node and new flowering stems will develop, rising between each pair of leaves and the main stem.

Care

In a drought, water every ten days to two weeks: overwatering encourages mildew. Where mildew is a problem, choose mildew-resistant cultivars. Cornell University research suggests that spraying with a solution of 1 tablespoon of ultrafine or horticultural oil plus 1 tablespoon of baking soda (sodium bicarbonate) per gallon of water protects against mildew.

Companion Planting and Design

Zinnias are ideal follow-on plants for spaces left empty by the passing of spring flowers. Dwarfs like 'Dasher' and 'Liliput' make colorful edgers. Ribbons of award-winning 'Peter Pan' zinnias, small plants with big flowers, brighten a garden path. Little *Z. angustifolia* is a spreading form to use in hanging baskets and as an edger. An annual that makes a delightful edger for zinnias is the pretty little creeping zinnia, *Sanvitalia procumbens*.

Our Personal Recommendations

For cutting and show, we like tall zinnias with blooms 4 to 5 in. across on 30-in. stems, and showy 'Candy Cane', 17-in. plants with semi-double and double flowers striped pink, rose, and cerise. The 12- to 14-in. 'Small World Pink' hybrid zinnias are pretty and billed as disease-resistant.

We love the zinnia's sparkling colors, wild and wonderful flower forms, and cut-and-come again attitude. One of the very best annuals for vibrant color and lasting vase life, it's a staple in our gardens. Zinnias are fun because there are so many varieties with which to experiment. These are upright plants that branch when harvested and they come in colors and sizes suited to every design purpose. The petals of some varieties are quilled like a cactus, others curl, and some are ruffled. There are flat-petaled forms, doubles, and singles. The large-flowered zinnias bloom less freely than the small-flowered forms, and need more time to come into bloom.

Bloom Period and Seasonal Color

When deadheaded, zinnias bloom summer through early fall. Colors include shades of red, pink, orange, magenta, yellow, white, and bi-colors.

Mature Height × Spread

$1/2$ to 3 ft. × 1 to $3^1/2$ ft.

Bulbs, Corms, and Tubers *for New England*

The earliest flowers come from bulbs, corms, and tubers planted September and October the fall before. The little bulbs open first, in March in our gardens that are in Zones 4 and 5. We plant these early risers under shrubs and trees that are tall enough to allow them dappled light. We edge flower beds with them, and woodland paths, and set them adrift in rock gardens. We plant lots of them near entrances where they keep us aware of the progress spring is making in New England. Each small bulb adds just a scrap of color to the winter landscape, so we plant them in drifts of twenty to 100. Many of these small bulbs thrive and perennialize even in lawns.

The next wave of color comes in late April and May from large bulbs planted in fall—depending on the severity of the winter and on how much heat early spring brings. Spring temperatures can be unpredictable: now and then in March and April, heat waves throw everything off. The earliest of the big bulbs to bloom are the perfumed hyacinths, which we plant near entrances. Then come the daffodils and the tulips. We plant dozens in flower borders accompanied by perennials (and annuals) that will grow up and hide the fading bulb foliage that must be allowed to ripen before it is removed. That's the major drawback of the big bulb flowers—for the larger bulb flowers to bloom well the following year, the foliage must be allowed to ripen (yellow) before it is removed. That takes weeks and the process is unsightly.

Oriental Lilies

The large spring bulbs are most effective planted in groups of ten in flower borders and naturalized in drifts of twenty or more.

The summer-flowering bulbs provide excellent screening for the fading foliage of the spring-flowering bulbs. They come into bloom when the nights turn warm—mid- to late June—and some go on until mid-September. Those that are winter hardy can be planted the fall before, while the tender bulbs are set out in the spring. To be effective these big bulbs need to be planted in sets of five or ten. In the flower borders, we like to add a few real tropicals, including canna and the ornamental banana, for their exotic foliage. They're available pot-grown in late spring, and some gardeners have luck wintering canna and other tropicals in their containers in a cool basement. We've tried wintering canna and bougainvillea in our root cellar, which theoretically stays at 42 degrees Fahrenheit year-round, but the bulbs rotted. Our bloom sequence list includes our favorite tropicals and a few exquisite bulbs that don't live through our winters and have to be lifted and stored. Some tender bulbs that shouldn't survive New England winters in the ground, do. We think it has to do with how much insulation is provided by deep snow cover. Tuberose, which was first discovered in Mexico, wintered over in Jacqui's first big garden, which was in Plainfield, in northern Vermont. Or was it a tender jonquil? Either way, that's an almost unthinkable thought, but the unpredictable and almost impossible are part of what makes gardening so fascinating in New England.

Bulbs that bloom in fall when all other flowers have gone by have a special place in the gardener's heart. The silky petals and tender colors look so fragile, but they endure cold rain and windstorms. The fall-flowering bulbs can be planted in summer—as soon as they're available. These small bulbs are most effective planted in groups of twenty and fifty.

When, Where, and How to Plant

Spring-flowering bulbs in waiting can be stored in the crisper or a cool garage or cellar. Do not store them with apples, which put out vapors that encourage ripening. If you can, plant them after the very first frost. Planted late they have shorter stems and bloom late. Most bulbs bloom earliest growing in full sun; in part shade they open later. Their first year, spring flowering bulbs will bloom planted in some shade. But to perennialize and bloom fully they need at least bright or dappled light under deciduous trees, or bright shade under a tall evergreen. Ideal is a sunny, sheltered location whose soil is dryish in summer and in winter. The small fall-flowering bulbs can be planted as soon as you have them.

The ideal soil for bulbs is light, very well drained, and improved by additions of organic matter such as peat moss, compost, or aged pine bark, along with an organic 4-10-6 fertilizer at the rate of 5 to 10 pounds per 100 square feet. The ideal pH range for most is 6.0 to 7.0. See Soil Preparation and Improvement in the Introduction. Set bulbs so the pointed tips are upright; set corms and tubers with the roots facing down. For bulbs under 2 inches in size provide holes at least 5 inches deep and 1 inch wide. Or, prepare a planting bed 5 to 6 inches deep. Set the small bulbs 2 inches apart. Plant bulbs 2 inches or larger in holes 8 inches deep and 3 inches wide. Or prepare a planting bed 8 to 10 inches deep. Set the bulbs 4 to 6 inches apart. To create drifts for naturalizing, dig an irregularly shaped planting bed, throw the bulbs out by the handful, and plant where they fall. Avoid leaving bits of bulb casings around the planting—squirrels notice.

Before planting bulbs, inventory the vole population. For voles your bulbs are the local gourmet counter. Squirrels shop there, too, and store their catch for later use. When they forget where they stored your bulbs, the flowers bloom in totally unexpected, sometimes delightful, places. To foil the sweet dears, plant your bulbs in pockets of VoleBloc™ or PermaTill®. Either one improves drainage, by the way. Place 2 inches of VoleBloc™ or PermaTill® in the bottom of the hole. Set the bulb on top of it, and fill in all around with VoleBloc™ or PermaTill® leaving just the tip exposed. Fill the hole with a mix of 50 percent

VoleBloc™ or PermaTill® and improved soil from the hole. Mulch with 2 inches of pine needles, oak leaves, composted wood chips, or with shredded bark. Daffodils don't need protection from voles, or, so far, from deer because they are toxic to wildlife.

Care

Most of the bulbs we recommend come back, at least for a season or two. Daffodils and some of the small bulbs are likely to return and to multiply indefinitely. Allow the stems and foliage of the other bulbs to ripen six to seven weeks before removing it. The foliage of the bulbs you plan to lift and store for winter also should be allowed to ripen before being removed. Tulip foliage may be cut when it yellows halfway down. If well fertilized, some tulips perennialize, but the following year many just put up puny foliage and fail to bloom. We dig and discard those. Most bulbs require ample moisture during the season of active growth, from the moment the first pip breaks ground. Once the foliage disappears the bulbs are dormant, and excess watering isn't good for them. After flowering, but before the foliage disappears, spread an organic, slow-release fertilizer over the bulb plantings at the rate of 4 to 6 pounds to 100 square feet. Large bulbs benefit from deadheading. Remove only the flower itself. Allowing the flower stem as well as the foliage to ripen adds nourishment to the bulb and that enhances next year's flowering.

Pink 'Maywonder' and red 'Ile de France' Tulips, interplanted with Grape Hyacinths, encircle a White Birch.

Bloom Sequence of Flowering Bulbs

Late Winter/Early Spring Bulbs

Early Crocus, *Crocus* spp.
Dwarf Beardless Iris, *Iris reticulata*
Glory-of-the-Snow, *Chionodoxa luciliae*
Grape Hyacinth, *Muscari* spp. and hybrids
Miniature Cyclamen, *Cyclamen coum*
Miniature Daffodils, *Narcissus* 'Tete-a-Tete'
    and other early daffodils

Snowdrops, *Galanthus nivalis*
Species Tulips, *Tulipa saxatilis, T. tarda,*
    T. turkistanica, and others
Squill, *Scilla mischtschenkoana*
Striped Squill, *Pushkinia scilloides*
Windflower, *Anemone blanda*
Winter Aconite, *Eranthis hyemalis*

Early/Mid-Spring Bulbs

Bearded Iris, *Iris* hybrids
Daffodils, *Narcissus*, early and
    midseason
Fritillaria, *Fritillaria imperialis*
    'Rubra Maxima'
Hyacinth, *Hyacinthus* hybrids
Late Crocus, *Crocus* spp.
Lily-of-the-Valley, *Convallaria majalis*

Mid- and Late Season Tulips,
    Tulipa spp. and hybrids
Silver Bells, *Ornithogalum nutans*
Starflower, *Ipheion uniflorum* 'Wisley Blue'
Wild Hyacinth, Wood Hyacinth,
    Hyacinthoides hispanica
    (syn. *Scilla campanulata*)
Wood Sorrel, *Oxalis adenophylla*

Summer Bulbs

Crocosmia, *Crocosmia* spp. and hybrids
Dahlia, *Dahlia* hybrids
Dwarf Canna, *Canna* × *hybrida*
Flowering Onion, *Allium giganteum*
Gladiola, *Gladiolus* hybrids
Lilies, *Lilium* spp. and hybrids
Peacock Orchid, *Acidanthera bicolor*

Peruvian Daffodil, *Hymenocallis narcissiflora*
    (syn. *Ismene calathina*)
Poppy Anemones, *Anemone coronaria*
Rain Lily, *Zephyranthes* spp.
Spider Lily, *Lycoris* spp.
Summer Hyacinth, *Galtonia* spp.
Tuberose, *Polianthes tuberosa*

Fall/Winter Bulbs

Colchicum, *Colchicum autumnale*
Hardy Cyclamen, *Cyclamen hederifolium*
Fall Crocus, Saffron Crocus, *Crocus sativus,*
    C. kotschyanus (syn. *C. zonatus*),
    C. speciosus

Lily-of-the-Field, *Sternbergia lutea*
Winter Daffodil, including Tenby Daffodils,
    Narcissus asturiensis and
    'Grand Soleil d'Or'

Late Blooming Bulbs and Tropicals:

Autumn Zephyr Lily, *Zephyranthes candidum*
    (Zones 6 to 9)
Canna, *Canna* × *generalis* (tropical)
Hardy Cyclamen, *Cyclamen hederifolium*
    (Zones 5 to 9)
Ornamental Banana, *Musa velutina* (tropical)
Peacock Orchid, *Acidanthera bicolor* (tropical)

Peruvian Daffodil, *Hymenocallis narcissiflora*
    (syn. *Ismene calathina*) (tropical)
Spider Lily, *Lycoris squamigera* (Zones 5 to 8)
Summer Hyacinth, *Galtonia candicans*
    (Zones 6-11)
Tuberose, *Polianthes tuberosa* (Zones 8 to 11)

Bearded Iris
Iris spp. and hybrids

A well-nourished, tall bearded iris in bloom is awesome. Successful everywhere in New England, these colorful spring to early summer flowers display the classic iris form—three upright standards that meet at the tips and three colorful bearded falls. The "beard" is a fuzz of filaments. The straight flower stalks end in branched stems bearing several buds. We use the dwarf bearded (about 15 in. tall) in flower beds and plant in groups for cutting; the tall bearded irises (28 to 40 in. high), are worthy of garden settings that feature each one. Many are ruffled or veined/laced with other colors. Their sword-shaped foliage anchors the garden when the flowers have gone by. Irises are beautiful in groups of three to five in a small garden or ten to twelve in a large garden.

Bloom Period and Seasonal Color
Spring to early summer; shades of white, yellow, apricot, rose, maroon, blue, lavender, purple, and bi-colors.

Mature Height × Spread
15 to 40 in. × 20 to 40 in.

Zones
3 to 8

When, Where, and How to Plant
Bearded irises develop from fleshy, horizontal, elongated stems called rhizomes: they look rather like long, thin potatoes. The best period for planting and transplanting bearded irises is midsummer to early fall. However, we've transplanted irises in spring and they survived. Bearded irises do not tolerate "wet feet"—don't place them in borders that require constant moisture. In the coolest regions of New England, you may need to protect them with winter mulch. Most irises prefer full sun and light, well-drained, rather sandy soil that has been worked to a depth of at least 10 in. See Soil Improvement in the Introduction. Two to three weeks before planting, work an organic, slow-release fertilizer into the top of the soil. Bury the rhizome with the top just barely beneath the surface of the soil but with the roots anchored deeply enough to be held firmly in place. Space the plants 8 to 18 in. apart, depending on the type—dwarf to tall bearded. Mulch 2 in. deep starting 3 in. from the crown or rhizome.

Growing Tip
Water a new planting of irises often enough to keep the bed slightly damp.

Care
Deadhead regularly, and when blooming is over, cut the stalk back to the crown. All irises are heavy feeders and need regular annual fertilization. Bearded irises need to be divided when the rhizomes begin to crowd each other—usually in two to three years. Midsummer, July or August, is the best time to divide and transplant bearded irises.

Companion Planting and Design
Dwarf bearded irises are good specimens for the rock garden and they naturalize and multiply quickly.

Our Personal Recommendations
We love 'Immortality', a tall bearded iris that is pure white, ruffled, blooms in midseason, and sometimes re-blooms later. A little beardless iris, *I. reticulata*—the very first flower of the year—is only 5 in. high, and many of the cultivars are fragrant.

Crocosmia
Crocosmia spp. and hybrids

When, Where, and How to Plant

Crocosmia may suffer in cold winters in Zone 6, so plant it in a protected area of the garden and provide it with a winter mulch. If your winters are colder than Zone 6, plan to lift and store the plants for the winter. Garden centers offer container-grown crocosmia in mid-spring, the planting season. In cool regions crocosmia needs full sun to be all it can be, but where summer gets very hot it may benefit from some protection from noon sun. Crocosmia is tolerant as to pH, but needs a well-drained site and humusy, fertile soil. See Soil Improvement in the Introduction and the planting instructions at the beginning of this chapter. Set the corms 3 in. deep and 5 in. apart. Plant container-grown crocosmia so that the crown is level with the ground. Mulch 2 in. deep starting 3 in. from the edge of the planting.

Growing Tip

Keep the soil nicely moist during the early growing season.

Care

Crocosmia does best given sustained moisture, but the plant is versatile. Crocosmia is self-cleaning and so it doesn't need deadheading. The flowers are followed by attractive seed capsules that can be left until fall, then the foliage should be cut down to a few inches above the crown. For winter protection in Zone 6, mulch with evergreen boughs or hay; in cooler regions lift the corms and store them for the winter in a frost-free area. Fertilize the bed between late winter and early spring with an organic, slow-release fertilizer at the rate of 6 pounds per 100 sq. ft.

Companion Planting and Design

Use crocosmia to screen the last of the foliage of the late spring bulbs: it will grow up and make a wonderful splash of color in the hot, dry months. Plant crocosmia in a flowering border in groups of five or ten toward the center of the bed. It needs lots of space all around.

Our Personal Recommendation

'Lucifer' is our favorite.

Crocosmia is a tall, exceptionally beautiful and showy, summer-flowering bulb that will remind you of a more refined gladiola. Like the gladiola it grows from a corm and sends up fresh, handsome, sword-shaped leaves followed by slender, branching spikes of flowers that provide many weeks of vivid color for the garden in the dull summer months. The blossoms are dearly loved by butterflies and hummingbirds. The most famous of the cultivated varieties is 'Lucifer', whose large, silky flowers are a vivid flame red. Crocosmia is a long-lasting garden perennial that lives through winters, even without snow cover, in Zone 6. In our warmest region, Zone 7, it's been known to perennialize and multiply. Crocosmia is also an excellent cutting flower.

Bloom Period and Seasonal Color
July and August; orange-red, red, yellow, apricot.

Mature Height × Spread
1¹/₂ to 2 ft. × 1¹/₂ to 2 ft.

Zones
6 to 10

Crocus

Crocus spp. and hybrids

There are both fall-blooming and spring-blooming crocuses. The late winter, early spring crocuses are planted the fall before, and begin to bloom about the same time as the snowdrops raise their tiny white bells. Often enough these early birds face up to and bloom through the last snowfall. The brightly-colored, little cup- or chalice-shaped flowers have vivid yellow anthers and come in many colors. Some have beautiful contrasting stripes or streaks. The grassy green leaves come up after the flowers and in some varieties have white or silver midribs. The fall crocuses (Zones 4 to 7) produce their elegant cup-shaped blooms in early and mid-fall. They are planted in summer. The following year the grassy leaves come up in the spring then die down in summer.

Bloom Period and Seasonal Color
Late winter and early spring; white, pink, lavender, purple, yellow, orange; many are striped or streaked with contrasting colors.

Mature Height × Spread
4 to 6 in. × 2 to 4 in.

Zones
3 to 8

When, Where, and How to Plant
Plant spring-flowering crocus in September or October, in full sun. Ideal is a sunny, sheltered place where the soil is dryish in summer and in winter. The ideal soil is light, well drained, and improved by additions of organic matter and a 4-10-6 bulb fertilizer. The ideal pH range is 6.0 to 7.0. See Soil Improvement in the Introduction and the planting instructions at the beginning of this chapter, including instructions on discouraging voles and squirrels. Provide holes 5 in. deep and 1 in. wide, or a planting bed 5 to 6 in. deep. Set the bulbs 2 in. apart. Avoid leaving bits of bulb casings around the planting: squirrels notice. Mulch the area.

Growing Tip
Mark the areas where crocuses are planted so that during their dormant period you don't accidentally dig them up as you are planting other things.

Care
After flowering, and before the foliage disappears, spread an organic, slow-release bulb fertilizer over the planted area at the rate of 4 to 6 pounds for every 100 sq. ft.

Companion Planting and Design
Plant crocus in drifts of twenty to 100. We keep lots of spring-blooming crocuses near house entrances, early reminders that spring is coming, and we set them at the very edge of flower beds, fronting shrub borders, and along woodland paths. Under tall trees and at the edge of our water garden we plant fall-blooming crocuses along with the "fall crocus" *Colchicum autumnale*.

Our Personal Recommendations
For spring bloom, we love the fragrant little snow crocus, historic *C. chrysanthus*, one of the very first to flower, that bears many stemless yellow, blue, or white blossoms with yellow anthers; *C. tommasinianus*, the most tolerant of moisture during dormancy, and somewhat squirrel-resistant; and *C. vernus*, the Dutch hybrids, which bear 3-in. flowers, some striped or feathered, and in cultivation since 1765. For fall-flowering we like *C. speciosus*, which blooms early, is the showiest, the easiest, and can stay in bloom until hard frosts; *C. kotschyanus* (syn. *C. zonatus*), which bears 4- to 6-in.-tall, rose-lilac flowers; and the later blooming saffron crocus, *C. sativus*.

Daffodil
Narcissus spp. and hybrids

When, Where, and How to Plant
Plant the bulbs in September or October in full or partial sun. The ideal soil is well drained and slightly acid. Provide well-worked fertile loam with excellent drainage. See the Soil Preparation section of the Introduction. Some of the bigger daffodil bulbs are two or three bulbs attached: don't separate them. Set the bulbs out following the instructions at the beginning of this chapter. Plant them 8 in. deep, about 3 to 6 in. apart, and mulch the area.

Growing Tip
To perennialize daffodils, after flowering and before the foliage disappears, spread an organic, slow-release bulb fertilizer over the area, 4 to 6 pounds for every 100 sq. ft.

Care
Deadheading isn't essential. Allow the foliage to yellow about six weeks before cutting it back. Don't bind the leaves: that cuts off light and oxygen. When daffodils get smaller and crowded, divide them just before the foliage has died. Replant them at once, or store them in well-ventilated trays at 50 to 80 degrees Fahrenheit and replant them in the fall. Cut daffodils last well: before combining just-cut daffodils (which contain toxic substances) with other flowers, soak them in water overnight and discard the water.

Companion Planting and Design
Plant daffodils in irregular drifts of ten, twenty, or more. Large daffodils are breathtaking perennialized in woods, fronting evergreens, edging meadows, and along the banks of ponds and streams. The miniatures are exquisite in rock gardens, containers, near boulders, in rocky nooks. By choosing bulbs that come up early, midseason, and late you can have daffodils from early spring until early summer.

Our Personal Recommendations
Nurseryman André Viette, whose father founded the famous Martin Viette Nursery on Long island, recommends for perennializing 'February Gold', 'Avalanche', 'Geranium', 'Hawera', 'Ice Wings', 'Quail', 'Sir Winston Churchill', and 'Tete-a-Tete'. Lynette Courtney, our consultant for New England bulbs, favors 'Ice Follies', fragrant 'Cheerfulness' and 'Tahiti', little 'Jack Snipe', 8-in. 'Minnow', which bears several flowers per stem, and split-corona 'Butterfly'. We find paperwhites reliable for forcing.

Daffodils are big bulb flowers that announce the arrival of spring with a splashy show of gold, cream, or bi-colored trumpets on straight 4- to 20-in. stems. In Zone 6 the early daffodils often bloom with the melting of the snow. In our Zones 5 and 4, early daffodils and early to midseason miniatures such as 'Tete-a-Tete' flower in early or late April, depending on the winter. Daffodils perennialize readily and are safe from squirrels and other animals because they are poisonous to them. The names "daffodil," "narcissus," and "jonquil" cause confusion: Narcissus is the botanical name, and the common name "daffodil" may be used in its place. Jonquils are a specific type of daffodil related to the species N. jonquilla, which are late bloomers that bear a cluster of flowers on each stem and are exquisitely scented. Not all species are hardy to Zone 3.

Other Name
Jonquil

Bloom Period and Seasonal Color
Spring; white, yellow, gold, orange, bi-colors.

Mature Height × Spread
4 to 20 in. × 3 to 5 in.

Zones
3 to 8

Dahlia

Dahlia cultivars and hybrids

The dahlia is one of the great flowers of late summer and early fall, an easy-to-grow, bushy perennial with lush foliage and many-petaled flowers in extraordinary forms and clear colors. The American Dahlia Society recognizes fourteen distinct types of this New World flower, discovered in the sixteenth century in the mountains of Mexico by members of the Cortez expedition. But for gardeners, there are two main groups: the seed-grown bedding plants sold in flats of mixed colors, and the big show dahlias grown as staked specimens in containers or at the middle or back of the border. The flowers range from 6- and 12-in. "dinner plates" to 1½- and 2-in. pom-pom charmers. The crisp, almost translucent petals catch the light and in paler shades can be luminous.

Bloom Period and Seasonal Color
Late summer, early fall; pastels and jewel tones of pink, salmon, white, cream, lemon, heliotrope mauve, red, bi-colors.

Mature Height × Spread
1½ to 5 ft. × 1 to 2½ ft.

Zones
5 to 9

When, Where, and How to Plant
Plant tubers, or container-grown dahlias, when the lilacs bloom. Provide an open sunny site and soil improved as described in the Introduction—light, fertile, well drained, humusy, pH 6.0 to 7.5. Set tubers, or container-grown plants, 18 to 24 in. apart. For 5-footers, provide sturdy, equally tall stakes. For tubers dig planting holes 6 to 8 in. deep with the eye portion nearest the stake, if there is to be one. Cover the tuber with 2 to 3 in. of soil. Water when a shoot appears about four weeks later. Then add a few inches more soil, water, and repeat at intervals as the plant grows until the hole is filled. When the stem is 12 in. tall, tie the stem to its stake. Tie on other branches as the plant matures.

Growing Tips
Dahlias require watering weekly or every ten days unless there's a good soaking rain. Harvest the blooms for flower arrangements or deadhead.

Care
Place cut dahlia stems in water at 150 to 160 degrees Fahrenheit to harden overnight then re-cut the stems and arrange them. In our warmer regions, given a deep winter mulch, dahlias may perennialize. But growers recommend digging and storing the tubers when the yellowing tops die back after the first killing frost. Lift the crown with a spading fork, remove the foliage, and wash off the dirt. Dry them out of direct sun for a day or so. Label and store them in cedar chips, vermiculite, sand, or peat moss in a cool dry place at 40 to 45 degrees Fahrenheit. In spring when the eyes begin to sprout, divide the tubers, providing each with at least one eye, and replant.

Companion Planting and Design
We plant dahlias in cutting and vegetable gardens: 5-footers get a row of their own. We use bedding dahlias to edge perennials and with blue salvia, mint, asters, lavender, purple basil, and statice. In the flower beds, we front tall dahlias with baby's breath, and grassy liriope.

Our Personal Recommendation
For cutting, we favor the long-stemmed cactus-flowered dahlias.

Fancy-Leaved Caladium

Caladium bicolor

When, Where, and How to Plant

We start caladiums indoors in a warm room about eight weeks before the weather turns warm enough to put out tropicals—55 degrees Fahrenheit. We lay them on 2 to 3 in. of peat moss or sterile soilless mix in big shallow trays, set about 8 in. apart with the knobble side up. The little straggle of dry roots should face down: planted upside down, they'll grow but may have smaller leaves. Caladiums are rather slow to start up but then they grow quickly. They develop well under grow lights and in a big sunny window. Once the tubers sprout, transplant them to beds or containers of potting or garden soil that is well drained, rich in humus or peat moss, and fertilized with a slow-release, organic fertilizer. You can set caladiums outdoors when nights are above 60 degrees and day temperatures are at or above 70 degrees Fahrenheit. They do best in a semi-sunny or a lightly shaded location. Deer love caladiums!

Growing Tip

Keep the soil evenly moist.

Care

As fall temperatures drop, let caladiums dry out and store them in dry peat moss, vermiculite, or perlite at 70 to 75 degrees Fahrenheit.

Companion Planting and Design

Caladiums are superb bedding and pot plants, glorious growing with impatiens whose colors complement the leaves: red impatiens with red-centered caladiums, white impatiens with white and green caladiums. For a showy garden display, plant caladiums in groups of four to six.

Our Personal Recommendations

The *C. bicolor* cultivars of great beauty include 21-in. tall, cool white and green 'White Christmas'; the lovely, light-as-air, 18- to 20-in., white and green-limned-red 'White Queen'; 18-in., dark green, white frosted rose and red 'Rose Bud'; solid red-bordered green 'Frieda Hemple'; rosy 15-in. 'Florida Sweetheart'; luminous, 16- to 18-in., shell pink touched with green 'Pink Symphony'; and 8-in. 'Miss Muffet'.

Caladiums, which grow from tubers, are not winter hardy in our area, but we can't imagine summer without these beautiful foliage plants to brighten semi-shaded areas with their incredible patterns. Unlike the time-bound show that flowers provide, the caladium's rich glow is with you all season long, growing more beautiful as the plants fill out. The leaves are large and shield-shaped, held on slender stalks 12 to 24 in. tall. The old-fashioned name for them is "dancing ladies" because they flutter in the wind. The fanciful leaf patterns are pink, red, and/or white on green, and in some varieties almost translucent. The leaves are used in flower arrangements; the flowers are insignificant and should be removed so the strength of the plant can go to the leaves.

Other Name
Dancing Ladies

Bloom Period and Seasonal Color
All season foliage color; green overlaid with patterns in white, pink, rose, salmon, crimson.

Mature Height × Spread
20 to 30 in. × 12 to 18 in.

Zones
9 to 11

Flowering Onion
Allium spp. and cultivars

The strap-shaped leaves of the flowering onions do smell like—onions—but several species have appealing flowers, and all are excellent pest-proof plants. There are two types of flowers. The most interesting are perfect spheres composed of many blue-purple or white-pink florets on leafless stalks above tufts of dark green, strap-shaped foliage. Think huge chives. The tallest is Allium giganteum, giant onion, whose round, 6-in., reddish purple flower heads top stems 35 to 45 in. tall. The flowers of A. tuberosum, which is known as garlic chives or Oriental garlic, are spreading clusters of fragrant white florets, typical of the other type of ornamental onion. The ornamental onions create striking accents in a mixed border. They're also lasting, eye-catching cut flowers and excellent for drying.

Other Name
Ornamental Onion

Bloom Period and Seasonal Color
Late spring and late summer; blue, purple, pink, white, yellow.

Mature Height × Spread
6 to 48 in. × 10 to 15 in.
Flower Heads: 1 to 12 in. across

Zones
3 or 4 to 8

When, Where, and How to Plant
Plant the bulbs for flowering onions in late fall in full sun or very light shade. The ideal soil is well drained, humusy, and fertile, with a pH of 6.0 to 7.5. You'll find instructions on improving soil for bulbs in the Soil Preparation section in the Introduction. Plant the bulbs, large or small, following the instructions at the beginning of this chapter. Set the bulbs, depending on their size, 3 to 5 or 8 in. deep, 3 to 6 or 8 in. apart. Mulch the area.

Growing Tips
Maintain moisture during the flowering onion's growth period; after that the soil can be average to dry. To encourage the plants to repeat, after flowering and before the foliage disappears, spread an organic, slow-release bulb fertilizer over the area, 4 to 6 pounds for every 100 sq. ft.

Care
Even in the cooler reaches of the flowering onions' hardiness range they repeat at least two or three years if the flower is removed after flowering and the foliage is allowed to mature fully before it is removed. Deadheading helps.

Companion Planting and Design
Plant flowering onions where the foliage of other flowers serves as a filler and screen for the onion foliage while it is ripening. The giant onion is striking in arrangements of flowers, fresh or dried.

Our Personal Recommendations
There are dozens of interesting ornamental onions. *A. aflatunense* is a smaller version of the giant allium and blooms earlier. Our bulbs consultant, Lynette Courtney, recommends drumsticks, *A. sphaerocephalum*, small, perfectly round, reddish-lavender flower heads on stalks 20 in. tall; starbursts, *A.* 'Globemaster', 'Purple Sensation', and 'Mars'; star of Persia's fireworks display, *A. christophii* and 'Lucy Ball', for huge, airy, round heads in burgundy through purple, lilac, and silvery pink; the lily leek, *A moly*, a summer bloomer also known as golden garlic; the heavenly azure blue globe onion, *A. caeruleum* (syn. *A. azureum*) Zones 4 to 7, which blooms in late spring on 20-in. stems; and fuschsia-rose *A. oreophylum*.

When, Where, and How to Plant

Gladiolas are usually planted in a full-sun cutting or vegetable garden. In Zones 3 through 6 gladiolas are handled as annuals, set out in mid-spring and lifted for the winter. In warm micro-climates and in sheltered gardens in warm Zone 7, and when protected by a winter mulch, the big gladiolas may live through the winter in the garden. Each corm produces a single flowering stem. For a continuous supply, plant groups of a dozen or so corms at two-week intervals from mid-spring through June. Gladiolas thrive in well-drained, rich soil with lots of peat moss. See Soil Preparation in the Introduction and the planting instructions at the beginning of this chapter. Set the corms 5 in. deep, 4 in. apart. Very tall gladiolas may need staking, especially in a windy location. Mulch 2 in. deep between corms.

Growing Tips

Water at planting time, and maintain moisture in the soil as the plants begin to grow.

Care

Fertilize the bed every year with a slow-release, organic fertilizer at the rate of 6 pounds per 100 sq. ft. After harvesting the flowers, allow the foliage to ripen. When it has died down, dig the corms and store them for the winter at 50 degrees Fahrenheit in a cool, dry place with good air circulation—wire trays or mesh bags are best.

Companion Planting and Design

Glads are especially nice in a kitchen garden.

Our Personal Recommendations

We plant the big hybrid glads for summer bouquets, but in Zones 5 and warmer, petite modern *G. × colvillei* is perennial. A miniature, 18 in. tall, that blooms in early summer in white, salmon-pink, red, and in bi-colors, it is winter hardy above -20 degrees Fahrenheit.

Several hybrids are in the background of the hundreds of beautiful, big, modern, elegant, and long-lasting gladiolas grown as annuals, primarily for cutting, in New England and northward. The elegantly tapering flower stems, 36 in. tall and more, rise from sword-shaped foliage, and are studded with flowers that may be 4 to 7 in. across. The blossoms open one by one starting at the bottom—and fade away starting at the bottom, while those higher up on the stem continue to open until all have bloomed. The blossoms of some varieties look like perched butterflies and have striking throat markings. The bloom time varies according to type. Gladiolas last longest when cut as the first flower colors.

Other Names
Corn Flag, Sword Lily, Glads

Bloom Period and Seasonal Color
Sixty to 100 days from planting; all colors, including green, and bi-colors.

Mature Height × Spread
3 to 4 ft. × 8 to 10 in.

Zones
7 to 10

Grape Hyacinth
Muscari spp.

The most familiar grape hyacinths are blue as blue can be, a tribe of little bulb flowers that bloom toward mid-spring almost anywhere there is sun or dappled light. Muscari *perennializes and naturalizes readily, and growing in good soil in open sunny woodlands, will eventually carpet the earth with an extraordinary "river" of blue. The tiny flowers of the grape hyacinth are thickly clustered on stems 6 to 8 in. high. In some forms the flowers are open and fertile, so they look a little like miniature hyacinths. Other types are sterile and the unopened buds look like tiny grapes enveloping the stems. Some varieties combine both fertile and infertile flowers. The leaves are grassy. There are white varieties. Some have a faint spice-and-grape fragrance, especially M. macrocarpum, a rather rare yellow species.*

Bloom Period and Seasonal Color
Early to mid-spring; many shades of blue, white, yellow.

Mature Height × Spread
6 to 8 in. × 4 to 6 in.

Zones
3 to 7 or 8

When, Where, and How to Plant
Plant grape hyacinths in September or October, in full or part sun. The ideal soil is light, well drained, and improved by additions of organic matter and 4-10-6 bulb fertilizer. The ideal pH range is 6.0 to 7.0. See Soil Preparation in the Introduction and the planting instructions at the beginning of this chapter, including instructions on discouraging voles and squirrels. Provide holes 5 in. deep and 1 in. wide, or a planting bed 5 to 6 in. deep. Set the bulbs 2 in. apart. Mulch the area.

Growing Tip
To encourage grape hyacinths to multiply, after flowering and before the foliage disappears, spread a slow-release bulb fertilizer over the area, 4 to 6 pounds for every 100 sq. ft.

Care
Plant blue grape hyacinths in large groups, drifts of twenty to 100. White grape hyacinths stand out more, so fewer can be effective. There's no dead-heading. Grape hyacinths will multiply if they are well fertilized after blooming every year.

Companion Planting and Design
Grape hyacinths add solid blue to the front of flower beds. We like them naturalized in drifts, along paths, and at the foot of stone walls and white picket fences. They're pretty at the edge of the lawn, as a carpet between larger bulbs, in bulb baskets or shallow pots, and as underplanting for large white daffodils. 'Blue Spike' is lovely with the daffodils white 'Thalia' and early pale yellow 'Hawera'.

Our Personal Recommendations
The most commonly grown is *M. armeniacum*; we like 'Blue Spike', whose flowers are light blue and double. *M. azureum* has both infertile flowers (buds) and fertile, open flowers, with a darker stripe of blue on the lobes. It is the muscari usually chosen for planting in "rivers." The feather hyacinth, *M. comosum* 'Plumosum' (Zones 6 to 8) has fluffy double mauve-lilac flowers on 6-in. stems and is the last to bloom here. It's a historic bulb flower used in restoration gardens. *M. latifolium* is great for rock gardens. The small blue-purple flowers bloom on 10- to 12-in. stems and produce just one large leaf, quite distinctive and unusual.

Hyacinth
Hyacinthus orientalis

When, Where, and How to Plant
Plant hyacinth bulbs in September or October in full sun. Some shade can prolong the hyacinth's flowering but in our cooler regions full sun is recommended. Provide well-worked fertile loam with excellent drainage. Look up the information about soils for bulbs in the Soil Preparation section in the Introduction. Plant following the instructions at the beginning of this chapter. Set the bulbs 8 in. deep, about 3 to 4 in. apart, and mulch the area.

Growing Tip
To encourage hyacinths to return, after flowering and before the foliage disappears, spread a slow-release bulb fertilizer over the area, 4 to 6 pounds for every 100 sq. ft.

Care
Hyacinths repeat at least two or three years if the flower is removed after flowering and the foliage is allowed to mature fully before it is removed. Maintain moisture in spring, but avoid it in summer and winter.

Companion Planting and Design
Plant early, midseason, and late types in groups along paths, and in pockets near patios and entrances. In flower beds, plant hyacinths in groups of five to fifteen; in containers, plant the bulbs in sets of three to five. For bedding, choose slightly smaller bulbs: they'll have outstanding blooms the first year and a looser cluster the second. For forcing indoors, choose the largest bulbs of very fragrant white 'Carnegie', 'Violet Pearl', deep blue 'Ostara', and clear pink 'Anna Marie'.

Our Personal Recommendations
Generally, white hyacinths seem to be the most fragrant. The pastels are next in line, but some deeply colored hyacinths have a powerful scent. Light blue 'Cote d'Azure' is unsurpassed for perfume. Among notably scented large doubles are the white 'Mme Sophie' and 'Ben Nevis' and the luscious pink 'Chestnut Flower'. Related species we like are endymion, *Hyacinthoides*, a frost hardy European bluebell that naturalizes easily; the Spanish bluebell, or wood hyacinth, *H. hispanica*, is glorious in hard to fill shaded places; and the English bluebell, *H. non-scripta* (syn. *Scilla non-scripta*).

The Oriental hyacinths open with the daffodils and early tulips and they bring us spring's most extraordinary perfume. The plant puts up wide grass-like leaves and a thick fleshy flower stem rises up right out of the middle, completely covered with starry, outfacing bells. Hyacinths are rather rigid and that makes them somewhat difficult to fit into a casual garden design. But the perfume is worth the effort. Hyacinths grow from bulbs that are quite large, a fair handful. Some varieties bloom early, others at midseason, and some quite far along in spring, so you can, if you plan carefully, keep hyacinth perfume in your garden all spring. Hyacinths can be forced to bloom indoors long before they come into flower out in the garden.

Other Names
Oriental Hyacinth, Dutch Hyacinth

Bloom Period and Seasonal Color
Early to mid-spring; pure white, yellow, coral, pink, rose, shades of blue, purple, midnight purple.

Mature Height × Spread
8 to 12 in. × 4 to 6 in.

Zones
4 to 8

59

Lily
Lilium spp. and hybrids

The lilies are among the tallest of all garden flowers. They're also the stateliest, probably the most beautiful and, in the case of the Oriental lilies, the most exquisitely perfumed. A 6- or 7-ft. lily is a commanding plant, not at home everywhere. But there's a place in every garden for medium and small lilies which, planted in groups, provide welcome color when you need it most in summer. They bloom in a wide range of colors for three to four weeks beginning in June in most areas. The three major groups—Asiatic, Trumpet, Oriental—bloom in that order. Their periods of bloom overlap since there are late Asiatics and early Trumpets and Orientals. By thoughtful selection you can have lilies flowering from late spring until frosts.

Bloom Period and Seasonal Color
June to August; white, every color but the blue range; spotted, bi-colors, and with brush marks that replace the spots with blotches of solid colors.

Mature Height × Spread
$1^1/_2$ to 6 ft. × $1^1/_2$ to 2 ft.

Zones
4 to 9

When, Where, and How to Plant
A container-grown lily in bloom adapts to transplanting almost any time during the growing season. On the other hand, planting a bulb with a shoot over 2 in. long is certain death. Growers ship big dormant bulbs in damp peat—keep them there until planted, or in a crisper. Four to six hours of full sun, plus partial sun the rest of the day, is the rule of thumb; where temperatures soar over 90 degrees Fahrenheit, lilies benefit from protection from noon and afternoon sun. Pastel shades are more successful in partial shade. A lily requires perfect drainage and very fertile soil with enough humus to keep moisture around the roots. Most need rather acid soil and will fail where lime or wood ashes have been applied. The exceptions are the Martagons and the species *L. candidum* which thrive in alkaline soils. See Soil Preparation in the Introduction. Provide planting holes worked to a depth of 24 in. to guarantee good drainage, and space the big lilies 12 to 18 in. apart. Stake taller varieties. Water well. Mulch 3 in. deep.

Growing Tip
Lilies tolerate a dry period after flowering.

Care
As they fade, pinch blooms off the stalk. For bouquets, cut stems at less than a third of the overall height, or the lily will be smaller next year. When flowering is over, cut the stalks to just above the leaves; when the leaves yellow, cut the stalks to the ground—or leave them to mark the locations. In fall and again in late winter fertilize the bed with an organic, slow-release fertilizer at the rate of 6 pounds per 100 sq. ft. and mulch. Move or divide lilies every four years in the fall.

Companion Planting and Design
All lilies enjoy cool feet. A mulch of ground covers such as alyssum or petunias or short marigolds does that job beautifully. For tubs or flower beds, group mid-size lilies in sets of three, five, or seven. For big borders, mass taller lilies in sets of ten to fifteen.

Our Personal Recommendation
An extraordinarily fragrant, beautiful lily is pure white, 3-ft. 'Casa Blanca', which has wide petals and colorful stamens (that stain!). It blooms mid-season. The deer haven't eaten ours yet.

Tulip
Tulipa spp. and hybrids

When, Where, and How to Plant
Plant tulips in September or October. They perform well with six hours of morning or afternoon sun. Tulips prefer slightly acid, well-drained, and deeply dug soil, enriched with compost and humus. You will find information about soils for bulbs in the Soil Preparation section in the Introduction. Plant tulips following the instructions at the beginning of this chapter, including tips for discouraging voles and squirrels. Avoid leaving bits of bulb casings around the planting—squirrels notice. Set large tulips 4 to 6 in. apart, 8 in. deep; set small bulbs 3 to 4 in. apart, 4 to 5 in. deep. Deeper planting can be successful but is not recommend below 10 in. Mulch the area.

Growing Tip
To encourage tulips to perennialize, after flowering and before the foliage disappears, spread a slow-release bulb fertilizer over the area, 4 to 6 pounds for every 100 sq. ft.

Care
In ideal conditions, a few tulips perennialize and multiply. Some come back under most conditions for about four years. Deadheading helps: take just the bloom, leaving the stem intact. Allow the foliage to yellow about seven weeks before cutting it back. Don't bind the leaves—that cuts off light and oxygen. If in the following year all you get is foliage, discard the little bulbs that produce it.

Companion Planting and Design
Plant the little early botanical or species tulips with other small bulbs and miniature daffodils. Plant a series of early, midseason, and late tulips for a long season of bloom. The big annuals—tall snapdragons, big marigolds, and zinnias—make fine screening for ripening tulip foliage.

Our Personal Recommendations
Our favorite tulips for show and bouquets are fragrant 'Ballerina', yellow/red/orange; 'Fancy Frills', fringed rose/white; 'Queen of Night', purple-maroon; 'Aleppo', fringed raspberry/rose/apricot; 'Marilyn', a lily-flowered tulip, white with rose-red streaks rising from the base toward the top; 'Burgundy Lace', fringed purple; gorgeous, stately, 'Duke of Wellington', a big, handsome pure white; 'Temple of Beauty', a lily-flowered Darwin hybrid that is deep pink with warm orange edges.

Tulips bloom from very early spring to late spring. There's every size, shape, almost every color, including midnight purple, and almost every combination of colors you can imagine. Tulips can bloom in your garden for months on end. We group them for design purposes according to their season of bloom. The earliest are the low-growing little species (botanical) tulips—bright, perky, and informal. The big cup-shaped tulips on round jade-green stems are showstoppers from late March through May. Some bloom as singles; others are bunch-flowering. There are early, midseason, and late bloomers in a range of colors and forms that are a delight to explore. Though most tulips aren't fragrant, many Single Early tulips are fragrant, and the vivid orange, lily-flowered (Zones 4 to 7) 'Ballerina' has scent. Deer adore tulips, so avoid easy access.

Bloom Period and Seasonal Color
Late winter to late spring; every color but blue.

Mature Height × Spread
4 to 24 in. × 6 to 8 in.

Zones
3 to 7 or 8

Conifers *for New England*

Evergreens are key foundation plants. In this chapter we've grouped together the needled and scale-leaved evergreens, large and small. The shrub sizes of familiar species—pines, yews, cedars, junipers, spruces, and hemlocks—are discussed on the same pages as the tree sizes.

We find the small, shrubby conifers extremely useful for anchoring color and as backgrounds in flower beds and shrubbery borders. The shrubby evergreens also make the best dense hedges and wind-

Cedar of Lebanon

breaks, and provide sturdy edgers for paths and driveways. For tall privacy screening and windbreaks we use big, naturally columnar evergreens, such as American arborvitae. To furnish neglected corners, and for mid-height or low screening, we like the bold branching of the sprawling dwarf junipers, and upright little yews like 'Pygmaea', which stay under 2 feet. Elegant columnar junipers, such as 'Skyrocket', are ideal where a stylish accent is wanted, and they make great verticals for small spaces. A big, needled evergreen that has considerable presence in New England landscaping is the fast-growing native white pine. The Canadian hemlock, a pyramidal conifer with short needles, is another handsome shade tree for our region (though it has severe problems in Rhode Island), and a hemlock hedge can be pruned for decades before the central stems become too thick to be attractive. White pine, hemlock, and blue spruce make a lovely background for the white-barked birch that flourishes here, and for azaleas and ornamental grasses. A hurry-up tree for really tall screening is the Leyland cypress, which grows at least 3 feet a year. It can be pruned for many years without losing its beauty. Mature, it becomes a big stately tree with graceful, feathery, bluish green, scale-like foliage and red-brown bark. Weeping evergreens, like the blue Atlas cedar, *Cedrus libani* ssp. *atlantica* 'Glauca Pendula', add grace notes to the landscape.

Planting and Pruning Conifers

Delayed leaf drop is one of the advantages you gain by planting evergreens: practically no leaves to gather and grind in the fall. It's reassuring to know that yellowing needles most often are a normal part of a needled evergreen's cycle and not symptomatic of a problem. The term "evergreen" is misleading. Every plant must renew its foliage. White pines shed aging needles every year. Most other evergreens shed *some* aging needles every year, but they don't, like the deciduous trees, lose *all* their older needles at once—so they appear to be "ever green."

Evergreens need well-drained soil—for some this is very critical—and most prefer an acid, or somewhat acid, pH. They are moderate drinkers. The information on planting and care for shrubs in the Shrubs chapter, and for trees in the Trees chapter, applies to evergreen shrubs and trees.

A collection of conifers, including Dwarf Alberta Spruce and False Cypress.

Most often we prune an evergreen only to shape the plant or to make it bushier. To encourage dense branching to the ground, begin pruning when the evergreen is three to five years old. Summer after its main spurt of growth is the time to prune an evergreen to slow, dwarf, or maintain its shape. The rule is to prune strong growth lightly, and weak growth hard. Never trim more than a third from an evergreen. You should not remove more of the top growth (the leader) than the growth of the last year or two. You can cut the main stem back to the first side shoots. This doesn't apply to trimmed hedges.

Light pruning of the branch ends of many evergreens, including hemlocks, junipers, and yews, is acceptable throughout the growing season, but not when they are dormant. Yews and junipers can take heavy pruning and fill out again very quickly. Firs, pines, spruces, and other evergreens whose growth is initiated by candles should be pruned in spring when the candles appear at the branch tips. Cutting back the new candles by one-half to two-thirds will make the tips branch. Heavy pruning in fall isn't a good idea, because the wounds heal more slowly in seasons of reduced activity and the pruning may stimulate a new flush of growth which could be damaged by winter weather.

Arborvitae
Thuja occidentalis

Arborvitae is perhaps the most beautiful of all the formal conifers. A tall shrub, it is used as a specimen, wind-break, hedge, and foundation plant. Densely clothed with lovely scale-like, lacy leaves in flat sprays that are a good deep green and aromatic when crushed, the plant is symmetrical, slow growing, long lived, and can be sheared repeatedly. The fruits are charming little erect cones. In cultivation, the height of this species is between 12 and 15 ft. Arborvitae is easy to grow. Cultivars in many shapes and shades are available. There are narrow forms, round forms, and broadly pyramidal forms, cultivars in shades of blue-green and yellow tones. 'Emerald', 5 to 6 ft. tall by 2 ft. wide, maintains its brilliant color in winter as does 15-ft. 'Techny'. 'Holmstrup' is a slow-growing arborvitae that stays under 10 ft. Deer love them all, every one!

Other Names
American Arborvitae, Eastern Arborvitae

Bloom Period and Seasonal Color
Insignificant blooms; small, erect cones.

Mature Height × Spread
12 to 15 ft. × 3 to 5 ft.

Zones
2 to 7 or 8

When, Where, and How to Plant
Container-grown or balled-and-burlapped arbor-vitae transplants easily in early spring and fall. The plant adapts to light shade but unless it is growing in full sun it loses the furry texture that is one of its major assets. It flourishes in soil that is slightly acid, pH 6.0 to 7.0, and tolerates clay and lime-stone soil as long as it is fertile, well drained, and sustains moisture. See Soil Preparation in the Introduction, and planting instructions in the Trees chapter. Provide a planting hole three times the width of the rootball and twice as deep. Set the rootball so the crown will be an inch or two above ground level. Shape the soil around the crown into a wide saucer. Water slowly and deeply. Apply mulch 3 in. deep starting 3 in. from the crown.

Growing Tips
The first year, unless there's a soaking rain, in spring and fall slowly and gently pour two to three bucketsful of water around the roots every two weeks; in summer every week or ten days. Maintain the mulch throughout the summer.

Care
Using a slow-release organic fertilizer, fertilize lightly in fall and again in spring. Replenish the mulch. Water deeply in periods of drought. Arborvitae generally does not need pruning. A heavy snowfall can open up the tight branching at the top: to avoid that, tie the top together in the fall. Any pruning should be done before spring growth begins.

Companion Planting and Design
Arborvitae is excellent as a formal specimen in the lawn, as a backdrop for deciduous trees and flowering shrubs, and in windbreaks and hedges. Deer crop arborvitae to the core at grazing height: the radical solution is to surround the plants with 8-ft. wire fencing. Other deer deterrents are discussed in the Appendix.

Our Personal Recommendations
In areas of New England in Zone 6, a smaller species, 18- to 25-ft. Oriental arborvitae, *T. orientalis*, succeeds; the grass-green foliage matures to a darker green. The foliage of the 8-ft. cultivar 'Blue Cone' has a blue cast.

Blue Atlas Cedar
Cedrus libani ssp. *atlantica* 'Glauca'

When, Where, and How to Plant

The true cedars are difficult to transplant, so set out a *young* container-grown plant in early spring. Handle the rootball with great care. While the cedars require a lot of space all around as they develop, they should be placed where they have protection from prevailing winds, especially weeping forms, according to Rhode Island Master Gardener Roseanne Sherry. The Atlas cedar tolerates partial shade but the other species named below need full sun. The cedars as a group do best in soil that is acid, pH 5.0 to 6.5, but the Atlas cedar withstands some alkalinity in the soil. It tolerates clay and sandy soils as long as they are well drained. See Soil Preparation in the Introduction, and planting instructions in the Trees chapter. Provide a planting hole three times the width of the rootball and twice as deep. Set the tree so the crown will be about 1 or 2 in. above ground level. Shape the soil around the crown into a wide saucer. Water slowly, deeply, thoroughly. Apply mulch 3 in. deep starting 3 in. from the main stem.

Growing Tips

The first year, unless there's a soaking rain, in spring and fall slowly and gently pour two to three bucketsful of water around the roots every two weeks; in summer every week or ten days. Maintain the mulch throughout the summer.

Care

Using a slow-release organic fertilizer for acid-loving plants, fertilize lightly in fall and again in spring. Replenish the mulch as needed.

Companion Planting and Design

Use as a handsome specimen tree in a large landscape.

Our Personal Recommendations

If you like picturesque plants, you should also consider the deodar cedar, *C. deodara*, which is native to the Himalayas and has needles that are light blue or grayish green—silvery at times. The leader must be staked. Zone 7 is the northern end of its hardiness range but the variety 'Kashmir' is recommended as hardy to -25 degrees Fahrenheit. *C. libani*, the legendary cedar of Lebanon celebrated since biblical times, hardy in Zone 5, is like the blue Atlas cedar in form, but has dark green needles; *C. libani* var. *stenocoma* can withstand severe winters.

The cedar is a needled evergreen: when mature, it is perhaps the most beautiful of the large evergreens, especially when featured as a specimen in a large landscape and surrounded by green lawn. Unfortunately, the cedars aren't winter hardy in the colder areas of New England, Zones 3 and 4. The blue Atlas cedar, which withstands winters in Zone 5, is the most cold hardy of the lot. The form is narrowly pyramidal in youth, and with maturity becomes a picturesque flat-topped tree 40 to 60 ft. tall, with slightly drooping horizontal branches, steel blue needles, and handsome upright cones. It grows quickly when young. In Zone 6, a smaller weeping form, 'Glauca Pendula', is hardy. The drooping branches are 15 to 20 in. wide and have icy blue foliage.

Bloom Period and Seasonal Color
Insignificant blooms; 3-in. upright cones.

Mature Height × Spread
40 to 60 ft. × 25 to 30 ft.

Zones
5 to 9

Canadian Hemlock

Tsuga canadensis

Long-lived, shearing-tolerant, and easy to transplant, the Canadian hemlock is a superb evergreen for screening, shade, and display as a specimen. The shape is pyramidal and the branches are graceful, feathery, slightly drooping, and covered with short, aromatic, deep green needles that have two white bands beneath. It's a favorite nesting place for birds. The fruits are pretty little coppery-brown cones a half to an inch long. Over time the cinnamon-brown bark becomes attractively ridged and deeply furrowed. The Canadian hemlock grows to between 40 and 70 ft. in cultivation, but in the Midwest, Northeast, and the Appalachian regions it can reach 100 ft. and more. The boughs are harvested for Christmas decorations and roping. Roseanne Sherry, Rhode Island Master Gardener, says neither Canadian nor Carolina hemlock are recommended for Rhode Island because of a high infestation of woolly adelgid; she suggests Leyland cypress as a replacement.

Other Name
Eastern Hemlock

Bloom Period and Seasonal Color
Insignificant blooms; the cones are coppery-brown.

Mature Height × Spread
40 to 70 ft. × 25 to 36 ft.

Zones
3 to 7

When, Where, and How to Plant

Plant a young balled-and-burlapped or container-grown hemlock in fall before Indian summer, or in early spring. Canadian hemlock does well in full sun or in partial shade. It thrives in cool, moist acid soil, pH 5.0 to 6.5. It also succeeds on rocky bluffs provided there is shelter from icy winds, and in sandy soil if there's enough humus in it to keep moisture around the roots. See Soil Preparation in the Introduction, and planting instructions in the Trees chapter. Provide a planting hole three times the width of the rootball and twice as deep. Set the tree so the crown will be an inch or two above ground level. Shape the soil around the crown into a wide saucer. Water slowly and deeply. Apply mulch 3 in. deep starting 3 in. from the crown.

Growing Tips

The first year, unless there's a soaking rain, in spring and fall slowly and gently pour two to three bucketsful of water around the roots every two weeks; in summer every week or ten days. Maintain the mulch throughout the summer.

Care

Using a slow-release organic, acid fertilizer, fertilize lightly in early spring. Replenish the mulch as needed. Prune away dead wood any time of year; light pruning or shearing of new growth on the branch ends is acceptable after the main spurt of growth and throughout the growing season, but not after the plant becomes dormant.

Companion Planting and Design

Canadian hemlock is an excellent tall foundation plant. Limbed up, it becomes a graceful evergreen shade tree. Trimmed, it makes a superb 6 ft. hedge that can be maintained for decades.

Our Personal Recommendations

The eye-catching variety 'Sargentii' is a spreading, weeping tree. 'Pendula', weeping Canadian hemlock, is a dark green prostrate form that takes decades to reach 5 ft. by 8 to 10 ft. and thrives in shade. Prostrate 'Cole' can handle winters in Zone 2.

Colorado Blue Spruce

Picea pungens 'Glauca'

When, Where, and How to Plant

Plant a balled-and-burlapped or container-grown spruce in early fall or in early spring. They have spreading root systems, so large specimens can be transplanted successfully. The Colorado blue spruce needs full sun to color well and does best in well-drained, moderately moist soil in the acid range, pH 5.0 to 6.0. See Soil Preparation in the Introduction, and planting instructions in the Trees chapter. Provide a planting hole three times the width of the rootball and twice as deep. Set the tree so the crown will be about 1 or 2 in. above ground level. Shape the soil around the crown into a wide saucer. Water slowly and deeply. Apply mulch 3 in. deep starting 3 in. from the main stem.

Growing Tips

The first year, unless there's a soaking rain, in spring and fall slowly and gently pour two to three bucketsful of water around the roots every two weeks; in summer every week or ten days. Maintain the mulch throughout the summer.

Care

In early spring before growth begins, broadcast a slow-release organic fertilizer for acid-loving plants. Replenish the mulch. To encourage density, or to change the shape of the plant, periodically prune the tips back by half.

Companion Planting and Design

The Colorado blue spruce is best featured as a specimen out in the open in a large landscape: parked in a small lawn it soon grows out of scale with the dwelling. Grouped with smaller evergreens and planted at a distance from a dwelling it becomes the anchor for a beautiful evergreen screen.

Our Personal Recommendations

Our favorite compact Colorado blue spruces are 'Glauca Globosa', just 3 ft. high at maturity; 'Montgomery'; and 'Fat Albert', which reaches 10 ft. by 7 ft. in ten years. For shade, windbreaks, and tall screening, we recommend the fast-growing, green-needled Norway spruce, *P. abies* (Zone 2). There's a weeping form, *P. abies* forma *pendula*, and a dwarf, bird's-nest spruce, 'Nidiformis', which grows to just 4 to 6 ft. high.

The spruces are the aromatic, symmetrical, conical evergreens we buy for Christmas trees, both cut and live. The needles are thin, rigid, 1/2 to 1 1/4 in. long with four sides and sharp points. The 2- to 4-in. cones start out green and turn light brown. A hardy native of the high Rocky Mountains, it lives 600 to 800 years. Majestic 'Glauca' has soft blue-gray foliage that turns silver-gray to blue-green as the tree grows slowly to from 30 to 50 ft. There's a gorgeous weeping form, 'Glauca Pendula', and several other cultivars with special characteristics: 'Hoopsii' has the bluest needles; 'Moerheimii' is a narrow, conical, blue tree; 'Thompsenii' has whitish silver-blue foliage and is considered one of the best of the blue spruces. Master Gardener Roseanne Sherry does not recommend Colorado blue spruce for Rhode Island, as it succumbs to a fungus as it matures.

Bloom Period and Seasonal Color
Insignificant blooms; cones are green and mature to light brown.

Mature Height × Spread
30 to 50 ft. × 10 to 20 ft.

Zones
3 to 8

Douglas Fir
Pseudotsuga menziesii

The Douglas fir is a stately pyramidal evergreen, straight as a spear in maturity, and one of North America's most important timber trees. It's also used as a cut or live Christmas tree. A dramatic landscape ornamental 40 to 50 ft. tall, in the wild it towers to heights of 250 to 300 ft. and lives 800 to 1,000 years! When young, the upper branches of the Douglas fir are ascending while the lower branches are somewhat drooping, a characteristic that becomes accentuated as the tree matures. The needles are flattish and blue green. The pendulous cones are 3 to 4 in. long and bear seeds: when they mature in late summer they become an important source of food for small mammals and birds.

Other Name
Green Douglas Fir

Bloom Period and Seasonal Color
Insignificant blooms; 3- to 4-in. seed-bearing cones.

Mature Height × Spread
40 to 50 ft. × 12 to 20 ft.

Zones
4 to 6

When, Where, and How to Plant
Balled and burlapped, or container grown, the Douglas fir transplants well in early spring. The ideal site is open and sunny with moist air and space all around it. It does not succeed in dry, windy locations. Plant a Douglas fir where the soil is well drained, with enough humus to maintain moisture around the roots, and slightly acid, pH 6.0 to 7.0. See Soil Preparation in the Introduction, and planting instructions in the Trees chapter. Provide a planting hole three times the width of the rootball and twice as deep. Set the tree so that the crown will be about 1 or 2 in. above ground level. Shape the soil around the crown into a wide saucer. Water slowly and deeply. Apply mulch 3 in. deep starting 3 in. from the main stem.

Growing Tips
The first year, unless there's a soaking rain, in spring and fall slowly and gently pour two to three bucketsful of water around the roots every two weeks; in summer every week or ten days. Maintain the mulch throughout the summer.

Care
Using a slow-release organic fertilizer, fertilize lightly in fall and again in early spring. Replenish the mulch as needed.

Companion Planting and Design
The Douglas fir is a dramatic ornamental tree for large parks, golf courses, and estates.

Our Personal Recommendation
The beautiful Douglas fir *P. menziesii* var. *glauca*, Rocky Mountain Douglas fir, grows more slowly and makes a long-lasting live Christmas tree. The needles are a beautiful shade of soft blue. Unfortunately, after Christmas it often gets lovingly planted on a small front lawn where it soon grows out of scale in proportion to the grounds and the dwelling.

Dwarf Hinoki Cypress
Chamaecyparis obtusa 'Nana Gracilis'

When, Where, and How to Plant

Plant a young container-grown cypress in the fall before Indian summer, or in early spring, while the shrub is still dormant. The Hinoki cypress requires full sun and does best with some protection from wind. It prefers soils that are well drained, with enough humus to maintain moisture around the roots, and neutral to slightly acid, pH 6.0 to 7.0. See Soil Preparation in the Introduction, and planting instructions in the Shrubs chapter. Provide a planting hole three times the width of the rootball and twice as deep. Set the shrub so the crown will be 1 or 2 in. above ground level. Shape the soil around the crown into a wide saucer. Water slowly and deeply. Apply mulch 3 in. deep starting 3 in. from the crown.

Growing Tips

The first year, unless there's a soaking rain, in spring and fall slowly and gently pour two to three bucketsful of water around the roots every two weeks; in summer every week or ten days. Maintain the mulch throughout the summer.

Care

Using a slow-release organic fertilizer for acid-loving plants, fertilize lightly in late fall and again in early spring. Replenish the mulch as needed. Pruning is hardly ever needed.

Companion Planting and Design

This is a first-rate, shrub-size evergreen—great for use in hedges, as background to a shrub border of azaleas, or as a foundation plant. The golden foliage of the cultivar 'Cripsii' is striking against darker evergreens.

Our Personal Recommendations

A fascinating relative is the blue- or gray-green weeping Nootka, or Alaska, cypress, *C. nootkatensis* 'Pendula' (Zone 5), a variety with drooping branches. It can live to be over 1,000 years old. In cultivation it reaches 30 to 45 ft. A yellow species that is hardier than 'Cripsii' and holds its striking yellow hue in summer, is the 8- to 12-ft. golden threadleaf sawara, or Japanese, cypress, *C. pisifera* 'Filifera Aurea' (Zone 4).

Many shrubby forms of the beautiful Hinoki cypress, Chamaecyparis obtusa, are first-rate landscape plants. The dwarf 'Nana Gracilis' is an exceptionally graceful shrub, 4 to 6 ft. tall, with deep green, lustrous foliage that is white on the underside, flat, and scale-like. The branch tips turn down in an interesting half-twist that gives the plant an appealing texture and the appearance of greater softness than is usual in an evergreen. An excellent yellow form is the golden cypress, C. obtusa 'Crippsii', a dense, pyramidal evergreen, whose branchlets are tipped a rich yellow-gold. It's a slow-growing shrub that in a decade or two will reach 8 to 10 ft. but can eventually reach 30 ft.

Other Name
Dwarf False Cypress

Bloom Period and Seasonal Color
Insignificant blooms; bluish cones changing to red-brown.

Mature Height × Spread
6 ft. × 3 to 4 ft.

Zones
4 to 8

Eastern White Pine

Pinus strobus

You can distinguish a pine from similar conifers by its needles, which are soft, thin, 2- to 5-in. long, and grow in bundles of two to five. The eastern white pine is one of the hardiest and most attractive of the big evergreens used in landscaping in New England. A native of the U.S. and Canada, it grows straight as a ship's mast, has long, soft, bluish green needles, 6- to 8-in. cones, a regal presence, and in cultivation grows rapidly to 50 to 80 ft. The pine group includes dwarf, compact forms that are useful in landscaping, as well as tall, pyramidal trees. The drooping branches of the variety 'Pendula' sweep the ground in a picturesque fashion. 'Nana' is a very slow-growing dwarf that can take 75 years to reach a height of 15 ft.

Bloom Period and Seasonal Color
Insignificant blooms; cones are 6 to 8 in. long.

Mature Height × Spread
50 to 80 ft. × 40 ft.

Zones
2 to 8

When, Where, and How to Plant
Pines have taproots and are best moved as *young* container-grown or balled-and-burlapped plants in early spring. Most pines require full sun and well-drained, acid soil, pH 5.0 to 6.0; the beautiful lacebark pine mentioned below tolerates some alkalinity. See Soil Preparation in the Introduction, and the planting instructions in the Trees chapter. Provide a planting hole three times the width of the rootball and twice as deep. Set the shrub so the crown will be an inch or two above ground level. Shape the soil around the crown into a wide saucer. Water slowly and deeply. Apply mulch 3 in. deep starting 3 in. from the crown.

Growing Tips
The first year, unless there's a soaking rain, in spring and fall slowly and gently pour two to three bucketsful of water around the roots every two weeks; in summer every week or ten days. Maintain the mulch throughout the summer.

Care
Using a slow-release fertilizer for acid-loving plants, fertilize lightly in fall and again in early spring. Replenish the mulch. To encourage density, or to change the shape of a pine, in June when new candles are fully grown, cut them back by half.

Companion Planting and Design
Eastern white pine makes an excellent specimen plant, a first rate divider, screen, windbreak, and dense tall hedge: set the trees in a row zigzag fashion and allow at least 20 ft. between plants. Pines do well by the shore. Coastal gardeners love the Japanese black pine, *P. thunbergii*, a picturesque, salt-tolerant tree that is sometimes used as a sand binder. It will grow to between 20 and 80 ft. depending on the environment.

Our Personal Recommendations
Multiple-stemmed lacebark pine, *P. bungeana*, tolerates urban conditions, and has beautiful exfoliating bark (Zone 4). For edging urban gardens and anchoring perennial beds we use dwarfs of the mugo pine, *P. mugo* (Zone 2), which have small, attractive, dark green bundles of needles.

Juniper

Juniperus spp. and hybrids

When, Where, and How to Plant

The junipers have a spreading root system that transplants easily. Set out container-grown plants in spring or fall. Plant in full sun: they accept some shade when young, but will get open and ratty unless growing in full sun. The hardy eastern red cedar, *J. virginiana*, does well in acid and in alkaline soils, but most junipers prefer soil in the pH 5.0 to 6.5 range that is light, even sandy, and moderately moist. But they are tolerant of dry clay soils and pollution. See Soil Preparation in the Introduction, and planting instructions in the Shrubs chapter. Provide a planting hole three times the width of the rootball and twice as deep. Set the shrub so the crown will be 1 or 2 in. above ground level. Shape the soil around the crown into a wide saucer. Water slowly and deeply. Apply mulch 3 in. deep starting 3 in. from the crown.

Growing Tips

The first year, unless there's a soaking rain, in spring and fall slowly and gently pour two to three bucketsful of water around the roots every two weeks; in summer every week or ten days. Maintain the mulch throughout the summer.

Care

Using a slow-release organic fertilizer for acid-loving plants, fertilize lightly in fall and again in early spring. Replenish the mulch as needed. Minimize shearing and pruning by choosing junipers whose growth habit fits your purpose. The best time to prune junipers to minimize growth or enhance their shape is just after a spurt of new growth.

Companion Planting and Design

There's a juniper to fill every garden need: tough ground cover, stately specimen, columnar accent, or graceful focal point.

Our Personal Recommendations

Graceful creeping juniper, *J. horizontalis* 'Plumosa' (Zone 3), is 3 to 4 ft. tall, with dropping branches, and 'Compacta' has foliage that turns purplish in winter. *J. scopulorum* 'Pathfinder' (Zone 3) is an elegant, narrow columnar 20-ft. tree. Red cedar, *J. virginiana* (Zone 2) is a dense 40- to 50-ft. tree that thrives by the sea.

The junipers are really tough conifers that come in amazingly variable shapes, from 60-ft. trees to 2-ft. ground-hugging plants like the creeping juniper, Juniperus horizontalis, described in the Ground Covers chapter. Juvenile growth has awl-shaped needles and the adult growth is scale-like: when this transition occurs depends on the variety. The male cones are yellow, and resemble catkins; the female fruits are berry-like cones. Many superb shrubs have been developed from the Chinese juniper, J. chinensis, (Zones 4 to 9) whose foliage may be bright green or blue- or gray-green. 'Hetzii' is a beautiful gray-green shrub about 10 ft. by 10 ft. at maturity. 'Mint Julep' is a compact bright green fountaining shrub, 4 ft. by 6 ft. 'Pfitzeriana', the most hybridized, has drooping branches, bright green foliage, and averages 5 ft. by 7 ft.

Bloom Period and Seasonal Color
Insignificant blooms; berry-like cones.

Mature Height × Spread
Variable, according to species and variety.

Zones
2 to 9

Leyland Cypress
× *Cupressocyparis leylandii*

The Leyland cypress is a stately columnar hybrid of the cypress family, a group of narrow shrubs and trees with flat, scale-like leaves. It has graceful branches and bluish green, feathery foliage, and bears small, roundish cones that are dark brown. The red-brown bark is a nice warm color, and is interestingly scaly. In addition to its grace, what makes the Leyland cypress unusual is that it grows to 60 or 70 ft. tall very quickly—3 ft. a year. That makes it an exceptionally good evergreen for screening. It tolerates heavy shearing, and makes a fine tall hedge. It also tolerates salt, and is used along the coast as a screen to protect the garden from salt spray.

Bloom Period and Seasonal Color
Insignificant blooms; roundish, dark brown cones.

Mature Height × Spread
60 to 70 ft. × 25 to 30 ft.

Zones
5 to 10

When, Where, and How to Plant
Plant a container-grown or balled-and-burlapped tree in fall before Indian summer, or in early spring. In shade, the branching is more open and informal; in full sun the foliage grows densely and close to the trunk. Leyland cypress adapts to a variety of soils, acid or alkaline, but grows most rapidly in moist, humusy, fertile soil. See Soil Preparation in the Introduction, and planting instructions in the Trees chapter. Provide a planting hole at least three times the width of the rootball and twice as deep. Set the tree so the crown is 1 or 2 in. above ground level. Shape the soil around the crown into a wide saucer. Water slowly and deeply. Apply mulch 3 in. deep starting 3 in. from the main stem.

Growing Tips
The first year, unless there's a soaking rain, in spring and fall slowly and gently pour two to three bucketsful of water around the roots every two weeks; in summer every week or ten days. Maintain the mulch throughout the summer.

Care
Using a slow-release organic fertilizer, fertilize in fall and again in early spring. Replenish the mulch. Maintain soil moisture during droughts. Periodically prune or shear a Leyland cypress during July. For a formal hedge, allow the tops to grow 6 to 12 in. beyond the intended height, then cut the leaders off to just above a lateral branch 6 in. below the intended height.

Companion Planting and Design
Give Leyland cypress plenty of room as it is too vigorous for narrow spaces that restrict growth. In a new landscape, Leyland cypress is sometimes planted with a desirable but slow-growing evergreen, and removed when the second plant attains a desired height.

Our Personal Recommendations
Several appealing varieties have been named. One of the most graceful of the Leylands is 'Naylor's Blue', an open, loosely branched, narrow cultivar, 30 to 40 ft. at maturity, whose bright, gray-blue foliage is most intensely colored in winter. The new growth of 'Castlewellan Gold', a narrow upright form about 20 ft. tall, is tipped yellow-gold and turns to bronze in winter.

When, Where, and How to Plant

The best time to plant an umbrella pine is in early spring. Buy a *young* container-grown or balled-and-burlapped plant and handle the roots with great care. The site can be in partial shade or in full sun as long as there is protection from the hot late afternoon sun and from sweeping winds. The umbrella pine does not tolerate pollution or drought. The ideal site is a steep, rocky, well-drained place that has rich, moist, and somewhat acid soil. See Soil Preparation in the Introduction, and planting instructions in the Trees chapter. Provide a planting hole three times the width of the rootball and twice as deep. Set the tree so the crown will be about 1 or 2 in. above ground level. Shape the soil around the crown into a wide saucer. Water slowly and deeply. Apply mulch 3 in. deep starting 3 in. from the main stem.

Growing Tips

The first year, unless there's a soaking rain, in spring and fall slowly and gently pour two to three bucketsful of water around the roots every two weeks; in summer every week or ten days. Maintain the mulch throughout the summer.

Care

Using a slow-release fertilizer for acid-loving plants, fertilize lightly in fall and again in early spring. Replenish the mulch. Carefree, the umbrella pine should not be sheared and should not need pruning.

Companion Planting and Design

The umbrella pine is best used as an accent tree in a group of trees and shrubs, or as a specimen out in the open. It isn't easy to find but well worth the effort if you are looking for an evergreen accent for a special place in the garden.

Our Personal Recommendation

Plant the species.

Consider an umbrella pine if you'd like something different in an evergreen. It's a rather small tree with a strongly textured look that to some seems primitive, as though it belonged to an earlier time. Considered unique and artistic in appearance, it has two types of needles: one type is small and scale-like and arranged at the tips of the twigs, and the other type consists of 2- to 5-in.-long, dark green needles bunched at the ends of the branches. When the tree begins to mature, the bark turns orange to red-brown and begins to peel in plates and strips. A young umbrella pine has a compact pyramidal shape and the branches are stiff, twiggy, and spread in whorls. As it matures, the branches droop and loosen. It grows very slowly.

Other Name
Japanese Umbrella Pine

Bloom Period and Seasonal Color
Insignificant blooms; green 2- to 4-in. cones turning to brown.

Mature Height × Spread
20 to 30 ft. × 15 to 20 ft.

Zones
4 to 8

White Fir

Abies concolor

The firs are long-lived, stately trees native to the Rockies. Pyramidal conifers similar to the spruces, they also are used as live Christmas trees, and the boughs are sold to make Christmas decorations. In silhouette, the conical white fir looks like a blue spruce, but it's more refined. The silvery, blue-green needles are flatter than those of the spruces, soft, 2 to 3 in. long, and they have two pale, bluish bands underneath. The cones are 3 to 5 in. long and greenish when new, shading to purple. Most other fir species are big forest trees that live at high altitudes and do poorly in hot, dry cities. The white fir has some tolerance for long, hot summers and it resists city conditions, cold, and drought.

Other Names
Colorado Fir, Silver Fir, Concolor Fir

Bloom Period and Seasonal Color
Insignificant blooms; cones are 3 to 5 in., green shading to purple.

Mature Height × Spread
30 to 50 ft. × 15 to 30 ft.

Zones
3 to 7

When, Where, and How to Plant

Plant a *young* container-grown or balled-and-burlapped tree in early spring. The white fir prefers full sun, but tolerates all-day bright filtered light. Firs do best in acid soil, pH 5.0 to 6.0. The white fir can live on almost bare rock, but it does poorly in heavy clay soils. Ideal soil is a rich, moist, sandy loam. Prepare the soil well! See Soil Preparation in the Introduction, and planting instructions in the Trees chapter. Provide a planting hole three times the width of the rootball and twice as deep. Handle the rootball with great care. Set the tree so the crown will be about 1 or 2 in. above ground level. Shape the soil around the crown into a wide saucer. Water slowly and deeply. Apply mulch 3 in. deep starting 3 in. from the main stem.

Growing Tips

The first year, unless there's a soaking rain, in spring and fall slowly and gently pour two to three bucketsful of water around the roots every two weeks; in summer every week or ten days. Maintain the mulch throughout the summer.

Care

Using a slow-release organic fertilizer for acid-loving plants, fertilize lightly in fall and again in early spring. Replenish the mulch.

Companion Planting and Design

The evergreen needles make a handsome backdrop for ornamental plants and in fall and winter they lend life to the sleeping garden. It is generally used as a specimen in lawns and parks.

Our Personal Recommendations

In addition to the white fir, we recommend the graceful Caucasian, or Nordmann fir, *A. nordmanniana*, whose tiered branches sweep downward and then curve up. It's a big tree, 40 to 60 ft., whose needles are a lustrous black-green. The ideal pH for the Caucasian fir is soil in the 5.8 to 7.0 range. It needs full sun, a very well-drained site, and it does best in a somewhat sheltered situation.

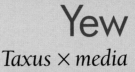

When, Where, and How to Plant

Plant a balled-and-burlapped or container-grown yew in fall before Indian summer, or in early spring. A yew does well growing in full sun or bright shade, but the needles will brown in winter if the plant is exposed to strong, cold winds. They generally prefer somewhat alkaline soil, but *T.* × *media* needs an acid loam. The ideal site has excellent drainage (yews do not tolerate wet feet at all) and fertile, humusy soil. See Soil Preparation in the Introduction, and planting instructions in the Trees chapter. Provide a planting hole three times the width of the rootball and twice as deep. Set the tree so the crown will be about 1 or 2 in. above ground level. Shape the soil around the crown into a wide saucer. Water slowly and deeply. Apply mulch 3 in. deep starting 3 in. from the main stem.

Growing Tips

The first year, unless there's a soaking rain, in spring and fall slowly and gently pour two to three bucketsful of water around the roots every two weeks; in summer every week or ten days. Maintain the mulch throughout the summer.

Care

Using a slow-release organic fertilizer, fertilize lightly in fall and again in spring. Prune away dead wood any time of year, but do not cut beyond the area where green needles are growing. Yews accept shearing of the branch ends throughout the growing season. To keep it compact, follow an early spring pruning by the removal of the soft new summer growth. To create a natural looking hedge, remove the longest growth every other year.

Companion Planting and Design

Yews are enduring foundation plants.

Our Personal Recommendations

The tree form we favor is 'Capitata', a pyramidal 40- to 50-ft. cultivar of the very hardy, light green Japanese yew, *T. cuspidata* (Zone 4). A single plant that can make a low hedge almost all by itself is 'Repandens', a cultivar of the big English yew, *T. baccata* (Zone 6), which grows 2 to 4 ft. tall and 10 to 15 ft. wide. It has beautiful dark or black-green foliage.

The yews are the most adaptable, durable, and useful of evergreens. Dark needled shrubs and trees with reddish brown, scaly bark, they bear pea-sized fleshy red berries. Native to the Northern hemisphere, the yews are disease resistant. They grow slowly and are tolerant of extensive pruning, so they're often used for clipped hedges, green screens, and walls, archways, topiaries, and foundation plantings, small and tall. Yews come in almost all sizes and shapes. Among of the very best for hedges, screening, and foundation planting are pyramidal 10- to 12-ft. by 10-ft. 'Hatfieldii'; columnar 'Hicksii'; low, spreading, 4- to 5-ft. 'Densiformis'; and rounded, 6-ft. 'Brownii'. The seeds and foliage contain toxic compounds.

Other Names

Intermediate Yew, Anglojap Yew

Bloom Period and Seasonal Color

Insignificant blooms; fleshy red berries in winter.

Mature Height × Spread

Cultivars vary in size. Many are as wide as, or wider than, they are tall.

Zones

4 to 8

Ground Covers *for New England*

Ground covers create a unified field that harmonizes and pulls together the various elements of the landscape—shrub borders, flower beds, and specimen trees. A ground cover can be any height: even daylilies can be a ground cover. Those we recommend here are low-growing, need almost no maintenance once established, can do what lawn grasses do where mowers can't go, and can replace lawns you are weary of mowing. The most attractive and enduring ground covers for New England landscapes are the plants on the pages that follow, but not every one of these is perfect for every site. They are designated as ground covers because, like weeds, most of them spread rapidly: so think twice about planting any of these where they might later invade stands of native plants or woodlands we are trying to preserve.

Periwinkle

The toughest evergreen ground covers are ajuga, vinca, ivy, and creeping juniper. Ajuga and vinca bear sweet little flowers in early spring and can be walked on—with discretion. Ivy can take months to expand, but once started spreads irrepressibly. Creeping juniper withstands sun, heat, drought, and salt, and it's a good bank holder.

A beautiful plant that lightens shaded places is dead nettle, which produces masses of small hooded flowers in spring. Leadwort has handsome glossy foliage and in late summer bears long-lasting gentian-blue flowers. For cooler regions, dappled light, and a formal look, pachysandra is the perfect choice. The ferns we recommend also do well in dappled light and are lovely in transitional areas edging woodlands.

Combining several compatible ground covers adds texture to an area and is a safeguard should one of the plants run into difficulties. For a richly varied lawn substitute we like drifts of small winter-flowering bulbs, over-planted with aromatic Greek oregano and thyme, ajuga in the sunny places, vinca in part sun, and dead nettle under the trees.

Planting Ground Covers

We recommend starting a ground cover with flats or pots of rooted cuttings. If you will be planting in an area covered by turf or unwanted weeds, in early spring or fall when the soil is dry, spray the area with herbicide, or remove the top layer. Top the area with 2 or 3 inches of compost or decomposed leaves, and broadcast over it slow-release fertilizers, along with greensand (with its thirty-two micro-nutrients) and rock phosphate. Follow the rates recommended on the packages. Rototill all this 8 inches deep, three times over a two-week period. If you are installing an invasive ground cover such as ivy or ajuga, bury a 6-inch metal barrier to keep it from overrunning neighboring plantings.

At planting time, cover the area with 3 inches of mulch and plant the ground cover seedlings through it. Working in even rows and starting at the widest end, dig a row of evenly spaced planting pockets 8 to 14 inches apart. Set the plants into the pockets and firm them into place. If you are planting on a slope, set the plants so their backs are a little lower than their fronts. Position the second row plants zigzag style between those of the first row. For row three, repeat row one, and for row four repeat row two. Maintain the mulch until the ground cover has grown so dense that it shades out weeds. Plan on at least two years for the plants to grow enough to cover well.

If weeding won't be possible, plant your ground cover through a porous landscape fabric. Push the edges of the fabric sheet into the ground and weight them with rocks, or use your heel to push them in. Make rows of X-shaped slits in the fabric, and insert the plants through the slits with a trowel. Landscape fabric slows the rooting of the above-ground branches, so plant densely.

In fall clear your ground cover of the thickest drifts of fallen leaves with a blow-vac. Certain ground covers when fully mature benefit from shearing every year or two in early spring before growth begins.

Other Good Options

The plants on the following pages are the best of the best, but we have other favorites:

Groundcovers:

Bloody Cranesbill, *Geranium sanguineum*

European Ginger, *Asarum europaeum*

Golden Star, *Chrysogonum virginianum*
    (Zones 5 to 9)

Mountain Pink, *Phlox subulata* (Zones 2 to 9)

Soapwort, *Saponaria officinalis* 'Rosea Plena'

Snow-in-Summer, *Cerastium tomentosum*

Sweet Woodruff, *Galium odoratum* (Zones 4 to 9)

Ferns:

Beech Fern, *Thelypteris hexagonoptera*

Cinnamon Fern, *Osmunda cinnamomea*

Deer Fern, *Blechnum spicant* (Zones 5 to 8)

Japanese Shield Fern, *Dryopteris erythrosora*
    (Zones 5 to 9)

Maidenhair Fern, *Adiantum pedatum*

Marsh Fern, *Thelypteris palustris* forma *pufferae*

Massachusetts Fern, *T. simulata*

New York Fern, *T. noveboracensis* (Zones 2 to 8)

Royal Fern, *Osmunda regalis*

Variegated Liriope

Barrenwort
Epimedium spp. and hybrids

The barrenworts are spring-flowering plants that, given time, carpet the earth under trees, shrubs, and in woodlands with clumps of beautiful, long, heart-shaped leaves that are evergreen in Zones 7 but not usually in New England. The foliage colors reddish or gold in cold weather, bringing new vitality to the fading fall scene. In spring, exotic little flowers rather like columbines, some long spurred, are borne in clusters on slim, gracefully arching stems. Among the several barrenworts that work well in New England, the hardiest is red alpine epimedium, Epimedium × rubrum (Zones 4 to 8), whose graceful sprays of flowers are red with yellow or white. Another good one is bi-color barrenwort, E. × versicolor 'Sulphureum' (Zones 5 to 9), which bears delicate yellow flowers with long rosy spurs. E. pinnatum (syn. E. colchicum) (Zones 5 to 8) has handsome brownish foliage and bears up to twenty-four short-spurred, yellow flowers.

Other Name
Bishop's Hat

Bloom Period and Seasonal Color
Spring; flowers in yellow, pink, orange, rose, lavender, white, bi-colors. Fall foliage is reddish or gold.

Mature Height × Spread
6 to 10 in. × 12 to 18 in.

Zones
4 to 9

When, Where, and How to Plant
You can set out container-grown epimediums at any time during the growing season. The plants do best in bright shade. In the cooler regions of New England epimediums can tolerate full sun, but they grow well in semi- to full shade, even in Vermont. Epimediums need to be planted in well-drained, rich soil with an acid pH 4.5 to 5.5. This is an ideal ground cover for land that was forest and for wooded areas. Follow the planting instructions at the beginning of this chapter, and provide planting holes 8 to 12 in. deep. Space the plants, which are slow to establish, about 12 in. apart. Spread a permanent 1-in. mulch of pine needles, or rotted leaf mold.

Growing Tips
Keep the plants well watered the first two months, and weekly thereafter unless you have a good soaking rain. Established epimediums can handle some drought, but they need sustained moisture to get off to a good start.

Care
In early spring fertilize and re-establish the mulch in new beds: once established, epimediums make dense mats so they will need no mulch in subsequent years. In early spring just before new foliage emerges, shear old foliage. You can multiply your holdings by dividing mature clumps of epimediums in very early spring or toward the end of summer.

Companion Planting and Design
The barrenworts are beautiful ground covers under trees, shrubs, and in woodlands. We love seeing them bordering a woodland path planted with fall-flowering anemones, ferns, and hostas. They're handsome growing with hellebores in the shade of a tall shrub border.

Our Personal Recommendation
We especially like *E. × versicolor* 'Sulphureum' because it is beautiful and grows vigorously.

Bearberry
Arctostaphylos uva-ursi

When, Where, and How to Plant

Set out container-grown plants in very early spring. If local people do not carry bearberry, you will find it in catalogs like Ray and Peg Prag's Forest Farm Nursery, in Williams, Oregon. Do not dig bearberry in the wild—it is protected in many states and will likely die anyway. An ideal ground cover for land that was forest and for wooded areas, it does best where it receives some direct sun and some shade. Though it succeeds in neutral and even in limestone soils, it prefers well-drained, infertile soil with an acid pH of 4.5 to 5.5. Bearberry is difficult to transplant and the plants are fairly costly, so put the effort necessary into soil preparation. Follow the soil preparation and planting instructions at the beginning of this chapter, omitting the fertilizer. Dig generous planting holes, spacing the plants 12 to 24 in. apart. Water well. Apply a permanent mulch of pine needles, or rotted leaf mold.

Growing Tip

Water a new planting every week or two the first season.

Care

Replenish the mulch in early spring until the plants have spread widely enough to shade out weeds. Do not fertilize. Pruning is rarely needed. Once the plants are established, local rainfall should be enough to keep bearberry healthy and growing, except during our mid- and late August droughts.

Companion Planting and Design

Bearberry is used as a soil stabilizer on sandy banks beside highways and at the shore as it survives without much water in poor, sandy, or gravelly soil, and hot sun. It is especially attractive as a ground cover for hillside terraces, and we love to see it rambling over stony slopes.

Our Personal Recommendations

A. uva-ursi 'Radiant' is taller than most, 18 in., and has beautiful red berries in fall. It is an excellent shore plant. Little 'Wood's Compact' is just 4 in. high. 'Bear' is large and tinged with red in winter. 'Wood's Red' is a dwarf with unusually large red fruits. 'Massachusetts' is very tolerant of wet conditions. 'Emerald Carpet' has pink flowers and tolerates shade.

Bearberry is one of the most beautiful of all low-growing, trailing ground covers. A broad-leaved evergreen, it is not used nearly as often as it should be because it is hard to transplant and slow to spread. But it is rugged, and in time can spread to 15 ft. The leaves are shiny and dark green in summer, bronze-red in cold weather. In spring, clusters of tiny pink or white flowers bloom, followed by lasting red berries that the birds love. It tolerates sandy soil, and makes an excellent ground cover for seashore gardens. Bearberry is a major asset for gardeners interested in creating a beautiful, natural looking, woodland ground cover that will need little maintenance. As far as we know, deer do not eat it.

Other Name
Kinnikinick

Bloom Period and Seasonal Color
Spring; tiny pink or white flowers.

Mature Height × Spread
$^1/_2$ to 1 ft. × 2 to 4 ft.

Zones
2 to 7

Blue Lily-Turf
Liriope muscari

Liriope looks like a graceful clump of grass, but is in the Lily Family. It produces lovely flower spikes, is as tough as any ground cover, and spreads rapidly. The grass-like leaves of Liriope muscari *are tall, coarse, and broad, about ¹/₂ to ³/₄ in. wide. The flowers appear in late summer and early fall. They look like tall, slim stems of grape hyacinths and bloom in shades of blue, purple, lilac, or white. The flowers are followed by attractive shiny black fruits that persist through early winter. A tough and resistant plant, it takes several seasons of growth to fill out, but once established, it's almost indestructible. Blue lily-turf,* Liriope muscari, *is hardy to Zone 5; a slimmer relative, creeping liriope,* L. spicata, *is hardy to Zone 4.*

Other Names
Liriope, Lily-Turf, *Liriope phatyphylla*

Bloom Period and Seasonal Color
August and September; blue, lavender, purple, white.

Mature Height × Spread
1 to 1¹/₂ ft. × 1 to 2 ft.

Zones
5 to 9 or 10

When, Where, and How to Plant
In early spring or early fall, set out container-grown root divisions. Liriope thrives in bright shade under tall trees, but spreads even in dense shade. It is not particular as to soil pH, tolerates high-alkaline soils, and succeeds in hot, dry locations. Following the planting instructions at the beginning of this chapter, prepare a planting bed, or planting holes twice the width of the container, with well-drained, moderately fertile soil. Set the plants 12 in. apart. Water thoroughly, and provide a permanent mulch.

Growing Tips
Keep the planting watered during droughts the first summer. Liriope withstands muggy weather and high humidity, and spreads as long as the soil doesn't dry out completely.

Care
In early spring, cut the foliage down to the crown to allow for fresh growth, and replenish the mulch. In continuing wet weather, slugs and snails may chew the edges of the leaves: the control is to wait until the soil dries then sprinkle diatomaceous earth around each plant. Repeat the treatment as necessary. We've also heard that slugs stay away from coffee grounds. Well-established clumps can be divided in early spring before growth begins.

Companion Planting and Design
We use liriope many different ways. We plant clumps of several together as filler for flowering borders. The white-flowered cultivar 'Monroe White' is lovely with variegated liriope. Lavender-flowered 'Gold Banded', has leaves with a gold stripe down the middle and forms a mound. 'John Burch' has variegated foliage and bears attractive crested, lavender flowers.

Our Personal Recommendations
For edging flower beds and garden paths, we like the effect of 'Christmas Tree', which produces a large, full flower spike in lavender-lilac. Another beauty is 'Royal Purple' whose flowers are deep purple. For ground cover foliage, the best of the variegated forms is 'Variagata'. Creeping lily-turf, *L. spicata*, spreads rapidly by underground stolons and is excellent as a bank holder and to cover very large areas. It is a slightly smaller species with ¹/4-in. leaves and pale violet or white flowers.

Bugleweed
Ajuga reptans

When, Where, and How to Plant

Plant clumps of rooted plantlets in early spring or early fall. Where summers are muggy, ajuga does best in tall, bright shade under trees. In dense shade the leaves will be smaller and the runners will spread toward the light. The colored varieties are showiest growing in some direct sun. Rooted plants are fairly expensive, but you can minimize the cost by choosing the rapidly spreading species *A. reptans* and setting the plants 6 to 12 in. apart. You can also divide the clumps into individual plantlets and make more. Ajuga does best in well-drained, ordinary garden soil whose pH range is between 6.0 and 7.0. Follow the soil preparation and planting instructions at the beginning of this chapter, but omit the fertilizer. Prepare a planting bed 6 to 8 in. deep. Space slower-spreading ajuga species 3 in. apart and be prepared to divide the plants—or prune them back—the following summer. Mulch the area.

Growing Tip

Water a new bed every week to ten days the first season, unless rain is plentiful.

Care

Once established, ajuga can take a wide range of conditions. Too well fed, it will "melt out" with diseases. In early spring, scratch in a little slow-release fertilizer beside young plants. In the following years, when you fertilize your lawn, water in a long-lasting organic fertilizer. Clear away autumn leaves to avoid crown rot: if a fungal problem develops, ask your garden center to recommend a fungicide. Rooted plantlets of *A. reptans* can be cut from the parent and replanted during the growing season; divide other species in early spring.

Companion Planting and Design

We use ajuga to cover a small area with a low dense mat. Its growth is expansive—aggressive is probably more accurate—so avoid growing it close to flower beds and other areas easily invaded.

Our Personal Recommendations

For something different, plant *A. reptans* 'Alba', whose flowers are off-white, or 'Burgundy Glow', whose leaves are cream, pink, rose, and green. 'Rosea' has green leaves and showy rose-pink flower spikes. Where crown rot is a problem, choose *A. genevensis*.

Ajuga covers the ground with flat rosettes of colorful leaves 3 to 4 in. long, and it is an excellent ground cover for small, partially shaded areas, and poor soil. It's a tough plant that can be walked on in moderation, grows aggressively, and is semi-evergreen in our warmer areas. Fast-growing Ajuga reptans is our choice for quick cover. Some forms are green-leaved, while others are splashed with cream or pink or have a metallic sheen. In mid- to late spring ajuga is misted with blue florets on short, squarish flower spikes. When the weather turns cold ajuga takes on an attractive bronze-plum tint. Cold that persists without snow cover damages the leaf tips but in spring the plants soon fill out.

Other Names
Ajuga, Carpet Bugleweed

Bloom Period and Seasonal Color
Foliage may be green, or multicolored, rose and burgundy; in early spring flowers are white, red-blue, pink, deep blue, rose.

Mature Height × Spread
4 to 8 in. × 12 to 14 in.

Zones
4 to 9

Christmas Fern
Polystichum acrostichoides

Ferns have a cool graceful presence that other types of plants just don't have. The lush greens evoke woodlands and romantic glades. No cottage garden is complete without them. The Christmas fern is a forever plant, a lifetime fern with beautiful lance-shaped, leathery fronds up to 24 in. long by 5 in. wide, growing in arching, circular clusters from the crown. And it is evergreen here! A woodland native, it offers practical solutions to the challenges presented by the north side of a house, the north slope of a wooded stretch, and sun-dappled stream edges with poor drainage. It can tolerate more sun than most other ferns if given adequate moisture. Insist on purchasing only plants propagated by nurseries, not gathered from the wild.

Other Names
Dagger Fern, Canker Brake

Bloom Period and Seasonal Color
Evergreen crown of dark green foliage.

Mature Height × Spread
1 to 1¹/₂ ft. × 1¹/₂ to 2 ft.

Zones
3 to 8

When, Where, and How to Plant
Set out container-grown plants of Christmas fern after the last frost. They do best in partial shade. Some direct morning sun is acceptable if the soil has been well prepared. Like most ferns, the Christmas fern thrives in moist, humusy soil in the pH range 5.0 to 6.0. Follow the planting and soil preparation instructions at the beginning of this chapter, and enhance the soil mix by mixing in 50 to 75 percent of humusy forest soil or decayed shredded leaves and a natural, or slow-release, organic fertilizer for acid-loving plants. Since the fern lives long and multiplies all around, dig wide planting holes 20 to 25 in. apart. Set the rootball just a little higher than the level at which it was growing before. Mulch all around with pine needles, shredded leaves, or leaf compost.

Growing Tips
Maintain soil moisture for the first season. A little overhead watering in high heat and drought is helpful. Fern glades are often misted rather than watered.

Care
In following seasons, in early spring scatter a light application of organic slow-release fertilizer for acid-loving plants under the foliage. Allow the duff (layer of decaying vegetation that covers the soil) to remain undisturbed. Avoid cultivating next to the crown: pull weeds by hand.

Companion Planting and Design
This evergreen fern is a beautiful ground cover and it is especially lovely in a ferny glade planted with hostas and astilbes. Christmas fern fills its space throughout the year so it makes a charming background for wildflowers as well as other garden plants: begonias, columbine, lily-of-the-valley, primroses, Solomon's-seal, trilliums, and lady's-slippers. Shallow-rooted, Christmas fern competes successfully with tree roots and in rock gardens for moisture and space.

Our Personal Recommendations
Evergreen and long-lived, Christmas fern is a northland favorite. But in alkaline soils, you will do better with the shield, or holly, fern, *P. braunii*, a cousin to the Christmas fern. It is semi-evergreen with graceful, arching fronds to 36 in. long, and has twice divided leaves covered with hair-like scales at the edges. It needs cool, deep shade.

Creeping Juniper

Juniperus horizontalis

When, Where, and How to Plant

Container-grown junipers can be planted in any season. If the plants are root-bound, make shallow, vertical cuts through the binding roots, and slice 1 in. off the bottom. Junipers need six hours of direct sun; in shade they get thin and ratty. The creeping junipers do best in soil with a pH of 5.0 to 6.0, but can handle slightly alkaline soils. The shore juniper, *J. conferta*, can be planted in areas reached by salt spray. Juniper colors most intensely in infertile sandy loam that is somewhat moist. Follow the soil preparation and planting instructions at the beginning of this chapter but omit the fertilizer. Set the plants about 3 ft. apart in generous planting holes and spread out the roots. Water thoroughly. Spread a mulch 3 in. deep of pine needles, bark chips, or rotted leaf mold.

Growing Tip

Water a new planting every week or two the first season.

Care

Local rainfall should be enough for established plants. Do not fertilize unless the soil is extremely poor. Replenish the mulch in early spring. If the branches brown here and there, chances are spider mites are at work: apply a miticide according to label directions. Where branches are overlapping, prune in midsummer. Where branches touch the soil they will eventually root—in early spring you can sever rooted branches and replant them.

Companion Planting and Design

We plant creeping juniper as a bank holder, and as ground cover for neglected areas, among rocks, and edging masonry walls. These low-growing junipers can be interplanted with early daffodils and other medium-height spring-flowering bulbs.

Our Personal Recommendations

Among the finest junipers are gray-green 'Bar Harbour', 12 in. tall, which withstands salty shore conditions; 6-in. silver-blue 'Blue Rug'; 12- to 28-in. shore juniper, *J. conferta*, which thrives by the sea; and little 6-in., dense, blue-green, moss-like *J. procumbens* 'Nana', dwarf Japanese garden juniper. For taller ground covers we use Chinese juniper, including 18-in. blue-green *J. chinensis* var. *sargentii*, and compact spreader, 4- to 6-ft. 'Sea Green'.

This is a creeping form of the familiar evergreen tree or shrub. It grows just 6 to 12 in. high, and the branches spread horizontally about a foot a year to 5 ft. and more. Tough, drought-resistant creeping juniper performs beautifully in sun-baked situations, saves hot dry slopes from erosion, makes a great small (prickly) lawn, and is a favorite for bordering paths and driveways. Along with the somewhat taller shore juniper, Juniperus conferta, it thrives in sandy soils. The junipers are either male or female plants: the females bear pea-sized, gray-blue or green, berry-like cones. Some varieties are dark green; others are shaded soft gray-green or blue-green, and there are gold- and silver-tipped forms. In cold weather, many varieties color plum to purple.

Other Name

Ground Cover Juniper

Bloom Period and Seasonal Color

The foliage turns plum in winter, or deeper green or deeper blue, depending on the variety.

Mature Height × Spread

6 to 12 in. × 5 to 8 ft.

Zones

3 to 9

Dead Nettle
Lamium maculatum

Beautiful but tender-leaved, dead nettle produces a froth of silvered leaves in the shade where even hostas and impatiens do poorly. A low, fast-growing creeper in the mint family, its dark green, oval leaves are splashed or striped silver or white along the midrib. Between late spring and midsummer, it sends up small hooded flowers. In summer, it throws 1- to 2-ft. horizontal stems that root at the nodes. The plantlets can revert to other foliage and flower colors. Dead nettle is evergreen in very mild winters, but in drought and sizzling heat and in very cold winters without snow cover, the new stems may die back; the rooted parent plants, however, will remain and re-grow in the spring.

Other Names
Lamium, Spotted Dead Nettle

Bloom Period and Seasonal Color
Spring; flowers are pink, lavender-pink, or white. The foliage is green and silver.

Mature Height × Spread
8 to 12 in. × 12 to 16 in.

Zones
4 to 8

When, Where, and How to Plant
Plant root divisions in early spring in partial shade. Lamiums can take full shade and they tolerate more direct sun in cool upland areas. They do well in almost any soil, but spread rapidly in light, well-drained loam. Follow the soil preparation and planting instructions at the beginning of this chapter. Prepare planting holes 6 to 8 in. deep and set the plants 12 to 18 in. apart. Water well. Mulch between the plants to keep weeds at bay until the plants completely shade the ground.

Growing Tips
For the first month or two, water weekly or bi-weekly, unless there is a good supply of rain. If the plants become straggly toward midsummer, cut them back to 6 to 8 in. to keep the growth full and within bounds.

Care
To keep the bed growing vigorously, water lamium as often as you do garden flowers. If lamium dries out repeatedly, the bed will die back to scatterings of rooted plantlets that will then need months to re-establish vigorous growth. Fertilize every two or three years in early fall or early spring by adding $1/2$ in. of compost and an application of a slow-release fertilizer. In spring, remove winter-damaged stems. Replenish the mulch if weeds begin to take hold. In late fall, remove dead stems and clear away fallen leaves, which can smother nettle's tender leaves. To multiply your holdings, dig rooted plantlets *that have not reverted to an unwanted color* and replant at once in moist, humusy soil. Terminal cuttings taken from parent plants during the growing season will root easily in water and can be planted once the heat of summer has gone by.

Companion Planting and Design
Lamium brightens dark corners and makes a nice contrast when planted with dark-foliaged ground covers such as wild ginger.

Our Personal Recommendations
'Album' has white flowers with a silver stripe down the middle of the leaves. Most beautiful for foliage is 'Beacon Silver', whose silver leaves are edged with a narrow band of green; the leaves of 'White Nancy' are a lovely pale jade with white blossoms.

English Ivy
Hedera helix

When, Where, and How to Plant

Plant flats of rooted cuttings in early spring or early fall in part shade or sun. Ivy grows most vigorously in fall and thrives in acid and non-acid soils with a pH range of 6.0 to 7.5. To encourage rapid growth, follow the soil preparation and planting instructions at the beginning of this chapter and provide a planting bed with soil that is rich, fairly humusy, and well drained. In sandy soil, mix in 40 percent humus. Set the plantlets 6 in. apart. Prune straggly stems back to 6 in. then soak the ground with water containing a liquid organic fertilizer such as seaweed or fish emulsion. Provide a permanent mulch of pine needles, rotted leaf mold, or bark. The vines can take two or three seasons to cover the area.

Growing Tips

The first season water the plants deeply every week in hot and dry weather. The second year keep the soil moderately damp until the plants are well established and the vines are running (growing).

Care

Do not fertilize established beds unless the foliage yellows. Water during droughts. Keep ivy trimmed, tidy, and well groomed and shear it back every three or four years to maintain the density of the foliage. To encourage ivy to root, peg a stem to the soil: when it shows new growth in the spring, dig it, sever it from the parent, and transplant.

Companion Planting and Design

Ivy is beautiful dripping from hanging baskets, urns, and in tall flower arrangements, and is a great edger between strips of pavement. But ivy-clad walls and trees are often in trouble because the density of foliage at the soil line can create humidity problems that can cause damage from freezing, or in hot, wet weather, rot. The solution is to remove the base foliage. Stop ivy from climbing walls and tree trunks by pruning it yearly.

Our Personal Recommendations

'Baltica' and '238th Street' withstand our winters and do not scald in winter sun. '238th Street' is a particularly resistant form. 'Glacier' is splashed with white and pale green.

Tough, reliable English ivy fills the bill where a vigorous ground cover is needed. It withstands hot sun, heat, drought, cold, or too much rain. Any vigorous non-native can become a pest, ivy in particular, so don't plant it where it can escape your control, and especially never near woodlands. It succeeds in shade under trees, though the vines will run toward better light, and it competes well with tree roots. Thickly planted, it makes a dense "lawn" 6 to 8 in. high. English ivy is a running or climbing woody vine that has an adult form that is shrub-like and not viny, if allowed to run. Ivy cultivars make beautiful container plants—especially variegated forms.

Bloom Period and Seasonal Color
Evergreen foliage. The flowers are insignificant

Mature Length
Strands can grow 25 to 50 and even 90 ft.

Zones
5 to 9

Foamflower
Tiarella cordifolia

The foamflower is a charming wildflower native to the rich moist woodlands of New England and eastern Canada. Evergreen here, it forms small clumps of overlapping crinkled leaves that spread by runners. In mid-spring the foliage is covered with a foam of fluffy little white flowers on tall stems. The blooms fade in a couple of weeks revealing fresh new foliage. Foamflower is easy to grow and spreads so energetically that it makes an excellent woodland ground cover. Breeding by Sinclair Adams has expanded the beauty of the foliage colors and markings so that now many interesting new hybrids are coming onto the market, some with flowers that are white, cream, pink, or deep rose.

Other Name
Allegheny Foamflower

Bloom Period and Seasonal Color
May; the species flowers are white.

Mature Height × Spread
6 in. (with 10-in. flower spikes) × 2 ft.

Zones
3 to 9

When, Where, and How to Plant
Plant root divisions or runners of foamflower in early spring in partial or full shade. Good-sized plants of the new varieties are now being offered by growers with many more anticipated in the years ahead. Foamflower thrives in soil with pH between 5.0 and 6.0 and is an excellent low ground cover for damp, shady places where the soil is rich in humus. Follow the soil preparation and planting instructions at the beginning of this chapter, mix in 50 to 75 percent of humusy forest soil or decayed shredded leaves, and fertilize with a slow-release organic fertilizer for acid-loving plants. Provide planting holes 6 to 8 in. deep, and 8 to 12 in. apart. Water well after planting and mulch 2 in. deep between the plants with shredded leaves, leaf compost, or peat moss.

Growing Tips
Maintain soil moisture for the first season. Mature plants tolerate brief periods of drought.

Care
In early spring scatter a light application of organic acid fertilizer under the foliage. Pull weeds by hand—selectively. *T. cordifolia* sends out runners that creep over or just under the surface soil, between fallen logs, and over or between rocks. You can control its growth by chopping off the runners, and you can multiply your holdings by clipping off rooted plantlets and transplanting those with good root systems.

Companion Planting and Design
With ferns, *Tiarella* makes a lovely living mulch for clematis. We use it as underplanting for drifts of bleeding heart along woodland paths and in sun-dappled glades. In shaded corners, it's pretty with hellebore, creeping phlox, and ferns. The new hybrids make attractive container plants.

Our Personal Recommendations
'Pink Brushes' is a new, very cold hardy *Tiarella* cultivar whose pink blooms gradually change to white. 'Pink Pearls' blooms over a long period. The foliage of both these cultivars acquires bronze-red tones in the fall. The leaves of 'Rambling Tapestry' are marked attractively with maroon veins; the leaves of 'Eco Running Tapestry' have wine-red centers. *T. wherryi* is a clump-forming foamflower—no runners—grown for the flowers.

Golden Moneywort
Lysimachia nummularia 'Aurea'

When, Where, and How to Plant
Set out container-grown plants any time after the last spring frost and before the first frost in autumn. It is versatile as to light. Moneyworts prefer somewhat neutral soil. If the planting bed is in or near woodlands, and somewhat acidic, apply lime to raise the pH to between 6.5 and 7.0. Follow the soil preparation and planting instructions at the beginning of this chapter. If the bed is not naturally moist, increase the humus content by digging in a 2-in. layer of peat moss or chopped leaves, along with a 1-in. layer of compost, or an application of a slow-release organic fertilizer. Set the plants 12 to 18 in. apart. Water thoroughly. Provide a permanent mulch of well-rotted leaf mold to keep weeds at bay until the plants cover the ground completely.

Growing Tips
Water a new planting every week unless the ground is naturally moist. Golden creeping Jenny spreads aggressively in moist conditions and can become invasive, so keep an eye on its development.

Care
Fertilize a new planting early in the spring after you set out the plants by scratching a slow-release organic fertilizer into the soil beside young plants. Prune the plants back if they are becoming matted. Once established, these plants do well on their own without fertilization or spraying. They are pest and disease resistant—but they will suffer if the soil surface is dry for days at a time. Maintain mulch until the plants spread enough to shade out weeds. You can multiply your holdings in early spring or in early fall by digging up and replanting rooted sections of the stems or small divisions of the crown.

Companion Planting and Design
'Aurea' is an excellent ground cover for wet, difficult places. It's lovely in rock gardens, where it can even become invasive, pretty between paving stones, and makes a nice edger for patio containers. It's attractive planted with golden-leaved coleus.

Our Personal Recommendations
For golden cover, we plant 'Aurea'. For green cover, we plant the species, which has round, medium green leaves, and abundant, bright yellow, cup-shaped flowers in summer.

A great galloping ground cover in shaded areas with moist soil, moneywort is a rapidly spreading perennial with round, dark green leaves. It bears masses of small, faintly fragrant, golden yellow, cup-shaped flowers and is an excellent ground cover for stream borders, wet banks, and the edges of damp woodlands. Moneywort is a European plant that has naturalized here. It rambles along the ground, rooting as it goes and forming a ruffled carpet. 'Aurea' produces rounded, penny-shaped, 1-in.-long leaves that start out yellowish in spring then turn toward lime-green in summer. In the shade, the foliage fairly glows. It can grow in water up to 2 in. deep.

Other Name
Golden Creeping Jenny

Bloom Period and Seasonal Color
Early summer; blooms in yellow.

Mature Height × Spread
1 to 2 in. × indefinite spread

Zones
3 to 8

Japanese Painted Fern
Athyrium nipponicum 'Pictum'

Members of the genus Athyrium are among the easiest of all ferns to grow in part shade. Japanese painted fern is a strikingly beautiful specimen plant for the wild garden, or a flower bed. An exotic looking variegated fern, it has gray-silver, lance-shaped fronds with wine red stems and a graceful weeping habit. It is slow to take off but grows vigorously and easily in partial shade almost anywhere. Unlike the Christmas fern, which is evergreen here, the Japanese painted fern dies down in winter, but it stands up to a lot of cold, greening wooded lots long after the trees have dropped their leaves. In a suitable habitat— partially shaded, moist soil—it grows lusher every year, doubling and tripling its size and competing successfully with tree roots.

Other Name
Painted Fern

Bloom Period and Seasonal Color
Blended silver-green and maroon fronds.

Mature Height × Spread
14 to 24 in. × 18 to 30 in.

Zones
3 to 8

When, Where, and How to Plant
Root divisions of Japanese painted fern are available from nurseries and through garden catalogs. Set them out after the last frost in partial to deep shade. Some direct morning sun is acceptable if the soil has been well prepared. This fern thrives in moist, humusy soil in the pH range 5.0 to 6.5. It lives long and multiplies all around, so dig wide planting holes 25 to 30 in. apart. Follow the soil preparation and planting instructions at the beginning of this chapter and improve the soil by mixing in 50 to 75 percent of humusy forest soil or decayed shred-ded leaves fertilized with a slow-release organic fertilizer for acid-loving plants. Set the rootball a lit-tle higher than it was growing before and mulch with shredded leaves, leaf compost, or peat moss.

Growing Tips
Maintain soil moisture for the first season. A little overhead watering in high heat and drought is helpful.

Care
In following seasons, in early spring scatter a light application of organic acid fertilizer under the foliage. Allow the duff (a layer of decaying vegeta-tion that covers the soil) to remain undisturbed— pull weeds by hand. Protect new growth if unusu-ally early spring weather is likely to be followed by frosts: it is as sensitive to frost as impatiens. Japanese painted fern can be divided in early spring or fall by digging and separating the crown into smaller divisions.

Companion Planting and Design
We love Japanese painted fern paired with white impatiens and with wild ginger and creeping thyme. We have edged a water garden set in a rocky outcropping with Japanese painted fern, astilbes, white bleeding heart, and Japanese irises and they are pretty together.

Our Personal Recommendations
The silvery Japanese painted fern is our first choice, and 'Pictum Red', which has a reddish tinge in the fronds. We also recommend the Japanese painted fern's green cousin, the lady fern, *A. filix-femina*, which forms thick clumps of grace-ful, lacy fronds 24 in. long that appear throughout the growing season. It spreads at a moderate rate in moist conditions but is tolerant of fairly dry soils.

Japanese Spurge
Pachysandra terminalis

When, Where, and How to Plant
Plant rooted cuttings in the early spring or early fall in the bright shade of tall trees or in daylong dappled light. In direct sun, especially where summers are hot and muggy, pachysandra has problems. Humusy, well-drained, acid soil, pH 4.5 to 6.0, is best. Follow the soil preparation and planting instructions at the beginning of this chapter and mix in a 2-in. layer of peat moss or chopped leaves along with a 1-in. layer of acidic compost. Provide planting holes 6 in. deep and set the cuttings 4 to 6 in. apart. Water thoroughly. Spread a mulch 3 in. deep of shredded pine bark, pine needles, or rotted oak leaves. Cuttings of new growth taken in summer will root in damp sand tented with plastic; mist often for six weeks. Clumps of pachysandra dug with lots of soil attached transplant well in early spring; keep the transplants well watered.

Growing Tip
For the first season, water your planting well every week, especially where pachysandra is competing with the roots of trees and shrubs.

Care
Remove fallen autumn leaves. In late fall, apply a slow-release organic fertilizer for acid-loving plants. Maintain the mulch. Especially when growing in sun, pachysandra is susceptible to volutella stem blight, and to scale and mites: for the stem blight, use a copper fungicide, and use ultrafine or horticultural oil to control scale and mites. Keep the bed airy and cool by thinning and cutting. If leaves wilt where soil is reasonably moist, treat the area with a fungicide.

Companion Planting and Design
Pachysandra is perfect as a ground cover for formal plantings anywhere, beautiful under rhododendrons, azaleas, tall trees, and in open woodlands.

Our Personal Recommendations
The most attractive variety is deep-green 'Green Carpet', which has wide, compact, rather smooth leaves. Glossy 'Green Sheen' has a more formal look. 'Variegata' and 'Silver Edge' are beautiful but tolerate less direct sun and are less vigorous.

Pachysandra is a beautiful, rather formal, low-growing evergreen ground cover that does best in light shade. It makes a handsome "lawn," though it cannot be walked on, and succeeds under tall shrubs and even under maples, beeches, and sycamores whose roots are shallow and competitive. The plant consists of upright rosettes of rich-green, scalloped, or saw-toothed leaves on fleshy stems 8 to 10 in. tall. In early spring, there is a flush of light-green new growth and small green-white flower spikes appear. The flowers can reappear in fall when Indian summer warmth follows a cold snap. We can't do without pachysandra, but we've learned that it suffers if planted where it receives several hours of direct sun in summer. Snow cover is definitely a benefit.

Other Name
Japanese Pachysandra

Bloom Period and Seasonal Color
Spring; flowers are insignificant. Evergreen foliage.

Mature Height × Spread
8 to 10 in. × indefinite spread

Zones
4 to 8

Leadwort
Ceratostigma plumbaginoides

This is a beautiful ground cover for small, sunny, or partly shaded areas and it bears one of the bluest of all blue flowers in late summer and fall. The plants form sprawling mats of glossy leaves, 6 to 8 to 12 in. high. The peacock-blue flowers tip new growth from midsummer to frost, perfectly set off by rusty-red calyxes and bracts. With frost plumbago dies, leaving behind a tangle of not very attractive brown stems. Plumbago takes a year or two to get under way, but once it's established, it will throw new growth in every direction, overwhelming lower-growing ground covers such as pachysandra and periwinkle. It is a favorite of butterflies, large and small.

Other Names
Plumbago, *Plumbago larpentae*

Bloom Period and Seasonal Color
Summer and early fall; bright blue flowers.

Mature Height × Spread
8 to 12 in. × 12 to 18 in.

Zones
5 to 9

When, Where, and How to Plant
In early spring, plant rooted divisions or container plants in full sun, or moderate shade. Plumbago needs a well-drained site. It does best in rich, acidic loam but will tolerate other soils. Follow the soil preparation and planting instructions at the beginning of this chapter, but omit the fertilizer. Make the planting holes 6 to 8 in. deep. Set the divisions 9 to 15 in. apart as plumbago will eventually spread rapidly. Water well. Mulch with salt hay, straw, or compost to keep weeds at bay until the plants shade the ground so completely weeds cannot get started. This will take two or three seasons to happen.

Growing Tips
For the first three or four weeks after planting, it is important to maintain soil moisture. Overhead watering is suitable.

Care
Half an inch or so of compost applied in late fall every two or three years keeps plumbago a good green. Cut plumbago back after frost wilts the leaves to keep the bed tidy and healthy, and to promote the new growth on which flowers will appear the next season. Plumbago blooms on new growth. If you do not cut it back, you will get lots of foliage but you will miss out on its really beautiful flowers. We shear the tops of plumbago growing in an all-plumbago bed in winter and then mow with a sharp rotary mower. Plumbago spreads by underground shoots, rooting as it rambles. It gets matted in time, and every three or four years benefits from dividing. To multiply your holdings, in early spring cut all around rooted clumps to free them from the parent plants, then dig them and replant.

Companion Planting and Design
We like plumbago combined with other flowering ground covers, such as periwinkle and lamium. It's lovely with flowering perennials but in time can take over the bed. To prevent this from happening, confine it to 3-gallon pots.

Our Personal Recommendation
Plant the species.

Lenten Rose

Helleborus orientalis

When, Where, and How to Plant

Set out large container-grown plants in early spring or early fall where they will receive morning sun or all day dappled light. The hellebores thrive in well-drained, humusy, nearly neutral woodland soil. Follow the soil preparation and planting instructions at the beginning of this chapter and, unless you are planting in woodland soil, mix in 50 to 75 percent of humusy forest soil or decayed shredded leaves mixed with a slow-release organic fertilizer. Make the planting holes twice as wide and as deep as the container. Set the rootball a little higher than the level it was originally growing. Water well and mulch with shredded leaves or leaf compost.

Growing Tip

During the first six weeks after planting, water often enough to keep the soil damp to the touch.

Care

Fertilize the plants in fall and remove any deteriorating foliage. Established clumps are relatively drought tolerant. Lenten rose self-sows: eventually you'll find seedlings growing under and around the plants. Lift them with as much soil as you can take along, and transplant them to a similar environment. Baby the seedlings with sustained moisture and yearly feedings of an organic fertilizer until they are growing lustily. August to September 10 is the best time to divide the plants.

Companion Planting and Design

The hellebores are especially handsome under tall evergreen shrubs. To make sure you get to fully enjoy this lovely early flower, plant hellebores along well-used paths and where they can been seen from a window. They're especially attractive growing with daffodils, skimmia, hostas, and *Pulmonaria saccharata* 'Mrs. Moon'.

Our Personal Recommendations

Hellebores come in a wide array of strains and colors, but the Lenten rose and its cultivars are the best of the best. In Zones 4 and 5, musty-smelling stinking hellebore, *H. foetidus*, lives through winters, and bears panicles of drooping, bell-like, pale apple-green flowers edged with red.

Imagine a flower blooming in the cold of late March and early April! That's the Lenten rose, the best of the hellebores, and one of the toughest and hardiest ground covers we have. Growing in lightly shaded areas, under rhododendrons and other tall shrubs for example, the plants develop dense stands of shining, leathery, deeply divided foliage that is as beautiful in winter as it is in summer. Unique nodding flowers appear in late winter. In clear colors, or speckled, mottled, or streaked, these are the finest, most long lasting of any winter flower. Rather like small nodding roses, they are composed of 5 petal-like sepals and persist for two to three months. Undisturbed, beautiful colonies of Lenten rose will expand and self-sow.

Other Name
Hellebore

Bloom Period and Seasonal Color
Early through mid-spring in all but the warmest areas; hybrids range from green-white through rose to maroon, pink, and black-maroon.

Mature Height × Spread
1 to 1 1/2 ft. × 1 1/2 to 3 ft.

Zones
3 or 4 to 8

Lily-of-the-Valley
Convallaria majalis

One of the world's great perfumes, Joy, is derived from lily-of-the-valley, a slim stem of pure white bells topping foliage that starts out looking like a tiny furled umbrella. The leaves pop up in early spring, and the flowers rise up through them a few weeks later. Lily-of-the-valley is loved for its fragrance and it also is a great ground cover in our area. In light woodlands and shaded wild gardens it naturalizes, and rapidly colonizes on deep—hard to eradicate—underground roots. You can get lily-of-the-valley to put up flower stems tall enough to cut easily by interplanting it with pachysandra—but we enjoy pulling them gently from their foliage. Pre-cooled pips of lily-of-the-valley can be forced into bloom early indoors. Lily-of-the-valley is listed among toxic plants.

Bloom Period and Seasonal Color
Spring; white, pink cultivars.

Mature Height × Spread
10 to 12 in. × indefinite spread

Zones
2 to 7

When, Where, and How to Plant
You can plant container-grown lily-of-the-valley any time. Bare-root divisions or rhizome segments are best planted in early spring or early fall. Lily-of-the-valley is most successful in sun and in dappled light. The cooler the region, the more sun it can handle. It thrives in somewhat acid soil that is well drained, humusy, and moist. Follow the soil preparation and planting instructions at the beginning of this chapter. Set planting holes for bare-root divisions 6 to 8 in. apart and place the pointed tips (called "pips") just below the surface with the roots bunched up underneath. Space plants from 4- or 5-in. containers 8 to 10 in. apart. Water well. Provide a 2-in. mulch for the area.

Growing Tip
During the first six weeks after planting, water often enough to keep the soil damp to the touch.

Care
If the foliage browns in late summer, spider mites are at work: apply a miticide according to label directions. Fertilize in fall with a light topdressing of slow-release organic fertilizer for acid-loving plants. Water when you water your lawn. If the flowers become smaller and less fragrant, it means the roots are crowded: dig out clumps in the fall, and replant them elsewhere with space all around. Lily-of-the-valley roots go deep, so push your spading fork way down and make sure you get all the roots. Fill the empty space with improved soil and the plants all around will move into the new ground.

Companion Planting and Design
Well-tended, lily-of-the-valley stays a fresh green all during the growing season and is charming as a ground cover for various garden plants including wildflowers. It is delightful in a woodland garden with columbines, primroses, Solomon's-seal, trilliums, and lady's-slippers. Keep it out of any flower beds where its aggressive nature will be a problem.

Our Personal Recommendations
We recommend the cultivar called 'Fortin's Giant', a tall, full-flowered white that has larger flowers than the species. If you are planting for the beauty of the flowers, plant 'Plena', a double-flowered variety, and little 'Rosea', a less fragrant variety whose flowers are lavender-pink.

Periwinkle
Vinca minor

When, Where, and How to Plant
Set out flats of rooted cuttings of *V. minor* in early spring or fall. Vinca does best in bright shade under tall shrubs or trees and in the partial shade created by a building. It prefers well-drained soil with a pH between 5.5 and 7.2 that is well worked, fertile, and loamy. Follow the soil preparation and planting instructions at the beginning of this chapter. Provide planting holes 6 to 8 in. deep and space the plants 8 in. apart. Water thoroughly. Mulch with pine needles or composted leaf mold.

Growing Tip
Do not allow vinca to dry out the first season.

Care
In early spring before growth starts, use a mower or shear the vinca to keep the bed thick. Scratch in a slow-release organic fertilizer. Water the plants during extended droughts. To multiply your holdings, divide and replant rooted stems as growth resumes in early spring, or during wet weather in late summer and fall. You can also bunch up root divisions or offsets and plant them.

Companion Planting and Design
For small areas we like the look of ground covers grouped in richly varied combinations rather than in single-species displays. A combination that has everything—flowers, fresh foliage, fall color—is *V. minor*, pachysandra, plumbago, and ferns. It includes plants for shade, semi-shade under tall trees, and sun. In planters we sometimes combine variegated forms of the tender species *V. major*, which we treat as an annual, and *V. minor*. *V. major* has larger leaves, is a paler green or is variegated, and produces 3- to 4-ft.-long branches that are lovely trailing over the edges of containers.

Our Personal Recommendations
Some of the most beautiful cultivars are: *V. minor* 'Alba', which has creamy white flowers and is somewhat less vigorous than the species; 'Bowlesii', which has large blue flowers; 'Miss Jekyll', which bears small white flowers; and 'Sterling Silver', which has midnight blue flowers and beautiful white margins around the leaves.

Small-leaved Vinca minor *is a low, flowering, evergreen plant with trailing branches and dainty, shiny, dark-green leaves. It creates a beautiful green carpet for open woodlands, rocky slopes, and shrub borders. Though it tolerates only a little foot traffic, it's a handsome lawn substitute. Vinca stems root every few feet, but, unlike ivy, vinca does not cling to masonry so it can be used for edging walls and terraces. The little flowers that appear in very early spring are a real asset: almost flat, wide open, a beautiful periwinkle-blue, they're lovely against the dark green foliage. Like other rapidly spreading ground covers, vinca can crowd out desirable natives and exotics, so plant it only where you are sure it will remain under your control.*

Other Names
Vinca, Myrtle

Bloom Period and Seasonal Color
March through May; shades of periwinkle blue, white.

Mature Height × Length
3 to 6 in. × 2 to 3 ft.

Zones
4 to 9

Herbs *for New England*

In the long ago and far away, our forebears grew aromatic kitchen herbs alongside roses, cinnamon-scented pinks, spicy nasturtiums, and the other perfumed flowers with which they flavored food—so the old-time herb garden was a place of beauty and fragrance. But enhancing food was just one of the ways in which herbal plants improved life. You can get a sense of the past—and present—importance of herbs by visiting the U.S. National Arboretum in Washington, D.C. There The Herb Society of America has established a beautiful two-acre herb garden planted in medicinal and dye herbs, early pioneer and Native American herbs, industrial and fragrance herbs, and Oriental and beverage herbs. Herbal trees and shrubs occupy the center of this grouping. Caprilands Herb Farm, in Coventry, Connecticut, the home of the late, great lady of herbal lore, Adelma Grenier Simmons, is a mecca for New England gardeners interested in knowing more about herbs. Planted together, herbs become an aromatic sprawl of greens. The knot garden at the National Arboretum illustrates the classical solution to herb sprawl, which is to group herbs within ribbons of low boxwood hedges. "Knot garden" originally referred to any garden with an intricate design, but has become almost synonymous with the growing of herbs.

The most indispensable kitchen herbs are the twelve on the following pages. We grow our cooking herbs in beds of ornamentals handy to the kitchen door. The lush greens of parsley and cilantro enhance the flower borders. Low-growing thyme makes an aromatic edger for the path to the kitchen steps. Basil hides the yellowing foliage of small spring bulbs. Dill adds grace to the flower-filled tub by the door.

Lavender 'Hidcote'

When to Plant, and How to Harvest and Dry

Seeds of most perennial herbs are slow to germinate and growing the seedlings can be a challenge. So, unless we need many plants of one kind—such as basil for bouquets, or creeping thyme for between stepping-stones—we buy potted plants, rooted cuttings, or seedlings and generally set them out in mid-spring after all danger of frost has passed. Most herbs thrive in full sun and well-drained soil with a pH between 5.5 and 7.0. A few kitchen herbs do well here in part sun, among them dill and basil. To prepare soil for herbs, see Soil Preparation and Improvement and Planting in the Introduction.

To encourage an herb to bush out and be more productive, early on pinch out the tips of the main stems. Remove herb flowers as they develop—they're edible and make charming garnishes. When the plants have filled out, you can harvest the tender sprig tips of the youngest branches at will without harming the plant. Never strip a plant of more than a third of its foliage or it will have trouble maintaining itself. In summer's high heat (especially in a very warm summer) herbs go into semi-dormancy. During this season, herbs should be picked sparingly, as the plants are unable to replace the missing foliage and will look awful and be slow to recover.

Herbs are most flavorful harvested in the early morning, before the sun dissipates the essential oils that give them flavor. Rinse herbs

Chives

only if they're muddy. You won't have to rinse the foliage if you surround your herbs with mulch. We find that herb foliage stays fresh for a week or so when we seal it in a vegetable bag lined with a damp paper towel and store it in the crisper.

To dry herbs, harvest clean, healthy stems, 12 to 14 inches long, and strip off the lower leaves. Tie them loosely in small bunches and hang them upside down in an airy, dry, preferably dark place. Direct sunlight fades the foliage. When they're crackling dry, strip off the leaves and discard the stems. Rub the leaves between your palms to break them up. Pour the leaves into labeled jars then seal them. We try to find time to renew our supply every season: old herbs lose much of their flavor.

Other Options

Some of the many other herbs we include in ornamental gardens for both their beauty and fragrance are these:

Catmint, *Nepeta × faassenii* (Zones 3 to 9)

Fennel, *Foeniculum vulgare* (tender perennial)

Feverfew, *Chrysanthemum parthenium* (Zones 4 to 9)

Lemon Grass, *Cymbopogon citrates* (tender perennial)

Rue, *Ruta graveolens* 'Jackman's Blue' (Zones 6 to 10)

Sweet Woodruff, *Galium odoratum* (Zones 4 to 9)

Basil
Ocimum basilicum

The basils are vigorous upright annuals or short-lived perennials with light-green, often slightly puckered, leaves that have the cool strong bite of mint (a close relative), with hints of anise or sweet licorice, clove, and thyme. The leaves are used to flavor Mediterranean dishes, raw tomatoes, salads, pasta sauces, and sauces for lamb, fish, and beef. We wouldn't be without basil for cooking, but we also plant basil for the aroma, color, and texture both ordinary basil and colorful varieties add to garden plantings. For fragrant bouquet fillers we plant opal basil, which has purplish leaves with green markings, and 'Dark Opal' basil, which has little green markings, red stems, and a sweet, anise-like flavor. 'Red Rubin', purple leaf basil, is a European selection that holds its color well.

Bloom Period and Seasonal Color
Summer; lavender flower spikes.

Mature Height × Spread
1 to 2¹/₂ ft. × 10 to 15 in.

When, Where, and How to Plant
Pots of seedlings can be set out after the weather has warmed and all danger of frost has passed. You can start seeds indoors four to six weeks before that, or sow basil seeds in the garden once night temperatures stay above 50 degrees Fahrenheit. See Starting Seeds Indoors in the Appendix. Basil prefers full sun but will tolerate some afternoon shade. Avoid planting basil near roses because roses attract Japanese beetles, which also enjoy basil. Basil does well in well-drained, humusy soils whose pH is between 6.0 and 7.0. See Soil Preparation and Planting in the Introduction. Provide planting holes 8 to 12 in. deep, and allow 6 to 8 in. between plants. Basil wilts quickly and easily in summer heat, so apply a 3-in. layer of mulch starting 3 in. from the stem to help keep in moisture.

Growing Tips
Pinch out the central leader and harvest branch tips and flowers early and often to encourage leaf production. To promote rapid growth, water often enough to sustain the soil moisture for the first few weeks. After that, water weekly unless you have a soaking rain.

Care
At midseason, cut the plants back by about half. Pick sprig tips at will when the leaves are still young. Big harvests can begin when flower spikes start to form. We find it keeps fresh for at least a week in the fridge, sealed into a plastic bag. Basil will continue right up until the first frost.

Companion Planting and Design
The purple varieties especially are beautiful tucked into flower borders and growing in containers planted with flowers in pastel colors. They're lovely in bouquets of cosmos. In window boxes and for edging containers use tiny bush basils like 'Spicy Globe', which grows between 6 and 12 in. tall: the flavor is quite good.

Our Personal Recommendations
Our favorite basils for flavoring are common sweet basil and holy basil, *O. sanctum*. We plant purple-leaved basils, which aren't very flavorful, for the rich color they bring to flower beds and bouquets. The opal basils and 'Purple Ruffles', an All-America Selections winner, are our current favorites.

Chives

Allium schoenoprasum

When, Where, and How to Plant

Chives can be started from seed indoors six to eight weeks before the last frost date: they grow best at temperatures around 75 degrees Fahrenheit. The clumps enlarge over the years so unless you are planting lots for floral display, we suggest you buy a few potted seedlings. Potted chives can be planted spring, summer, or early fall. They thrive in full sun and in soils between pH 6.0 and 7.0. Choose a well-drained site—chives hate puddles—and work the soil to a depth of 8 to 12 in. See Soil Preparation and Planting in the Introduction. For each plant mix in a handful of either compost or composted manure. Set the plants 12 to 18 in. apart and water with diluted fertilizer. Mulch all around 2 in. deep.

Growing Tips

To promote rapid, unchecked growth, for the next two or three weeks after planting, water often enough to sustain soil moisture. After that, water deeply only during prolonged droughts. Keep weeds away: they're hard to get out of a clump once the chives are well established.

Care

In early spring, fertilize the bed with a slow-release organic fertilizer. To encourage more foliage, keep the flowers pinched out. Use sharp, clean scissors to harvest chives and cut no lower than 2 in. from the crown. Never take more than a third of the plant at one time and harvest sparingly in summer's high heat. Divide chives every three to four years in early spring or early fall. In late summer, you can pot chives in a clay container and bring a clump indoors for modest winter harvests.

Companion Planting

Chives are pretty little plants that are lovely in bloom and attractive tucked into a flowering border or edging an herb or a vegetable garden. They do well in large containers.

Our Personal Recommendations

For cooking, we recommend the variety called 'Fine Chives'. There are interesting other allium species. One we plant for cooking and for its flowers is *A. tuberosum*, the tall garlic, or Chinese, chives. The leaves are flat, not round, and the flowers are white.

Chives are perennials. They develop attractive mounds of perfectly round, hollow, dark-green leaves that at first glance look like grass. Beginning in June, pretty, dryish, lavender-pink globes appear and these, too, are edible. It's a charming display that continues all summer long. Chive leaves impart a mild onion flavor. They're used chopped as a garnish and flavoring agent for salads, dips, stews, and casseroles, and laid full size over fish or meat that will be roasted. Chopped chives puts a flavorful finishing touch to one of the world's great cold soups, vichyssoise, and the flowers, pulled apart, make an elegant garnish for eggs Benedict. Though they are best fresh from the garden, chives keep well frozen, or dried on a screen, and sealed into airtight containers.

Bloom Period and Seasonal Color
Spring and summer; mauve-lavender to pink.

Mature Height × Spread
8 to 12. in. × 12 to 15 in.

Zones
3 to 9

Dill
Anethum graveolens

Dill is a willowy annual with foliage as fine as asparagus fern. It looks a lot like fennel, Foeniculum, to which it is related, and tastes of parsley-carrot-lemon-anise. The foliage is called "dill weed." Yellow-green flower heads resembling Queen-Anne's-lace develop as the season warms. The flowers are edible and eventually produce seeds that can be dried and bottled for winter seasoning of casseroles and stews, and for pickling. Dill foliage dries quickly on screens and also can be bottled for later use. Snipped fresh dill weed is excellent in salads and with salmon, potatoes, green beans, salads, and in chicken soup. It's also a very pretty garnish. We use whole stems of aromatic dill weed as a garnish for platters of cold cuts, salmon, tomatoes, and cheese.

Bloom Period and Seasonal Color
Late summer; yellow-green flower heads.

Mature Height × Spread
2 to 3 ft. × 8 to 12 in.

When, Where, and How to Plant
You can start dill from seed indoors six to eight weeks before the last frost. See Starting Seeds Indoors in the Appendix. Dill's taproot doesn't transplant easily, so sow the seeds in peat pots and transplant the seedlings in their pots. Or, after the ground has warmed sprinkle the seeds over the soil where the plants are to grow. Dill needs sunshine but deteriorates in noon sun in prolonged, intense heat. Avoid growing dill where walls or white-painted surfaces intensify the heat. Dill prefers soil in the acid range, pH 5.5 to 6.5. See Soil Preparation and Planting in the Introduction. Work the soil 8 to 12 in. deep and set seedlings about 12 in. apart. Water with diluted fertilizer. Apply a 2-in. mulch starting 3 in. from the stem.

Growing Tips
To promote rapid, unchecked growth, for the first several weeks water often enough to keep the soil moist. Pinch out sprig tips regularly to encourage branching.

Care
Water deeply every week or ten days unless you have a soaking rain. Harvest sparingly in high heat. If dill deteriorates when heat comes, discard it and plant new seedlings in early September. Keep the flower heads picked until the end of the season. Dill may self-sow if the soil around the parent plants is cultivated and moist. To have dill seed for cooking, when the seedheads yellow or brown, but before they dry, shake the seeds into a paper bag and dry them on paper towels on screens.

Companion Planting and Design
Dill's feathery foliage lends grace to the kitchen garden, and to herb and cutting gardens. In choosing a place for dill, take into account that it may die out when high heat arrives. Dwarf dill varieties do well in containers.

Our Personal Recommendations
'Dukat' and 'Tetra' dill have a delicate, rather sweet flavor and are slow to bolt. 'Bouquet' has especially large seed heads. 'Fernleaf' dill, a 1992 All-America Selections winner, is a lovely, blue-green, 18-in. dwarf with excellent flavor. 'Mammoth' is an aromatic 4-ft. dill for pickling.

When, Where, and How to Plant

You can start oregano from seed, but all the seeds sold do not produce plants with a satisfactory flavor. When selecting the seedlings, first gently rub the leaves together, sniff, and choose only the most fragrant plants. If you choose to propagate from seed, keep only the most fragrant seedling. We prefer to start oregano from root divisions of plants whose flavor we have tested. Plant oregano in midspring or in late summer. It will be most productive growing in full sun. It can take a lot of heat and resists drought. Partially shaded, it also grows well. Oregano does best in slightly alkaline soil, but any well-drained, well-worked soil will do. See Soil Preparation and Planting in the Introduction. Space the plants 12 to 15 in. apart. Maintain a 2-in. mulch to keep the leaves clean for cooking.

Growing Tip

Keep the roots fairly moist until the plant is growing lushly.

Care

Keep the flower spikes pinched out. Water when you water the flower beds. Italian oregano will invade nearby garden space with long trailing stems that root. So, either plant it where it can go wild or cut established plants back by about a third after their first flush of growth in mid-spring. Multiply Italian oregano by dividing established plants in early spring or by digging up and replanting rooted branches any time. Every two or three years use several of the existing rooted stems to start new plants since the parent plant will begin to deteriorate.

Companion Planting and Design

We plant Italian oregano in front of the fence surrounding the kitchen garden, and we use ornamental types as edgers in the perennial beds.

Our Personal Recommendations

For drying and bouquets we plant Italian oregano. For salads we prefer the small leaves of Greek oregano, *O. vulgare* ssp. *hirtum* (*O. heracleoticum*), which develops into a green mat, and the tender perennial called sweet marjoram, *O. majorana*. 'Kent Beauty' is an ornamental with pink flowers and modest flavor. *O. vulgare* 'Compactum Nanum', a creeper about 2 ft. high, is great between stepping-stones. It is not much for flavor.

The oreganos form graceful clumps 1 to 2 ft. high with bright green, sometimes woolly, wedge-shaped leaves, charming as an edger and in small bouquets and centerpieces. Hardy Italian oregano, and its close relative, cold-tender sweet or annual marjoram, Origanum majorana, are creeping relatives of mint that produce panicles of whitish, pink, or lavender florets. The leaves of Italian oregano, O. vulgare, have a bold, peppery bite like that of thyme but milder, and they add a delicious sharp flavor to salad dressings, tomatoes, pizzas, and Mediterranean dishes. The plant is upright but somewhat sprawling and is attractive planted as an edger in a mixed, flowering border. Deer don't trouble it, and it withstands drought and neglect and goes right on growing. The yellow-leaved varieties are quite beautiful.

Other Names

Oregano, Marjoram, Pot Marjoram

Bloom Period and Seasonal Color

Summer; panicles of faintly fragrant, whitish, pink, or lavender florets.

Mature Height × Spread

6 to 10 in. × 6 to 12 in.
Dwarf and creeping varieties: 2 to 6 in. × 2 to 3 ft. or more

Zones

3 to 9

Lavender

Lavandula angustifolia

Lavender's sweet, lasting scent has been a source of fragrance for thousands of years. It's a shrubby evergreen whose every part is intensely fragrant—flower spikes, stems, and needle-like, gray-green leaves. Lavender stems are harvested before the buds open, dried, and the buds are stripped and used to scent linens and lingerie, sleep pillows, and other tools of aromatherapy. The buds, dried or fresh, are also used to add a sweet mint-anise-rosemary flavor to herbes de Provence, honey, dessert butters, savory sauces, grilled fish and steaks, marinades for game, and to stews and soups. We plant lavender so it will sprawl across paths and near roses, where we will brush against it often, releasing its wonderful aroma. Deer dislike it.

Other Name
English Lavender

Bloom Period and Seasonal Color
June, sometimes repeats in August, especially if many of the first set of flowers were harvested; lavender, deep purple, blue-gray, pink, white.

Mature Height × Spread
2 to 4 ft. × 2 to 2¹/₂ ft.

Zones
5 to 9

When, Where, and How to Plant
We recommend you set out container-grown plants in early spring, late summer, or early fall. Lavender does best here in full sun in soil whose pH is above 6.0. It needs a well-drained site, and flourishes growing on a sandy south-facing slope. See Soil Preparation and Planting in the Introduction. Work the soil to a depth that is twice the height of the container to assure good drainage. Set the plants 15 to 30 in. apart. Water well. Apply a 2-in. mulch starting 3 in. from the stem.

Growing Tips
Water often after planting to sustain soil moisture. After that, water deeply every ten days or so unless you have a soaking rain.

Care
Lavender often re-blooms in late summer if the first set of flowering stems has been harvested. Harvest lavender stems just before the buds begin to open, tie them in loose bunches and hang them upside down to air dry, then strip off the buds and store them in a sealed container. In spring when new growth appears on old stems, prune 1 to 2 in. from the branch tips of established plants, and remove old flowering stems. Every two to three years shear the bush back to about 6 to 8 in. Do not cut lavender to the ground, as you do perennials, and do not prune it after late August or in winter.

Companion Planting and Design
Lavender looks great in a rock garden, and makes a wonderful ground cover for sunny orchards. We plant the English lavender cultivar 'Hidcote', which withstands more cold than other types, for its deep purple flowers. The beautiful purple-pink French, or Spanish, lavender, *L. stoechas*, isn't hardy even in our warm Zone 6, but it makes a pretty pot plant.

Our Personal Recommendations
The lavender we use in dry perfumes and for flavoring is the English type, *L. angustifolia* ssp. *angustifolia*. If you garden in a region colder than Zone 5, try 'Hidcote' in a sunny, sheltered spot.

Mint
Mentha spicata

When, Where, and How to Plant

Mint spreads relentlessly, so gardeners are eager to share rooted divisions. Plant only a mint whose flavor you have tasted and like, or one you will use in bouquets. Garden centers offer many container-grown varieties. You can plant rooted mint in almost any season in full sun or in filtered or bright shade. It is very invasive, so unless you are planting in poor or clay soil, confine the roots to a large bottomless plastic pot or coffee tin and plant the container. Mints do best in slightly acid soil, pH 5.5 to 6.5, but any well-drained soil will do. Space the plants 12 to 15 in. apart. Water well. The sprawling mints get muddied during rainstorms, so stake a few branches to have clean leaves available for cooking. Apply a 2-in. mulch starting 3 in. from the stem.

Growing Tip

To get the plants off to a good start after planting, water often enough to sustain the soil moisture for the next two or three weeks.

Care

Water the small-leaved mints when you water the flower beds. Harvest only sparingly in summer's high heat. Shear mint to keep it looking neat and to produce fresh new growth. Mint growing in a container should be divided every year or two in the spring or early fall. Six-inch tip cuttings root readily in damp potting soil, sand, or water.

Companion Planting and Design

Centuries of growing mint has resulted in more than 500 species and cultivars. They are diverse in appearance and aroma and make an interesting collection for garden hobbyists. As an edger along walkways and in containers we like the beautiful, variegated pineapple mint, *M. suaveolens* 'Variegata': the flavor is negligible but this mint is somewhat less invasive than other species and really beautiful.

Our Personal Recommendations

We grow a few spearmint plants to use fresh to flavor food and to dry for making mint tea. And, because we love the aroma of mint in bouquets, we let *M. arvensis*, which has broad, hairy leaves, grow wild in our kitchen flower bed.

The mints are upright or sprawling herbs, 1 to 3 ft. tall, with intensely aromatic, crinkly green leaves (hairy in some species), that are pungent when brushed against. One of its many distinguishing features is its square stems. In summer, fuzzy mint-scented flower spikes appear. This species, Mentha spicata, has small, pointed, dainty leaves and a truly fine sweetish mint flavor. It is our choice for use as a culinary herb—for teas, juleps, vinaigrette, lamb sauce, desserts (use fresh tiny tips), jellies, soups, and Indian and Middle Eastern foods. It is also used dried in potpourris. Stepped on, mint sprawling onto a garden path becomes a carpet of magical fragrance. Bees will happily graze mint diligently all day long.

Other Name
Spearmint

Bloom Period and Seasonal Color
Summer; purplish, white, pink, mauve, lilac.

Mature Height × Spread
1 to 3 ft. × 2 ft.

Zones
3 to 9

Parsley
Petroselinum crispum

We plant three parsleys: curly parsley and flat-leaved, or Italian, parsley, which are varieties of Petroselinum crispum, and Chinese parsley, Coriandrum sativum, more commonly known as cilantro. All three are low, very green, leafy plants. Curly and flat-leaved parsley are pungent, winter-hardy biennials. Their earthy carrot-celery flavor blends other flavorful ingredients. Rich in chlorophyll, they kill odors and sweeten the breath. Curly parsley is the most beautiful for garnish and the quickest to mince. Flat Italian parsley, P. crispum var. neapolitanum, is more richly flavored. Cilantro is a cold-tolerant annual that grows to a foot or two in a season. It adds a unique flavor to Latin and Oriental recipes. Its dried ripe seed is the ancient Asian spice called coriander, which imparts a sweet lemony flavor and a hint of sage.

Other Names
Curly Parsley, Italian Parsley, Cilantro, Chinese Parsley, Fresh Coriander

Bloom Period and Seasonal Color
Summer; grown for its foliage; once it flowers, its season for usable leaves is past.

Mature Height × Spread
12 to 18 in. × 12 to 18 in.

When, Where, and How to Plant
Parsley is a biennial—that is, it lives two years. It stays green through New England winters, flourishes mightily through most of spring, then when heat comes it quickly goes to seed. To have a steady supply of parsley, plant two or three parsley seedlings in early spring, and the following fall plant a new batch near the veterans. Discard the veterans when they bolt (flower)—or let them grow their greenish flower heads and enjoy watching the butterflies flocking to them. Planting time for cilantro seedlings is after the air has warmed. All three parsleys do best in full sun in well-drained, neutral soil, between pH 6.0 to 7.0. See Soil Preparation and Planting in the Introduction. Dig planting holes 8 to 12 in. deep and set the plants 8 to 10 in. apart. Water well. Provide a 2-inch mulch.

Growing Tip
To promote rapid, unchecked growth, water often for the first two to three weeks.

Care
The parsleys can be harvested as soon as the plants have grown a substantial number of stems. Use scissors to harvest the outer stems and make the cut at the base. Never take more than a quarter to a third of one plant at a time. When curly and Italian parsley are growing lushly, harvest, mince, and freeze some for winter use.

Companion Planting and Design
From an ornamental point of view, the parsleys can be planted wherever a low-growing mound of bright green is desirable. Curly parsley makes a handsome edging for bright red geraniums, and it thrives in window boxes and large containers. We like to keep a little bouquet of red geraniums and curly parsley in the kitchen.

Our Personal Recommendations
'Clivi' is a mossy, dwarf curly parsley to use in window boxes. 'Krausa' parsley is a moss variety we like for flavor. 'Triple Curled' is thickly ruffled. 'Giant Italian' is a 3-ft., deep green parsley with a full, mellow flavor excellent fresh or dried. Cilantro labeled "slow bolt" is best for foliage: if you'd like to grow your own coriander seeds, plant varieties called just "coriander."

When, Where, and How to Plant

In Zones 6 and 7, rosemary is grown as an annual and over-wintered indoors. To germinate, the seeds need nights at 75 degrees Fahrenheit, and can take three months to sprout. So we start with container-grown plants. The time to plant rosemary is after danger of frost is over. It needs full sun. A native to the Mediterranean, it withstands high heat and drought once established, and can be grown where it will be neglected. Rosemary does best in well-drained soil, acid or neutral. See Soil Preparation and Planting in the Introduction. Work the soil 8 to 12 in. deep and set baby plants 6 to 8 in. apart, shrub sizes 12 to 24 in. apart. Water well. Provide a 2-in. mulch starting 3 in. from the stem.

Growing Tips

To promote rapid, unchecked growth, water often enough to sustain the soil moisture for the first two or three weeks. Harvest 1- or 2-in. sprigs from young branch tips often to encourage the plant to bush out.

Care

Water established plants only during long droughts. Before winter, pot the plant in sandy, humusy soil and bring it indoors to a sunny window; water regularly but don't keep the soil moist. Mist several times each week. Rosemary will last longest in bright light in a room at 50 degrees Fahrenheit. Put the plant out in the spring after all danger of frost has passed.

Companion Planting and Design

Rosemary is a good bonsai and pot plant, and specimen to place near entrances, windows, and garden seats where you can enjoy its fragrance.

Our Personal Recommendations

For flavoring we recommend the species, *R. officinalis*. Ornamental rosemaries, though not the best for cooking, are lovely in the garden and include: 'Benenden Blue', which has handsome blue flowers; 'Lockwood de Forest', which has brighter leaves and bluer flowers; 'Kenneth's Prostrate' and 'Huntington Carpet', which are superior creeping forms; and variegated 'Golden Prostratus'.

An age-old symbol of remembrance and beloved of bees, rosemary is a shrub-like perennial that has hauntingly aromatic gray-green needles. It's not hardy in New England, even in Zones 6 and 7, but it may be wintered indoors and sometimes grows well enough from year to year to be trained as a Christmas tree topiary. The pungent needles impart a sweet, hot, piney, nutmeg taste used to flavor many foods—polenta and potatoes, fruit, cookies, breads and biscuits, grilled meats, and fish. Olive oil infused with rosemary makes a delicious dipping and sautée oil. Rosemary is the base for many men's colognes and for potpourris. A circlet of rosemary branches makes a great foundation for an herb wreath. Sprigs of rosemary add aroma to bouquets of fresh flowers.

Bloom Period and Seasonal Color
Summer; pale lavender-blue flower spikes.

Mature Height × Spread
2 to 4 ft. × 2 to 3 ft.

Sage
Salvia officinalis

Common sage is a small, beautiful woody perennial whose grayish leaves have the texture of crepe. Some colorful varieties are beautiful enough to be grown as ornamentals. The leaves impart a subtle flavor—sweet pine, camphor, and citrus. Minced fresh sage is used to flavor bread and pasta sauces, and with roasted pork, chicken, and vegetables. Dried sage enhances fatty meats and is used in stuffing for poultry. The flavor of fresh sage becomes more potent the longer it cooks—so use it with caution in delicate sauces. Sage stays fresh for a week sealed in a vegetable bag in the crisper. The leaves dry well in a microwave oven, on screens, or tucked into a wreath.

Bloom Period and Seasonal Color
Midsummer; violet, blue, white.

Mature Height × Spread
1 to 2 ft. × 1 to 2 ft.

Zones
4 to 9

When, Where, and How to Plant
Set out container-grown plants or root divisions in early spring after all danger of frost is past. Sage does best in full sun, but tolerates afternoon shade. Provide very well-drained, ordinary, neutral soil, around pH 7.0. See Soil Preparation and Planting in the Introduction. Work the soil 8 to 12 in. deep and dig generous planting holes 2 ft. apart. Water well. Stake stems that sprawl to avoid having to rinse the foliage, robbing it of some of its flavorful oils. Apply a 2-in. mulch starting 3 in. from the stem.

Growing Tips
For the first two or three weeks after planting water often enough to sustain the soil moisture. The flower spikes are edible, and removing them improves the appearance and growth of the plant.

Care
Water deeply when you water the flower beds. Harvest tender sprig tips at will. In the fall trim sage back to a tidy mound to avoid root rot—a problem where drainage is poor. Sage can be harvested sparingly in winter. To multiply your holdings, divide well-established older plants in spring or early fall. Sage can also be grown successfully indoors as long as it gets sun at least six hours a day and has proper drainage; the plant should be pruned to no more than 12 in. If it starts to look leggy and the leaves grow pale and are thinly spaced, the plant isn't getting enough light.

Companion Planting and Design
For their texture and beauty, we plant colorful cultivars of *S. officinalis* toward the front of flowering borders and in the herb and the kitchen gardens. Sage is pretty in a planter, set so it droops over the edge. Several varieties of sage grouped together are striking. Sage's camphor aroma is said to deter garden insects.

Our Personal Recommendations
The species is best for flavoring food, but some of the more colorful sages have flavor, though less than *S. officinalis*. 'Tricolor', the showiest, has leaves splattered with deep pink, silver gray, cream, and purple. 'Icterina' has beautiful gray leaves splashed with gold.

Tarragon
Artemisia dracunculus

When, Where, and How to Plant

True French tarragon cannot be grown from seed: buy a container-grown plant or rooted cutting that meets your taste test. It may not winter over in exceptionally cold winters. One or two plants will satisfy your needs. Plant tarragon in mid-spring in full sun—it tolerates a few hours of afternoon shade. It can take a lot of heat and resists drought, so you can plant it where it may be neglected. Don't plant tarragon in a kitchen garden where rototilling might disturb it. Tarragon thrives in ordinary, neutral soil between pH 5.5 or 6.0 and pH 7.0. Good drainage, especially in winter, is essential. See Soil Preparation and Planting in the Introduction. Dig planting holes 8 to 12 in. deep and 8 to 12 in. apart. Water well. Apply a 2-in. mulch starting 3 in. from the stem.

Growing Tips

Once planted, water often enough to sustain soil moisture for the first two or three weeks. Harvest sprig tips often in spring to promote growth of tender branches—the leafy tips are the tastiest.

Care

Water established plants deeply when you water the flower beds. Cut the plants back in summer when they begin to flower in order to promote new growth. In time tarragon's roots become crowded and tangled, resulting in a less productive plant. Renew your plant by dividing the clumps in the spring before growth begins. Carefully separate 3-in. pieces with shoots intact and replant. Discard any woody roots.

Companion Planting and Design

For all of its elegant flavor, tarragon is not a very jazzy looking plant. We recommend placing it in an out-of-the-way place in your herb garden surrounded by other tall, more interesting looking plants. It's useful as a filler in a flower border or a container garden.

Our Personal Recommendations

We grow the species for flavoring, and two of its aromatic cousins for their appeal in the garden and in bouquets. One is true wormwood, *A. absinthium*, and the other is southernwood, *A. abrotanum*, a beautiful foliage plant with finely divided, strongly scented leaves.

Tarragon is a perennial that grows into a good-sized, rather weedy shrub in our region. The slim, delicately flavored leaves impart a heavenly aroma of sweet anise or sweet licorice, and camphor. It is used for its flavor and scent in vinegars, dressings, French and Southern European dishes, and in potpourris. Tarragon is what gives Béarnaise sauce its flavor and it is an essential ingredient in fines herbes for stocks, broths, and Green Goddess salad dressing. There are two main tarragon groups, French and Russian. French tarragon has an addictive, hauntingly sweet aroma, and that's what makes the plant worth looking for. Taste before buying! Russian tarragon can grow to 5 ft. tall and doesn't do much for food, but is handsome in the garden.

Bloom Period and Seasonal Color
Summer; whitish green florets.

Mature Height × Spread
1 to 2 ft. × 2 to 3 ft.

Zones
5 to 9

Thyme
Thymus spp. and hybrids

The thymes are small, prostrate, evergreen perennials with graceful trailing branches 6 to 10 in. long. The tiny dark green leaves have a sharp aroma and flavor, and an earthy mint taste. The flavor combines well with bay leaf, parsley, and onion. The leaves are used dried or fresh in stuffings for pork, lamb, and in salads, soups, stews, creole dishes, gumbos, and fish and seafood broths. Parisians sprinkle thyme on steaks before broiling. The leaves are so small they don't need to be minced, just bruised to release the flavor. Herb fans brew thyme to make an herbal tea. To dry thyme for storing, pick sprig tips, air dry them on screens until crisp, then strip off the leaves, and bottle and cap them. The thymes are excellent basket and container plants.

Other Names
French Thyme, Summer Thyme, Garden Thyme

Bloom Period and Seasonal Color
Early summer; pale pink, white, lilac, purple.

Mature Height × Spread
2 to 8 in. × 2 to 3 ft.

Zones
4 to 9

When, Where, and How to Plant
For an early crop, in mid-spring set out container-grown thyme. Plant it in full sun for the best flavor. Thyme tolerates considerable drought and abuse, so it can be planted where it is likely to be neglected. It does well in ordinary soil that has a pH above 6.0. See Soil Preparation and Planting in the Introduction. Provide a well-drained site and generous planting holes 8 to 12 in. deep and 12 in. apart. Water well. Mulch the area 2 in. deep.

Growing Tips
For a week or two after planting, promote rapid growth by watering often enough to sustain soil moisture. After that, water deeply during droughts.

Care
Harvest thyme sparingly in summer's high heat. Every year in early spring shear established plants back mercilessly, and fertilize them with a handful of a slow-release organic fertilizer. To multiply your holdings, divide mature plants in spring or early fall.

Companion Planting and Design
Two or three thyme plants will likely meet your needs for fresh and dried thyme. Good culinary thyme makes a neat dark-green edger. A nice combination in a hanging basket is thyme with white-splashed pineapple mint, white petunias, and pink geraniums. Creeping thyme, *T. serpyllum*, is tough enough to be walked on and can be used between flagstones. Colorful when in bloom, varieties of this species—white-flowered 'Albus', crimson 'Coccineus', and red 'Splendens'—are suitable ground covers for sunny slopes and attractive planted where they will trail over garden walls. For edging, we plant varieties whose leaves are splashed silver or gold; the names usually include 'Argenteus' or 'Aureus'.

Our Personal Recommendations
The sweetest culinary thymes are *T. vulgaris* and its cultivars, 'Wedgewood English', an excellent taller form, and 'Orange Balsam', which has a hint of citrus. We also grow lemon thyme, *T.* × *citriodorus*, and caraway-flavored *T. herba-barona*.

Winter Savory
Satureja montana

When, Where, and How to Plant

Set out root divisions of winter savory in mid-spring. Winter savory seeds can be started indoors six to eight weeks before the last frost date and then transplanted to the garden when you sow the summer savory seeds. Do not cover the seeds since they require light to germinate. You can sow seeds or plant seedlings of summer savory where they are to grow. Thin seedlings so that they are 7 in. apart. Summer savory prefers light, fertile soil while winter savory prefers poorer soil. Plant both savories where they will receive full sun and have well-drained, neutral soil. Savory tolerates drought, so it can be planted in an area where it may be neglected. Set plants into the garden 6 to 8 in. apart and water well.

Growing Tips

To promote rapid, unchecked growth after planting, water often enough to sustain the soil moisture for the first two to three weeks. After that, the plants will tolerate considerable drought. If you have planted seeds, weed around the seedlings until they have grown large enough to shade weeds out.

Care

Harvest sprig tips of savory at will while the plants are growing. Harvest branch tips sparingly in summer's high heat. In August, harvest young sprigs of winter savory, hang them upside down until dry, strip the leaves, bottle, and cap. To multiply winter savory, in early spring, hill up a little humusy soil around the plant: new shoots ready to transplant will appear in four to six weeks.

Companion Planting and Design

Summer savory can be grown almost anywhere, and lends texture and interest to container, flower, vegetable, and herb gardens. Winter savory, the traditional plant of formal knot gardens, is best grown with other perennial herbs where it won't be disturbed. We use the savories as edgers and in sunny corners of some perennial beds.

Our Personal Recommendations

One plant of summer and one of winter savory will provide lots of leaves for fresh use and for drying. *S. montana* 'Nana', or 'Pygmaea', is a dwarf winter savory about 4 in. tall that looks charming in a wall garden.

There are two savories, one perennial and one annual. Both are low-growing aromatic herbs with glossy, narrow, dark green leaves that bear spikes of dainty flowers in the summer. Winter savory, Satureja montana, *is perennial, and is the savory dried for flavoring liqueurs and vinegars, pork products, poultry, fish, and cheese. In most of New England it is hardy and grows into a woody little evergreen that bears white or blue flowers and grows well even in rocky nooks and crannies. The flavor of the leaves is peppery, rather like thyme, pine, or a sweet camphor. Minced fresh leaves add a pleasant tang to soups, meat casseroles, sauces, and salads. Summer savory,* Satureja hortensis, *is an annual herb 12 to 18 in. tall. The flavor is milder and finer than that of winter savory, and we prefer it for use fresh.*

Bloom Period and Seasonal Color
Winter Savory: Summer; spikes of white or blue flowers. Summer Savory: Summer; spikes of dainty pink-lavender or white flowers.

Mature Height × Spread
12 to 18 in. × 12 to 15 in.

Zones
4 to 9

Ornamental Grasses *for New England*

Windblown, untamed, graceful, 1 to 12 feet tall and more, the ornamental grasses are the signature plants of today's naturalistic landscaping, and they need little maintenance. The sight and sound of wind whispering through tall grasses is refreshing on a hot summer day—a country sound very welcome in a city garden. Airy, luminous seedheads develop late in the season and remain lovely through fall and early winter.

The low-growing ornamental grasses add texture to the front of flower beds and to pocket wild gardens. Those 6 feet and more can replace a high-maintenance espalier fronting a masonry wall. Planted among native trees and shrubs, grasses become part of a handsome low-maintenance screen. The mid-height ornamental grasses are the natural transition plants to woodland or water, and, in combination with native wildflowers, make a beautiful flowering meadow. The recommended ratio for a meadow garden is one-third flowers to two-thirds ornamental grasses for sunny places, and one-third grasses to two-thirds flowers for shade.

The first consideration in choosing a grass, after you have checked its hardiness in your zone, is how the end-of-season height and width of the plant will fit the site. The very tall grasses must be featured as specimens and nearby plantings chosen to complement them. Then consider the overall form. Some

Reed Grass

grasses clump, some mound, some fountain. The texture of the leaves and their color is important—fine, coarse, bold, bluish, greenish, reddish, gold, striped, variegated. For contrast, combine both fine- and coarse-textured grasses. When you have thought all that through, then you can consider which of the flower heads you are going to fall in love with. Grouping many plants of a few varieties is more effective than planting a few of many.

Writer Carole Ottesen classes the grasses into cool-season and warm-season plants, and it's a useful concept. The cool-season grasses shoot up in the spring, so they're cut back in early spring. Their early growth makes them the best choice when you want a grass that will be highly visible, the main show, all year round. The warm-season grasses begin to grow later, so you can wait until mid-spring to cut them back. A warm-season grass is a good choice when you're considering combining grasses and flowers: interplant them with big, early spring-flowering bulbs that will bloom after the grasses' annual haircut and hide the bare crowns while the grass is growing up. The grass will soon grow tall enough to hide the ripening bulb foliage.

Chinese Silver Grass and Hostas

When, Where, and How to Plant

Like the perennial flowers, the ornamental grasses begin to fill out the second year. They may be planted in early spring, summer, or early fall. At garden centers they are sold in containers. Mail order suppliers may ship some ornamental grasses bare root; these plants must be soaked thoroughly before planting. Most of the ornamental grasses thrive in acid to neutral soil that is one-half to one-quarter humus, and most need a well-drained site. See Soil Preparation and Improvement and Planting in the Introduction. Set the crowns $1/2$ to 1 inch higher than the soil surface. Surround the plants with 1 to 2 inches of mulch.

The annual haircut is just a matter of shearing for the low-growing grasses. When a big grass matures, before cutting it back use sisal twine to rope the leaves together all the way to the top so that it ends up looking like a telephone pole; then saw the top off a few inches above the crown. If you use a chain saw take care not to catch the twine in the teeth!

Most ornamental grasses need annual fertilization. The time for it is when new growth appears. Apply a slow-release organic fertilizer. In prolonged droughts, water slowly and deeply.

Other Good Options

In addition to the grasses recommended in this chapter, we like:

Hakone Grass, *Hakonechloa macra* (Zones 4 to 9), 'Aureola' (Zones 5 to 9)

Korean Feather Reed Grass, *Calamagrostis brachytricha (Achnatherum brachytricha)* (Zones 5 to 9)

Leather Leaf Sedge, *Carex morrowii* 'Goldband' (Zones 5 to 9)

Ravenna Grass, Plume Grass, *Saccharum ravennae* (Zones 4 to 8)

American Beach Grass
Ammophila breviligulata

American beach grass is a native grass 2 to 3¹/₂ ft. high that grows wild all along the coast of New England, and continues its range as far south as North Carolina. It is highly desirable as a sand stabilizer and is very valuable for ground cover in dry sandy soils, especially along the seaboard. The plant survives salt spray and spreads quickly on creeping rootlets, which makes it an excellent choice for preventing wind erosion on beaches and dunes. The grass is unique in that its response to being buried is to send up a new underground stem from which a new shoot emerges above ground. In effect, the grass traps blowing sand and so maintains and even creates dunes. It has good fall color and produces seeds, but the flowers are unremarkable.

Other Name
Beach Grass

Bloom Period and Seasonal Color
Fall; rust-colored leaves.

Mature Height × Spread
2 to 3¹/₂ ft. × up to 10 ft. annually

Zones
4 to 8

When, Where, and How to Plant
Set out containers of American beach grass in early fall or early spring. It requires full sun and sandy, well-drained soil. If you are planting by the sea, the row closest to the ocean must be 100 ft. above the average high tide line. The U.S. Department of Agriculture Natural Resources Conservation Service recommends planting beach grass in strips no less than 20 ft. wide and ten rows deep to permit the planting to trap the blowing sand and build a dune. The spacing between rows should be 18 in., 12 in. where erosion is severe. Set out two 18- to 24-in. stems in holes 7 to 9 in. deep. Firm the sand around the plants and water well. Protect the planting by placing a snow fence or burlap around it.

Growing Tip
Keep the planting moist if you can until there are signs of new growth.

Care
In early spring, every year, fertilize with an organic, long-lasting lawn fertilizer.

Companion Planting and Design
Plant to stabilize beach areas.

Our Personal Recommendations
The U.S. Department of Agriculture Natural Resources Conservation Service recommends 'Cape' and other improved varieties. Please do not rip up your dunes without first seeking advice. You will find beach grass offered at local conservation-minded nurseries.

Blue Fescue
Festuca glauca

When, Where, and How to Plant

Set out dormant, container-grown plants as soon as the ground can be worked in spring. Plant blue fescue in full sun or in very bright shade. Without enough light, the blue will be less intense. Avoid damp spots. The foliage has a bluish gray, waxy coating that protects it from water loss, and wet feet can cause problems. The fescues thrive in a range of soils from pH 5.5 to 6.5. They develop the bluest color in soil that is not especially fertile, and on the dry side. See Soil Preparation and Planting in the Introduction. Provide roomy planting holes and set the plants an inch above the soil level about 2 ft. apart. Water well. Mulch 2 in. deep around and between the plants.

Growing Tips

Water a new planting every week or two the first season. Blue fescue grows rapidly during cool weather, but in hot, dry periods it sulks. Do not try to force growth by watering or fertilizing. Wait for cool weather and it will revive.

Care

The plant is fairly drought-resistant, so once it is established, local rainfall should be enough to keep it growing except during our mid- and late-August droughts. Allow the seedheads to ripen and stand through fall and winter. Toward the early spring, prune the plant back to the crown. Replenish the mulch until the plants have spread widely enough to shade out weeds. This grass benefits from division every few years. You can divide and replant this grass in fall, but not in summer.

Companion Planting and Design

Blue fescue is attractive planted as edging for beds of shrubbery, walks, naturalized areas, and grass gardens. It is sometimes used as a ground cover, but we find the clumps too compact, and the foliage too stiff—it never seems quite comfortable in the role. It looks well, and grows well, with lavender, salvia, and Russian sage.

Our Personal Recommendation

'Elijah Blue' (to Zone 5) has the most intense blue of all the fescues.

Blue fescue forms low rounded tufts or hummocks of slender, metallic blue-green blades that are evergreen in most areas of New England. It's a cool-season grass, that is, it starts to grow soon after the spring haircut, which is all the maintenance it needs. The flowers are loose, lacy panicles on stems that reach well above the foliage. The contrast between the relatively small, stiff clump and the thin, gracefully arching and gently swaying flower stalks is charming. It's widely used in perennial borders where it adds a welcome blue accent. The genus includes familiar lawn grasses as well as big, handsome ornamentals.

Other Names
Festuca ovina var. glauca, Blue Sheep's Fescue

Bloom Period and Seasonal Color
Tan flower heads rise in mid- to late spring; the blue foliage is attractive all season.

Mature Height × Spread
8 to 12 in. × 8 to 10 in.

Zones
4 to 8

Blue Oat Grass

Helictotrichon sempervirens

This is a lovely, steely blue grass a little taller than blue fescue, and it maintains its color through late winter. A cool-season grass, it starts growing very quickly after its early spring haircut, forming compact, spiky tufts of striking silvery blue-green leaves. In May or June delicate, golden, oat-like flowers sway far above the foliage on graceful, erect or arching stems that extend 1 ft. or more beyond the foliage, swaying and bobbing in the wind. In summer, the blue-gray flower heads turn to a bright tan that contrasts beautifully with the foliage. It's a good specimen for informal, open landscapes, terraces, and rock gardens.

Other Name
Avena Grass

Bloom Period and Seasonal Color
Blue-gray inflorescences turn to tan in summer; the metallic blue leaves are attractive all season.

Mature Height × Spread
2 to 3 ft. × 25 in.

Zones
4 to 8

When, Where, and How to Plant

As soon as the ground can be worked in early spring, set out container-grown plants or rooted divisions. Plant blue oat grass in full sun or in bright shade. Without enough light, the blue will be less intense. Avoid damp spots. Blue oat grass thrives in rich soil and succeeds in a wide pH range, from acid 3.0 to neutral 7.0. See Soil Preparation and Planting in the Introduction. Provide roomy planting holes and set the plants an inch above ground level and about 2 ft. apart. Water well. Mulch 2 in. deep around and between the plants.

Growing Tip

Water a new planting every week or two the first season.

Care

Once established, local rainfall should be enough to keep blue oat grass growing except during our mid- and late-August droughts. Allow the spikelets to ripen and stand through fall and winter. In early spring prune the plant back to the crown. Trim the plant back earlier if storms flatten the flower stems, or if it becomes less appealing. Replenish the mulch in early spring until the plants have spread widely enough to shade weeds out. You can divide and replant this grass in fall, but not in summer. Dig the crown, cut it apart, and replant the pieces.

Companion Planting and Design

Blue oat grass has many uses in the home landscape. Planted toward the middle of a large perennial border, it makes a colorful textural accent and it is beautiful massed and naturalized. We've seen it combined very effectively in wild gardens near the shore with silvery plants like artemisia, catmint, and lamb's ears.

Our Personal Recommendations

The species is beautiful, though there are a few cultivars available, including 'Saphirsprundel', which is supposedly wind resistant.

Chinese Silver Grass

Miscanthus sinensis

When, Where, and How to Plant
Set out container-grown plants as soon as the ground begins to warm. Most Chinese silver grass cultivars grow best in six or more hours of direct sun, but some, including the lovely maiden grass, 'Gracillimus', make do with three to four hours of direct sun. Given a constant supply of moisture, *Miscanthus* thrives, but established plantings sustain modest growth in drier soil. *Miscanthus* is not particular as to pH, and adapts to reasonably fertile soil. See Soil Preparation and Planting in the Introduction. Provide generous planting holes and plant with 3 to 4 ft. between the centers. Water well. Mulch 2 in. deep.

Growing Tip
Water a new planting every week or two the first season.

Care
Water during droughts until the plants are fully matured. Established cultivars can do with less moisture—the leaves roll if they need more. This warm-season grass starts its growth when air and soil warm up, so wait until mid-spring to cut it back to the crown. Replenish the mulch. To multiply, divide before new growth begins. Lift and carefully use an axe to cut the crown apart, giving each section at least one growing point.

Companion Planting and Design
Some cultivars are planted as specimens, others as transitional plants by the water. We think it's most beautiful growing in groups, or massed.

Our Personal Recommendations
For the smaller home garden we recommend 4- to 7-ft. maiden grass, 'Gracillimus' (Zones 4-5), which has narrow, arching leaves and a conspicuous white midrib; 5- to 7-ft. 'Cabaret', whose broad leaves have a silver stripe; 5-ft 'Cosmopolitan', whose wide leaves have white margins; and 4-ft. 'Morning Light' (Zone 5), which is striped green and white and has a silvery look. In larger landscapes we like 6- to 8-ft. silver zebra grass, 'Zebrinus', a striking upright grass banded horizontally; refined 6- to 8-ft. 'Silberfeder' ('Silver Feather') (Zones 4-5), which bears beautiful silver plumes. Giant silver grass, *M. floridulus* (Zone 6), is a wide-leaved, coarse species 10 to 14 ft. tall that fills with silvery light when the wind catches it.

Chinese silver grass is one of the most desirable and versatile of the big landscape grasses, a 6- to 7-ft. grass to use boldly, in big spaces. Beautiful fall and winter, it is a warm-season grass that grows slowly in spring and then rapidly, producing robust, open, upright clumps of gracefully arching leaves that develop into dense, effective screening. In late summer and fall, silky silvery pale pink flower clusters open on panicles up to 1 ft. long. With cold weather, the foliage and the plumes turn to silver and tan. Long grown in Japan and China, beloved of the Victorians who called it eulalia, the species has given rise to many cultivars considered the most beautiful of the ornamental grasses. In northern New England the varieties don't attain the heights common in warmer areas.

Other Name
Eulalia

Bloom Period and Seasonal Color
Pale pink flower clusters in late summer, fading with the foliage to silver and gold in fall.

Mature Height × Spread
6 to 8 ft. × 3 to 5 ft.

Zones
5 to 9

Feather Reed Grass
Calamagrostis × *acutiflora* 'Karl Foerster'

The feather reed grass 'Karl Foerster', named the Perennial Plant Association Plant of the Year in 2001, is an upright cool-season grass that shoots up after its early spring haircut, and remains attractive through hot summers. Feather reed grass is a cross between reed grass, Calamagrostis arundinacea, and wood small-reed, C. epigejos. The seeds are sterile, so it never is invasive. Through most of spring the plant is a solid mass of medium- to dark-green foliage. By the time the late-blooming daffodils have gone it is 4 ft. tall and producing pale, feathery, bronze-purple, foot-long panicles of florets that stand straight up on wiry green stems and gradually turn tan colored. With the coming of frost, the foliage fades to gold and platinum unless winter storms flatten the stems, and it remains beautiful until it is cut back.

Bloom Period and Seasonal Color
In spring, purple-tinted flower heads that change to tan; with frost the foliage fades to gold and platinum.

Mature Height × Spread
5 to 6 ft. × 20 in.

Zones
5 to 9

When, Where, and How to Plant
Set out dormant, container-grown plants as soon as the ground can be worked in early spring. It requires full sun: without enough light the flower heads will flop over. A pH range between 6.0 and 7.0 suits feather reed grass. It grows well in dry or wet soil and isn't particular as to fertility. See Soil Preparation and Planting in the Introduction. Provide generous planting holes and set the plants an inch above ground level and about 2 ft. apart. Water well. Mulch 2 in. deep around and between the plants.

Growing Tip
If the plants are in dry soil, water every week or two the first month, or until you see signs of vigorous growth.

Care
Allow the seedheads to ripen and stand through fall and winter. Cut the plant back to the crown in early spring. Trim it earlier if storms flatten the flowering stems. Replenish the mulch. Feather reed grass grows rapidly during cool weather, but in hot, dry periods it may sulk. Do not try to force growth by watering or fertilizing. The plants will not need dividing for eight to ten years or more. When they do, dig the crowns, and chop them apart with an axe. You can divide and replant this grass in spring, but not in summer or fall.

Companion Planting and Design
In a smaller landscape, we like this grass in mass plantings. It's beautiful as a specimen or a hedge against a masonry wall and also lovely interplanted among shrubs and evergreens. Its meadowy, autumn golds are beautiful backing black-eyed Susans, *Sedum* 'Autumn Joy', pale and dark purple asters, boltonia, and fronting taller varieties of *Miscanthus*.

Our Personal Recommendation
In a very small garden, a good choice would be *C.* × *acutiflora* 'Overdam', which has arching, white-striped foliage about 1 ft. high. Its flowers are 3-ft. pink plumes that age to gold.

Northern Sea Oats
Chasmanthium latifolium

When, Where, and How to Plant
Set out container-grown plants of this warm-season grass in spring as the ground begins to warm. It will be fullest and most colorful growing where it receives at least six hours of sun daily. It thrives in partial shade, but the less light it receives the more it will sprawl. A pH range of between 6.0 and 7.0 suits it, and it does best where the soil has sustained moisture without being soggy. It does, however, tolerate dry soil. See Soil Preparation and Planting in the Introduction. If the soil is sandy, work in one-quarter compost, peat moss, chopped leaves, or other organic material. Provide generous planting holes 2 to 3 ft. apart. Set the plants about an inch above ground level and water well. Mulch 2 in. deep around and between the plants.

Growing Tip
To encourage rapid growth, water a new planting every week the first season.

Care
Once established, local rainfall should be enough to keep northern sea oats growing except during droughts, but it spreads most quickly if it doesn't dry out. Allow the seedheads to ripen and stand through fall and winter. This warm-season grass will start new growth only when the cold has ended, so wait until early spring to cut the plant back to the crown. Trim the plant back earlier if storms flatten the stems, or it becomes less appealing. Replenish the mulch in early spring until the plants have spread widely enough to shade out weeds. Sea oats self-sows in the right environment: you may have to rogue out the volunteers.

Companion Planting and Design
Northern sea oats is an excellent transitional plant that can be positioned to create screening. It looks best when it is massed. Ornamental plants that flourish in the same environment include Japanese anemone, lobelia, and toad lily. Sea oats are especially lovely growing on a slope where the seedheads can catch the light and be seen against a darker background.

Our Personal Recommendation
Plant the species.

This is a beautiful, tall, woodland grass that grows in narrow, upright clumps and produces fresh green leaves that, like bamboo leaves, are held perpendicularly at intervals on stiff, wiry stems. It is a warm-season grass. Though northern sea oats reach maximum size when grown in full sun, they also flourish in semi-shade at the edge of woodlands, and in the shadow of tall buildings. The flower heads are eye-catching spikelets of flat fruits with oat-like heads. As much as an inch wide and an inch long, they are green in summer and gradually mature to shades of pink and copper. Spangled over wiry drooping stems that stand well above the foliage, they rustle and shimmer in a breeze.

Other Names
River Oats, Wild Oats, *Uniola latifolia*

Bloom Period and Seasonal Color
Green in summer, gradually changing to pink and copper.

Mature Height × Spread
3 to 4 ft. × 2 to 3 ft.

Zones
3 or 4 to 8

Switch Grass
Panicum virgatum 'Heavy Metal'

North American switch grass, a prairie native, is an upright, narrow, arching, clump-forming warm-season grass that lifts a mist-like ethereal cloud of pale blooms on 4- to 5-ft. stalks in summer. The inflorescences are spikelets on long open panicles held high above the foliage. With frost the foliage turns a warm gold and that color and its handsome structure remain until cut back. In the garden we plant the 5-ft.-tall cultivar 'Heavy Metal' whose leaves are a beautiful metallic blue-green; the flowers are tinged pink and the upright structure is useful for introducing contrast into the garden. The species itself occurs naturally in most of the country and is an excellent choice for naturalizing.

Bloom Period and Seasonal Color
In summer 'Heavy Metal' produces pink inflorescences; flowers and foliage are gold fall and winter.

Mature Height × Spread
5 ft. × 2 to 3 ft.

Zones
3 to 8

When, Where, and How to Plant
Switch grass develops from rhizomatous roots and spreads quickly. Set out container-grown plants or root divisions in mid-spring or early fall. It will be most colorful where it receives direct sun. Though it thrives with fairly constant moisture, switch grass is so deeply rooted it can withstand drought, as well as high heat and bitter cold. Any well-worked soil will do, and it is tolerant of sandy soils. See Soil Preparation and Planting in the Introduction. Provide generous planting holes and space the plants 16 to 18 in. apart. Water well. Mulch 2 in. deep around and between the plants.

Growing Tips
Water a new planting every week or two the first season. The grass will do well if you maintain soil moisture at the roots even if the surface dries between waterings.

Care
Switch grass does best in moist soil, so even after the plants are established and spreading, water when late-summer drought stresses your flowers. This warm-season grass will start new growth only when air and soil warm, so wait until spring to cut the plant back to 4 to 5 in. above the crown. Fertilize with a light application of slow-release organic fertilizer. Replenish the mulch until the plants have spread widely enough to shade out weeds. To multiply, divide the plants in spring before new growth begins. Lift and gently break or cut the clump apart, giving each section a few growing points.

Companion Planting and Design
Naturalize switch grass with flowers that stand some neglect, such as foxtail lilies, Joe Pye weed, black-eyed Susans, asters, boltonia, and sedums. It is attractive planted as a specimen, and quite beautiful set out in large sweeps in transitional spaces near water.

Our Personal Recommendation
'Heavy Metal' is one of the most beautiful of the grasses that add a strong blue accent to the landscape—and you can plant it where the drainage isn't very good, a definite advantage!

Tufted Hair Grass

Deschampsia caespitosa

When, Where, and How to Plant

Set out container-grown plants or root divisions in early spring. It can handle full sun with adequate moisture, but will not survive in hot, dry locations. Tufted hair grass thrives in part shade and prefers moist, somewhat acidic soil. Too much shade will result in fewer flowers. It prefers rich, well-worked soil. See Soil Preparation and Planting in the Introduction. Provide generous planting holes and space the plants 2 to 3 ft. apart. Water well. Mulch 2 in. deep around and between the plants.

Growing Tips

Water a new planting every week or two the first season. The grass will do well if you maintain soil moisture at the roots.

Care

In late summer or early fall when the plant's beauty has gone by, shear the whole clump back to the crown. New foliage will form fresh green clumps by mid-fall and will remain evergreen through most winters. If the plant is situated in rich soil it shouldn't need fertilizer. Tufted hair grass may need dividing every three to four years.

Companion Planting and Design

Tufted hair grass looks best in groups or massed. We like clumps in the perennial bed. Some flowers we like with it are low-growing bergenia, epimediums, hostas, and *Ligularia*.

Our Personal Recommendations

Some plants recommended by the National Arboretum are: 'Goldschleier' ('Golden Veil'), a light green whose flowers are a brighter gold, and whose stalk rises to 30 in.; and 'Bronze Haze'. 'Tautraeger' ('Dew Carrier'), has darker green foliage and is a rich bloomer whose flowers can be 3 ft. tall.

Although tufted hair grass starts as a modest 1-foot clump of arching dark-green foliage, it goes on to produce a nearly 3-ft. high cloud of delicate flowers. The flowers arrive in late spring, presenting a soft, silky, bronze-green halo, but later stiffen and form a billowing mass of yellow or gold. In its full glory in midsummer it makes a beautiful backdrop for garden flowers. The show lasts until blasted by winter winds. Tufted hair grass is a cool-season plant, well suited to New England's unpredictable springs and partially cool summers. This vigorous versatile grass naturalizes readily.

Bloom Period and Seasonal Color
Early June; yellow and gold.

Mature Height × Spread
2 to 3 ft. × 2 ft.

Zones
4 to 9

Perennials *for New England*

Perennial flower and foliage plants give our gardens continuity. Annuals live one season: some perennials come back for just a few years, but many live ten to fifteen, and peonies can go on for more than a hundred. When we're planning a garden, our first selections are a series of hardy perennial flowers whose sequence of bloom will carry color through the bed all season long. Within most species' stated bloom period, you can find varieties that come into flower early, midseason, or late. To avoid late spring frostbite in cool regions, choose late-blooming varieties of spring-flowering species; where frosts can come early in fall, choose early-blooming varieties of perennials that bloom in late summer. Most hardy perennials are resistant to surface frosts unless temperatures go below freezing (32 degrees Fahrenheit).

Flower border with perennial Geraniums and pink Lupines.

Once we've chosen the flowers for a garden, we look for foliage plants that will complement or contrast with the flowers. Colorful foliage—silver, blue, yellow, or red—placed to reinforce, or to be a foil for, the colors of nearby blooms, add depth to the design. Think of the effect of spiky globe thistle and furry lamb's ears. Two lovely blue foliaged plants are the blue fescue and blue oat grass. Variegated foliage lightens the deep greens of summer. At a distance, white variegated foliage appears jade green or soft gray; yellow foliage looks like a splash of sunshine and fills the same role as flowers for color. We add ferns for the romance they lend to shaded spots, and ornamental grasses tall and small that dance, whisper, and bring sound and movement as well as contrasting texture to the garden.

In a large mixed border we include the big, dramatic leaves and striking architectural forms of a few bold-foliaged perennials, like the large hostas. In the shadow of tall perennials, these shade-lovers thrive even in a sunny border. Giant tropical foliage plants—dwarf canna and the hardy banana—add drama. These "tender perennials" won't winter over, but the effect they create is worthwhile. We also like to set two or three dwarf needled evergreens in strategic places. Their solid forms and strong color anchor flower beds in early spring and, with the ornamental grasses, they maintain a sense of life when the garden falls asleep.

Finally, we look for places to tuck in a few aromatic herbs and very fragrant flowers. Low-growing, fuzzy, white-splashed pineapple mint and silver variegated thyme lighten the bed and release their fragrance as you brush by. Aggressive plants like the mints can be set out in buried containers. Some flowering bulbs and many important perennials have fragrant varieties. The most fragrant of the spring flowers are the hyacinths, in the Bulbs chapter, but there are fragrant varieties of many perennials not noted for scent. Two examples are 'Myrtle Gentry', a scented peony, and 'Fragrant Light', a scented daylily.

When, Where, and How to Plant

If you are interested in experimenting with a flowering meadow or a wild garden, you'll need hundreds of plants. Try your hand at starting the perennials indoors from seed. See Starting Seeds Indoors in the Appendix. Plants that are the species, rather than an improved or named variety, will come true from seed. But when you want named varieties, we strongly recommend you choose container-grown perennials grown from root divisions and rooted cuttings. Here's why: the named varieties (hybrids and cultivars) are superior plants selected from among thousands. Growers propagate them from cuttings or root divisions and so they bloom true to the parent plants. Buy one plant, divide it into three plants, repeat for three years and you will have twenty-seven plants, in five years 243 plants, ad infinitum—so a perennial bed of the best can be inexpensive.

Perennials in 1-quart containers planted in the spring produce some blooms the first season: those sold in 2- to 3-gallon containers will make a bigger show. Most container-grown plants can be set out spring, summer, or fall. In spring, growers ship some perennials bare root—astilbes, for instance. These often flower fully only the second or third season. A perennial that blooms early in the spring—columbine, for example—gives the best show its first year when it is planted the preceding late summer or early fall.

The surest way to provide soil in which perennials will thrive for many years is to create a raised bed. In the Soil Preparation and Improvement section of the Introduction you'll find instructions for creating a raised bed and for bringing the soil to pH 5.5 to 7.0, the range for most flowers. Our recipe for a raised bed includes long-lasting, organic fertilizers.

The spacing of perennials depends on the size the mature plant will be: we've offered suggestions with each plant. Always provide a generous planting hole, one twice the width and twice as deep as the rootball. Before you plant, unwind roots that may be circling the rootball, or make shallow vertical slashes in the mass, and cut off the bottom $^1/_2$ inch of soil and rootball. Soak the rootball in a big bucket containing starter solution. Half fill the hole with improved soil. Then set the plant a little high in the hole, fill the hole with soil, and tamp firmly. Water slowly and deeply, then mulch around the planting following our suggestions in the Introduction. Staking protects very tall flowers in a storm. But most, if correctly fertilized and given plenty of space all around, won't need it. Tall, weak growth is often the result of force-feeding with non-organic fertilizers. Wide spacing also improves air circulation, reducing the risk of disease and mildew. Water a new planting, slowly, deeply, every week or ten days for a month or so unless you have soaking rains. And water any time the plants show signs of wilting.

Care

After summer, we like to leave in place seed-bearing perennials with woody upright structures, like black-eyed Susans, because they look interesting in winter, and feed the birds. Some self-sow and will replenish the planting. In late fall we clear away collapsed foliage that will grow slimy after frost. When you remove dead foliage, cut it off, don't pull it off because that may damage the crown beneath. In late winter or early spring, after the soil has dried somewhat, it is time to clear away the remains of last year's dead foliage: watch out for burgeoning stems while raking through perennials such as lilies. Every year in spring, and again in September to October, we fertilize established perennial beds, not individual plants, by broadcasting slow-release, organic fertilizer: an acid-type fertilizer at the rate of 4 pounds per 100 square feet for acid lovers, 6 pounds of a non-acid fertilizer for the others.

Daylily 'Silent Entry'

Dividing for Productivity

To remain productive and showy, most perennials should be divided and replanted every four or five years. Dividing also gives you plants for the development of new gardens and to give away as gifts. On the plant pages that follow we explain when each is likely to need dividing. But the perennials themselves indicate when the time has come: the stems become crowded and leggy, the roots become

matted, and there are fewer and smaller blooms. As to timing, the rule of thumb is to divide spring-flowering perennials a month before the ground will freeze in the fall, or before new growth begins in early spring; divide autumn-flowering perennials, such as chrysanthemums, in spring before any sign of growth appears. More specific instructions are given with each plant.

Other Good Options

The perennials described in this chapter are the best of the best for New England gardens. Other perennials that we think very highly of include:

Adam's Needle, *Yucca filamentosa* 'Bright Edge' (Zones 4 to 9)

Blazing Star, Gayfeather, *Liatris spicata* 'Kobold' (Zones 3 to 9)

Brunnera, *Brunnera macrophylla* (Zones 4 to 7)

Butterfly Weed, *Asclepias tuberosa* (Zones 3 to 9)

Candytuft, *Iberis sempervirens* hybrids (Zones 4 to 8)

Cranesbill (True Geranium), *Geranium macrorrhizum* 'Ingwerson's Variety' (Zones 3 to 8), 'Spessart' (Zones 4 to 8)

Goatsbeard, *Aruncus dioicus* (Zones 3 to 6)

Heliopsis, *Heliopsis helianthoides* and cultivars (Zones 3 to 9)

Jacob's Ladder, *Polemonium caeruleum* (Zones 2 to 7)

Lungwort, *Pulmonaria* spp. and cultivars (Zones 4 to 8)

Meadow Rue, *Thalictrum aquilegifolium*, *T. flavum* ssp. *glaucum*, *T. rochebrunianum* (Zones 4 to 8)

Silver King Artemisia, *A. ludoviciana* var. *albula* (Zones 5 to 9)

Speedwell, *Veronica* spp. and cultivars (Zones 4 to 8)

Spurge, *Euphorbia polychroma* (Zones 5 to 9)

Tickseed, *Coreopsis verticillata* 'Moonbeam' (Zones 3 to 9)

Aster

Aster spp., cultivars, and hybrids

In New England wild asters bloom along the sides of the roads in early to late summer depending on the zone. Garden asters are planted for fall blooming. Tiny daisy-like blossoms are borne singly or in sprays, and cover the plants. The light blue Aster novi-belgii 'Professor Anton Kippenburg', which is only 15 to 18 in. tall, can have as many as 300 to 400 small flowers on one plant. They are wonderful with autumn's earthy brown, russet, gold, orange, and crimson. The aster serves as a leafy bush, and, depending on height, is handsome at the back or front of a small border, and is a good green filler during the months before it comes into bloom. Pale pink asters are especially lovely with the big pale and deep pink dahlias that bloom in late summer and fall.

Other Names
New England Aster, New York Aster, Michaelmas Daisy

Bloom Period and Seasonal Color
Late summer and early fall; blue, dark purple, lavender, pink, rosy red, white.

Mature Height × Spread
1 1/2 to 6 ft. × 3 to 5 ft.

Zones
3 to 8

When, Where, and How to Plant
Perennial asters grow so vigorously they are considered weeds in some areas. In spring sow seed for bloom the following year. For bloom this year set out root divisions. Site them in full sun in well-drained, somewhat acidic soil—moderate fertility is best for most types. Plants growing in very fertile soil may need staking. Asters require good drainage—wet winter soils rot most of them but they can succeed in slightly damp meadows. See Soil Preparation in the Introduction. Dig generous planting holes and space plants 12 in. apart. Mulch 2 in. deep between plants.

Growing Tips
Water regularly until plants are established, then water during dry spells. Always water at the base of the plant to avoid mildew.

Care
Pinch the shoot tips back 2 to 3 in. once in spring and again a month later to keep the plants stocky and avoid the need to stake. Some asters that flower in summer may re-bloom if deadheaded. Taller types may need staking to stand upright. Divide aster plantings every two or three years. Discard the main section and replant the outer portions. In areas where powdery mildew is a problem choose resistant cultivars.

Companion Planting and Design
Beautiful in naturalized plantings with ornamental grasses and Russian sage. Also lovely fronting or behind an old stone wall. Set shorter types at the front of the border and the taller sorts at the back. The height of tall fall asters can be reduced a little by pinching or shearing in the spring when they are 6 to 8 in. high.

Our Personal Recommendations
A. novae-angliae 'Purple Dome' is 18 in. high with a spread of 36 in. The flowers are semi-double with deep violet ray florets surrounding a bright yellow central disk and in bloom from August to frosts. 'Alma Potschke' has rose-pink flowers on stiff stems that are 3 ft. tall. This is one of the showiest, most striking asters, and well worth planting. The New York aster, *A. novi-belgii*, is a smaller plant hardy in Zones 4 to 8.

When, Where, and How to Plant

Nurseries ship bare-root astilbes in early spring: they'll take a couple of years to mature. Container-grown astilbes can be planted in mid-spring or late summer. *Astilbe* thrives in light shade in well-drained, rich, moist, humusy soil. *A. chinensis* (Zones 3 to 8) tolerates drought; most astilbes need sustained moisture but suffer in soil that is soggy in winter. Slightly acid pH is best. See Soil Preparation in the Introduction. Follow the planting instructions at the beginning of this chapter, spacing the plants 18 in. to 3 ft. apart, according to the variety. Water well. Mulch 2 to 3 in. deep starting 3 in. from the outer leaves.

Growing Tips

Water astilbes deeply every week to ten days unless you have a soaking rain. The keys to success—particularly in the warmer reaches of New England—are sustained moisture and summer mulches.

Care

Fertilize the bed between late winter and early spring, and again in September to October, with a slow-release organic fertilizer at a rate of 6 pounds per 100 sq. ft. We don't deadhead: the drying flower spikes are attractive. Replenish the mulch in the spring. You can divide astilbe crowns every three years if you wish, between early spring and August.

Companion Planting and Design

Astilbes are excellent fillers for the middle or back of the border and lovely edging a woodland path, stream, or pond. Massed, astilbes in a range of colors make a lovely low tapestry. In summer and early fall the little Chinese astilbe, *A. chinensis*, raises tall mauve-pink flower heads, spreads rapidly by underground stolons, and is very attractive as edging or a ground cover in part shade.

Our Personal Recommendations

Some favorites of our New England consultants are *A. × arendsii* 'Cattleya', a 36 in. orchid-pink that combines vigorous growth with slightly nodding plumes. Another is 'Fanal', 24 in., with bronze leaves and red flowers, one of the earliest and most popular, and great in containers. Little *A. simplicifolia* 'Sprite', 12 in. (Zones 4 to 8), is the 1994 Perennial Plant Association Plant of the Year. It has bright green foliage with masses of light pink florets.

The shade-loving astilbes are beautiful plants whose flowers are tall, graceful plumes composed of masses of small florets in mostly pastel shades. The deeply cut, fern-like, green or bronzed foliage is attractive both before and after flowering. Over the years, plantings spread to make large, dense mats. Cut, the flowers are long lasting and they dry well. Although most astilbe cultivars flower from June through the middle of July, you can achieve a lasting show of color by planting early, midseason, and late bloomers. For instance, plant the white early-blooming favorite Astilbe japonica'Deutschland', and red A. × arendsii 'Fanal' and pink 'Europa'; with midseason A. thunbergii 'Straussenfeder' ('Ostrich Plume'); and late bloomers such as the lilac A. chinensis 'Pumila' and var. taguetii 'Superba'.

Bloom Period and Seasonal Color
Late spring and early summer; creamy white, pale pink, lilac, coral, red.

Mature Height × Spread
1 to 5 ft. × 2 to 3 ft.

Zones
4 to 8

Bellflower
Campanula spp.

These graceful flowers bear gossamer cups in shades of blue and white, sometimes lavender, sometimes pink, and they can be from a few inches to 6 ft. tall. They are known as bellflowers, but in some of the small forms the flowers are more star-like. Bellflowers have been loved and bred for centuries, and there are more than 250 species—making them a popular subject for plant collections. Erect forms such as the popular 2- to 3-ft. Campanula persicifolia, *the willow bellflower, are featured in mixed flower borders and are good cutting flowers. Bellflowers can be in bloom for two and even three months in late spring or early summer and into fall, depending on the species and the climate. They're long-lived perennials and many of the most popular species multiply and even naturalize.*

Mature Height × Spread
2 to 3 in. × 6 in.
2 to 6 ft. × 2 to 3 ft.

Bloom Period and Seasonal Color
Late spring to early fall; blue, white, lavender, pink.

Zones
3 to 8

When, Where, and How to Plant
Bellflower seed sown indoors develops well and transplants readily. See Starting Seeds Indoors in the Appendix. In early spring rooted cuttings and root divisions are offered at nurseries—these transplant readily. Or, you can set out root divisions in summer for blooms next spring. Most flower best in full sun here in cool New England, but they bloom in part sun, too. In Zone 7, bellflowers need rich, well-drained, moist, humusy soil, and morning rather than noon and afternoon sun. Provide well-worked, neutral pH range, fertile garden soil. Set the plants 12 to 18 in. apart, depending on the species. Taller forms may benefit from staking, especially if they are growing in part sun. Water very well. Provide a permanent 2-in. mulch starting 3 in. from the crown.

Growing Tip
Water new plants deeply every week the first season unless you have a good soaking rain.

Care
Fertilize the bed between late winter and early spring, and again in September to October, with a slow-release, organic fertilizer at a rate of 6 pounds per 100 sq. ft. In spring replenish the mulch. Maintain soil moisture. Deadhead the taller forms only when *all* the buds on a stem have faded. Divide only if the plants stop performing well.

Companion Planting and Design
Taller forms of bellflower are lovely paired with Siberian iris and perfect for cottage gardens. They are attractive planted with gray artemisias and white or pink flowers of any sort. We like shade-loving, 24- to 40-in. 'Kent Belle' planted with blue-tinted hostas.

Our Personal Recommendations
The lovely upright cultivars of *C. persicifolia*, white 'Grandiflora Alba', and light lavender-blue 'Telham Beauty', are a spectacular pair. For edging shaded beds, we like *C. portenschlagiana* (Zone 4,) which bears up-facing lavender flowers in spring on clumps 4 to 6 in. tall. The tall, old-fashioned biennial called Canterbury bells is the bellflower species *C. medium*, which is a good cutting flower. In warmer New England, and by the ocean, plant drought-tolerant, old-fashioned balloon flower, *Platycodon grandiflorus* 'Mariesii', instead of bellflowers.

When, Where, and How to Plant

The best time for planting bleeding hearts is just as active growth begins in early spring. Set out big, healthy, container-grown plants. Bright shade is the ideal exposure. In cool areas where soil moisture is retained evenly, bleeding hearts accept some (but not much) exposure to full sun. They do best in well-drained, rich, moist, humusy soil in the pH range of 5.0 to 6.0. See Soil Preparation in the Introduction. Follow the planting instructions at the beginning of this chapter. Space planting holes for old-fashioned bleeding hearts 2 ft. apart; space holes for wild bleeding hearts 15 to 18 in. apart. Water well. Provide a permanent 3-in. mulch starting 3 in. from the outer stems.

Growing Tips

Water bleeding hearts deeply every week to ten days for a month or so unless you have a soaking rain. The keys to a long bloom period—particularly in the warmer reaches of New England—are sustained moisture and mulch.

Care

Fertilize the bed between late winter and early spring, and again in late September to October, with a slow-release, organic fertilizer for acid-loving plants, at a rate of 4 pounds per 100 sq. ft. In spring, replenish the mulch. When the foliage of the old fashioned species looks ragged, cut the plant back to the ground. Cutting to the ground flowering stems of wild bleeding hearts that have finished blooming prolongs flowering; wait for several killing frosts before cutting back the foliage. In spring, if late frosts threaten, cover bleeding hearts with Remay cloth, old blankets, or burlap. The roots are brittle, so divide bleeding hearts only if needed. Established plants resent being disturbed but with care they can be successfully divided in early spring.

Companion Planting and Design

Mass bleeding hearts, especially *D. spectabilis*, among ferns, hostas, and Solomon's seal. Delightful in shady gardens, with wildflowers, and in rock gardens.

Our Personal Recommendations

Pierre Bennerup, owner of Comstock, Ferre and Co. in Wethersfield, Connecticut, recommends 'Snow Drift', 'Luxuriant', and 'King of Hearts'.

Bleeding heart is an old-fashioned, shade-loving plant named for the shape of its blossoms. The blossoms are pretty pink, white, or red heart-shaped flowers that dangle from arching stems above beautiful lacy foliage. The loveliest flower is borne by the species Dicentra spectabilis, a shrub-like, spring-flowering perennial that grows to 36 in. across and bears up to twenty or more arching racemes from which dangle perfect little pink or white hearts. It is long-lived, a true aristocrat, though the foliage dies back when heat comes. The wild bleeding heart, D. eximia, is a smaller ever-blooming variety that flowers throughout the summer and until frost: it is one of the best choices for Vermont gardens according to Master Gardener Judith Irven.

Bloom Period and Seasonal Color

Spring, or summer to fall, depending on the species; *D. spectabilis* cherry red and white; *D. eximia* pink, cultivars white.

Mature Height × Spread

D. spectabilis: 2 ft. × 3 ft.
D. eximia: 9 to 24 in. × 18 in.

Zones

3 to 9

Blue False Indigo
Baptisia australis

Baptisia is a bold, 3- to 4-ft. plant that in early spring produces multiple stems of beautiful gray-green foliage. By mid-spring the foliage is topped by 1- to 2-ft. flowering spikes that are a magnificent indigo blue color. The flowers last about a month. The leaves and the individual blossoms resemble those of the pea vine but they are much larger, showier, and more substantial. Handsome blue-black seedpods, 1 or 2 in. long, follow the flowers and usually remain handsome until at least the first hard frost. They're lovely in dried arrangements. Baptisia is a long-lived perennial—a little slow to get under way but it seems to go on practically forever. And it's a great indigo blue flower for climates too hot to grow delphiniums.

Other Names
Baptisia, Plains False Indigo, Wild Blue Indigo

Bloom Period and Seasonal Color
Mid-spring; indigo blue.

Mature Height × Spread
3 to 4 ft. × 4 ft.

Zones
3 to 8

When, Where, and How to Plant
Baptisia seeds are fresh when they first start to rattle around in the pod: plant fresh seeds in late summer if you want to start from scratch. Setting out root divisions of young plants in early spring is recommended because baptisia is slow to establish itself and doesn't transplant easily. Baptisia does best in full sun, but can take a little filtered shade and still be productive. In partial shade it will probably require staking, or support from a peony ring. It tolerates drought but cannot stand soil that is soggy in winter. Blue false indigo thrives in humusy, somewhat acid soil, pH range 5.5 to 6.5, but can tolerate higher pH. See Soil Preparation in the Introduction. Follow the planting instructions at the beginning of this chapter, spacing the plants about 3 ft. apart. Water well. Mulch 1 in. deep starting 3 in. from the crown.

Growing Tip
Water new plants deeply every week to ten days the first month or so unless you have a soaking rain.

Care
Fertilize the bed between late winter and early spring, and again in September to October, with a slow-release, organic fertilizer for acid-loving plants, at a rate of 4 pounds per 100 sq. ft. In spring replenish the mulch. If you cut the plant back by a third after flowering, it will fill in a few weeks later and become a handsome background "shrub" for the flower bed. But you lose the seedpods. Removing spent flowers may encourage a few more blooms, but we like to let the end-of-season spikes of seedpods remain for a fall and winter show. Cut baptisia to the ground when frosts blacken the foliage. You needn't divide it for ten years or more unless you want to multiply your holdings.

Companion Planting and Design
Baptisia's medium-tall mound of foliage and its indigo blue flowers create strong vertical lines at the middle or back of a large flowering border. It's one of those very substantial plants used to anchor other flowers, and it's an excellent meadow plant.

Our Personal Recommendation
Plant the species.

When, Where, and How to Plant

You'll find catmint offered as a container plant in early spring. If you are planning to use it for edging, you'll need lots of plants and we recommend starting it from seed. We grew our own, and found it very easy to start and transplant. See Starting Seeds Indoors in the Appendix. Or, look for a neighbor who is willing to share some catmint root divisions. Catmint does best in full sun but can handle some shade—but not a lot—and still look great. The ideal soil is light, moderately fertile, and well drained. See Soil Preparation in the Introduction. For information on planting root divisions and container-grown plants, follow the planting instructions at the beginning of this chapter. Allow at least 18 in. between plants. Water well, and apply 2 in. of mulch all around the plants.

Growing Tip

Maintain moisture during the first several weeks until the plants are growing lustily.

Care

Once established, we have found catmint tolerates drought. To keep the plants looking well, it is necessary to shear them back after they have finished blooming. Author Tracy DiSabato-Aust recommends shearing the plants back by two-thirds. We find shearing encourages some re-blooming but its main purpose is to keep the plants from getting straggly. As the plants mature, they tend to fall open in the middle. That's a sign they should be divided. In our gardens catmint self-sows modestly. We cut it back to the crown in mid-fall.

Companion Planting and Design

Catmint makes a lovely flowering mound useful for edging, as a ground cover with roses, to carpet sunny woodland paths, and sunny shrub borders. It's pretty alternating with coreopsis 'Moonbeam'.

Our Personal Recommendations

We planted the species and are pleased with it. 'Six Hills Giant' is a larger variety, 3 ft. tall and 3 ft. wide.

Catmint grows with the enthusiasm of mint, to which it is related, from early to mid-spring, and creates rounded 12- to 15-in. mounds of deliciously fragrant, grayish green foliage. Then, in mid- to late spring, the mounds are topped by slender, fuzzy spikes beaded with tubular, deep or pale lavender-blue florets. Don't confuse this with the species called catnip (and also catmint), Nepeta cataria, which is the one beloved of cats: we planted catnip three times in the garden and each time it was eaten to the crown by neighborhood cats. But N. × faassenii thrives here without interference, and we use it everywhere as an edger and ground cover under bare-legged shrubs such as roses, and in the wild garden. Deer don't bother it. Cut it back after flowering for a second season of bloom.

Other Name

Persian Ground Ivy

Bloom Period and Seasonal Color

Late spring, early summer; blue-purple.

Mature Height × Spread

12 to 15 in. × 24 to 30 in.

Zones

3 to 8

Chrysanthemum
Dendranthema spp. and hybrids

We divide mums into three groups: the hardy garden mums we grow for fall color and retain when we're especially pleased with the variety; florists' mums for collectors and connoisseurs that are too demanding for us; and the summer-flowering species with daisy flowers—the big, beautiful, single or double shasta daisies, pyrethrum (Zones 3 to 7), and feverfew (Zones 4 to 9). For garden mums for September color in the colder regions of New England, our Vermont consultants recommend 'Clara Curtis' and 'Mary Stoker'. For milder regions they recommend the semi-double, pink 'Mei Kyo', 'Pumpkin Harvest', pale pink 'Venus', and 'Viette's Apricot Glow'. The sparkling white shasta daisies, Leucanthemum × superbum (Chrysanthemum maximum), 'Becky' and 'Snowcap' do well even in Vermont.

Other Names
Mum, Daisy, Shasta Daisy

Bloom Period and Seasonal Color
Shasta daisies bloom in early summer; white. Hardy mums bloom September and October; many colors.

Mature Height × Spread
Shasta Daisies: 2 to 4 ft. × 3 to 4 ft.
Garden Mums: 15 in. × 3 ft.

Zones
Shasta Daisies: 5 to 9
Garden Mums: 3 to 9

When, Where, and How to Plant
Set out container-grown plants in early spring, summer, or early fall. The single shastas need full sun; shasta doubles do well in light shade. We plant dozens of hardy mums in the spring in the cutting garden and transplant them throughout the beds in late August. The hardy mums tolerate some drought but cannot stand soil that is soggy in winter. A wide range of soil types are suitable but a slightly acid pH is best. See Soil Preparation in the Introduction. Follow the planting instructions at the beginning of this chapter, spacing the plants about 2 ft. apart. Water well. Mulch 2 in. deep starting 3 in. from the crown.

Growing Tip
For a month or so after planting, water deeply every week to ten days unless you have a good soaking rain.

Care
Fertilize the bed with a slow-release organic fertilizer between late winter and early spring, and again in early summer—6 pounds per 100 sq. ft. Replenish the mulch. After the first flush of bloom, deadhead shastas back to the nearest side buds; when these have bloomed, cut the plants down to the basal foliage, which will remain attractive until frosts. Mums need to be divided every two or three years to remain fully productive: the best time is early spring or after the plants become dormant in fall.

Companion Planting and Design
Shasta daisies are handsome in perennial beds and flowering borders. For a filler plant we like the related, old-fashioned feverfew, *Tanacetum parthenium*, which bears masses of little 1-in., daisy-like, white or yellow button flowers with yellow centers. For glorious fall color, interplant perennials with hardy garden mums.

Our Personal Recommendations
Other shastas we like are: long-lived, 2-ft. 'Switzerland', a big, beautiful Viette nursery introduction that blooms in June and July, and long-blooming 'Ryan's White', which flowers from June to September. 'Becky', a single shasta, is one of our favorites too.

Columbine

Aquilegia spp. and hybrids

When, Where, and How to Plant

Fresh seed gathered from plants sown in late spring or early summer produces flowers the following year. For bloom this year, in early spring set out container-grown plants or root divisions any time after the ground can be worked. Columbines succeed in sun in moderate climates, but prefer some noon shade in warmer regions. *Aquilegia* needs well-drained, rich, evenly moist soil. See Soil Preparation in the Introduction. Follow the planting instructions at the beginning of this chapter, spacing the plants 12 to 15 in. apart in groups of at least three to five. Taller varieties may need staking. Water well. Mulch 2 in. deep starting 3 in. from the outer stems.

Growing Tip

Water new plants deeply every week to ten days for a month or so unless you have a soaking rain.

Care

Fertilize the bed between late winter and early spring, and again in late September to October, with a slow-release organic fertilizer, 6 pounds per 100 sq. ft. Replenish the mulch. Leaf miners attack the foliage in some areas. The solution is, after the flowers have bloomed, cut the foliage way back, almost to the crown; it will grow back and make a beautiful low foliage filler for the rest of the season. Columbines generally live only four or five years, and need no dividing. They often self-sow: dig out those you don't want and transplant them elsewhere.

Companion Planting and Design

Because columbines do well in part shade, they are often naturalized along sun-dappled woodland paths. The old-fashioned garden columbine, *A. vulgaris*, or granny's bonnet, is a favorite cottage garden flower. The native Canadian columbine, *A. canadensis*, is usually resistant to the leaf miner that defaces the foliage of less hardy breeds; it self-sows so it's a good choice for naturalizing. Carol Schminke, owner of Down To Earth Gardens in Garrison, New York, recommends this one.

Our Personal Recommendations

Among our favorites are varieties of *A. flabellata*, the fan columbine, which grows to 8 to 10 in., needs no staking, and is longer lived than other species. 'Nora Barlow' is a beautiful pink and white double-flowered columbine.

The columbine is one of the most beautiful of our mid- to late spring and early summer flowers, loved as much for its foliage as for its long-lasting, intricate blossoms. These nodding or upright flowers, usually in two shades, end in "spurs," and they stand out against the fresh blue-green scalloped foliage. Superb hybrids are available in a variety of heights, and in many colors and amazing bi-colors. Some have huge spurs—'Spring Song' and the Music series for example. There are double-flowered strains of columbine for the perennial beds, and dwarfs, which are charming in a rock garden. The leaves make a beautiful addition to the foliage plants in a perennial border.

Bloom Period and Seasonal Color
April; white, yellow, blue, rusty pinks, lavenders, purples, reddish orange, bi-colors.

Mature Height × Spread
1 to 3 ft. × 1 1/2 ft.

Zones
3 to 8

Coneflower
Rudbeckia fulgida var. *sullivantii* 'Goldsturm'

The showy perennial coneflower 'Goldsturm' is probably the finest of the yellow black-eyed Susan types. It blooms freely throughout midsummer and well into fall on compact, bushy plants, 18 to 30 in. high. The ray florets are deep yellow and the cone-shaped centers a deep brown-black. Heat- and drought-resistant, the foliage stays in good condition no matter how hot it gets. 'Goldsturm' is such a superior performer it was chosen as the 1999 Plant of the Year by the Perennial Plant Association. It self-sows aggressively so it's a good choice for wild gardens. Removing spent blooms early in the flowering season encourages repeat flowering. The flowers dry well. Leave a few for the birds, for winter interest, and to reseed.

Other Name
Black-Eyed Susan

Bloom Period and Seasonal Color
Summer into fall; dark gold with a dark eye.

Mature Height × Spread
1 1/2 to 2 1/2 ft. × 2 to 2 1/2 ft.

Zones
3 to 9

When, Where, and How to Plant
You can plant *Rudbeckia* from seedlings started indoors, or as seed in the open garden, anytime after the ground can be worked in spring. You will have bigger plants sooner if you set out container-grown plants or root divisions. *Rudbeckia* withstands high heat and thrives in full sun: in bright or partial shade it blooms well but tends to grow toward brighter light. Well-drained, light, fertile soil is best, pH 5.0 to 6.5. See Soil Preparation in the Introduction. Follow the planting instructions at the beginning of this chapter, spacing the plants 8 to 12 in. apart. Water well. Mulch 2 in. deep starting 3 in. from the crown.

Growing Tip
Water a new planting deeply every week to ten days the first season unless you have a good soaking rain.

Care
Fertilize the bed in early spring and again in September to October, with a slow-release organic fertilizer for acid-loving plants at a rate of 4 pounds per 100 sq. ft. *Rudbeckia* is drought-resistant, so, once established, local rainfall will be enough to maintain it. After the first flush of blooms, deadhead down to the next pair of buds. The plants are rhizomatous, and create large colonies. Divide the planting in early spring every four years to keep the bed full and flowery.

Companion Planting and Design
'Goldsturm' self-sows and is a good naturalizer. It's a very tough plant that glows gold throughout the summer; an excellent edger for ornamental grasses, meadow gardens, and sunny flower borders. Let the black seedheads stand when flowering dwindles as cold weather approaches: you will provide food for birds, and add interest to the garden in the winter months.

Our Personal Recommendations
'Goldsturm' is our first choice. Mark Viette has introduced a new edger, *R. fulgida* var. *speciosa* 'Viette's Little Suzy', just 12 to 14 in. tall, whose foliage turns a lovely mahogany in cold weather. And we're excited about the new 2003 All-America Selections winner, *R. hirta* 'Prairie Sun', a 3-ft.-tall coneflower with 5-in. blooms that are golden tipped with primrose yellow and have light green central cones.

Coral Bells
Heuchera spp. and hybrids

When, Where, and How to Plant
Set out container plants or root divisions any time after the ground can be worked in spring. Plants that are still near-dormant or just beginning to grow will give the best performance. 'Palace Purple' can stand more direct sun in cooler regions. Heuchera is drought-resistant, but the leaves scorch if the plant dries out. It needs well-drained, slightly acid soil, pH 5.5 to 6.5. See Soil Preparation in the Introduction. Follow the planting instructions at the beginning of this chapter, spacing the plants 12 to 18 in. apart. Water well. Mulch 2 to 3 in. deep starting 3 in. from the outer leaves.

Growing Tip
The first month or so water new heucheras deeply every week to ten days unless you have a good soaking rain.

Care
In cold climates, mulch with branches of evergreens after the first solid frost. Fertilize the bed in early spring, and again in September to October, with a slow-release organic fertilizer for acid-loving plants at a rate of 4 pounds per 100 sq. ft. *Heuchera* is fairly drought-resistant, so water when you water the other perennials. Deadhead if you want to prolong the flowering. If your main interest is the foliage, remove the flowers before they grow. In late summer cut off leaves that are less than perfect and allow the new foliage to develop and stay for winter. Divide every four or five years in the early spring.

Companion Planting and Design
Heuchera foliage is low to the ground, so the plant is used at the front of a flower border, or to edge a path, whether the plant is being grown for its foliage or its flowers.

Our Personal Recommendations
'Bressingham Bronze' has deep purple leaves and off-white flowers borne in late spring. 'Palace Purple' is our favorite for foliage. 'White Cloud' blooms May to July, and bears white flowers.

In late spring and early summer, coral bells' dainty, eye-catching panicles of tiny bell-shaped flowers sway on 1- to 2-ft. wiry stalks arching high above the foliage. The Bressingham hybrids bloom in shades of coral to deep red, pink, and white. The leaves of the species are low-growing, evergreen, dark green, scalloped clusters that remain attractive most of the year. But these days the excitement generated by Heuchera has to do with cultivars with colorful foliage. In 1991 Heuchera micrantha 'Palace Purple' was named Plant of the Year by the Perennial Plant Association. It introduced a heuchera planted primarily for its foliage. Its ivy-shaped leaves are mahogany-red above, beet-red below, and especially handsome with the tans and reds that dominate in the fall. The flowers are off-white.

Other Name
Alumroot

Bloom Period and Seasonal Color
May to July; coral, deep red, pink, white.

Mature Height × Spread
15 to 20 in. × 18 to 20 in.

Zones
3 to 8

Daylily
Hemerocallis spp. and hybrids

Daylilies are a favorite all-summer flower and bloom from July through August throughout most of New England. Extensive hybridizing for enhanced performance has given rise to a whole new breed of these easy-care, long-lived flowers. The blossoms range from $2^1/2$ in. to huge 8-in. trumpets. Large-flowered daylilies typically open one to three blossoms per stem every day; the miniatures open three to seven blossoms per stem every day. The daylilies classed as "tetraploids" have intense color, heavily textured petals, and strong stems: 'Viette's Cranberry Red' and 'Viracocho' are examples. Those labeled as "diploids" are very showy but smaller than the others: 'Stella d'Oro', the miniature famous for its multiple blooms, is a diploid, and is recommended by all of our New England consultants.

Bloom Period and Seasonal Color
July through August; near-white, creamy yellow, orange, gold, purple, pink, fiery red, lavender, bi-colors.

Mature Height × Spread
Standards: 2 to 4 ft. (a few reach 5 ft.) × 2 to 4 ft.
Miniatures: 12 to 14 in. (some reach 40 in.) × 1 1/2 to 2 ft.

Zones
3 to 8

When, Where, and How to Plant
The best planting time is spring. Soak tuberous roots for two to six hours before planting. You can plant container-grown daylilies anytime, but early spring is best. Daylilies are adaptable: they will bloom most fully in full sun but also bloom well in bright shade. They thrive in clay, loam, or sandy soils, and tolerate heat, wind, cold, and seashore conditions. See Soil Preparation in the Introduction. If you are planting bare-root daylilies, fan the tuberous roots out in the planting hole, and set the crown so it is about 1 in. below the soil surface. Plant container-grown daylilies following the planting instructions at the beginning of this chapter. Space daylilies 24 in. apart. Water well. Mulch with pine needles, pine bark, or hardwood bark 2 to 3 in. deep starting 3 in. from the crown.

Growing Tips
Water deeply every week for the first two weeks. Once the plants are growing well, water deeply in lasting droughts.

Care
After a couple of hard frosts remove the foliage. In mid-fall and again in late winter fertilize established beds with a slow-release organic fertilizer at a rate of 6 pounds for every 100 sq. ft. Maintain the mulch. Water in prolonged periods of drought. Divide in mid-spring or early fall every four to five years.

Companion Planting and Design
With daylilies we like *Rudbeckia*, ornamental grasses, sunny *Heliopsis* and *Helianthus*, *Crocosmia*, and poppies. Other good companion plants are fall-blooming asters and mums that will take over as the daylilies begin to fade away.

Our Personal Recommendations
For a long season of bloom, look for "re-blooming" daylilies that flower early, and again in late summer or early fall, or from summer into frosts. For small gardens, our New England consultants all love little 'Stella d'Oro', which bears somewhat fragrant, $2^3/4$-in. gold flowers with green throats. A three-year-old plant produces literally hundreds of blooms. Among daylilies with a marked fragrance are 'Fragrant Light', 'Hyperion', 'Ida Jane', and *H. citrina*. Another favorite is 'Happy Returns'.

Globe Thistle
Echinops ritro 'Taplow Blue'

When, Where, and How to Plant
Set out container-grown plants in the spring. Globe thistle blooms fully given six hours of full sun, and benefits from afternoon shade, especially in warmer regions. Echinops is not particular as to soil pH, as long as the soil is well drained. It spreads in moist, rich soil, which may or may not be a blessing. See Soil Preparation and Planting in the Introduction. Follow the planting instructions at the beginning of this chapter, spacing the plants 20 to 24 in. apart. Water well. Mulch 2 to 3 in. deep starting 3 in. from the outer leaves.

Growing Tip
Water new plants deeply every week or ten days for the first month or so unless you have a soaking rain.

Care
Established globe thistles tolerate drought. To encourage re-bloom, deadhead flowering stems back by a third or a half to a pair of basal leaves: if cut back twice, they often bloom a third time. At the end of the season leave the flower heads for the birds. In early spring cut back to the crown. Fertilize the bed between late winter and early spring, and again in late September to October, with a slow-release organic fertilizer for acid-loving plants at a rate of 4 pounds per 100 sq. ft. Maintain the mulch. Division is usually not needed—and difficult—but can be successful undertaken in early spring. If you let the flower heads remain over the winter, globe thistle may self-sow.

Companion Planting and Design
The globe thistles are handsome massed in a wild garden, and fronting tall shrubs. We grow a stand with ferns, astilbes, and Japanese irises as a backdrop to rocks encircling a small water garden. Attractive companion plants are plumey ornamental grasses, Siberian irises, peonies, yuccas, and coneflowers.

Our Personal Recommendations
'Taplow Blue' is a favorite. The flower heads produced by 'Veitch's Blue' are a deeper blue; if flowers are your main interest, this one is a good choice because it often re-blooms.

When you are looking for a plant that will add texture and variety to the perennial border, consider the globe thistle. It is a stately, erect, thistle-like plant, 2 to 4 ft. tall with big, beautiful spiny leaves that are gray-green and hairy on the underside. The foliage is handsome—reason enough for growing the plant. From July through August the globe thistle raises handsome, spiky, perfectly round flower heads that last for a couple of months. An added benefit is they attract goldfinches and nocturnal moths. The flowers of Echinops ritro 'Taplow Blue' are steel blue, and about 2 in. across. They add interesting texture and color to arrangements of fresh flowers, dry easily, and look great in dried winter arrangements. 'Taplow Blue' is the most popular of the cultivars.

Bloom Period and Seasonal Color
June to August; steel blue.

Mature Height × Spread
3 to 4 ft. × 2 to 3 ft.

Zones
3 to 8

Hosta

Hosta spp. and hybrids

Hostas are clump-forming foliage plants—the finest of all foliage plants for shaded places. Low mounds of bold leaves, hostas raise slender flower stems studded with bell-like blooms in summer. The flowers of some species are fragrant. Newer hybrids, like 'Aphrodite', have remarkably beautiful double flowers. There are dwarfs 7 in. across, giants 5 ft. across, and the leaves may be narrow or broad, smooth textured, quilted, puckered, or semi-twisted. The colors range from rich or muted shades of blue-green to yellow-white. The countless colorful variegations light up dim corners. There are green leaves with narrow or broad, white or gold edges, or interior splotches, and yellow-green leaves with dark-green splotching and edgings. Deer, alas, love hostas as much as we do; pay close attention to where you plant them because they will need to be protected from grazing.

Other Names
Plantain Lily, Funkia

Bloom Period and Seasonal Color
Summer to early fall; white, lavender, purple flowers, and foliage that may be green, chartreuse, blue, blue-green, gold, white, or gold variegated.

Mature Height × Spread
4 to 36 in. × 7 to 56 in.

Zones
3 to 8 or 9

When, Where, and How to Plant
Catalog nurseries ship hostas bare root in early spring, which are slow to develop. Container-grown plants can be set out anytime after the ground has warmed. Hostas thrive in filtered light; yellow foliage and variegated forms tolerate more sun. Where there are late frosts, hostas are safer under tall trees. Adaptable as to pH, hostas need well-drained, moist, humusy, fertile soil. See Soil Preparation in the Introduction. Follow the planting instructions at the beginning of this chapter, setting the plants an inch or two below ground level. Space small-leaved varieties 18 to 24 in. apart, and large-leaved forms 24 to 36 in. apart. Water deeply, and mulch well.

Growing Tips
Water a new planting every week or ten days for a month or two unless you have a good soaking rain. Don't overdo: moisture encourages slugs.

Care
In the fall clean the beds: fallen leaves can harbor slugs. In early spring and mid-fall fertilize with slow-release organic fertilizer, 6 pounds per 100 sq. ft. If late frosts threaten, cover hostas with Remay cloth, old blankets, or burlap. Maintain soil moisture the first two or three years; established plants tolerate drought. Harvest the flowers for bouquets. Hostas need three years to mature: the older they get the more impressive they become. Divide them if you wish in early spring or fall. In prolonged rainy weather slugs attack hostas; sprinkle diatomaceous earth, silica gel, or Sluggo® around the plants. You also can trap them with small saucers of beer.

Companion Planting and Design
Mass hostas in a woodland garden using a single type. Or, combine contrasting colors and sizes to create exciting textures. Small white-variegated hostas make a neat edging for shaded paths. The hostas start up rather late, so they're good companion plants for spring bulbs.

Our Personal Recommendations
We love the bold hostas, especially big 'Sum and Substance,' and new 'Blue Mammoth', which has 4-ft. foliage. We also love perfumed *H. fortunei* 'Fragrant Bouquet', and *H. plantaginea*. But, the deer limit our hosta plantings mightily.

Japanese Anemone

Anemone tomentosa 'Robustissima'

When, Where, and How to Plant

Plant a container-grown Japanese anemone after the ground has warmed in spring. Japanese anemone does best in morning sun or all-day bright shade. The Japanese anemone needs well-drained soil, and does well in pH 5.5 to 6.0. See Soil Preparation in the Introduction. Follow the planting instructions at the beginning of this chapter, spacing the plants at least 24 in. apart. The tallest cultivars will need staking. Water well. Mulch 2 in. deep starting 3 in. from the outer leaves.

Growing Tip

For the first month to six weeks, water a new plant every week to ten days unless there's a soaking rain.

Care

Deadhead to keep the plant attractive. When the foliage dies down, cut the plant back to the crown. In zone 4, it's a good idea to provide winter mulch. Fertilize the bed between late winter and early spring with a slow-release organic fertilizer for acid-loving plants at a rate of 4 pounds per 100 sq. ft. Replenish the mulch. Established clumps are fairly drought-resistant, but best results are obtained when plants are well watered during dry periods. These plants need two or three seasons to become established, and they resent disturbance; divide every ten years to refresh the clump.

Companion Planting and Design

The Japanese anemones are lovely growing at the edge of a woodland with ferns, hostas, and barrenworts. We've seen white Japanese anemones blooming as follow-on plants in a bed for spring bulbs with a formal gray stone wall in the background, and that was quite a sight! Anemones are lovely backed by a tall ornamental grass.

Our Personal Recommendations

'Robustissima' is the hardiest but there are beautiful forms of *A. × hybrida* if your winters are mild enough: historic 'Honorine Jobert' (Zones 5 to 6) is a gleaming white, single-flowered anemone, 3 to 4 ft. tall. 'Margarette' (Zones 5 to 6) is smaller and produces masses of double or semi-double, bright rose-pink blooms on stems 2 to 3 ft. tall. 'Queen Charlotte' (Zones 5 to 6) is an exquisite semi-double pink.

For New England gardeners the Japanese anemone, Anemone tomentosa 'Robustissima', is the most reliable of all the beautiful fall blooming anemones. Low, attractive clusters of divided leaves that are crimson on the reverse side appear first, then tall multi-branched stems begin to develop. Towards late summer the plants rise to 2 or 3 ft. and for many weeks silvery buds open to airy flowers 2 to 3 in. in diameter. The single-flowered types have five rounded petals surrounding a central heart of bright yellow stamens. There are doubles. We've seen the seemingly delicate stems withstand whipping winds. A. × hybrida (Zones 5 to 8) varieties are larger and more beautiful, and have been bred to many forms and colors.

Bloom Period and Seasonal Color
August to September; white, pink, deep rose.

Mature Height × Spread
2 to 4 ft. × 2 ft.

Zones
4 to 8

Lady's Mantle
Alchemilla mollis

Lady's mantle is a beautiful foliage plant, 12 in. high or taller, used for edging and massing in shaded gardens and under trees or along walls. The plant forms a rounded mound of scalloped, silvery foliage that holds shimmering drops of rain after a shower. In early to late summer in our region, lady's mantle raises sprays of tiny, chartreuse-yellow, star-shaped flowers that stand high above the leaves. This is a very effective foliage accent plant in the front of a flower border and a favorite old-fashioned herb believed to possess magical powers. The dwarf lady's mantle, Alchemilla erythropoda, is choice for edging small borders or to tuck at the base of steps. Much like A. mollis, it's a miniature about 6 in. high.

Other Name
Alchemilla

Bloom Period and Seasonal Color
Early to late summer; chartreuse-yellow.

Mature Height × Spread
1 to 1 1/2 ft. × 2 ft.

Zones
4 to 7

When, Where, and How to Plant
Alchemilla thrives in climates with cool, moist summers, and so it is a favorite for New England gardens. You can start alchemilla from fresh seed sown in late summer, or set out container-grown plants in early to mid-spring or early fall. A site in part sun is best, but alchemilla does well in shade, and well enough growing in full sun, provided that it is given some protection from hot noon and late afternoon sun. The ideal soil is well drained, humusy, and rich, with ordinary pH. See Soil Preparation in the Introduction. For container plants, follow the planting instructions at the beginning of this chapter, spacing the plants about 24 in. apart. Water well. Mulch 2 to 3 in. deep starting 3 in. from the outer leaves.

Growing Tips
Water lady's mantle deeply every week to ten days unless you have a soaking rain. The key to success—particularly in the warmer reaches of New England—is sustained moisture.

Care
To keep the foliage beautiful, you must remove fading flower heads: if you yank the stem rather than cutting it at the base, you may pull out a small chunk of the crown, and that can, with luck, transplant successfully. Growing in full sun, and if it hits a period of drought, some of the leaves may brown: cut them out to keep the clump looking fresh. Early spring is the time to divide and replant alchemilla. Fertilize in early fall and again in early spring with a slow-release organic fertilizer at the rate of 6 pounds per 100 sq. ft.

Companion Planting and Design
We plant groups of three or five of the species *A. mollis* to accent corners and mark curves of flower beds. It is very effective repeated as an edger along paths and walks, and in woodlands. In smaller borders, we prefer the dwarf, *A. erythropoda*. Lady's mantle is attractive with fennel, rue, sage, and with low colorful grasses such as blue fescue.

Our Personal Recommendation
The cultivar 'Auslese' has more upright flowers and a prettier form.

Lamb's Ears
Stachys byzantina

When, Where, and How to Plant
Set out container-grown plants or root divisions in early spring or in early fall. Lamb's ears grows well in full sun or part shade. It is not particular as to soil pH, but requires a very well-drained site and light, fertile, humusy soil. See Soil Preparation in the Introduction. Follow the planting instructions at the beginning of this chapter, spacing the plants 12 to 24 in. apart and an inch above ground level. Water slowly and deeply. Use a fine-textured mulch (something like cocoa hulls or pine needles) 1 in. deep, starting 3 in. from the outer leaves.

Growing Tips
Water a new planting three times every thirty days, slowly and deeply. Lamb's ears tolerates drought once it's established; wetting the foliage, especially in hot weather, may encourage rot. Avoid overhead sprinkling and frequent shallow watering.

Care
Remove the flower spikes that lamb's ears sends up to keep the plants looking beautiful; letting the flowers open and go to seed will cause the foliage to deteriorate. Cut out leaves and stems anytime there are signs that the foliage is beginning to rot on the underside. Leave healthy foliage in place for the winter, and remove it before growth begins in spring.

Companion Planting and Design
Lamb's ears is a good container plant, and will give pleasure wherever you plant it. It's a delight when inter-planted with *Sedum* 'Ruby Glow' and 'Vera Jameson', and lovely nestled in fallen leaves. To make a show, you need to plant lamb's ears in groups of at least three plants. The leaves dry well and can be included in tussie mussies and dried wreaths.

Our Personal Recommendations
We love 'Helen von Stein', whose silvery leaves are twice the size of other varieties and better able to withstand the heat and humidity. The non-flowering, 8-in.-high 'Silver Carpet' spreads rapidly and is choice for cooler regions.

Lamb's ears is often included in flowering borders for its unusual texture and the striking silvery light it brings to the dominant greens of other plants. The plant develops a mound of long, oval, semi-evergreen leaves that are so furry they invite stroking, and so luminous they catch moonlight. From midsummer until frosts lamb's ears produces fuzzy, semi-upright spikes of small flowers that are usually violet or white. Most gardeners remove the flowering spikes as they begin to develop to keep the mound low, and the focus on the leaves. The plant has been a favorite long enough to have acquired a number of common names, including lamb's tongue and lamb's tails, which describes the shape of the leaves.

Other Names
Woolly Betony, Lamb's Tongue, Lamb's Tails

Bloom Period and Seasonal Color
Furry, silvery foliage all season long; in summer, violet or white flower spikes.

Mature Height × Spread
12 to 15 in. × 12 to 18 in.

Zones
4 to 8

Marsh Rose Mallow
Hibiscus moscheutos

The two most familiar hibiscus flowers used to be the tropical shrub Hibiscus rosa-sinensis, a gorgeous funnel-shaped flower that lasts just a day, and the lovely old-fashioned rose-of-Sharon, shrub althea, H. syriacus, a woody flowering shrub or small tree described in the chapter on Shrubs. The huge blooms of the marsh rose mallow have captured the imagination of many gardeners. It's a shrubby perennial that in midsummer bears funnel-shaped flowers 7, 10, and 12 in. across. In late spring, the plant's new growth shoots up 3 to 6 ft. Even though the canes eventually sprawl, the plant does not need staking—just lots of sprawl space. When in bloom, it's eye-catching even at some distance. The dried pods are handsome.

Other Names
Common Rose Mallow, Swamp Rose Mallow

Bloom Period and Seasonal Color
Midsummer to frosts; red, white, pink, bi-colors.

Mature Height × Spread
3 to 8 ft. × 5 ft.

Zones
5 to 9

When, Where, and How to Plant
Set out container-grown or bare-root plants in early spring in full sun: in part shade, it won't produce as many flowers. Rose mallow does well in moist situations, and in a wide range of soils. It does best where the pH is between 5.5 and 7.0. See Soil Preparation in the Introduction. Follow the planting instructions at the beginning of this chapter. Provide a hole twice the size of the rootball and 6 in. deeper. Set the crown 2 in. below the soil surface. If you plant more than one, allow at least 3 to 4 ft. between plants. Rose mallow doesn't have to be staked, but it benefits from the support of a wall, or a fence corner where it also gets air. Water deeply. Mulch 2 to 3 in. deep with pine needles or decayed leaves starting 3 in. from the crown.

Growing Tip
Water a new plant deeply every week to ten days the first season unless you have a good soaking rain.

Care
The blooms, like tropical hibiscus, last a day then turn to brown mush. Removing them keeps the plant more attractive. Late in the season we allow seedheads to form and stay on the plant through winter. Rose mallow resists some drought once it's established, so local rainfall should be enough to keep it growing. Fertilize the bed in fall and again between late winter and early spring with a slow-release organic fertilizer at a rate of 6 pounds per 100 sq. ft. Cut the stems to the ground in early spring: in late spring new stems will appear. To keep the plant groomed, author Tracy DiSabato-Aust recommends cutting the stems back by half when they are 18 in. high.

Companion Planting and Design
Rose mallow is handsome in a corner, and beautiful blooming through and over a low metal fence.

Our Personal Recommendations
Red 'Lord Baltimore' bears masses of flowers and has beautifully lobed leaves. 'Appleblossom' has light pink flowers with deeper rose margins. 'Cotton Candy' is a bi-color with soft pink-on-white flowers.

When, Where, and How to Plant

Set out container plants or root divisions in the spring, summer, or fall. Monarda blooms fully in direct sun, or with afternoon shade, even in cooler regions. It thrives in well-drained, moist, humusy soil that is slightly acid, pH 5.0 to 6.5. See Soil Preparation in the Introduction and follow the planting instructions at the beginning of this chapter. The plant is susceptible to mildew so plant it where it has plenty of space and good air circulation all around—it will fill its space quickly. Water well. Mulch 2 to 3 in. deep starting 3 in. from the crown.

Growing Tip

Water new plantings of monarda deeply every week to ten days for a month or so unless you have a soaking rain.

Care

Fertilize the bed between late winter and early spring with a slow-release organic fertilizer for acid-loving plants at a rate of 4 pounds per 100 sq. ft. In spring, replenish the mulch. Maintain soil moisture during dry spells. Deadheading extends the period of bloom. If the plant shows signs of mildew after flowering, cut the stems back to just above the fresh new foliage at the base. Monarda spreads thanks to underground stems that can quickly fill a considerable area: planting it in 3- to 5-gallon containers keeps it under control. You can divide the planting every two to three years in late summer—just pull individual stems from the center of the planting and replant them with space all around.

Companion Planting and Design

Scarlet monardas make an extraordinary statement—even from afar, when planted in a clump growing against a wall. We love it in perennial borders, meadows, wild gardens—anywhere that we get to see the wildlife it attracts. It's a good cut flower, but when you are harvesting bee balm, watch out for bees that may think it belongs to them.

Our Personal Recommendations

We recommend mildew-resistant varieties, such as 48-in. 'Jacob Kline', which has large, dark red flowers; 36-in 'Marshall's Delight', a compact pink-flowered variety; and an exciting new dwarf, 15-in. 'Petite Delight', which has lavender-pink flowers.

In the past monarda was more typically known as "bee balm" and grown primarily for its herbal properties. This plant is now often called "monarda" and modern varieties are grown with perennials and in wild and meadow gardens for their beauty and long season of bloom. The tips of young shoots were—still are—used as garnishes for drinks and salads. An herb tea was, and is, made of the pointed, bright green leaves that have the scent of mint-bergamot. Middling tall, the attractive globelike flower heads are made up of whorls of shaggy, tubular, red flowers surrounded by red-tinted bracts. They bloom throughout the summer on stiff stems above neat plants and are wildly attractive to hummingbirds, butterflies, and bees. Monarda is a native American plant. It is an excellent cut flower.

Other Names
Bee Balm, Bergamot, Oswego Tea

Bloom Period and Seasonal Color
July and August; scarlet, pink, cerise, red, white, violet.

Mature Height × Spread
2 to 4 ft. × 2 to 4 ft.

Zones
4 to 9

Oriental Poppy
Papaver orientalis

Poppies come in all sizes. Silky, shiny, and colorful, they're a mainstay of sunny gardens everywhere. The stars of the poppy domain are the big, crinkled-silk Oriental poppies. A spangle of these brilliant, beautiful blossoms lifts a garden from ordinary to extraordinary. The blossoms measure between 5 and 8 to 10 in. across, and they unfold in spring and early summer in vibrant colors and color combinations. The petals of some are splotched at the base in a contrasting color, usually black or mahogany, and others have contrasting edges. Though the wiry stems bend to even a little wind, the flowers withstand storms of amazing proportions. The fuzzy pods are attractive in dried arrangements. The deeply cut foliage dies after the flowers have bloomed, and new foliage appears in the fall.

Bloom Period and Seasonal Color
Spring and early summer; red, orange, salmon, pink, white, bi-colors.

Mature Height × Spread
2 to 4 ft. × 2 ft.

Zones
3 to 7

When, Where, and How to Plant
Set out sturdy container-grown plants in early spring. Poppies need full sun, but can be productive in filtered shade. They succeed in bright shade under tall trees. Poppies tolerate a range of soils as long as they are well drained, deeply dug, light, somewhat sandy but humusy enough to hold moisture, and a pH of 6.0 to 7.5. See Soil Preparation in the Introduction. Follow the planting instructions at the beginning of this chapter. Set the crowns 1½ in. below the soil level and space the plants about 2 to 3 ft. apart. Water deeply. Mulch 2 to 3 in. deep starting 3 in. from the crown.

Growing Tips
Maintain moisture during the growing and flowering period, but don't force watering during the dormant period that follows. The big, decorative seedheads should be removed: it's better for the plant.

Care
When poppies die the foliage deteriorates: allow it to yellow and brown, then gently remove it from the crown. When the foliage begins to re-grow in the fall, fertilize with a slow-release organic fertilizer, 6 pounds per 100 sq. ft. In late winter replenish the mulch. Oriental poppies have a fleshy taproot that is difficult to dig and transplant. They're very long-lived and rarely need dividing; the best time to dig a poppy is after it goes dormant. These are gorgeous cut flowers: a poppy will last longer if you sear the bottom of the stem with a hot flame before putting it into water.

Companion Planting and Design
Don't plant poppies with flowers requiring moist soil in summer. The Oriental poppies are unsightly as the foliage is dying, so they belong toward the back of the border fronted by plants that will grow big as they fade away—dahlias, asters, and chrysanthemums, for example.

Our Personal Recommendations
The most beautiful and easiest poppies to grow are 'Cedar Hill', light pink; 'Maiden's Blush', a ruffled white poppy with a blush-pink edge; brilliant 'Raspberry Queen'; and fringed 'Turkenlouis', a fiery orange red.

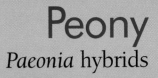

When, Where, and How to Plant

Set out container-grown peonies in early September or in early spring. They require a minimum of six hours of sun and are most successful in well-drained, fertile, humusy, neutral or slightly alkaline soils, pH 6.0 to 7.5, but tolerate mildly acid soils. See Soil Preparation in the Introduction. Do not use barnyard or composted manure with peonies. Provide a hole 24 in. wide and 18 in. deep and follow the planting instructions for container-grown plants at the beginning of this chapter. Space peonies 36 in. apart. Water well. Do not mulch.

Growing Tip

Water plants every week or ten days for the first month or so, unless you have a soaking rain, then water as needed.

Care

In fall and early spring, fertilize the bed with a slow-release organic fertilizer, 6 pounds per 100 sq. ft. In late summer and early fall, we spread wood ashes around the peonies. Water established peonies during droughts. Remove invasive ground covers and weeds by hand, and the seedheads of single peonies. Harvest slow-to-open side blooms: they may open in vase water. It's a healthy practice to cut the foliage of herbaceous peonies to the ground in fall and burn it. Fall is a good time to divide or transplant peonies, but we've had complete success transplanting peonies in early spring. Provide each piece of the crown with three to seven eyes, and plant so the eyes are 2 in. below ground level. Transplanted peonies need a year or two to re-establish themselves.

Companion Planting and Design

Plant peonies in groups of four to eight in beds of their own in lawns—that's the Victorian way—or in groups of two or three to anchor large flowering borders. In snow country they often are planted in rows to hedge walks, and even driveways, because the foliage dies away in fall, leaving space to pile up snow, which a woody shrub would not allow.

Our Personal Recommendations

Some famous peonies that have been loved for decades are: 'Gay Paree', 'Sword Dance', 'Sea Shell', the Lobata hybrids, 'Jan Van Leuven', 'Tomate Boku', 'Nick Shaylor', and fragrant 'Philippe Revoire'. 'Myrtle Gentry' is also scented.

There are two main types of peonies—the herbaceous perennials that are one of the glories of spring in New England, and woody flowering plants classed with shrubs, and known as tree peonies. Revered in the Orient for 2,500 years, thousands of elegant modern peonies attract collectors, botanists, taxonomists, horticulturists, and beginning gardeners. The herbaceous peonies often outlive the gardeners who plant them. The showy flowers bloom in late April and May for four to six weeks, producing huge heads of crinkled silk flowers—single, semi-double, fully double—that make awesomely luscious bouquets. The double-flowered forms are the most popular, but interest is growing in the exotic single-flowered and Japanese peony cultivars. Peonies must have a chilling period at below 40 degrees Fahrenheit to flower—not a problem in New England.

Bloom Period and Seasonal Color
Spring; white, shades of pink and rose, coral, deep crimson, and bi-colors.

Mature Height × Spread
3 ft. × 3 ft.

Zones
3 to 8

Phlox

Phlox paniculata 'David'

The full flower heads of Phlox paniculata *filled old-time midsummer gardens with luscious pastels and the special scent of phlox. An American native, this upright species bears big rounded heads of open-faced, silky-soft florets. It was the backbone of summer borders until its vulnerability to mildew—and strong self-sowing tendencies to regress back to magenta—became deterrents. Phlox is back, featuring healthy and beautiful hybrids such as 'David', which was named Plant of the Year for 2002 by the Perennial Plant Association. The bright white, delightfully fragrant flowers bloom from mid-July to September and its resistance to powdery mildew, according to PPA, is better than that of others. The creeping phlox species carpet New England slopes and rocky ledges with pastel blossoms for weeks in spring, and they spread quickly: P. stolonifera, 5 to 12 in. tall, thrives in semi-shade or shade; the moss pink, P. subulata, just 6 in. tall; P. divaricata, 9 to 15 in., hardy only to zone 4, produces lovely lavender-blue flowers.*

Other Names
Summer Phlox, Perennial Phlox, Fall Phlox

Bloom Period and Seasonal Color
July to September; white.

Mature Height × Spread
35 to 40 in. × 2 ft.

Zones
3 to 8

When, Where, and How to Plant
Set out container-grown plants in early fall or in the spring, in full sun or in partial sun. Phlox is tolerant of a wide range of pH but thrives best in well-drained, moist, fertile soil rich in compost and humus. See Soil Preparation in the Introduction. Follow the planting instructions at the beginning of this chapter, spacing the plants 24 in. or more apart: good air circulation deters mildew. Water deeply. Mulch 2 in. deep starting 3 in. from the crowns.

Growing Tips
For the first two months water new plantings weekly unless you have a soaking rain: unchecked growth contributes to healthy plants. To prolong the flower display, early on pinch back one or two weaker stems in each clump so secondary flowers will be growing as the main stems fade.

Care
Rogue out seedlings and remove the seeded flower heads so that the plants will bloom again and won't self sow. Cut them down to the crown at the end of the season or in early fall, and destroy the stems. Fertilize the bed between late winter and early spring with a slow-release organic fertilizer, 6 pounds per 100 sq. ft. Maintain soil moisture to keep the plants growing lustily. Keep them vigorous by dividing the crowns every three years in spring before growth begins. Discard the center of the crown, and provide each piece with three to four vigorous shoots.

Companion Planting and Design
Plant phlox near asters that will come into bloom as the phloxes fade in late summer, or with fall-flowering Japanese anemone. In mid-fall, heel in potted cushion mums in white and lavender.

Our Personal Recommendations
Old-fashioned 'Katherine', lavender-blue with white eyes, was discovered in an old Connecticut garden and has been reintroduced by André Viette's nursery. 'Flamingo', 'Robert Poore', and 'Eva Cullum' are mildew resistant. White *P. maculata* 'Miss Lingard' and dark pink 'Rosalind' are beautiful together.

Pinks

Dianthus spp. and hybrids

When, Where, and How to Plant

Flats and container-grown plants are available in early spring and early fall. Full sun is best, but pinks bloom in part sun, too. They do best in well-drained, even sandy, soil whose pH is between 6.0 and 7.5. Excellent drainage in winter is essential. See Soil Preparation in the Introduction, and for the pinks, be a little stingy with the humus. For container-grown plants follow the planting instructions at the beginning of this chapter. Space pinks 12 to 15 in. apart and set them a little higher than the soil level. Water well. Spread a light, fine mulch such as cocoa hulls 2 to 3 in. deep starting 3 in. from the crown.

Growing Tips

Water new plantings every week or ten days unless you have rain. After the first flush of bloom, deadhead or shear off the faded flowers. If the plants show brown tips in August, cut them off, and make sure the plants don't go dry. They will freshen when fall comes, and can go on blooming until frosts.

Care

Fertilize the bed between late winter and early spring with a slow-release organic fertilizer at a rate of 6 pounds per 100 sq. ft. Replenish the mulch. Pinks are drought-resistant once established. They don't like wet feet. The little pinks divide and transplant easily in spring or early fall.

Companion Planting and Design

We use pinks as edgers, and position them where the fragrance can be experienced readily.

Our Personal Recommendations

For edging, we like the tiny 6 to 9 or 12 in. high cheddar pink, *D. gratianopolitanus*, which is famous for fragrance: 'Bath's Pink' and 'Tiny Rubies' are popular varieties. The 'Zing' group—'Zing Rose' for example—are 6-inchers that bloom all summer. We love the promise of an exciting new annual dianthus, such as the 2003 All-America Selections winner, 12- to 14-in. 'Can Can Scarlet', whose double blooms can fill a room with spicy fragrance.

Pinks are members of the ancient Dianthus *tribe, which includes carnations and sweet Williams. Annuals, biennials, and perennials, they are loved for their sweet, spicy clove scent and prolific bloom. The perfume is strong in the little cottage and grass pinks that fill New England gardens with sparkling colors spring, summer, and fall. Pinks range in size from 6 to 24 in. and the fresh grassy foliage, evergreen in most, is an all-season asset. There are double-flowered forms. Many varieties will bloom for months if deadheaded or sheared after the first flush of bloom. For cutting we plant cultivars of D.* × *allwoodii, the Allwood pink, which bears very fragrant fluffy carnations 2 to 2^1/$_2$ in. across, 8 to 15 in. high, in blends of pink, red, and white. The old-fashioned sweet William, D.* barbatus, *a great annual cutting flower, is spicily scented, too: cut it back after flowering and it may come back next year.*

Other Names
Miniature Carnation, Cottage Pink, Grass Pink, Sweet William, Cheddar Pink

Bloom Period and Seasonal Color
Spring, summer, early fall; pink, red, salmon, white, yellow (*D. knappii*), often with a contrasting eye, bi-colors.

Mature Height × Spread
6 to 24 in. × 8 to 12 in.

Zones
3 to 9

Purple Coneflower
Echinacea purpurea 'Magnus'

This big, bold coneflower with huge, mauve, daisy-like blooms is one of the showiest, toughest, and longest-lived natives for meadow gardens. It grows 2 to 4 ft. tall, and has coarse, dark green foliage. In 1998, 'Magnus' was named Plant of the Year by the Perennial Plant Association. The petals sweep back from a deep orange-bronze cone and are a rich, dusky rose-purple. Purple coneflower blooms in early summer: deadheaded, it goes on intermittently into fall. There are white varieties but they don't have quite the eye-catching appeal of the purple. Purple coneflowers last well as cut flowers, they dry easily, and the cones alone (minus the petals) look terrific in dried winter flower arrangements. Butterflies love purple coneflower.

Bloom Period and Seasonal Color
Late spring, early summer; mauve pink petals surround orange-bronze cones.

Mature Height × Spread
2 to 4 ft. × 2 ft.

Zones
3 to 8

When, Where, and How to Plant
For flowers the first season, set out container-grown plants or root divisions any time after the ground can be worked in spring. Purple coneflowers need full sun, but they will take a little filtered shade and still be productive, especially in the warmer parts of New England. It tolerates drought and can't stand soil that is soggy in winter. The ideal soil is in the somewhat acid range, pH 5.5 to 6.0. Over-fertilized soil makes for tall, leggy plants that need staking. See Soil Preparation in the Introduction, and reduce the fertilization recommendations by half. Follow the planting instructions at the beginning of this chapter, spacing the plants 18 to 24 in. apart. Water well. Mulch 2 to 3 in. deep starting 3 in. from the outer leaves.

Growing Tips
The first six weeks, water purple coneflower every week unless you have a soaking rain. Given time to become established, it will tolerate drought.

Care
In reasonably fertile soil, spring fertilization may not always be necessary. Deadheading keeps the plants from self-seeding and reverting to inferior forms. Whether you deadhead or not, new blossoms keep coming. We keep some stands of purple coneflower deadheaded, and allow some to form seedheads to feed the birds that relish the seeds: next year you can rogue out the self-sown plantlets that will appear in abundance in the spring. When harvesting flowers for bouquets, cut the stem just above the next flower bud so the stem can produce more blooms.

Companion Planting and Design
Virtually pest- and disease-free, and tolerant of considerable drought, the purple coneflower is an excellent choice for naturalizing. It's the backbone, the showpiece, the eye catcher, of a meadow garden! It also makes a great summer-long show planted in groups of five to seven in the center or toward the back of a formal border.

Our Personal Recommendations
For the cutting garden, plant 'Leuchtstern' ('Bright Star'), which is a rosy-pink coneflower with a maroon center. The cream-white varieties with orange centers, like 'White Lustre' and 'White Swan' are attractive growing with black-eyed Susans.

Russian Sage

Perovskia atriplicifolia

When, Where, and How to Plant

Set out container-grown plants anytime; set out rooted softwood cuttings in early spring or fall. While not overly demanding, Russian sage requires full sun to do its best, and a very well drained site. It thrives in moderately fertile soil in the neutral range. See Soil Preparation in the Introduction. Follow the planting instructions at the beginning of this chapter, spacing the plants 24 in. apart. Water well. Mulch 2 to 3 in. deep starting 3 in. from the crown.

Growing Tip

For the first two months, water deeply and thoroughly every week to ten days, unless you have a good soaking rain, then water as needed.

Care

Russian sage is a sub-shrub with a woody base. Cut the stems back to about 6 in. above the ground in the spring and new buds will start from these stems. In cooler regions the stems may die to the ground: as long as your winters are no colder than Zone 4, or if the plants are planted where they have some protection from the full sweep of north winds, the plants will likely re-grow. If unusually late frosts damage the stems, trim off the spoiled branch tips. In warm areas where Russian sage blooms early, you can try cutting the branches back by two-thirds after they have flowered and hope that will produce a new flush of blooms in fall. Russian sage hardly ever needs dividing.

Companion Planting and Design

We like Russian sage at the back of a perennial border, in groups of three or five or seven, backed by evergreens that will show off their lovely winter color. It is beautiful massed with boltonia, sedums, and ornamental grasses in naturalized settings, both in bloom and later, when the stems turn silvery. It's also a great shore plant.

Our Personal Recommendations

'Filigran' is just 40 in. tall and blooms from July to October. 'Longin' is more upright and narrower than the species.

Russian sage keeps a cloud of that coveted color, blue—a beautiful, soft, powdery lavender blue—in the garden for a long time in summer and early fall. Very tall, so airy they're cloudlike at a distance, the silvery stems and the grayish foliage are topped by spikes of tiny florets of a lovely, subtle shade of blue. When the foliage is brushed, you get a whiff of the clean, warm scent of sage. In winter the branches are a beautiful cloud of silvery white. One of the most heat- and drought-resistant of all the perennials, in 1995 Russian sage was named Plant of the Year by the Perennial Plant Association. It should be planted in groups of three or four in order to properly appreciate its presence.

Bloom Period and Seasonal Color
July through September; powder-blue florets.

Mature Height × Spread
3 to 4^1/$_2$ ft. × 3 to 4 ft.

Zones
4 to 9

Salvia 'May Night'

Salvia × sylvestris 'May Night'

This species is known as perennial salvia. It's a tough plant that winters over even in Zone 3. Square-stemmed like its kissin' cousin Salvia splendens, *described in the chapter on Annuals, perennial salvia has a different look, more that of a small upright shrub with dark green pointy leaves. The slim flowering spikes of 'May Night' are a rich, wonderful, midnight violet-blue. Growing in full sun the flower spikes rise straight up like a candelabra and they bloom for weeks, followed by reddish bracts that are attractive in their own right. In less light, 'May Night' grows taller and sprawls so widely you'd hardly recognize it. Deadheading extends the flowering period. 'May Night' was chosen Plant of the Year by the Perennial Plant Association in 1997.*

Other Names
Perennial Salvia, *Salvia × sylvestris* 'Mainacht',
Salvia nemorosa 'May Night'

Bloom Period and Seasonal Color
June to August; midnight blue.

Mature Height × Spread
1¹/₂ to 3 ft. × 2 ft.

Zones
4 to 7

When, Where, and How to Plant
Set out container-grown plants anytime; set out rooted divisions in early mid-spring or late summer. Salvia needs full sun to stay trim looking, but, while it sprawls widely in partial shade, it still blooms well. Perennial salvia is tolerant as to pH, but needs a site that is well drained, and soil that is fertile and humusy. See Soil Preparation in the Introduction. Follow the planting instructions at the beginning of this chapter, spacing the plants 24 to 30 in. apart. Water well. Mulch 2 to 3 in. deep starting 3 in. from the crown.

Growing Tip
For the first two months, water newly planted perennial salvia every week to ten days unless you have a soaking rain.

Care
Deadhead down to a pair of lateral leaves, and perennial salvia re-blooms beautifully. If the plant falls open and gets stringy looking after blooming, you can cut it down to the crown and it will usually re-grow and, depending on your climate, may have time to re-bloom. After such radical treatment it's a good idea to fertilize the plant and make sure the soil doesn't go dry. Fertilize the bed between late winter and early spring with a slow-release organic fertilizer at a rate of 4 pounds per 100 sq. ft. In spring, replenish the mulch. Water only as needed. Dividing, which isn't often necessary, is best undertaken in early spring.

Companion Planting and Design
Perennial salvia is the perfect plant for the middle of the border between dainty *Coreopsis* 'Moonbeam', chunky yarrow, and tall airy summer flowers like boltonia. We use it to anchor clumps of flowers with light variegated foliage.

Our Personal Recommendations
'May Night' is a favorite but more colors are coming because it is a very useful border plant. Recently introduced *S. × superba* 'Rose Wine' is similar to 'May Night' but rose-pink. And now there's a white perennial salvia from Germany called *S. × sylvestris* 'Snow Hill', which makes a striking show planted in part shade.

Scabiosa
Scabiosa columbaria 'Butterfly Blue'

When, Where, and How to Plant
In early spring set out container-grown plants or root divisions. In cooler regions, scabiosa does best in full sun but in warm regions it flowers well given noon shade. Scabiosa thrives in soil close to neutral, pH 7.0, and very well drained. Excellent drainage in winter is essential. See Soil Preparation in the Introduction. Follow the planting instructions at the beginning of this chapter, spacing the plants 12 to 15 in. apart. Water well. Mulch 2 to 3 in. deep starting 3 in. from the crown.

Growing Tip
For the first two months, water new plantings every week to ten days unless you have a soaking rain.

Care
In cooler regions, provide a light, dry winter mulch of pine boughs or hay. Fertilize the bed between late winter and early spring, and again in September with a slow-release organic fertilizer, 6 pounds per 100 sq. ft. In spring, replenish the mulch. Water only as needed. Deadheading prolongs blooming, but is complicated by the fact that the fading blooms can be mistaken for the emerging flower buds. Deadhead by cutting a finished flowering stem down to a new lateral flowering stem present in the basal foliage. If the stems do not branch, just cut down to the crown. When scabiosa begins to put up just one central leader, cut it down to the basal foliage. Before winter, cut back old flowering stems but leave the basal foliage in place; in spring before growth begins, remove dead foliage. Every three to four years, if the plants seem crowded, divide the crowns any time in early mid-spring up to when active growth begins. The flowers last longest harvested half-open.

Companion Planting and Design
Plant scabiosa toward the front of the perennial bed with space all around.

Our Personal Recommendations
We like 'Butterfly Blue'. The other lovely scabiosa is *S. caucasica*, which has very large flowers and is grown specifically for cutting. It's large, with grayish ferny foliage, and pale blue, white, or lavender flowers summer to frosts. 'Fama' is the clear intense sky blue version, and 'Alba' is the white form. 'Pink Mist' is a lavender-pink version of 'Butterfly Blue'.

'Butterfly Blue' scabiosa is a beautiful cultivar of a long-blooming old-time favorite, the "pincushion" flower—and the blossoms do look like sweet little pincushions surrounded by curving petals. Actually, the blooms are domed heads composed of tiny flowers, surrounded by leafy bracts. It's an excellent flower for cutting and for drying. 'Butterfly Blue' can take the cold all the way to Zone 3 and keep flowering into fall if it is consistently sheared, or deadheaded. A heavy-blooming dwarf perennial, it produces 2-in. flowers in amazing abundance from mid-spring until mid-fall. The color is beautiful, the plant itself a neat compact mound, and the masses of flowers are amazing. The Perennial Plant Association named 'Butterfly Blue' Plant of the Year for 2000.

Other Name
Blue Pincushion Flower

Bloom Period and Seasonal Color
May to October; blue.

Mature Height × Spread
1 to 1¹/₂ ft. × 1 ft.

Zones
3 to 7

Sedum

Sedum spp. and hybrids

Indestructible, heat- and drought-resistant, sedums are valued for their succulent, evergreen, light-green foliage and for the beautiful late summer color of the flowers of some tall hybrids. The flowers are tiny, star-shaped, and in taller forms cluster in showy flat-topped flower heads. 'Autumn Joy' is considered by perennial experts to be among the top fifteen perennials. Its jade green foliage is evergreen. In spring new stems rise, followed in early summer by fresh apple-green, broccoli-like flower heads. These change to rich pink, then rose, salmon, bronze, and finally to rosy russet. Critters (we haven't figured out which ones) sometimes eat sedum foliage but leave the flowers intact. The little ground-hugging sedums, Sedum acre and others, are used in rock gardens, between stepping-stones, in wall crannies, and by steps.

Other Name
Stonecrop

Bloom Period and Seasonal Color
Summer to fall; yellow, pink, white, red.

Mature Height × Spread
2 to 24 in. × 1 to 2 ft.

Zones
3 to 10

When, Where, and How to Plant
Set out container-grown plants spring, summer, or fall. Plant root divisions anytime after the ground can be worked in spring, or in late summer. Many smaller sedums are invasive, and even tall varieties, if not deadheaded, self-sow. The plants flourish in full sun in cold Zone 6 and all the way to Zone 3. The idea soil is pH 6.0 to 7.5, very well drained, humusy, and fertile. Most seem to prefer dry soil, but tolerate moisture. See Soil Preparation in the Introduction. Follow the planting instructions at the beginning of this chapter, spacing the plants according to their size at maturity. Water well. Mulch 2 to 3 in. deep starting 3 in. from the crown.

Growing Tips
Sedum withstands heat and drought even in sand and by the sea. Watering if there's no rain is a good idea but necessary only until you see vigorous new growth.

Care
Fertilize the bed between late winter and early spring, with a slow-release organic fertilizer at a rate of 2 pounds per 100 sq. ft. and replenish the mulch. Sedums need average moisture during active growth but can stand a lot of drought later. Don't deadhead the taller sedums, like 'Autumn Joy'—the flowers change color as they go to seed and provide a beautiful rust color accent in the garden throughout fall and winter. Cut stems off just above the basal foliage in late winter. Divide clumps to multiply your holdings anytime; to refresh the plants divide clumps in early spring every six to ten years.

Companion Planting and Design
The taller cultivars are superb growing with ornamental grasses in naturalized plantings that include *Rudbeckia* 'Goldsturm', purple coneflower, and Russian sage.

Our Personal Recommendations
'Autumn Joy' is the favorite. Another handsome sedum is 'Ruby Glow', a slightly smaller plant whose flower heads are iridescent ruby-red. 'Frosty Morn' is a beautiful new sedum whose leaves are edged with cream and which bears cream-pink flowers that look blush-pink at a distance. Another new sedum is *S. telephium* 'Matrona', which has wine red stems and soft pink flowers.

Siberian Iris
Iris sibirica

When, Where, and How to Plant
Plant container-grown Siberian irises any time; growers ship rhizomes bare root in early spring. The irises are successful growing in full sun in cold, wet climates; in warmer regions they tolerate light shade or late afternoon shade. They adapt to pH 5.0 to 7.5, but prefer moderately acid soils. They tolerate poor, dry soil but bloom best in well-drained, rich, evenly moist garden loam with good drainage. Once established, they can stand some drought. See Soil Preparation in the Introduction. For container-grown plants follow the planting instructions at the beginning of this chapter, allowing a good 18 in. between crowns. Plant rhizomes with the roots on the underside, and the tops just below the soil surface, and space them 18 to 24 in. apart depending on the size of the iris: they soon grow into a solid, deep-rooted clump. Water well. Mulch 2 to 3 in. deep starting 3 in. from the outer edges of the planting.

Growing Tip
Water the planting every week for a month to six weeks, unless you have a soaking rain.

Care
Fertilize the bed between late winter and early spring with a slow-release organic fertilizer, 6 pounds per 100 sq. ft. Water as needed. Deadhead, leaving a third of the handsome seedheads in place to extend the plant's season. Remove dead foliage in spring before growth begins. Divide and transplant in late summer to early fall, or in early spring. Get the rhizomes into the ground as soon as possible; keep them *moist* until planted.

Companion Planting and Design
One or two slim, elegant Siberian irises are beautiful beside a water garden and are lovely in a Japanese garden. Siberian iris, with sedum 'Autumn Joy', and a bramble of coreopsis keep color in the garden in fall and winter.

Our Personal Recommendations
'Butter and Sugar', a new yellow and white variety, has gardeners excited. 'Caesar's Brother' is a deep, rich violet. 'Creme Chantilly' is a superb white.

We love the Siberian irises—they're so easy to maintain and have so few problems. Breeders agree, and are enhancing the colors, range, and bloom times of these exceptionally graceful plants. Depending on the zone, Siberian irises bloom in late spring to early summer. Clusters of two or three flowers top tall slender stems above slim grassy leaves that turn lovely shades of rust in winter. The flowers stand a little taller than the bearded irises (see Bulbs), from 24 to 40 in., and come in as many colors and forms as anyone could want—from white to yellow, blue, some edged with silver, and there's a pansy purple with white lines. Some are ruffled, some have huge flaring blossoms. It's an excellent flower for cutting and very lovely massed in a large border. The dried pods are handsome.

Bloom Period and Seasonal Color
In late spring to early summer; blue-purple, lavender, maroon, white, off-pink, yellowish tones.

Mature Height × Spread
8 to 40 in. × 10 to 24 in.

Zones
3 to 8

Solomon's Seal

Polygonatum spp.

Solomon's seal is truly a superb flower and foliage plant for woodland gardens and naturalized corners of the landscape. It's a native aristocrat that is now propagated and sold by nurseries all over New England. The species gardeners grow are graceful spring-bloomers that originated in damp, light woodlands, so they're reliable performers for a shade garden. In spring, rows of dangling, bell-shaped, green or cream-white flowers (usually in pairs) line the arching stems and are followed by blue-black berries. Pretty if not spectacular, and the flowers of some are fragrant. The foliage turns an appealing yellow-brown in fall and persists. Solomon's seal thrives in domesticity as long as it is provided with light and soil approximating its native haunts.

Other Name
King Solomon's Seal

Bloom Period and Seasonal Color
Mid- to late spring; creamy white flowers.

Mature Height × Spread
2 to 3 ft. × 18 to 20 in.

Zones
4 to 8

When, Where, and How to Plant
Set out nursery-grown root divisions in fall or spring: do not dig Solomon's seal growing in the wild as it is protected. *Polygonatum* volunteers in full sun where there is moisture in cool Zones 5 and 6, and in quite deep shade in woodlands farther north, so it is adaptable. In regions where summers are very hot, a partially shaded site is best. Solomon's seal thrives in well-drained, deeply dug, rich, humusy, somewhat acid soil, pH 5.0 to 6.0. See Soil Preparation in the Introduction. Follow the planting instructions at the beginning of this chapter, spacing the plants 18 to 20 in. apart. Water well. Mulch 2 to 3 in. deep starting 3 in. from the outer leaves.

Growing Tip
Keep the soil moist while the plant is establishing itself, and water deeply during droughts.

Care
Fertilize the bed between late winter and early spring with a slow-release organic fertilizer for acid-loving plants at a rate of 4 pounds per 100 sq. ft. Once a planting is established you can dig and transplant the rhizomes while still dormant in late winter: divide the rhizomes with a knife, allowing each section at least one healthy bud. Set the rhizomes 2 to 3 in. deep with the bud facing upward and pointing in the direction in which you want the plant to grow.

Companion Planting and Design
Plant Solomon's seal along a woodland path with ferns, columbines, fragrant lily-of-the-valley, primroses, trilliums, hostas, and lady's-slippers. *P. commutatum*, a magnificent 5-footer at maturity, belongs in a large wild garden.

Our Personal Recommendations
In addition to the native Solomon's seals, there are several with non-native parentage. The 30-in. *P. odoratum* 'Variegatum', a superb variegated Solomon's seal that is exquisitely fragrant, is recommended as "well behaved" by Master Gardener Judith Irven. It was introduced to gardeners by legendary nurseryman Martin Viette. His son André Viette introduced the 6-in. dwarf species *P. humile* (Zones 4 to 7), a gift he had received from a friend. Another favorite is *Polygonatum multiflorum*, a beautiful, graceful, deep green Solomon's seal.

When, Where, and How to Plant

In spring or late fall set out container-grown plants or root divisions. Yarrow requires full sun, even in hot regions. It thrives in very well-drained, sandy soils, and in poor soils: very rich or moist soils encourage lax growth and cause fern-leaved *A. millefolium* cultivars to become invasive. Yarrow handles drought but can't stand soggy soil in winter. See Soil Preparation in the Introduction but halve the fertilization recommendations. Follow the planting instructions at the beginning of this chapter. Yarrow is a wide-spreading plant, so space the plants 18 to 24 in. apart. Water well. Mulch to keep weeds down 2 to 3 in. deep starting 3 in. from the crown

Growing Tips

Yarrow requires watering for the first few weeks after planting; once it shows signs of vigorous growth, it should do well with ordinary rainfall.

Care

Prune spent flowers down to the first pair of buds, and these will bloom. Yarrow, especially fern-leaved yarrow, *A. filipendulina*, makes a delightful dried flower, so harvest the last round of blooms for winter bouquets. Fertilize the bed lightly between late winter and early spring, applying a slow-release organic fertilizer at the rate of 2 pounds per 100 sq. ft. In spring, replenish the mulch. Before growth begins in spring, gently remove the dead foliage. Every four or five years—or if the plant becomes less productive—divide in early spring before growth begins.

Companion Planting and Design

Yarrow's ferny foliage adds texture to perennial beds and is very attractive in naturalized plantings.

Our Personal Recommendations

Golden cultivars 'Coronation Gold' and 'Moonshine' have superb long-lasting blooms; 'Feurland'('Fireland') opens blood red with gold centers and gradually fades to deep pink, salmon, and eventually to soft gold. Durable *A. millefolium*, a slightly smaller species that self-sows, comes in many attractive shades: 'Cerise Queen' is cherry red; 'Paprika' is hot pink; 'Red Beauty' is rose red; 'Terra Cotta' starts out peach colored and matures to a rich terra-cotta hue. The fern-leaved yarrow, *A. filipendulina*, which has deeply divided silvery foliage, thrives by the sea and in sandy places.

Long known for its leaves' medicinal qualities, yarrow is a flower for all seasons and all locations, from the formal perennial border to the casual herb garden. It was so prized for its healing properties, the French called it "herb aux charpentiers," because they made poultices of it to heal the bruised fingers of carpenters. From spring through midsummer, the large, flat-topped flower heads of modern cultivars in strong yellow, gold, off-pink, cerise, and off-white, stand above woolly gray-green foliage, 8 to 36 in. high. The ferny foliage of this ancient herb is strongly scented and makes a great filler. Yarrow is showy naturalized with ornamental grasses in meadow gardens, and a wonderful textural accent in perennial borders. The cut flowers are very long lasting in fresh bouquets. They also dry quickly, preserve excellent color and much of their volume, and are a mainstay of winter arrangements.

Other Name
Milfoil

Bloom Period and Seasonal Color
June through August; yellow, gold, off-pink, cerise, red, rust, salmon, off-white.

Mature Height × Spread
1 to 4 ft. × 2 to 3 ft.

Zones
3 to 7 or 8

Roses *for New England*

The rose was designated the nation's floral emblem in 1987. Gardeners fall in love with the beautiful form and seductive fragrance of varieties like the green-eyed, white, old garden rose 'Madame Hardy', and David Austin's English rose 'Graham Thomas'. Do fall in love, but confine your passion to roses billed as "disease resistant." We count on roses that hold awards from the All-America Rose Selections and the American Rose Society to be disease resistant.

Planting and Pruning

For roses to produce a dazzle of flowers and fragrance, nearly all need eight hours of morning sun, or six hours of afternoon sun. They need a well-drained site, and for most a pH of between 5.5 and 7.0. See Soil Preparation in the Introduction. The key to success is thorough and deep soil preparation—deeply dug planting holes 24 inches wide and 24 inches deep, and humusy, fertile soil. Apply an organic fertilizer three times a year: in late winter or early spring, in early midsummer, and in early fall.

You can plant a container-grown rose in early or late spring, and in summer or fall before Indian summer. If the rootball is encircled by roots, untangle them gently. If they can't be unwound, make four shallow vertical cuts in the wall of roots and slice off the matted roots on the bottom. Half fill the planting hole with improved soil, and pack it down very firmly. Set the rootball into the hole so that it's about 1 inch above ground level. For hybrid roses, position the plant so that the bud union is 2 to 3 inches above ground level. Half fill the remainder of the hole with improved soil, and pack that down firmly. Finish filling the hole with improved soil and pack it down firmly again. Make a saucer around the plant, and water it slowly and deeply. You plant bare-root roses the same way, but soak the roots in water for twelve hours before planting, and drape them over a firm mound in the center of the hole.

'Double Delight'

Deadheading, and harvesting, big-flowered show roses keeps them blooming. When cutting roses for bouquets, leave a five-leaf sprig on each shoot as a base for new flowering shoots. Make all pruning cuts $1/2$ inch above an outside bud eye or sprig. Do not prune roses after the wood has hardened for the winter. Before growth begins in early spring, cut out diseased and damaged canes. Prune roses that bloom on new wood to the desired shape in early spring. Prune roses that bloom on wood from the previous season— some shrub and climbing roses—after they have flowered. Cut the oldest canes of recurrent bloomers back to two or three bud eyes, and remove twiggy ends. As new canes grow, tie them to fencing or trellising. To encourage growth of flowering laterals, cut side branches back to short spurs.

Winter protection for roses is a necessity in Zones 3 and even 4, unless the grower has certified the rose for those zones. Even with that promise, if snow cover fails, your rose will suffer. Roses whose winter hardiness is doubtful in our zone we plant facing south, with the house behind them blocking the north wind. A house creates a microclimate that can be a zone or two warmer than the prevailing

Bush and Climbing Roses in a cottage garden.

climate. Hybrid teas and miniatures are especially likely to require winter protection. Cover the plants with pine boughs or hill soil over the lower stems. Don't mulch with leaves or anything that creates a cozy habitat for field mice (voles): they'll girdle the roses and kill them.

Rose Problems

If you run into the big three problems with *Rosa*—Japanese beetles, blackspot, and powdery mildew— what we have learned may help. One approach with Japanese beetles is to spray plants under attack with rotenone, an OK spray. Another is to apply milky disease spores to the gardens and the lawn. Effective the second year, this natural deterrent kills the larvae. Also, in early morning the beetles are sluggish, and you can knock them into a pot of soapy water. Letting loose native parasitic wasps and flies that go for the beetles, helps. Do not crush the beetles as that releases pheromones that will draw more Japanese beetles to the garden.

For blackspot, which loves hybrid teas, floribundas, and grandifloras, try the spray recommended by Cornell University research: 1 tablespoon of baking soda (sodium bicarbonate) and 1 tablespoon of ultrafine horticultural oil to 1 quart of water. And, remove infected vegetation from the plant and the ground. Spraying with the Cornell University research solution may also minimize powdery mildew. Ask your garden center about new, environmentally safe controls. Concerning deer—well, sprays containing very bitter Bitrex® may keep deer away for a time. The only sure protection is to screen the bushes with chicken wire, which isn't noticeable at a distance.

Climbing Rose
Rosa spp. and hybrids

The roses we call "climbers" put forth long canes that can be trained to cover an arch, an arbor, a trellis, a wall, a fence, or to climb a tree. "Training" means being tied— roses don't climb on their own. The floweriest climbers are ramblers that bear clusters of small blooms on pliant canes that rise annually from the base. Climbers that are tall shrubs with stiff, not pliant, canes bear large flowers singly or in clusters. There are large climbing roses and miniature climbing roses. The large types are usually included as backdrops for rose gardens—trained to an arch, a pergola, or a wall. The miniatures require little space at the base and succeed in containers with winter protection: they are ideal for small patios and porches.

Other Name
Pillar Rose

Bloom Period and Seasonal Color
Bloom period depends on the variety; hues of all colors, except true blue.

Mature Height × Spread
6 to 20 ft. x 3 to 6 ft.

Zones
Varies according to cultivar.

When, Where, and How to Plant
Plant bare-root roses before the last frost. Plant container-grown roses in early to mid-spring, summer, or early fall. Most roses need full sun, but climbers whose branches are in the sun will bloom with their roots in shade. Climbers attach themselves with thorns to trees, but must be trained (tied) to other supports. Plant a rose meant to climb a tree so that prevailing winds blow the branches toward the tree. Leave 12 in. between a climber and a house wall, and provide a trellis for support. The ideal planting soil is well drained, fertile, humusy, with a pH between 5.5 and 7.0. See Soil Preparation in the Introduction. Follow the planting instructions at the beginning of this chapter. Water well. Apply a mulch 3 in. deep beginning 3 in. from the main stem.

Growing Tips
The first year, unless there's a soaking rain, in spring and fall pour a bucketful of water slowly and gently around the roots every two weeks; in summer every week or ten days. Maintain the mulch throughout the summer.

Care
Apply a slow-release organic rose fertilizer in late winter or early spring, again in early midsummer, and again in early fall. Renew the mulch. Every year remove one of the oldest canes, and save two or three of the new canes for next year: five or six heavy canes are all a climbing rose can support.

Companion Planting and Design
A climbing, or pillar, rose can be trained into a 10- to 12-ft. pillar. To cover an arch, a pergola, or a wall, choose a large-flowered climber. Climbing roses trained to grow horizontally along fences tend to flower more abundantly. Climbing roses, and floribundas, are the roses used to create standard or tree forms. To hide a climber's bare legs plant a bushy companion, catmint or lavender for example.

Our Personal Recommendations
For pillar roses with recurrent bloom, we recommend fragrant 'Golden Showers', an AARS winner; blush pink 'New Dawn' and its white version 'White Dawn'. 'Don Juan' is very fragrant. Rosarian Donna Fuss recommends for New England: 'Fourth of July', 'Gertrude Jekyll', 'Heritage', 'Othello', 'Fisherman's Friend', and especially 'Pilgrim'.

Garden Rose

Rosa spp. and hybrids

When, Where, and How to Plant

Plant bare-root roses before the last frost. Plant container-grown roses in early to mid-spring or early fall. Most roses need full sun: when a rose can do well with less, it is usually stated in the grower's description. Leave 12 in. between a rosebush and a house wall because the ground there tends to stay dry even in hard rain. The ideal planting soil is well drained, fertile, humusy, with a pH between 5.5 and 7.0. See Soil Preparation in the Introduction. Follow the planting instructions at the beginning of this chapter. Water well. Mulch 2 to 3 in. deep starting 3 in. from the main stem.

Growing Tips

The first year, unless there's a soaking rain, in spring and fall slowly and gently pour a bucketful of water around the roots every two weeks; in summer every week or ten days. Maintain the mulch throughout the summer.

Care

Apply a slow-release organic rose fertilizer in late winter or early spring, again in early midsummer, and again in August. Renew the mulch. If an English rose sends out an excessively long shoot, cut it back hard any time. As the buds swell in spring, prune English roses back by about a third of their height, and cut polyanthas and floribundas back a third of their size. Remove the oldest flowering canes and leave the plants open in the center, creating a vase-shaped framework.

Companion Planting and Design

English roses are most effective planted in groups of three or more of one variety. The floriferous little polyantha roses grow into dense impenetrable low hedges, so you may need only one or two. The pretty, slightly fragrant, seashell pink 'The Fairy' makes a dense flowery hedge all by itself. A floribunda favorite for edging fences is 'Betty Prior', a vivid pink whose emerald foliage stays fresh all summer.

Our Personal Recommendations

Among our favorite David Austin English roses are the pink 'Cottage Rose' and pristine white 'Fair Bianca'. Rosarian Donna Fuss recommends for New England: 'Scentimental', 'Travemunde', 'Sunsprite', 'Iceberg', 'Blueberry Hill'.

The English roses, the polyanthas, and the floribundas (meaning many-flowered) are cluster-flowering garden roses whose beauty rivals hybrid teas. Modern, disease-resistant plants, they produce blooms almost all season long and many of them are fragrant. The many-petaled David Austin English roses bear 2$\frac{1}{2}$- to 5-in. blooms that recall the full, fragrant roses our grandparents used to grow, but the shrubs are compact and easily managed. The polyanthas are 2 to 3 ft. tall, and bear clusters of charming little seashell-like flowers under 2 in. across. The floribundas are 4 or 5 ft. tall with 2- to 5-in. blooms that, like the polyanthas, are borne in clusters. Some have blooms in the same form as the hybrid tea rose. In Europe, they landscape many roadsides and parks.

Other Names

English, Polyantha, and Floribunda are classed as Garden Roses.

Bloom Period and Seasonal Color

Recurrent all-season bloom; hues of all colors, except true blue.

Mature Height × Spread

English Rose: 3 to 8 ft. x 4 to 5 ft.
Polyantha: 2 to 3 ft. x 2 to 3 ft.
Floribunda: 2 to 5 ft. x 2 to 5 ft.

Zones

Varies according to cultivar.

Ground Cover Rose
Rosa spp. and hybrids

Ground cover roses spread outward rather than upward to carpet slopes, edge shrub borders and gardens of shrub roses, and they are grown as low hedges. Best known are the Meidilands, which reach 2 to 3 ft. in height. They bloom from early summer until fall, have natural resistance to rose blights, and the only maintenance they need is pruning in late winter. The typical flower colors are white, cherry pink, and scarlet, but there is a pearly-white blushed with pink called 'Pearl Sevillana'. Recently introduced, the new "carpeting" roses grow on their own roots. They add coral to the colors available. Just 2 to 2 1/2 ft. tall, they can spread in a season to 4 ft. across.

Other Names
Landscape Rose, Carpet Rose

Bloom Period and Seasonal Color
All season; white and hues of pink, rose, and coral.

Mature Height × Spread
2 to 3 ft. x 3 to 4 ft.

Zones
Varies according to cultivar.

When, Where, and How to Plant
Ground cover roses are generally offered growing in containers. They are best planted in early spring a few weeks before the last frost, but will succeed planted any time in early to mid-spring to early fall. They produce the most blooms in full sun but will bloom in some shade. The ideal planting soil is well drained, fertile, humusy, with a pH between 5.5 and 7.0. See Soil Preparation in the Introduction. Follow the planting instructions at the beginning of this chapter. Water well. Mulch 2 to 3 in. deep starting 3 in. from the main stem.

Growing Tips
The first year, unless there's a soaking rain, in spring and fall slowly and gently pour a bucketful of water around the roots every two weeks; in summer every week or ten days. Maintain the mulch throughout the summer.

Care
Apply a slow-release organic rose fertilizer in late winter or early spring, again in early midsummer, and again in early fall. Renew the mulch. Deadheading isn't necessary. As buds begin swelling in spring, shear the plants back to 1 1/2 to 2 ft. high.

Companion Planting and Design
The modern ground cover roses are just what they are called: excellent ground cover. Some sprawling or trailing miniature roses can also serve as ground cover roses. Some leggy shrub roses, like the bourbons, are trained as ground covers by pegging the sprawling branches to the ground with a forked stick or a bent wire—interesting, but it's a high-maintenance endeavor!

Our Personal Recommendations
The best-known ground cover rose is 'Flower Carpet' whose flowers are lavender-pink, and slightly perfumed. 'Jeepers Creepers' is a white version, and there's a light pink called 'Baby Blanket'. The native Virginia species rose, spring-blooming, rose-magenta *R. virginiana*, which is hardy as far north as our Zone 3, can be used as ground cover for sandy gardens and slopes along the coast. The autumn foliage is brilliant. Rosarian Donna Fuss recommends for New England: 'Scarlet Meidiland', 'White Meidiland', and 'Starry Night'.

When, Where, and How to Plant

Plant bare-root roses before the last frost; set out container-grown plants in early to mid-spring, summer, or early to mid-fall. They need full sun. Leave 12 in. between the bush and a house wall because the ground there tends to stay dry. The ideal planting soil is well drained, fertile, humusy, with a pH between 5.5 and 7.0. See Soil Preparation in the Introduction. Follow the planting instructions at the beginning of this chapter. Water well. Mulch 2 to 3 in. deep starting 3 in. from the main stem.

Growing Tips

The first year, unless there's a soaking rain, in spring and fall slowly and gently pour a bucketful of water around the roots every two weeks; in summer every week or ten days. Maintain the mulch throughout summer.

Care

Apply a slow-release organic rose fertilizer in late winter or early spring, again in early midsummer, and again in early fall. Renew the mulch. As the buds swell in spring, remove diseased and damaged canes. For a rugosa rose, to encourage vigorous new growth, beginning the fourth season in early spring remove all canes that have flowered.

Companion Planting and Design

If space allows, plant several different types of roses for blooms at different times during the season, and colorful rose hips in fall.

Our Personal Recommendations

New England Rosarian Donna Fuss says her favorite old garden roses are 'Salet'; 'Madame Hardy', a fragrant old white rose with a green-button eye, one of the world's most beautiful roses; 'Rose de Rescht'; 'Baronne 'Prévost'; 'Celsiana'; and the ancient 'Rosa Mundi'. Donna loves all the rugosa roses except 'Topaz Jewel'. For brilliant rose hips in fall, we suggest *R. rugosa* 'Alba', 'Rubra', and 'Belle de Provins', which has almost-double pink flowers. The 4-ft. light pink cultivar 'Fru Dagmar Hastrup' can be pruned repeatedly without diminishing much the production of flowers. 'Therese Bugnet' grows to 5 or 6 ft. and bears large, flat, slightly fragrant, deep pink flowers, with some repeat. Almost thornless 'Linda Campbell' grows 5 to 8 ft. and produces large clusters of crimson flowers.

For hedging and impressive specimen planting, we recommend the repeat-blooming hedge and shrub roses, along with the old garden and rugosa roses, and the cluster-bearing polyantha and floribundas described on preceding pages. Many varieties have flowers shaped like hybrid teas. The shrub roses and the old garden ("romantica") roses are robust growers, and bear gorgeous flowers. The romantica roses tend to bloom profusely but only in spring; modern shrub roses may repeat bloom. The modern rugosa, or Japanese roses, hybrids of Rosa rugosa, bear clove-scented single or double flowers in spring with some repeat, followed in fall by colorful foliage and shiny coral-orange rose hips high in vitamin C. Tall, stiff, and spiny, they're effective as hedges and thrive by the sea.

Other Names
Shrub Rose, Old Garden Rose, Rugosa Rose

Bloom Period and Seasonal Color
Profuse bloom in spring, modern hybrids repeat; colors are white, and all hues of pink, rose, and red.

Mature Height × Spread
4 to 8 ft. x 3 to 6 ft.

Zones
Varies according to cultivar.

Hybrid Tea Rose
Rosa hybrids

The hybrid tea roses are long-stemmed cutting flowers, large, high-centered, pointed, and semi- or double-flowered. The best, like the exquisite and enduring yellow-and-rose 'Peace', are perfumed. Most bloom in June, throw a few flowers throughout summer, and bloom well from September until cold. Though the shrubs are leggy, need attention, and many are hardy only to Zone 5, these are the most popular roses. The tea rose form appears in small polyantha roses, large-flowered floribunda roses, miniature roses, and climbing roses. To set the florist's single-stemmed, large-flowered hybrid tea rose apart, its classification has recently been changed to "large-flowered bush rose," but time will pass before most nurseries and catalogs call them anything but hybrid tea roses.

Other Name
Large-Flowered Bush Rose

Bloom Period and Seasonal Color
Spring and sporadically through the season; many colors.

Mature Height × Spread
3 to 6 ft. x 3 to 6 ft.

Zones
Varies according to cultivar.

When, Where, and How to Plant
Plant bare-root roses before the last frost; set out container-grown hybrid teas in early to mid-spring, summer, or before mid-fall. They need full sun. Leave 12 in. between the bush and a house wall because the ground there tends to stay dry. The ideal planting soil is well drained, fertile, humusy, with a pH between 5.5 and 7.0. See Soil Preparation in the Introduction. Follow the planting instructions at the beginning of this chapter. Water well. Mulch 2 to 3 in. deep starting 3 in. from the main stem.

Growing Tips
The first year, unless there's a soaking rain, in spring and fall slowly and gently pour a bucketful of water around the roots every two weeks; in summer every week or ten days. Maintain the mulch throughout the summer.

Care
Apply a slow-release organic rose fertilizer in late winter or early spring, again in early midsummer, and again in early fall. Renew the mulch. As the buds swell in spring, remove diseased and damaged canes, and the oldest flowering canes, leaving an open structure of four to five strong canes 5 or 6 in. long, with the uppermost buds pointing outward. Remove spent flowers, fallen petals and leaves, and suckers as they occur. Cut roses and spent blossoms at a point just above a five-leaf stem. Every seven to ten days, and after heavy rainfalls, apply an all-purpose rose spray that controls insects and diseases. Even if your hybrid tea is hardy in winters in your zone, providing winter mulch might be a good idea.

Companion Planting and Design
Hybrid teas are most often grown in a bed of their own with lavender or leafy annuals disguising their legginess.

Our Personal Recommendations
Some fragrant favorites are: orange 'Tropicana', AARS 1963; 'Miss All-American Beauty', AARS 1968, a rose-pink; 'Fragrant Cloud', a coral-red; 'Double Delight', AARS 1977, whose white flowers are blushed with a red; 'Touch of Class', AARS 1986, a slightly fragrant pink, coral, and cream rose usually raised for show. Rosarian Donna Fuss recommends: 'Dublin', 'Elina', 'Olympiad', 'Queen Elizabeth', 'Electron', and 'Earth Song'.

When, Where, and How to Plant

Miniature roses are usually sold growing in containers. They may be planted any time in early to mid-spring, summer, or early fall. They produce the most blooms in full sun but will bloom in some shade. The ideal planting soil is well drained, fertile, humusy, with a pH between 6.5 and 7.0. Space the plants 2 ft. apart. See Soil Preparation in the Introduction. Follow the planting instructions at the beginning of this chapter, but make the holes twice the width of the rootball and 12 to 15 in. deep. Set the roses so they are at ground level. Water well. Mulch 2 to 3 in. deep starting 3 in. from the main stem.

Growing Tips

The first year, unless there's a soaking rain, in spring and fall slowly and gently pour a bucketful of water around the roots every two weeks; in summer every week or ten days. Maintain the mulch throughout the summer.

Care

Apply a slow-release organic rose fertilizer in late winter or early spring, again in early midsummer, and again in August. Renew the mulch. Deadheading isn't necessary. As buds begin swelling in spring, remove dead, weak, and discolored canes and canes that cross. Trim all the branches back by about a third, enough to maintain a pleasing form. Even if your little rose is hardy in winters in your zone, providing winter mulch may be a good idea.

Companion Planting and Design

We like miniature roses as edging for beds of leggy shrub roses. Those sold as climbers make beautiful tree-form roses, and are lovely dripping from containers. Some of the very dense miniature roses make delightful edgers for paths and driveways. Holly has luck growing them indoors on a sunny kitchen windowsill.

Our Personal Recommendations

Rosarian Donna Fuss recommends: 'Jean Kenneally', 'Jeanne Lajoie', 'Magic Carrousel', 'Cachet', 'Raindrops', 'Black Jade', and 'Ruby Pendant'. For fragrance we recommend yellow 'Rise 'n Shine', a recipient of the American Rose Society Award for Excellence. For hanging baskets we like 'Red Cascade', a miniature, and 'Starina', a fragrant, orange-red that holds an ARS Award for Excellence.

The miniature roses are offspring of 'Roulettii', a selection of the China rose 'Minima', the fairy rose, which blooms all season. Those sold as climbers can also be trained as tree-form, basket, and container plants. The minis flower modestly from June to frost, and bear flowers less than 1³/4 in. in diameter, often shaped like hybrid teas or cabbage roses. Too small to be effective as specimen plants, they're delightful as edging plants and in rock gardens and containers. Miniature roses will bloom for a time indoors on very sunny windowsills. They also flourish in containers set in the sun on a patio or porch, but to be safe for the winter they need to be in a spot protected from the wind.

Bloom Period and Seasonal Color
Spring, and repeat bloom; white, and all hues of yellow and pink through red.

Mature Height × Spread
1 to 1¹/2 ft. x 1¹/2 to 2 ft.

Zones
Varies according to cultivar.

Shrubs *for New England*

Shrubs wed the other elements of the landscape to the buildings and the trees. Given a minimum of maintenance they provide flowers, foliage, fragrance, fruits, and interesting structures—pyramidal, columnar, arching, rounded, upright, or sprawling.

The leaf-losing flowering shrubs bring color to the garden early in the year. Forsythia turns to gold in March and the beautiful quinces follow. The spicily fragrant viburnums bloom later. In mid-spring, mature mock oranges perfume our gardens and the roses described in the Roses chapter come out full force. Summer has its stars, among them shore-loving hydrangeas, and butterfly bush—a prime attraction for those beautiful insects. Daphne fills summer afternoons with perfume. The foliage of some deciduous flowering plants also contributes to the beauty of the garden. When shrub borders are a mass of dark green in summer, the colorful foliage of variegated daphne lightens the overall effect. In cold weather spirea and the silver-backed leaves of willowleaf cotoneaster, *Cotoneaster salicifolius* 'Autumn Fire', take on a purplish cast that blends beautifully with autumn's russet tones. The structure of the deciduous shrubs is an important winter asset, especially very twiggy plants like the barberries.

A few broadleaved evergreens flourish here, and we recommend them highly because they not only add color, they green the garden at other seasons. Evergreen rhododendrons and mountain laurels bloom in spring. Boxwood can be sheared for centuries, literally, so it's ideal for topiary accents, low hedges, and to edge formal beds. The needled evergreen shrubs we find most beautiful and valuable are included in the Conifers chapter.

Oakleaf Hydrangea

When, Where, and How to Plant

When we are choosing shrubs, our first concern is whether the places we have in mind will suit them as they mature. To develop well a shrub needs air and space. Small young shrubs may look cozy in a deep, airless corner, but they become cramped as they mature, and can fall prey to certain insects and diseases under the stressful conditions. Light isn't usually a problem. Many are "understory" plants that developed in partial shade of taller trees, so they thrive in partial sun.

Early spring and fall before Indian summer are the best planting seasons; early spring is best for shrubs that don't transplant easily. Container-grown plants can be set out any time, spring, summer, or fall. Mail order suppliers deliver some shrubs bare root and in time for spring planting—the roots need to be soaked six to twelve hours before planting. Young shrubs tend to be more vigorous than bigger, older plants that may have been in their containers for some time. Before buying a bargain plant, make sure the rootball has a healthy, earthy smell and is vigorous looking, not irretrievably locked in wound-around roots. When the color of a shrub's blossoms or its foliage is important to you, buy a plant whose flower or leaf color is evident.

A generous planting hole is the best send-off you can give a plant. Make the hole three times as wide and twice as deep as the rootball and plant the shrub so the crown will be an inch above the ground level. Loosen the soil on the sides, and blend the soil taken from the hole with the organic amendments described in Soil Preparation and Improvement in the Introduction. Never replace existing soil with potting soil. Half fill the bottom of the hole with the improved soil, and tamp it down to make a firm base for the shrub to rest on. Then proceed with the planting.

Before placing a bare-root shrub in its planting hole, make a firm mound in the center of the hole. Drape the plant roots over and around the mound and proceed with the instructions for planting a container-grown shrub. To free a containerized shrub, tip the container on its side and roll it around until the rootball loosens, or slit the pot open. If roots wrap a rootball, before planting make four deep vertical cuts in the sides and slice the matted roots off the bottom 1 to 2 inches. Set the shrub in the hole and half fill with amended soil. Tamp it down firmly. Fill the hole with improved soil and once more tamp it down firmly. Shape the soil around the crown into a wide saucer. Water the soil slowly, gently, and thoroughly with a sprinkler, a soaker hose, a bubbler, or by hand. You need to put down $1^1/2$ inches of water measured in a regular sized coffee can, or 10 to 15 gallons of water poured slowly from a bucket. Mulch newly planted shrubs 2 to 3 (for bigger shrubs) inches deep starting 3 inches from the main stem. Replenish the mulch as needed to maintain it 2 to 3 inches deep.

Care

For a shrub's first season, unless there's a soaking rain, in spring and fall slowly and gently pour two to three bucketsful of water around the roots every two weeks; in summer every week or ten days. Even after summer heat is gone, and cold sets in, during fall droughts continue the watering program sufficiently to keep the soil from drying out. Once established, most shrubs will require less extra watering than perennials; they slow their growth in high heat so they adapt unless forced by shallow watering and inappropriate fertilizing to grow when the weather isn't supporting growth. Fertilize shrubs twice a year. Early spring is the time to apply the slow-release organic fertilizers we recommend (see the Appendix); repeat in early fall. Avoid fertilizing flowering shrubs with chemical fertilizers shortly before blooming: that stimulates growth at a time when you want the plants to direct their energy into flowering. After early spring fertilization, renew the mulch. Nourish the soil as the forest does with fall's harvest of leaves—gather, shred, allow to age, and return them to the garden in the form of leaf mold or compost.

Pruning

You can reduce the amount of pruning your shrubs will need by selecting dwarf and slow-growing varieties. But even dwarfs grow, albeit slowly, and they need some pruning to maintain their size. Pruning—reducing leaf surfaces—limits the sugar synthesized and sent to the roots, and that limits next year's growth. Pruning also stimulates growth. Pruning young, just-developing shrubs when they are growing actively encourages growth and makes growth bushier. Fresh, young shoots that are cut back by half immediately begin to grow lateral shoots.

Japanese Kerria

The season to prune flowering shrubs depends on their bloom habit: in late winter or early spring, well before growth begins, it is time to prune shrubs that bloom on the current season's wood. Prune a shrub that blooms in summer on current growth—butterfly bush for example—shortly before growth begins in spring. Those that bloom on last season's wood—such as azaleas, flowering quince, and forsythia—should be pruned as soon after their flowering period as possible, because the next thing they do is initiate buds for the following season. To stop a plant at its current height, prune after it has completed its growth for the season. To encourage branching that produces more foliage in broadleaf evergreens, cut succulent new shoots in half while they are actively growing.

Make the cut 6 to 10 inches from the ground. To rejuvenate a multi-stemmed shrub, before growth begins in spring, take out a third to a quarter of the oldest of the branches and the suckers crowding young branches. Repeat the process for the next three to four yeears.

162

Witch-Hazel in fall color.

More Options

Other beautiful shrubs that flourish here include:

Amur Privet, *Ligustrum amurense*
    (Zones 4 to 9)

Golden Privet, *L.* × *vicaryi* (Zones 4 to 9)

California Privet, *L. ovalifolium*
    (Zones 5 to 8)

Bayberry, *Myrica pensylvanica*

Bush Cinquefoil, *Potentilla fruticosa*
    'Abbottswood'

Harry Lauder's Walking Stick, *Corylus avellana*
    'Contorta' (Zones 4 to 8)

Highbush Blueberry, *Vaccinium corymbosum*

Inkberry Holly, *Ilex glabra* (Zones 4 to 9)

Winterberry, *I. verticillata* 'Red Sprite',
    male pollinator 'Jim Dandy'

Merserve Holly, *I.* × *merserveae* 'Blue Boy' and
    'Blue Girl' (Zones 4 to 8)

Korean Stewartia, *Stewartia koreana*
    (Zones 5 to 8)

Oregon Grape Holly, *Mahonia aquifolium*
    (Zones 5 to 8)

Red Twig Dogwood, *Cornus sericea*

Slender Deutzia, *Deutzia gracilis*
    (Zones 4 to 8)

Scotch Broom, *Cytisus scoparius* (Zones 5 to 9),
    'Moonlight'

Warminster Broom, *C.* × *praecox*
    (Zones 5/6 to 8)

Spicebush, *Lindera benzoin* (Zones 4 to 8)

Weigela, *Weigela florida* 'Variegata'
    (Zones 4 to 8)

Witch-Hazel, *Hamamelis* × *intermedia*

Blue Spirea
Caryopteris × clandonensis 'Blue Mist'

Blue spirea 'Blue Mist' is a small, easy deciduous shrub or sub-shrub that in summer bears spikes of airy flowers in delightful shades of blue. The blue spireas produce long arching branches covered with silvery foliage and the leaves, stems, and flowers are delicately aromatic. 'Blue Mist' grows quickly to 2 ft., and develops an open, airy, twiggy shape very appealing in flowering borders, and attractive edging walks and paths. The fringed blue flowers bloom on new wood at or after midsummer when most other flowering shrubs have gone out of bloom, and they attract hordes of butterflies. Both foliage and flowers are used in bouquets, fresh and dried. Even with winterkill in dry, cold winters, 'Blue Mist', and other blue spirea cultivars, are wonderful shrubs. Deer aren't interested.

Other Names
Blue-Mist Shrub, Bluebeard

Bloom Period and Seasonal Color
Midsummer; shades of blue.

Mature Height × Spread
2 to 3 ft. × 3 to 4 ft.

Zones
5 to 9

When, Where, and How to Plant
Container-grown blue spirea transplants easily in early spring or in early fall. The flowering will be most satisfactory in full sun but it also will do well in some shade. Almost any soil will do as long as it is well drained, loose, or loamy, with enough humus to maintain moisture. See Soil Preparation in the Introduction, and the planting instructions at the beginning of this chapter. Provide a planting hole three times the width of the rootball and twice as deep. Set the shrub so the crown will be an inch or two above ground level. Shape the soil around the crown into a wide saucer. Water slowly and deeply. Apply mulch 3 in. deep starting 3 in. from the crown.

Growing Tips
The first year, unless there's a soaking rain, in spring and fall slowly and gently pour two to three bucketsful of water around the roots every two weeks; in summer every week or ten days. Maintain the mulch.

Care
Using a slow-release organic fertilizer, fertilize lightly in fall and again in early spring. Replenish the mulch. Blue spirea blooms on new wood: to improve flowering, in spring, just as the buds are breaking, prune back to within an inch of the living wood all the growth that starts from the short woody branches at the base of the plant. Severe pruning in early spring vastly improves the flowering.

Companion Planting and Design
Include blue spirea in your butterfly plantings. Its summer blooming habit and wonderful blues make it an excellent addition to flowering borders.

Our Personal Recommendations
We recommend 'Blue Mist', but 'Dark Knight' is also very appealing. It is a 3-ft. shrub with a spread of 3 to 4 ft., which bears very fragrant dark purple-blue flowers that attract butterflies and hummingbirds. 'Worcester Gold' has blue flowers and bright yellow to chartreuse foliage. 'First Choice' is a small shrub, 2 ft. tall by 2 to 2 1/2 ft. wide, which bears cobalt blue flowers from midsummer till fall.

Boxwood
Buxus spp. and cultivars

When, Where, and How to Plant

Plant a container-grown boxwood in spring, summer, or fall. Transplant established boxwood just before growth begins in spring, but first treat it with an anti-dessicant (wilt-proofing) spray that will help the foliage retain its moisture. Established plants thrive in full sun or light shade and tolerate some drought. Boxwood doesn't tolerate salt or wet feet. It needs well-drained, humusy, loose soil, pH 6.0 to 7.0. See Soil Preparation in the Introduction, and planting instructions at the beginning of this chapter. Provide a hole three times the width of the rootball and twice as deep. Set the shrub so the crown will be an inch or two above ground level. Shape the soil around the crown into a wide saucer. Water slowly and deeply. Apply mulch 3 in. deep starting 3 in. from the crown.

Growing Tips

The first season, unless there's a soaking rain, in spring and fall slowly and gently pour two to three bucketsful of water around the roots every two weeks; in summer every week or ten days. Maintain the mulch to keep the temperature even around the roots.

Care

Using a slow-release organic fertilizer, fertilize lightly in early fall and again in spring. Protect for winter with a burlap screen. Replenish the mulch as needed. Weed by hand. Prune elongated shoots in late spring after new growth is complete to keep boxwood bushy. To reshape overgrown shrubs, in early spring cut the plants back to within 18 in. of the ground.

Companion Planting and Design

Boxwood is used as a foundation plant, as a topiary specimen, in hedges, and to edge rose beds and knot gardens. A group of tiny, clipped boxwood globes makes a charming accent in a flowering border.

Our Personal Recommendations

For a formal edging, use dwarf box *B. sempervirens* 'Suffruticosa' (Zone 6), a slow-growing shrub. Where winters are hard, Korean littleleaf box, *B. microphylla* var. *koreana* is best. Our consultant Judith Irven recommends 'Green Mountain', 'Green Velvet', and 'Verdant Hills' for Vermont: they must be planted in a sheltered spot.

Historically, boxwood was used as a tailored edging for flower beds, knot gardens, and for hedges. It has dainty evergreen leaves, grows slowly, is long lived, and can be clipped and pruned forever to almost any shape. Clippings are used to make Christmas roping and Christmas tree topiaries. English boxwood, Buxus sempervirens, is the species used in the clipped hedges that defined gardens on the great estates and palace grounds in England, France, Renaissance Italy—all of Europe. The trim hedges outlining the parterres at the Palace of Versailles are clipped box. In our climate to maintain the beauty of English boxwood, which is hardy only to Zone 5 or 6, you must provide real protection in winter. For Zones 4 and 5, a better choice is littleleaf boxwood, B. microphylla, whose natural height is 4 to 6 ft., with an equal spread. It's not as refined, but somewhat hardier. Deer avoid boxwood: chewing the leaves has caused the death of animals.

Other Name
Box

Bloom Period and Seasonal Color
Spring blooms are insignificant.

Mature Height × Spread
4 to 10 ft. × 4 to 10 ft.

Zones
4 to 8

Butterfly Bush
Buddleja davidii

Butterflies and hummingbirds—and bees—really do love this shrub, but that's not the only reason we recommend butterfly bush. The flowers are a rich source of nectar. The species grows to between 6 and 8 ft. in a single season, and from late summer until frost the slim arching canes sweeping the ground are tipped with beautiful 4- to 10-in. spikes of delicately scented florets. The leaves range from green to gray-green to gray, and are narrow, 4 to 10 in. long, and silvery on the underside. Many beautiful cultivated varieties are available in a wide range of colors. Where winters are too cold for butterfly bush, many gardeners set out a container plant and grow it as an annual.

Other Name
Summer Lilac

Bloom Period and Seasonal Color
August through September; species flowers are lilac; cultivars are white, pink, lavender, dark purple, purple-red.

Mature Height × Spread
5 to 8 ft. × 4 to 7 ft.

Zones
5 to 9

When, Where, and How to Plant
Container-grown butterfly bush transplants easily in early spring or in early fall. It flowers best in full sun and thrives in humusy, fertile, well-drained soil with a pH of 5.5 to 7.0. See Soil Preparation in the Introduction, and the planting instructions at the beginning of this chapter. Provide a planting hole three times the width of the rootball and twice as deep. Set the shrub so the crown will be an inch or two above ground level. Shape the soil around the crown into a wide saucer. Water slowly and deeply. Apply mulch 3 in. deep starting 3 in. from the crown.

Growing Tips
The first year, unless there's a soaking rain, in spring and fall slowly and gently pour two to three bucketsful of water around the roots every two weeks; in summer every week or ten days. Maintain the mulch.

Care
Using a slow-release organic fertilizer, fertilize lightly in fall and again in early spring. Where *Buddleja* doesn't make it through New England winters, butterfly lovers set out large container-grown plants and treat them as annuals. After the winter fertilization, replenish the mulch. Prune last year's growth to 12 to 18 in. in early spring while the plant is still dormant. *Buddleja* blooms on new wood; it is slow to develop in spring, so be patient.

Companion Planting and Design
For a small garden, dwarf butterfly bush is the better choice. *B. davidii* var. *nanhoensis* 'Mongo', 'Petite Indigo', and 'Petite Plum' are 4-ft. dwarf forms with attractive grayish foliage; they are small enough to plant next to the kitchen steps. For a large garden, or for the back of a flowering border, consider *B. alternifolia*, a graceful 20-ft. butterfly bush with long, pendulous branches and flower spikes that are neat clusters of lilac-purple florets. It blooms early, in June.

Our Personal Recommendations
The species offers a range of colors that are attractive together: 'White Profusion', which bears white trusses 8 to 12 in. long; 'Pink Delight', whose trusses are up to 15 in. and a true pink; and 'Black Knight', which has very dark purple-violet flowers.

Cranberry Cotoneaster

Cotoneaster apiculatus

When, Where, and How to Plant

Set out a container-grown cotoneaster in early spring or early fall. It flowers well in full sun, four to six hours of sun, or all-day filtered light. Cotoneaster doesn't tolerate wet feet, but handles some drought. It succeeds in well-drained, humusy soil, acid or alkaline. See Soil Preparation in the Introduction, and planting instructions at the beginning of this chapter. Provide a planting hole three times the width of the rootball and twice as deep. Set the shrub so the crown will be an inch or two above ground level. Shape the soil around the crown into a wide saucer. Water slowly and deeply. Apply mulch 3 in. deep starting 3 in. from the crown.

Growing Tips

The first year, unless there's a soaking rain, in spring and fall slowly and gently pour two to three bucketsful of water around the roots every two weeks; in summer every week or ten days. Maintain the mulch.

Care

In early spring fertilize with a slow-release organic fertilizer. Replenish the mulch. Fertilize again in the fall. Minimal pruning is needed, and it's best undertaken after the berries are over. If the plant is growing against a wall, retain a few widely separated main branches and allow these to develop side branchlets. Keep an informal hedge in bounds by light selective pruning during the growing season. A formal hedge may be lightly sheared as needed.

Companion Planting and Design

Use cotoneaster for hedges, to clothe slopes, steps, and rocky places with attractive foliage, interesting branching, and bright berries.

Our Personal Recommendations

In addition to cranberry cotoneaster, for Zone 6 we recommend creeping cotoneaster, *C. adpressus*, a very compact dwarf form for ground cover; bearberry cotoneaster, *C. dammeri*, a low, prostrate evergreen ground cover; and spreading upright cotoneaster, *C. divaricatus* (Zone 5), a pink-flowered shrub, 6 to 7 ft. tall, which has smaller red berries and foliage that colors reddish purple in fall.

The cotoneasters are fine-textured, evergreen or semi-evergreen shrubs with layered branches and small white or pinkish flowers in the spring and summer. There are both tall and very low-growing members of the clan. Cotoneaster is a wide-spreading, semi-evergreen tiered mound of branches that creates an attractive herringbone pattern. The big show occurs in the fall with a display of vibrantly colored bright red or orange-red berries. The light pink flowers are followed in late summer by masses of persistent red fruits, most spectacular of all in the popular cranberry cotoneaster, Cotoneaster apiculatus, which bears large, bright red berries. The leaves are a shiny dark green color in the summer and usually turn scarlet-orange in the fall. Cotoneasters are good shore plants, and the fruits attract birds. Deer don't seem to care for them. Mid-size rockspray cotoneaster, C. horizontalis, is the most commonly planted species.

Other Name
Rockspray Cotoneaster

Bloom Period and Seasonal Color
Spring and summer; white or pinkish flowers; bright red berries; colorful fall foliage.

Mature Height × Spread
2 to 3 ft. × 5 to 8 ft.

Zones
4 to 8

Daphne 'Carol Mackie'
Daphne × burkwoodii 'Carol Mackie'

The daphnes are deciduous, semi-evergreen, or evergreen shrubs, low, wide, slow growing, and they bear fragrant flowers followed by brightly colored fleshy fruits. They are native to Europe, Asia, and northern Africa. The hardiest daphne is Daphne × burkwoodii and one of its loveliest and most cold hardy varieties is 'Carol Mackie'. 'Carol Mackie' is a very beautiful bushy shrub about 3 to 4 ft. tall by 3 ft. and a little more wide, whose narrow leaves are delicately edged with a band of cream or pale gold—and are evergreen or semi-evergreen in warm climates. In late spring, it opens masses of star-shaped, light pink flowers that are extremely fragrant. These are superb garden plants, with a dense, round, mounded form that works particularly well in a small garden. They are not easy to get established, but well worth the effort. And the deer mostly don't eat them.

Bloom Period and Seasonal Color
May; pale pink flowers; foliage is variegated cream or pale gold.

Mature Height × Spread
3 ft. × 3 ft. or more

Zones
4 to 8

When, Where, and How to Plant
Plant a container-grown daphne in early spring, and handle with care until new growth is evident. Choose a site with some protection from hot noon sun, and cold north winds. By the shore it may be able to take full sun. Daphne will do best in well-drained, sandy loam, with lots of leaf mold added, in the pH range between 6.0 and 7.0. See Soil Preparation in the Introduction, and the planting instructions at the beginning of this chapter. Provide a planting hole three times the width of the rootball and twice as deep. Set the shrub so the crown will be an inch or two above ground level. Shape the soil around the crown into a wide saucer. Water slowly and deeply. Apply mulch 3 in. deep starting 3 in. from the crown.

Growing Tips
The first year, unless there's a soaking rain, in spring and fall slowly and gently pour two to three bucketsful of water around the roots every two weeks; in summer every week or ten days. Maintain the mulch.

Care
Where snow cover is uncertain, protect for the winter with a cover of evergreen boughs. Using a slow-release organic fertilizer, fertilize lightly in fall and again in early spring. Replenish the mulch. To maintain daphne's shape, when it finishes blooming and before July, prune the branches back to outward-facing buds. This will also stimulate growth, and encourage the formation of flowering buds for the next season.

Companion Planting and Design
Plant daphne by garden paths and anywhere its fragrance can be appreciated.

Our Personal Recommendations
Daphne 'Carol Mackie' is a superb plant, but there are others we can recommend: D. × burkwoodii 'Somerset' (Zone 4) is a shrub 3 or 4 ft. tall and 6 ft. wide whose foliage is a shiny green; the daphne known as garland flower, D. cneorum (Zones 4 and 5), has tiny, dainty, dense foliage and is less than a foot high.

Deciduous Azalea
Rhododendron spp. and hybrids

When, Where, and How to Plant
Azaleas are shallow-rooted and transplant well even when quite large. Plant a balled-and-burlapped azalea in early spring or early fall; plant a container-grown azalea in spring, summer, or fall. Azaleas do best in bright dappled light, but they tolerate full sun if the soil is moist. Provide soil that is well drained, rich in humus, and between pH 4.5 and 6.0. See Soil Preparation in the Introduction, and the planting instructions at the beginning of this chapter. Provide a planting hole three times the width of the rootball and twice as deep. Set the shrub so the crown will be an inch or two above ground level. Shape the soil around the crown into a wide saucer. Water slowly and deeply. Apply mulch 3 in. deep starting 3 in. from the crown.

Growing Tips
The first season, unless there's a soaking rain, every two weeks in spring and fall slowly and gently pour two to three bucketsful of water around the roots; in summer every week or ten days. Maintain the mulch.

Care
Using a slow-release organic fertilizer for acid-loving plants, fertilize an azalea in early spring, and in the fall. Replenish the mulch. To keep an azalea shapely, stimulate growth, and encourage the formation of flowering buds, after blooming prune the branches back to outward-facing buds.

Companion Planting and Design
We like deciduous azaleas with broadleaved evergreen shrubs, such as rhododendrons and mountain laurels. They are especially nice with early blooming forsythia.

Our Personal Recommendations
In Zones 4 and 5, where summers and winters are cool, the Ghent and Mollis, as well as the Exbury strains do well. The Robin Hill azaleas are hardy to -20 degrees Fahrenheit. Low growing, wide 'Robin Hill Gillie' has 4- to 5-in. rosy salmon blooms and stays under 30 in., with a 40 in. spread. The University of Minnesota's Northern Lights series, including lovely 6-foot 'White Lights', are hardy in Zone 3, and can withstand cold up to -35 degrees.

Azaleas provide us with early color for semi-shaded places. A botanically distinct member of the Rhododendron genus, there are two kinds: evergreen and deciduous (leaf-losing). The evergreen azaleas don't perform well in most New England climates and the deer love them, so we recommend staying with the deciduous types. There are thousands of azalea hybrids, including some that bloom again in fall. The blooms may be single, semi-double, or double, hose-in-hose, and the colors include white and hues of yellow, pink, orange, purple, and red, and bi-colors. The Exbury hybrids have blooms as big as some rhododendrons, and they are hardy in Zone 5, as far north as warm coastal Maine.

Bloom Period and Seasonal Color
Early spring; pink, rose, rose-magenta, white.

Mature Height × Spread
4 to 8 ft. × 4 to 8 ft.

Zones
4 to 7

Dwarf Burning Bush

Euonymus alatus 'Compactus'

Euonymus is a member of the bittersweet family, a group that includes both leaf-losing and evergreen shrubs, small trees, and vines, which have beautiful foliage and colorful fall fruits. Dwarf burning bush is a slow-growing shrub with outreaching branches, a compact version of the winged spindle tree, Euonymus alatus, *whose flaming fall color rivals the sugar maple. When cold comes, every leaf on the species winged spindle tree, and on the dwarf burning bush, turns a glowing rosy crimson before falling. The show is enhanced by small clusters of tiny fruits that turn lipstick red. The birds love the fruits and usually pick the branches clean. "Winged" in the common name refers to corky ridges edging the branches. The ridges are most pronounced in the larger species, enough to have textural interest. Deer can be a problem.*

Other Name
Dwarf Winged Spindle Tree

Bloom Period and Seasonal Color
Fall foliage is a glowing crimson.

Mature Height × Spread
8 to 10 ft. × 8 to 10 ft.

Zones
3 to 8

When, Where, and How to Plant
Container-grown euonymus can be planted spring, summer, or fall. It succeeds even on dry, rocky slopes. The dwarf burning bush and the winged spindle tree color most brilliantly in full sun, but succeed in shade or part shade. Any soil that isn't swampy will do, pH 6.0 to 8.0. See Soil Preparation in the Introduction, and the planting instructions at the beginning of this chapter. Provide a planting hole three times the width of the rootball and twice as deep. Set the shrub so the crown will be an inch or two above ground level. Shape the soil around the crown into a wide saucer. Water slowly and deeply. Apply mulch 2 in. deep starting 3 in. from the crown.

Growing Tips
The first year, unless there's a soaking rain, in spring and fall slowly and gently pour two to three bucketsful of water around the roots every two weeks; in summer every week or ten days. Maintain the mulch.

Care
Fertilize with a slow-release organic fertilizer in fall and again in early spring. Replenish the mulch periodically. Burning bush is most attractive when it is allowed to develop naturally with some thinning to keep the plant structure open. To keep a hedge of euonymus to 4 to 6 ft., cut back branch tips of older wood in April or May. While all *Euonymus* are subject to scale, there's very little problem with *E. alatus*, either the dwarf or the species.

Companion Planting and Design
Dwarf winged spindle tree is used in informal hedges and as a featured lawn specimen. It is superb planted with evergreens and forsythias.

Our Personal Recommendations
In addition to recommending dwarf burning bush, a cultivar of the European euonymus, *E. europaeus* 'Red Cascade' bears bright red fruit and is hardy to Zone 3. *E. fortunei*, the winter-creeper euonymus planted for its silver-veined foliage, is a beautiful ground cover or vine, but has lots of problems, including deer, which love it.

Dwarf Fothergilla
Fothergilla gardenii

When, Where, and How to Plant
Plant a balled-and-burlapped fothergilla in early spring or early fall. If it's container grown, it can be planted spring, summer, or fall. Fothergilla flowers best and produces the brightest fall colors growing in full sun, but in hot areas it benefits from protection from noon sun in the summer. To succeed, fothergilla must have soil with an acid pH, under 6.0. It is not suited to alkaline or limey soil. See Soil Preparation in the Introduction, and the planting instructions at the beginning of this chapter. Provide a planting hole three times the width of the rootball and twice as deep. Set the shrub so the crown will be an inch or two above ground level. Shape the soil around the crown into a wide saucer. Water slowly and deeply. Apply mulch 2 in. deep starting 3 in. from the crown.

Growing Tips
The first year, unless there's a soaking rain, in spring and fall slowly and gently pour two to three bucketsful of water around the roots every two weeks; in summer every week or ten days. Maintain the mulch.

Care
Using a slow-release organic fertilizer for acid-loving plants, fertilize lightly in fall and again in early spring. Replenish the mulch. Before growth begins in spring, cut back to the ground old branches that are crowding others, taking care not to harm young shoots coming up from the base.

Companion Planting and Design
Fothergilla lights up small gardens, and is a huge asset in shrub borders planted with azaleas, rhododendrons, and evergreens. We like to place them near the house and along paths where the sweet honey scent of the flowers can be appreciated.

Our Personal Recommendations
The dwarf fothergilla is the best choice for small gardens, but where there's space for a larger plant, choose faster-growing *F. major* (Zone 4), the large fothergilla: it is similar to the dwarf but grows more upright and matures at 6 to 10 ft.

Fothergilla is native to the Allegheny Mountains and is rated as one of the top ten to twenty native American shrubs. Like witch-hazel, to which it is related, fothergilla blooms early, has fragrant blossoms, and the foliage colors brilliantly in fall. Dwarf fothergilla is a small bushy shrub, just as wide as it is high. In spring it bears rounded tufts of whitish bottlebrush flowers that have the sweet scent of honey. The flowers and the crinkly dark green foliage are reason enough to plant fothergilla, but the brilliant fall foliage is the star attraction. The leaves turn to yellow gold, orange, and scarlet, and usually with all three colors on the same bush.

Other Name
Dwarf Witch Alder

Bloom Period and Seasonal Color
Spring; white flowers in spring; fall foliage is yellow gold, orange, and scarlet.

Mature Height × Spread
2 to 4 ft. × 2 to 4 ft.

Zones
5 to 8

Firethorn

Pyracantha coccinea

Firethorn is a large, sprawling, beautiful broadleaved evergreen that is seriously thorny. The asymmetrical branches tend to spread vertically or horizontally, depending on the variety. The refined foliage is dark green and in fall and winter makes a dramatic background for clusters of brilliant orange or scarlet fruits. The flowers are modest, white, lightly scented, and bloom in mid-spring. The species grows to 10 ft. tall and is used most often as a vertical accent or draped over a stone wall. The species is susceptible to scale, but in recent years several improved varieties have been introduced. When you buy Pyracantha, insist on having a scale- and fireblight-resistant specimen.

Other Name
Scarlet Firethorn

Bloom Period and Seasonal Color
Late spring; white, somewhat scented flowers; bright, persistent, orange or red berries in the fall.

Mature Height × Spread
6 to 10 ft. × 8 to 10 ft.

Zones
5 to 9

When, Where, and How to Plant
Firethorn transplants with difficulty, so plant a container-grown shrub in early spring before growth begins. Firethorn flowers best and produces the brightest fruits growing in full sun. It thrives in any well-drained soil in a broad pH range, 5.5 to 7.5. See Soil Preparation in the Introduction, and planting instructions at the beginning of this chapter. Provide a planting hole three times the width of the rootball and twice as deep. Set the shrub so the crown will be an inch or so above ground level. Shape the soil around the crown into a wide saucer. Water slowly and deeply. Apply mulch 3 in. deep starting 3 in. from the crown.

Growing Tips
The first year, unless there's a soaking rain, in spring and fall slowly and gently pour two to three bucketsful of water around the roots every two weeks; in summer every week or ten days. Maintain the mulch.

Care
Using a slow-release organic fertilizer, fertilize lightly in the fall and again in early spring. Replenish the mulch. Firethorn becomes very wide spreading if left unpruned. If you wish to maintain the shape of this spring flowering shrub, shortly after it finishes blooming, prune the branches back to a pair of outward facing buds. Flower buds—and the fruit—form on old wood; as you prune, keep in mind that the flowers you don't prune off will provide you with a lovely show of berries in the fall.

Companion Planting and Design
Firethorn can be used as a freestanding specimen, and as a thorny protective hedge, but it is most striking espaliered against a blank masonry or wooden wall, or grown on a trellis where the asymmetrical branching and bright fall fruits stand out.

Our Personal Recommendations
Some recommended as scale resistant are orange-berried 'Rutgers', a 2- to 3-ft. hybrid that spreads widely; 'Mohave', an upright shrub 8 to 10 ft. tall that is hardy to 0 or -5 degrees Fahrenheit; and 'Fiery Cascade,' hardy to -10 degree Fahrenheit. *P. angustifolia* and its cultivar, orange-berried 'Monon', tolerate winters in Zone 4.

Flowering Quince
Chaenomeles speciosa

When, Where, and How to Plant
Plant a balled-and-burlapped quince in early spring or fall. Plant a container-grown quince spring, summer, or fall. Quince does best growing in full sun but succeeds with four to six hours of sun, or all-day filtered light. It thrives with pH 5.5, but can succeed in a broad range of soil types and pH as high as 7.5. See Soil Preparation in the Introduction, and the planting instructions at the beginning of this chapter. Provide a planting hole three times the width of the rootball and twice as deep. Set the shrub so the crown will be an inch or two above ground level. Shape the soil around the crown into a wide saucer. Water slowly and deeply. Apply mulch 3 in. deep starting 3 in. from the crown.

Growing Tips
The first year, unless there's a soaking rain, in spring and fall slowly and gently pour two to three bucketsful of water around the roots every two weeks; in summer every week or ten days. Maintain the mulch.

Care
Using a slow-release organic fertilizer for acid-loving plants, fertilize lightly in fall and again in early spring. Replenish the mulch. Quince flowers on wood grown the previous season and on a system of spurs. To keep the center open, when the blossoms fade, cut back older canes and suckers to the ground. As new wood hardens in summer, remove branches that cross or are badly positioned, and thin out older woody spurs. After the leaves fall, take the main branches back to two or three buds.

Companion Planting and Design
Flowering quince is attractive in an informal hedge. In spite of its beauty, flowering quince adds to the appeal of the garden only when in bloom, so in a small landscape it shouldn't be given space that could go to a plant with appeal in three or four seasons.

Our Personal Recommendations
There are innumerable named varieties. 'Texas Scarlet', and 'Toyo Nishiki' are popular for cutting and forcing. The single flowered forms have a kind of purity common to all singles and we prefer them to the doubles—although not everyone will agree.

Flowering quince in bloom is one of spring's most beautiful shrubs. The blossoms appear to sprout from the bark, like apple blossoms, and are perfectly arranged on the branches. There are exquisite single or double flowering forms that come in white and many beautiful coral and rose-red shades. The shrub is broad spreading, and produces a twiggy mass of rather thorny branches, quite extraordinary trained as an espalier or a pruned hedge. The branches are easy to force into early bloom and are remarkably lovely. The new foliage is red-rose-bronze that changes to glossy green leaves. This is not the quince grown for making preserves, though it also bears fruit— waxy, yellowish, 2-in. fruits that are fragrant. The quince grown for its fruit is common quince, Cydonia oblonga, a large shrub or small tree.

Other Name
Chinese Flowering Quince

Bloom Period and Seasonal Color
Early spring; flowers may be white, peach, pink, coral, rose, orange, red, ruby red.

Mature Height × Spread
6 to 10 ft. × 6 to 10 ft.

Zones
4 to 8

Forsythia
Forsythia × intermedia

Forsythia is the herald of spring everywhere. It pops a few golden blooms before the plum trees have even budded. The flower buds open before the leaves appear, covering the wide-spreading branches with small, showy, vivid yellow flowers. The small blooms last well, as long as there isn't a heat spell. When the cold comes in autumn, the leaves take on an orangey-plum hue before they fall. This is a fast-growing, arching shrub that roots where it touches the ground. It develops dense thickets unless it is pruned annually, and is used as a tall ground cover for slopes. Branches pruned in late winter as the buds swell are easily forced into bloom indoors. It can stand a lot of shearing, and can be espaliered. Most forsythias will grow but not bloom reliably north of Zone 5. 'Meadowlark' is considered hardier than others, worth a try in Zone 3. Snow cover makes a difference.

Other Name
Border Forsythia

Bloom Period and Seasonal Color
March and April; pale to deep yellow flowers.

Mature Height × Spread
8 to 10 ft. × 10 to 12 ft.

Zones
4 or 5 to 8

When, Where, and How to Plant
Container-grown forsythia transplants easily spring, summer, and fall; balled-and-burlapped shrubs, and rooted plantlets, transplant best in very early spring or in fall after the leaves drop. Forsythia flowers best in full sun but blooms in part shade. It thrives in almost any soil that is well drained, loamy, and has enough humus to maintain moisture, with a pH range of 6.0 to 8.0. See Soil Preparation in the Introduction, and the planting instructions at the beginning of this chapter. Provide a planting hole three times the width of the rootball and twice as deep. Set the shrub so the crown will be an inch or two above ground level. Shape the soil around the crown into a wide saucer. Water slowly and deeply. Apply mulch 3 in. deep starting 3 in. from the crown.

Growing Tips
The first year, unless there's a soaking rain, in spring and fall slowly and gently pour two to three bucketsful of water around the roots every two weeks; in summer every week or ten days. Maintain the mulch.

Care
Using a slow-release organic fertilizer, fertilize lightly in fall and again in early spring. Replenish the mulch from time to time. To keep forsythia in bounds, when it finishes blooming, prune mature branches back to buds that face outward and take out the oldest canes all the way down to the ground. Branches that touch the ground will root over time and can be transplanted.

Companion Planting and Design
Fast-growing forsythia is used for screening, in informal hedges, and as a tall ground cover. It is attractive featured as a specimen in the middle of a large lawn, or in a group with evergreens and other flowering shrubs. 'Arnold Dwarf' is used as a bank holder.

Our Personal Recommendations
'Meadowlark' is the hardiest. 'Spring Glory' is an upright rounded shrub that bears sulfur yellow flowers excellent for cutting and forcing. 'Primulina' has pale yellow flowers and golden fall foliage that turns to mahogany: it's an old time favorite.

Glossy Abelia
Abelia × *grandiflora*

When, Where, and How to Plant
The time to plant a container-grown abelia is in the fall before Indian summer, and in early spring while the shrub is still dormant. Abelia flowers best growing in full sun. However, like most shrubs, it succeeds with four to six hours of sun, or all-day filtered light. The ideal soil is well drained, humusy, sandy, and in the acid range, pH 5.5 to 6.5, but pH can be variable. See Soil Preparation in the Introduction, and planting instructions at the beginning of this chapter. Provide a planting hole three times the width of the rootball and twice as deep. Set the shrub so the crown will be about an inch or two above ground level. Shape the soil around the crown into a wide sauce. Water slowly and deeply. Apply mulch 3 in. deep starting 3 in. from the crown.

Growing Tips
The first year, unless there's a soaking rain, in spring and fall slowly and gently pour two to three bucketsful of water around the roots every two weeks; in summer every week or ten days. Maintain the mulch.

Care
Using a slow-release organic fertilizer for acid-loving plants, fertilize lightly in fall and again in spring. Replenish the mulch. Glossy abelia blooms on side branches of the previous year's growth, and on new wood, so in late winter prune back dead branch tips to outward facing buds. Prune winterkilled tips in early spring. Once the shrub has attained a size that is pleasing, you can keep it at that size by removing up to a third of the branch tips in a year. Prune to restrict its size when flowering is over.

Companion Planting and Design
Abelia is used as a twiggy asset in flowering borders, and as a bank cover. 'Edward Goucher' makes an informal hedge and is handsome enough on its own to be a featured specimen.

Our Personal Recommendation
For the foliage, we recommend the cultivar 'Prostrata', a compact, low-growing shrub with smaller leaves that turn burgundy-green in winter.

Glossy abelia's great asset is a summer-long show of flowers, May to frost. The small, slightly fragrant, funnel-shaped pink flowers come into bloom in early summer and go on blooming until the garden show is about over. The plant itself is a rounded, multi-stemmed, semi-evergreen shrub about 5 ft. tall, with twiggy branches, and dainty foliage that is a lustrous dark green in summer. The leaves take on a purplish-bronze cast in late fall and persist until early winter. The shrub's twiggy structure is an asset to the winter garden. There are many varieties. A tried and true favorite is 3- to 6-ft. 'Edward Goucher', a dense, arching shrub with orange-throated, lilac-pink flowers.

Other Name
Abelia

Bloom Period and Seasonal Color
June till frost; pink flowers, purplish foliage in fall.

Mature Height × Spread
3 to 6 ft. × 5 ft.

Zones
5 to 9

Hydrangea

Hydrangea spp. and cultivars

Hydrangeas are fast-growing deciduous shrubs with cane-like branches, large handsome leaves, and a mid- to late summer show of often huge flower heads composed of dozens of florets. The hortensia, or mophead, types have rounded flower heads of showy, wide-open (sterile) florets; lacecaps are composed of both the showy sterile flowers around the outer edge, and tiny fertile florets in the center, and may be cone-shaped or flattened. A favorite for home gardens is the bigleaf hydrangea, Hydrangea macrophylla, a seaside favorite that includes both lacecap and mophead varieties in cream, rose, pink, and light or dark blue: the color depends on soil acidity. The tall oakleaf hydrangea, H. quercifolia (Zone 5), is a magnificent plant with elegant cone-shaped flower heads in early summer and striking foliage that colors red-purple in the fall; especially nice are 'Snowflake', a double flowered form, and 'Snowqueen' (Zones 5 and 6), which bears enormous flower trusses. Deer love hydrangeas.

Bloom Period and Seasonal Color
Mid- to late summer; white, and shades of pink and blue.

Mature Height × Spread
3 to 5 ft. × 3 to 5 ft.

Zones
4 to 9

When, Where, and How to Plant
Plant container-grown hydrangeas in early spring in full sun, or in bright or dappled shade. *H. arborescens* 'Annabelle' and *H. quercifolia* are tolerant as to pH. *H. macrophylla* requires acid soil. It will color blue or pink according to soil pH: acid soil assures blue; pH 5.0 to 5.5 results in a soft blue; 6.0 to 6.5, or slightly higher, maintains pink. Hydrangeas need well-drained or sandy soil with enough humus to maintain moisture. See Soil Preparation in the Introduction, and the planting instructions at the beginning of this chapter. Provide a planting hole three times the width of the rootball and twice as deep. Set the shrub so the crown will be an inch or two above ground level. Shape the soil around the crown into a wide saucer. Water slowly and deeply. Apply mulch 2 in. deep starting 3 in. from the crown.

Growing Tips
The first year, unless there's a soaking rain, in spring and fall slowly and gently pour two to three bucketsful of water around the roots every two weeks; in summer every week or ten days. Maintain the mulch.

Care
Using a slow-release organic fertilizer, fertilize lightly in fall and again in early spring. Replenish the mulch. *H. arborescens* flowers on new wood: cut out the oldest canes between late fall and early spring. Prune bigleaf hydrangea, *H. macrophylla*, and *H. quercifolia*, right after flowering.

Companion Planting and Design
Hydrangeas should be featured specimens.

Our Personal Recommendations
A favorite of ours is the big peegee hydrangea, *H. paniculata* 'Grandiflora' (Zone 4), a graceful shrub to 20 ft., with smaller leaves, that bears huge conical flower clusters, creamy at first, changing to rose then bronze. Smooth hydrangea, 4-ft. *H. arborescens* 'Annabelle' (Zone 4), was selected for the 1995 Georgia Gold Medal Award. It produces white flower heads up to 12 in. across that turn a beautiful pale green with age.

Japanese Andromeda
Pieris japonica

When, Where, and How to Plant

A young container-grown or balled-and-burlapped andromeda transplants easily in early spring. The andromedas are known as shrubs for shady places, two to six hours of sun a day: Rhode Island Master Gardener Rosanne Sherry warns that in full sun andromeda is more susceptible to damage by azalea lacebugs. The ideal site, especially in cold Zone 5, is out of the wind, well drained, with humusy, moist soil that is acid, pH 4.5 to 6.0. See Soil Preparation in the Introduction, and planting instructions at the beginning of this chapter. Provide a planting hole three times the width of the rootball and twice as deep. Set the shrub so the crown will be an inch or two above ground level. Shape the soil around the crown into a wide saucer. Water slowly and deeply. Apply mulch 3 in. deep starting 3 in. from the crown.

Growing Tips

The first year, unless there's a soaking rain, in spring and fall and going into winter, slowly and gently pour two to three bucketsful of water around the roots every two weeks; in summer every week or ten days. Maintain the mulch. Removing spent blooms when the plant is young encourages growth and flower production.

Care

Using a slow-release organic fertilizer for acid-loving plants, fertilize lightly in fall and again in spring. Replenish the mulch. Ideally, andromeda's cascading branches are allowed to develop naturally. Damaged wood should be pruned back in March before new growth begins.

Companion Planting and Design

Andromeda has a rather formal appearance and is an excellent foundation plant. We like it in shrub groups with rhododendrons and azaleas whose need for acid soil it shares.

Our Personal Recommendations

There are some beautiful named varieties of Japanese andromeda. Among our favorites are 'Flamingo', whose flowers are deep rose-red bells; the semi-dwarf 'Variegata' (Zones 5 and 6), whose foliage is flushed pink when new, then margined with white; and 'White Cascade', which bears long, large panicles of pure white flowers that last weeks longer than the species.

Andromedas are handsome evergreen shrubs that do best in part shade and the acid soils that suit azaleas and rhododendrons. They're the first of the evergreen shrubs to bloom. In late winter and early spring they are covered with large clusters of waxy, cream-white buds that open into small urn-shaped flowers. The leaves are shiny green year-round, and the new foliage is a gleaming rose-bronze. Japanese andromeda is a beautiful species, whose branches cascade almost to the ground. The tips are dense with clusters of rather fragrant flowers in strands 3 to 6 in. long that last two to three weeks. The new foliage is bronze to wine red, and very showy in the newer hybrids. The native mountain andromeda, Pieris floribunda (Zone 5), is a better choice for naturalized situations, and for Vermont and the cooler, more exposed sites of Zone 6.

Other Name
Japanese Pieris

Bloom Period and Seasonal Color
March or April; white flowers, with pink buds in some varieties.

Mature Height × Spread
5 to 8 ft. × 6 ft.

Zones
6 to 8

Japanese Kerria
Kerria japonica 'Pleniflora'

Like forsythia, Japanese kerria covers itself for two or three weeks in spring with small masses of little yellow, flat-faced, 5-petaled flowers as bright and cheerful as sunshine. There's one species in cultivation and it comes from Central and Western China, though we call it Japanese kerria. It is a 3- to 6-ft. shrub that was once so popular you can still find it in the older parks of New England. Sometimes it will repeat its bloom in the summer. The variety 'Pleniflora', which is taller than the species, is the best for landscaping. It's a tough, vigorous, upright, bushy plant that bears masses of double golden yellow flowers. Cut, kerria lasts well in a vase.

Bloom Period and Seasonal Color
Spring; bright yellow.

Mature Height × Spread
6 to 8 or 10 ft. × 6 to 8 ft.

Zones
4 to 9

When, Where, and How to Plant
You'll find that balled-and-burlapped kerria transplants well in early spring or early fall. Container-grown kerria can be planted spring, summer, or fall. Kerria blooms well in sun and in part shade, even in dry urban gardens. Kerria isn't particular about soil—it will flourish in almost any well-drained soil that is moderately moist and fertile. See Soil Preparation in the Introduction, and the planting instructions at the beginning of this chapter. Provide a planting hole three times the width of the rootball and twice as deep. Set the shrub so the crown will be an inch or two above ground level. Shape the soil around the crown into a wide saucer. Water slowly and deeply. Apply mulch 3 in. deep starting 3 in. from the crown.

Growing Tips
The first year, unless there's a soaking rain, in spring and fall slowly and gently pour two to three bucketsful of water around the roots every two weeks; in summer every week or ten days. Maintain the mulch.

Care
Using a slow-release organic fertilizer, fertilize lightly in fall and again in early spring. Replenish the mulch periodically. Once it is well established, kerria seems able to tolerate summer heat and drought. To keep 'Pleniflora' shapely, when the flowers have completely faded, trim the old flowering stems back to strong young shoots or to ground level.

Companion Planting and Design
A traditional wall plant in cottage gardens, kerria is attractive massed in naturalistic plantings, on slopes, anywhere you have room for a good sized shrub and would like to see a sunny color in early spring and wonderful green foliage in summer heat. We like it where paths intersect—it makes a nice, tall marker.

Our Personal Recommendation
'Pleniflora,' a Japanese selection, is our choice.

When, Where, and How to Plant

Lilacs transplant easily in early spring and in early fall. They succeed in open, airy sites in full sun or light shade. The ideal soil is well drained, moist, and neutral—pH 7.0 to 7.5; we use an annual sprinkling of wood ashes or lime to keep ours growing in neutral soil. See Soil Preparation in the Introduction, and the planting instructions at the beginning of this chapter. Provide a planting hole three times the width of the rootball and twice as deep. Set the shrub so the crown will be an inch or two above ground level. Shape the soil around the crown into a wide saucer. Water slowly and deeply. Apply mulch 3 in. deep starting 3 in. from the crown.

Growing Tips

The first year, unless there's a soaking rain, in spring and fall slowly and gently pour two to three bucketsful of water around the roots every two weeks; in summer every week or ten days. Maintain the mulch.

Care

Using a slow-release organic fertilizer, fertilize lightly in fall and again in early spring. Replenish the mulch. Established lilacs tolerate some drought. Deadhead to encourage flowering. Regularly prune out the oldest branches and all but two or three strong suckers to keep the plants open and airy, a deterrent to mildew. The taller lilacs can be pruned to grow as single-stemmed or multi-stemmed plants.

Companion Planting and Design

A staple of Victorian shrub borders, lilacs are now featured lawn specimens, or used in tall hedges, and in allées called "lilac walks." Smaller forms do well in containers.

Our Personal Recommendations

We love late blooming, 9-ft. Manchurian lilac *S. reticulata* 'Miss Kim' which has fragrant icy blue flowers, good fall color, and is mildew resistant. And fragrant, compact, mildew-resistant, flowery, violet-purple Meyer lilac, *S. meyeri* 'Palibin', which blooms before the leaves appear. And the 20- to 30-ft. species Japanese tree lilac, *S. reticulata*, which blooms last with big plumes of creamy white florets, (alas, sharply scented as a privet hedge). 'Ivory Silk' is a lovely cultivar that will grow in acid soil.

Lilacs are multi-stemmed shrubs or small trees that bear panicles of single or double florets in late spring. The one most famous for fragrance is the 20-ft. common lilac, Syringa vulgaris, which came to New England with the colonists. In the late 1700s it was being hybridized in France to improve the flowers, so many of today's most beautiful double-flowered forms and unusual colors are known as French lilacs; not all are fragrant. If perfume is what you love, look for hybrids advertised as very fragrant, like 'Charles Joly', a double flowered form with deep wine-red flowers, and 'Ludwig Spaeth', a heavily fragrant, dark purple, single-flowered hybrid. Lilacs are subject to mildew, so look for the hybrids that are advertised as mildew-resistant.

Other Name
Common Lilac

Bloom Period and Seasonal Color
May; white to lilac, blue, lavender, purple, pink, wine red.

Mature Height × Spread
5 to 20 ft. × 8 to 20 ft.

Zones
3 to 8

Mock Orange
Philadelphus × virginalis

Mock orange is a big old-fashioned shrub with crisp white flowers whose beauty and perfume recall orange blossoms. The plant itself is large, and rather dull until May and early June, when it opens clusters of five to seven beautiful little 1- to 2-in. pure white flowers that have showy golden anthers. The perfume of fully fragrant plants permeates a garden. The modern varieties with old-fashioned fragrance are preferred. The cultivars of Philadelphus × virginalis are very fragrant and have semi-double or double flowers, which will quite often bloom for a second time in the summer. 'Glacier' has double flowers. 'Minnesota Snowflake' is a tall—9 ft.— plant with arching branches and big double flowers. In addition to perfume, another great virtue is that deer don't eat mock orange.

Bloom Period and Seasonal Color
May to June; white.

Mature Height × Spread
10 to 12 ft. × 12 to 16 ft.

Zones
4 to 8

When, Where, and How to Plant
To guarantee your mock orange will be as perfumed as you hope, buy a container-grown plant already in bloom. Plant a container-grown mock orange in spring, summer, or fall. It will flower most fully in full sun, but can handle some shade during the day. Mock orange succeeds in most any soil, but does best in a moist, well-drained site, pH 6.0 to 7.0. See Soil Preparation in the Introduction, and the planting instructions at the beginning of this chapter. Provide a planting hole three times the width of the rootball and twice as deep. Set the shrub so the crown will be an inch or two above ground level. Shape the soil around the crown into a wide saucer. Water slowly and deeply. Apply mulch 3 in. deep starting 3 in. from the crown.

Growing Tips
The first year, unless there's a soaking rain, in spring and fall slowly and gently pour two to three bucketsful of water around the roots every two weeks; in summer every week or ten days. Maintain the mulch.

Care
Using a slow-release organic fertilizer, fertilize lightly in fall and again in late winter or early spring. Replenish the mulch. An established mock orange tolerates some drought. The mock oranges flower on growth made on branches developed the previous year. Giving older branches a light annual pruning after they have bloomed helps keep it productive and well shaped. Woody stems that are more than five years old should be removed in winter or early spring.

Companion Planting and Design
Mock orange is a big shrub that needs a large garden to show off its beauty. It's usually grown as a specimen plant in the middle of the lawn. It's also attractive in a border for big shrubs such as weigela, forsythia, spirea, and deutzia.

Our Personal Recommendations
Other fragrant modern mock oranges are named varieties of *P. × lemoinei* (Zone 5), including 8-ft. 'Innocence', which is single flowered and perhaps the most fragrant, and 4-ft. 'Avalanche', a very fragrant single-flowered form.

Mountain Laurel

Kalmia latifolia

When, Where, and How to Plant

In poor, dry soil and full sun, mountain laurel develops leaf spot and dies. Plant a container-grown laurel in the fall before Indian summer, or in early spring while the shrub is still dormant. It needs a half-day of sun or bright shade all day to flower well and does best in light, open woodlands. It needs well-drained soil, one-third to one-half humus or leaf mold, and pH 4.5 to 6.0. See Soil Preparation in the Introduction, and planting instructions at the beginning of this chapter. Provide a planting hole three times the width of the rootball and twice as deep. Set the shrub so the crown will be an inch or two above ground level. Shape the soil around the crown into a wide saucer. Water slowly and deeply. Apply mulch 3 in. deep starting 3 in. from the crown.

Growing Tips

The first year, unless there's a soaking rain, in spring and fall slowly and gently pour two to three bucketsful of water around the roots every two weeks; in summer every week or ten days. Maintain the mulch.

Care

Using a slow-release organic fertilizer for acid-loving plants, fertilize lightly in fall and again in early spring. Replenish the mulch as needed. Remove flower heads as they fade. *Kalmia* recovers slowly from pruning, and it is unnecessary in healthy plants. To restore an overgrown mountain laurel, wait till flowering is over, and remove one or two of the less attractive branches each year over a period of three to five years.

Companion Planting and Design

Mountain laurel is used at the back of shaded shrub borders and is ideal for naturalizing at the edge of an open sunny woodland with rhododendrons and azaleas. Nothing is more beautiful than a shaded bank on the edge of a woodland with well-grown, fully-flowered mountain laurels in bloom.

Our Personal Recommendation

'Elf' is used as a landscape accent, to create an informal low hedge, and toward the front of an evergreen shrub border.

Mountain laurel is a tall, exceptionally handsome evergreen shrub with shiny, leathery leaves that make beautiful Christmas roping. It grows wild in the woodlands of New England and is the state flower of Connecticut. In mid- to late spring, mountain laurel bears clusters of white, pink, or red-variegated cup-shaped florets. The blooms of the species are pale pink; modern hybrids are showier, blooming in brighter pinks, reds, and bi-colors. 'Elf' is a slow-developing smaller mountain laurel, which eventually grows 4 to 6 ft. tall, and whose showy clusters of light pink buds open to white. The buds of 'Ostbo Red' are an intense crimson that open to pink. 'Bullseye' is one of several forms whose flowers are banded red inside. By the way, every part of the plant is toxic to people but not to wildlife—deer will nibble, usually only the laurels you plant, not those in the wild.

Other Name
Laurel

Bloom Period and Seasonal Color
Spring; white, pink, red, bi-colors.

Mature Height × Spread
7 to 12 ft. × 5 to 6 ft.

Zones
4 to 8

Purple Japanese Barberry
Berberis thunbergii 'Atropurpurea'

The barberries are low deciduous and evergreen shrubs whose twiggy branches are so thorny they make almost impenetrable hedges. Deciduous barberries, like Berberis thunbergii 'Atropurpurea' and 'Atropurpurea Nana', have pinkish or reddish new leaves in late spring and glowing shades of orange, yellow, and scarlet in fall. The twiggy winter silhouette is very textural, a real asset. In mid-spring, they bear small, attractive yellow flowers rather hidden by the foliage, followed by red, purplish, or bluish black fruits in late summer. The named variety 'Crimson Pygmy' has better color than the species, and is often the first to leaf out in spring. It is a low-growing, dense, rounded plant 2 to 3 ft. wide by 3 to 5 ft. tall, whose foliage emerges a rosy crimson in spring, and turns dark crimson in the fall.

Other Name
Japanese Barberry

Bloom Period and Seasonal Color
Flowers are insignificant; new foliage is pinkish or reddish in late spring, paler red in summer, and glowing shades of orange, yellow, and scarlet in fall.

Mature Height × Spread
2 to 3 ft. × 3 to 5 ft.

Zones
4 to 8

When, Where, and How to Plant
Plant a bare-root shrub before the buds start to break. A container-grown barberry can be planted in spring, summer, or fall. The barberries display the brightest fall color growing in full sun but succeed with four to six hours of sun. They do well in most any soil, but prefer soil that is slightly acid, well drained, loose or loamy, with enough humus to maintain moisture. See Soil Preparation in the Introduction, and the planting instructions at the beginning of this chapter. Provide a planting hole three times the width of the rootball and twice as deep. Set the shrub so the crown will be an inch or two above ground level. Shape the soil around the crown into a wide saucer. Water slowly and deeply. Apply mulch 3 in. deep starting 3 in. from the crown.

Growing Tips
The first year, unless there's a soaking rain, in spring and fall slowly and gently pour two to three bucketsful of water around the roots every two weeks; in summer every week or ten days. If you plant it close to a wall where it will miss normal rainfall, be sure to water it as directed above. Maintain the mulch.

Care
Using a slow-release organic fertilizer for acid-loving plants, fertilize lightly in fall and again in early spring. Replenish the mulch. Barberries bloom on old wood. Pruning to control the height or shape of a hedge should be undertaken shortly after the shrubs have flowered. You can remove up to a third of the branch tips in a year.

Companion Planting and Design
The barberries are used a great deal for hedges because the spiny leaves and thorns are wicked enough to discourage pets and wildlife. And gardeners as well, should you forget to wear gauntlet type garden gloves when handling barberries.

Our Personal Recommendations
'Crimson Pygmy' is our favorite. 'Rose Glow' is an excellent reddish-purple barberry that is a little larger. Another appealing variety is 3- to 4-ft. 'Aurea', whose new foliage is bright yellow in spring fading to light green in summer.

Rhododendron

Rhododendron spp. and hybrids

When, Where, and How to Plant

Plant a balled-and-burlapped or container-grown rhododendron in early fall or in early spring. To be sure of the flower color, buy one already blooming, or labeled with its cultivar name. Rhododendrons do best in the bright dappled light of tall trees with protection from high winds. Ideal soil is well drained, humusy, and acid, pH 4.5 to 6.0. See Soil Preparation in the Introduction, and planting instructions at the beginning of this chapter. Dig the hole three times the width of the rootball and twice as deep. Set the shrub so the crown will be an inch or so above ground level. Shape the soil around the crown into a wide saucer. Water slowly and deeply. Apply mulch 3 in. deep starting 3 in. from the crown.

Growing Tips

The first year, unless there's a soaking rain, in spring and fall slowly and gently pour two to three bucketsful of water around the roots every two weeks; in summer every week or ten days. Maintain the mulch.

Care

Apply a slow-release organic fertilizer for acid-loving plants lightly in fall and early spring. Replenish the mulch. As each flower truss withers, pinch or cut it off, taking care not to damage the tiny leaf buds just behind it. Prune a rhododendron after it has bloomed, removing individual branches that have grown ragged or as required to achieve the desired shape.

Companion Planting and Design

Use rhododendrons for the transitional area to a woodland, backing a border of acid-loving shrubs, for screening, and rural hedges.

Our Personal Recommendations

Showy, large-leaved, super hardy evergreen rhododendron hybrids that handle winters in our area include Catawba rhododendrons: 5- to 7-ft., bright red 'America'; compact 4- to 5-ft., white 'Boule de Neige'; 6-ft., white 'Catawbiense Album'; 6-ft., rosy pink 'English Roseum'; and 5-ft., red 'Nova Zembla'. And the hybrid rose-lilac 'Roseum Elegans', which does well in the sun. We like the hardy, small-leaved, lavender-pink PJM hybrids for their fall color.

These tall, handsome evergreen shrubs with their huge, airy globes of exquisite flowers are among the most valued of spring and early summer flowering shrubs. Native species growing in the wild reach 20 ft. and more, but in cultivation most reach 6 or 8 ft. Mature specimens of the popular large-leaved evergreen rhododendrons provide spectacular displays of their huge blossoms in mid- to late spring—providing you have planted a variety suited to your climate, your site, and your soil. The large-leaved evergreen rhododendrons you can count on to survive winters in Zone 4 include cultivars of the Catawba rhododendron, Rhododendron catawbiense, and the PJM hybrids. Lovely little apple-blossom-pink 'Yaku Princess', R. yakusimanum (Zone 4), has beautiful foliage and is said to be hardy to -25 degrees Fahrenheit. In winter, big, juicy rhododendron leaves are a magnet for deer.

Bloom Period and Seasonal Color
May to June; white, pink, rose, lavender, purple-red, yellow flowers, that may be flushed, splotched, or spotted with another shade or color.

Mature Height × Spread
3 to 8 ft. × 3 to 8 ft.

Zones
4 to 8

Rose-of-Sharon
Hibiscus syriacus

This is an old-fashioned, tall, spreading shrub, or small upright tree, that bears a profusion of flowers in July or early August and goes right on blooming until the end of September. The blossoms are trumpet shaped, like its relative the exotic tropical hibiscus, and about 4 to 6 in. across with ruffled petals crinkled on the margins. The usual colors are white, pink, crimson, and purple, most with an eye in a vivid contrasting color. Look for one of the new cultivars introduced through the U.S. National Arboretum by the late, great Dr. Donald Egolf. They are sterile triploids that have a longer blooming season and set less fruit, which can be a nuisance. The plant can be trained to a single trunk and allowed to develop into a small tree; pruned back heavily in spring it will retain a shrubby appearance.

Other Name
Shrub Althea

Bloom Period and Seasonal Color
July to September; pure luminous white, pink, lavender blue, lilac, deep red.

Mature Height × Spread
8 to 12 ft. × 6 to 10 ft.

Zones
4 to 10

When, Where, and How to Plant
Choose a young—under 6 ft.—container-grown shrub, and plant it in fall before Indian summer, or in early spring. Rose-of-Sharon flowers best growing in full sun. It thrives in a wide variety of soils, and a pH ranging between 5.5 and 7.0. Provide a site that is well drained and has about 50 percent leaf mold, peat moss, or acid humus. See Soil Preparation in the Introduction, and the planting instructions at the beginning of this chapter. Provide a planting hole three times the width of the rootball and twice as deep. Set the shrub so the crown will be an inch or two above ground level. Shape the soil around the crown into a wide saucer. Water slowly and deeply. Apply mulch 3 in. deep starting 3 in. from the crown.

Growing Tips
The first year, unless there's a soaking rain, in spring and fall slowly and gently pour two to three bucketsful of water around the roots every two weeks; in summer every week or ten days. Maintain the mulch.

Care
Using a slow-release organic fertilizer, fertilize lightly in fall and again in early spring. Replenish the mulch. In early spring before the buds break, prune the branches back heavily to the first or second pair of outward-facing buds. If you want larger flowers, prune the branches all the way back, so that only three or four outward-facing buds remain. Water at the same time you water flower borders during prolonged droughts.

Companion Planting and Design
Rose-of-Sharon looks great anchoring a corner of a mixed border, fronting a building, and backing groups of shrubs. It can be used for screening and to create a tall hedge.

Our Personal Recommendations
Our favorites are modern hybrids 'White Chiffon' and award winner 'Lavender Chiffon': they grow to about 6 ft. tall and 5 ft. wide and bear 4 and 5 in. blooms with lacy centers. 'Diana' is another gorgeous white.

Spirea
Spiraea japonica

When, Where, and How to Plant
Plant a balled-and-burlapped spirea in fall or in early spring; a container-grown plant can be set out spring, summer, or fall. Spirea flowers best in full sun and an airy site but it tolerates some shade. It handles all but very wet soil. The ideal pH is 6.0 to 7.0. See Soil Preparation in the Introduction, and the planting instructions at the beginning of this chapter. Provide a planting hole three times the width of the rootball and twice as deep. Set the shrub so the crown will be an inch or two above ground level. Shape the soil around the crown into a wide saucer. Water slowly and deeply. Apply mulch 3 in. deep starting 3 in. from the crown.

Growing Tips
The first year, unless there's a soaking rain, in spring and fall slowly and gently pour two to three bucketsful of water around the roots every two weeks; in summer every week or ten days. Maintain the mulch.

Care
Using a slow-release organic fertilizer, fertilize lightly in late fall and again in early spring. Replenish the mulch. To maintain the shape and to increase flowering of low, shrubby spireas, snip off stem tips before growth begins. For bridal wreath spireas, remove old or dead interior wood after the shrub has bloomed.

Companion Planting and Design
Shrubby spireas are used to cover sloping beds and banks. Their twiggy mass adds texture and color to perennial beds. The big bridal wreath spireas are a landscaping must for traditional New England homes.

Our Personal Recommendations
'Goldflame' is our favorite pink spirea. It's a smaller plant, 2 to 3 ft. high, with compact pink flowers, whose foliage is a fiery gold in spring and in fall turns to red, copper, and orange. We also like 'Neon Flash' which has chartreuse leaves and white flowers. We love the old-fashioned, 5-ft. bridal wreath spirea, *S. prunifolia* , whose arching branches are covered with showy, small white flowers in mid-spring. A smaller version, *S. nipponica* 'Snowmound', is replacing the bridal wreath your grandmother planted.

Japanese spirea is a low, very wide, twiggy shrub with dainty leaves and arching branches that literally cover themselves with rounded clusters of exquisite flowers in the summer. Undemanding, and one of the most successful of the spireas, it has been much hybridized. A long-time favorite variety is 3- to 4-ft. 'Anthony Waterer', whose 4- to 6-in. wide rose-pink flower heads open in July and remain in bloom into August. The new foliage has a pink tinge, and in fall the leaves turn to wine red. Several pink-flowered varieties with colorful foliage have been introduced. An interesting new Japanese spirea is 'Shibori', a 2- to 3-ft. shrub covered with white, red, and pink flower heads all summer. Bumald spirea, a dwarf with dark pink flowers, is another winner. Deer don't care for spireas.

Other Names
Japanese Spirea, Pink Spirea

Bloom Period and Seasonal Color
July and August; rose pink flowers; pink tinted foliage in spring, that turns to wine red.

Mature Height × Spread
2 to 4 ft. × 3 to 5 ft.

Zones
4 to 8

Sweet Pepper Bush
Clethra alnifolia

If you love fragrance in the garden, then consider planting sweet pepper bush, or summersweet. It's a tall shrub native to the Eastern U.S. that naturalizes readily in shady, damp places and coastal gardens. The dense, rather shiny leaves are an attractive green, and have a nice yellow-orange glow in the fall. The plant's shrubby silhouette is a winter asset. But summersweet's best gift is the masses of scented flowers it produces in July and August. The flowers are fuzzy little 6-in. spikes so fragrant just one or two plants can perfume a whole garden. Bees love them. The 2- to 3^1/$_2$-ft., white 'Hummingbird' is one of the finest compact deciduous shrubs available to the gardener. 'Rosea', 'Pink Spires', and 'Fern Valley Pink' are compact pink-flowered varieties. As far as we know, deer don't like Clethra!

Other Name
Summersweet

Bloom Period and Seasonal Color
July and August; white or pink flowers.

Mature Height × Spread
3 to 8 ft. × 4 to 6 ft.

Zones
3 to 8

When, Where, and How to Plant
Like so many of our native plants, summersweet takes a little time to get established in the garden. Choose a young container-grown plant and plant it in early spring, summer, or early fall. *Clethra* does well in either sun or shade. The ideal soil is rich, moist, mixed with 50 percent humus or leaf mold, and somewhat acid. But it tolerates wet feet, dryish soil, and salty seashore conditions. See Soil Preparation in the Introduction, and the planting instructions at the beginning of this chapter. Provide a planting hole three times the width of the rootball and twice as deep. Set the shrub so the crown will be an inch or two above ground level. Shape the soil around the crown into a wide saucer. Water slowly and deeply. Apply mulch 3 in. deep starting 3 in. from the crown.

Growing Tips
If the planting site is ordinary garden soil, unless there's a soaking rain, the first spring and fall slowly and gently pour two to three bucketsful of water around the roots every two weeks; in summer every week or ten days. If the planting site is rather moist, the extra watering may not be needed. But keep in mind that sweet pepper bush needs moisture at the roots. Maintain the mulch.

Care
Using a slow-release organic fertilizer for acid-loving plants, fertilize lightly in fall and again in early spring. Replenish the mulch. In winter, cut bare older branches back to ground level, and remove the weakest suckers. In ideal conditions, *Clethra* will colonize in its environment.

Companion Planting and Design
Clethra grows wild in moist places, so if you have a wild spot or a wet place, it's a good candidate. Summersweet's foliage makes it useful as a foundation plant, and we include it in large shrub borders and look for spots along paths and much frequented places where its perfume will be enjoyed.

Our Personal Recommendations
We recommend both the full size sweet pepper bush, and compact 'Hummingbird', and like them growing together.

186

When, Where, and How to Plant

Plant container-grown and balled-and-burlapped viburnums in fall before Indian summer, or in early spring. Viburnums thrive in full sun but they also do well in bright, all-day filtered light. Most species prefer well-drained, humusy soils that are slightly acid, pH 6.0 to 7.0. See Soil Preparation in the Introduction, and the planting instructions at the beginning of this chapter. Provide a planting hole three times the width of the rootball and twice as deep. Set the shrub so the crown will be an inch or two above ground level. Shape the soil around the crown into a wide saucer. Water slowly and deeply. Apply mulch 3 in. deep starting 3 in. from the crown.

Growing Tips

The first year, unless there's a soaking rain, in spring and fall slowly and gently pour two to three bucketsful of water around the roots every two weeks; in summer every week or ten days. Maintain the mulch.

Care

With viburnums, be sure to use low-analysis, natural organic fertilizers that don't force or stimulate excessive growth. Fertilize lightly in fall and again in early spring. Maintain the mulch. To keep the shape of the fragrant viburnums, shortly after they finish blooming, prune protruding branches back to outward-facing buds, and cut old branches to the ground.

Companion Planting and Design

Plant fragrant viburnums by a porch, patio, and near house windows, or along a well-traveled path. The doublefile viburnum needs plenty of space all around; it's a choice plant for the entrance to a property, by a stone wall, or cloaking a garage corner.

Our Personal Recommendations

Our favorite variety of Koreanspice viburnum, *V. carlesii*, is 'Aurora'. In a flowering border we like another hybrid, *V. × carlcephalum* (Zone 5), a tall, open shrub whose flowers change from pink bud to white when open. Our doublefile viburnum favorites are 'Shasta', a spectacular National Arboretum introduction by Donald Egolf, and 'Mariesii', which is lovely in bloom and spectacular in fruit.

The viburnums are magnificent spring-flowering shrubs. Two distinctly different forms are popular: the scented viburnums planted for their fragrance, and the large, strikingly handsome doublefile viburnums planted for their flower display. Both develop colorful berries and fall foliage. Our favorite fragrant viburnums are the cinnamon-scented Koreanspice viburnum, Viburnum carlesii (Zone 4), whose fall foliage is a cheerful red, and V. × burkwoodii 'Mohawk' (Zone 4 with protection), a National Arboretum introduction whose fall foliage is red-plum. In early spring both bear beautiful rounded clusters of deep pink buds that open to a cream pink. The perfume is intoxicating. The doublefile viburnum, V. plicatum 'Shasta' (Zone 5), is different altogether—a big, handsome bush with beautifully layered branches that are covered in mid-spring with a snowfall of white blossoms. Noted plantsman Michael Dirr has called it "possibly the most elegant of flowering shrubs."

Bloom Period and Seasonal Color

Spring; pure white or pink or scarlet; summer and fall fruits are red or black.

Mature Height × Spread

6 to 15 ft. × 9 to 12 ft.

Zones

4 to 9

Trees *for New England*

A tree is such a large presence in a landscape, its every aspect—habit, color, and texture—can contribute to your pleasure in fall and winter as well as in spring and summer. In this chapter we have included large and small deciduous trees, trees we plant for their flowers, for fall foliage color, and for beauty of bark and form. Needled evergreen trees and shrubs can be found in the Conifers chapter.

In choosing a tree, beauty is the first thing we look for, and we think of foliage. A maple's flaming fall color can be breathtaking. But when the leaves go, it's the bark, bole, and branch structure that lend beauty to your garden view. Imagine white birches against a stand of evergreens. A tree's silhouette, whether columnar, pyramidal, oval, vase-shaped, round, clumping, or weeping, also makes a deep impression. By repeating the same silhouette, color, and texture—the symmetry of paired blue spruces flanking an entrance, or an allée of columnar flowering apple trees—you create an air of gracious formality. By combining a variety of forms, such as a symmetrical incense cedar and a stylized Serbian spruce with a wide-branching maple and a clump of birches, you create a natural, informal effect, add a hint of mystery, a little excitement.

When it's shade we need, we look to wide-branched trees whose silhouettes are oval, pyramidal, vase-shaped, or round. Maples and oaks are excellent shade trees, and some evergreens make good shade trees too—hemlocks, for example. Limbed up, small flowering trees can provide all the shade a small urban garden needs—the dogwoods and some flowering fruit trees, for example.

For style and for the fun of something different, we look to columnar trees. Many species now are offered in this form—red maple, European hornbeam, beech, and apple. 'Princeton Sentry'® is a

Kousa Dogwood

'Heritage' River Birch

beautiful columnar ginkgo. Small columnar forms even grow well in big tubs, adding style to patios, roof gardens, and decks.

For romance, grace, and movement, weeping trees are tops. They're especially effective planted where their drooping branches will be reflected in water. The graceful weeping willow loves wet places. A weeping birch or a weeping beech, or the gorgeous weeping crabapple 'Red Jade', can be very beautiful. And weeping varieties of the flowering and the kousa dogwoods are lovely.

To create a seasonal parade that is a true delight, we plant small flowering trees. The flowering fruit trees— almond, plum, cherry, pear, crabapple, apple—open the season. Some flowering trees bear colorful fruits—the fruits of the dogwoods and flowering crabapples are among many that attract birds. For more choices than those we offer in this chapter, look into some of the tall shrubs in the Shrubs chapter—lilac, rose-of-Sharon, hydrangea, viburnum, and shrubs that can be trained as trees, or standards. Dwarf fruiting trees make pretty specimens too: dwarf apple, pear, peach, and plum. A few big trees rival the show staged by the small flowering trees. In early spring the maples are outlined in tiny garnet-red buds. In summer a mature Japanese pagoda tree bears showy panicles of creamy-white, fragrant, pea-like flowers followed by beautiful showers of winged, yellow-green seedpods. It takes years to bloom, but it's worth the wait.

Size can be an asset, or a debit. A tree that will grow out of scale with a dwelling is a debit. The heights we give in this chapter are for trees in cultivation—in the wild and in arboreta they can often be twice as big.

When, Where, and How to Plant

Young trees knit into their new environments quickly: a tree 7 to 8 feet tall can overtake the growth of a 15-foot tree set out at the same time. Early spring and early fall are the best planting seasons for trees. Fall-planted trees need two months of good weather ahead to begin to adjust. Choose early spring for trees difficult to transplant. Most large trees need full sun; many small flowering trees are understory plants that developed in the partial shade of a forest, and do well with part sun.

Make the planting hole for a tree three times as wide as the rootball and twice as deep. Mix into the soil from the hole the amendments described in Soil Preparation in the Introduction. Half fill the bottom of the hole with improved soil, and tamp it down to make a firm base for the tree to rest on.

Trees are sold balled and burlapped, or growing in containers. To free a containerized tree, tip the container on its side and roll it around until the rootball loosens, or slit the pot open. If roots wrap the rootball, before planting make four deep vertical cuts in the sides and slice the matted roots off the bottom 2 inches. A balled-and-burlapped tree goes into the hole in its wrapping, then you cut the rope or wires and remove as much of the burlap as you can. Set the tree in the hole so the crown will be 1 to 2 inches above ground level (the weight on unsettled soil will cause it to sink some after planting). Half fill the hole again with improved soil and tamp it down. Fill the hole to the top with improved soil and tamp it down firmly. Shape the soil around the trunk into a wide saucer. Water the soil slowly and gently with a sprinkler, a soaker hose, a bubbler, or by hand. Put down $1^1/_2$ inches of water measured in a regular sized coffee can, or pour 10 to 15 gallons of water slowly from a bucket.

Apply 3 inches of mulch starting 3 inches from the trunk and extending to the edge of the saucer. Stake a young tree so the trunk will grow up straight, and wrap the lower trunk to protect the bark from sunscald and deer rubbing. Remove the stake and wrapping as the trunk fills out. Or, paint the trunk with whitewash, which is calcium carbonate with resins in it.

Care

The first year, unless there's a soaking rain, in spring and fall slowly and gently pour two to three bucketsful of water around the roots every two weeks, in summer every week or ten days. Maintain the mulch. The slow-release organic additives mixed into the soil at planting time are sufficient fertilizer for that year. For flowering trees, use a slow-release organic fertilizer. For trees whose flowers are not the show, use a complete, slow-release, long-lasting lawn fertilizer. In the following years, in late winter or early spring apply one of these fertilizers from the drip line outward to a distance that equals the height of the tree, plus half again its height. And compost the leaves you rake up in the fall. The nutrients they contain should go to enriching your soil, not clogging a landfill!

Pruning Trees

Most new trees require periodic light pruning. The first few years are the most important times to prune and shape a new tree. When needed, remove branches growing into the center of the tree, or crossing other branches. Never remove more than 25 percent: such "dehorning" causes "water sprout" growth.

Before cutting a branch, find the collar or ring at its base, where it springs from the trunk. Taking care not to damage the ring, make the cut just to the outside of it. From the collar an attractive, healthy covering for the wounded area can develop. Current wisdom says "no" to painting or tarring these cuts. That said, our main consultant, nurseryman André Viette prefers to paint with orange shellac any wounds caused by removing big branches: it disinfects and seals the cuts.

The best time to prune is when the tree is dormant, just after the coldest part of the season. If sap starts to flow, never mind. It will stop when the tree leafs out. Light pruning in summer is not harmful, and you can see what you're doing. Pruning stimulates growth and you can use that to encourage bushier growth and more flowering stems. Prune a spring-flowering tree that blooms on last year's wood after the flowers fade. Prune a summer-flowering tree that blooms on current growth shortly before growth begins.

Nurturing a beautiful tree for years and then losing it leaves a gap in the heart as big as the gap in the garden. For an extra fee, nurseries will plant your purchase and guarantee replacement if it fails, but usually only the first year. The best protection against loss or disappointment is to choose disease-resistant trees and to plant, water, and feed them wisely.

Other Choices

While the trees in this chapter are recommended for New England gardens, here are a few others we like:

Small Flowering Trees
Carolina Silverbell, *Halesia tetraptera*
Chaste Tree, *Vitex agnus-castus* (Zones 6 to 9)
Mountain Silverbell, *Halesia monticola*
    (Zones 4 to 8)

Large Deciduous Trees
Kentucky Coffee Tree, *Gymnocladus dioicus*
    (Zones 4 to 8)
Yellowwood, American Yellowwood, *Cladrastis kentukea* (*C. lutea*) (Zones 4 to 9)

Sugar Maples in autumn.

American Beech

Fagus grandifolia

The American beech is a grand tree, a magnificent pyramidal native species that needs plenty of space all around it. Its magnitude cries out to be placed in park-like settings. It has silky silver-gray bark and beautifully symmetrical branches that reach to the ground, shading out weeds and creating a hiding place for nut-loving squirrels, and children. The American beech has shimmery green leaves that appear late in spring and later turn a russet-gold-brown in fall and cling to lower branches well into winter. The big oily seeds appeal to many species of birds and animals. This species is slow growing and rather difficult to transplant. The European beech, Fagus sylvatica (Zones 4 To 7), and its cultivars transplant more readily.

Bloom Period and Seasonal Color
April to early May; fall foliage is russet-gold-brown; bark is silky gray.

Mature Height × Spread
50 to 70 ft. × 60 ft.

Zones
3 to 8

When, Where, and How to Plant

Transplant a young container-grown or balled-and-burlapped tree with great care in early spring. Take care not to break the rootball—American beech does not transplant easily. It needs space all around and full sun, though it can handle dappled shade when young. The brow of a low hill, and toward the top of a slope is a likely site. It does best in soil in the somewhat acid range, pH 5.0 to 6.5, well drained, loose, and humusy enough to hold moisture. See Soil Preparation in the Introduction, and the planting instructions at the beginning of this chapter. Provide a planting hole three times the width of the rootball and twice as deep. Set the tree so the crown will be an inch or so above ground level. Staking might help the tree grow straighter, but remove it once the tree is established. Shape the earth around the crown into a wide saucer. Water slowly and deeply. Apply mulch 3 in. deep starting 3 in. from the stem.

Growing Tips

The first year, unless there's a soaking rain, in spring and fall slowly and gently pour two to three bucketsful of water around the roots every two weeks; in summer every week or ten days. Maintain the mulch.

Care

Apply a complete, slow-release, long lasting, organic lawn fertilizer in early spring from the drip line to a distance $1^1/2$ times the tree's height. Water it in. Replenish the mulch.

Companion Planting and Design

The American beech has high surface roots that are hard to cover, but they're attractive when inter-planted with small flowering bulbs.

Our Personal Recommendations

Though not as winter hardy as the American beech, the European beech is smaller and easier to transplant and many striking cultivars are available. 'Pendula' is a weeping form. The young leaves of the purple beech, 'Atropunicea' ('Purpurea'), are an extraordinary black-red that changes to purple-green. The purple leaves of the tricolor beech, 'Purpurea Tricolor' ('Roseo-marginata'), have an irregular edge of rose, and pinkish white.

Birch

Betula spp. and cultivars

When, Where, and How to Plant

The birches transplant easily in early spring or fall. They thrive in full sun, but accept bright shade. Most cultivated varieties grow well in somewhat wet or dry soils and are not particular as to pH. Provide soil that's fertile, humusy, and well drained, though that's not critical. See Soil Preparation in the Introduction. Follow the planting instructions at the beginning of this chapter. Staking might help the tree grow straighter, but remove it once the tree is established. Water well. Mulch 3 in. deep starting 3 in. from the main stem.

Growing Tips

The first year, unless there's a soaking rain, in spring and fall slowly and gently pour two to three bucketsful of water around the roots every two weeks; in summer every week or ten days. Maintain the mulch.

Care

Apply a complete, slow-release, long lasting lawn fertilizer in early spring from the drip line to a distance 1¹/₂ times the tree's height. Water it in. Replenish the mulch. In summer or fall prune out limbs that threaten to cross others or grow in the wrong direction.

Companion Planting and Design

Beautiful birches like 'Whitespire' are at their best standing alone as specimens with a background of evergreens.

Our Personal Recommendations

Other birches said to be resistant include: the Chinese paper birch, *B. albosinensis* (Zone 4), which is one of the most beautiful and whitest of all the birches—but not easy to find; the handsome bark of *B. nigra* 'Heritage' (Zone 4), river birch, peels to expose inner bark that may be salmon-pink to grayish, cinnamon, or reddish brown. The older bark of monarch birch, *B. maximowicziana* (Zone 5), is white, and it is represented as exceptionally resistant. Weeping birch, *B. pendula* 'Youngii' (Zone 3), has a graceful habit, but may be vulnerable to the birch bark borer.

As a group, the birches are fast growing, tall, slender trees known for beautiful bark. They have graceful crowns of dainty pointed leaves that move in every breeze and turn to yellow and yellow-green in fall. The birches are susceptible to birch leaf miner and bronze birch borer, so choosing a resistant cultivar is a wise move. The Himalayan birch, Betula utilis var. jacquemontii (Zone 5), has beautiful, strikingly white bark, and is said to be resistant. A beautiful single-trunked cultivar of the Japanese white birch, B. platyphylla var. japonica 'Whitespire', may have even better resistance. Introduced by John L. Creech, late director of the U.S. National Arboretum, it has chalk-white bark enhanced by contrasting triangles of black at the base of the branches. The bark doesn't peel off, like that of the beautiful native canoe birch, but the structure of the tree is very appealing.

Bloom Period and Seasonal Color
April; 2- to 3-in. catkins; chalk-white bark patterned with black triangles.

Mature Height × Spread
30 to 40 ft. × 12 to 15 ft.

Zones
2 to 6 or 7

Callery Pear
Pyrus calleryana

The flowering pear is a beautiful, pyramidal tree bigger than most of the flowering fruit trees. In early spring, before the leaves appear, it covers itself with clusters of small, white blooms. In fall, the glossy, green leaves turn an attractive orange to wine-red and stay on the tree into late October and November. The fruits are small and russet-colored and attract birds. The flowering pear has been widely planted as a street tree. The first flowering pear was 'Bradford', a beautiful tree that unfortunately tends to split as it matures. It is being replaced with stronger varieties such as 'Whitehouse'—magnificent trees that never have a broken branch. Most flowering pears are a little big for a small city garden, but handsome in a larger suburban landscape and as a street tree.

Other Name
Flowering Pear

Bloom Period and Seasonal Color
Early spring; white; foliage turns wine red in fall.

Mature Height × Spread
30 to 50 ft. × 15 to 20 ft.

Zones
4 to 8

When, Where, and How to Plant
Plant a balled-and-burlapped tree in late winter or early spring before the plant leafs out. A flowering pear blooms most fully and produces the brightest fruits when growing in full sun. The callery pears succeed in soils with a broad pH range, 5.5 to 7.5. See Soil Preparation in the Introduction, and the planting instructions at the beginning of this chapter. Provide a planting hole three times the width of the rootball and twice as deep. Set the tree so the crown will be an inch or so above ground level. The tree might grow straighter if it's staked, but remove the stake once the tree is established. Shape the earth around the crown into a wide saucer. Water slowly and deeply. Apply mulch 3 in. deep starting 3 in. from the trunk.

Growing Tips
The first year, unless there's a soaking rain, in spring and fall slowly and gently pour two to three bucketsful of water around the roots every two weeks; in summer every week or ten days. Maintain the mulch.

Care
Apply a slow-release, organic fertilizer in early spring to just beyond the drip line, at half the recommended rate and water it in. Replenish the mulch. In late winter or early spring cut away branches that will grow into the center of the tree or rub against other branches—keep it open a nd airy.

Companion Planting and Design
The callery pear is tolerant of urban conditions, and a superb street tree and park specimen.

Our Personal Recommendations
'Chanticleer' (which may be the same as 'Select' and 'Cleveland Select') (Zone 5) has a distinctive conical form ideal for street planting and lawns. 'Whitehouse', a larger National Arboretum introduction, is best for boulevards and parks: it has a strongly developed central stem, produces masses of pure white flowers, and colors red-purple early in the fall. 'Redspire', a narrow pyramidal form 30 to 35 ft. tall, tolerates urban conditions and is also recommended for street planting.

Common Smoke Tree

Cotinus coggygria

When, Where, and How to Plant

The smoke tree transplants readily in spring while the plant is still dormant, and in fall before Indian summer. It achieves the best color growing in full sun but grows well in part shade. Almost any soil will do; it can handle dry, rocky soils, but in well-drained loam it thrives. See Soil Preparation in the Introduction, and the planting instructions at the beginning of this chapter. Provide a planting hole three times the width of the rootball and twice as deep. Set the tree so the crown will be an inch or so above ground level. Shape the earth around the crown into a wide saucer. Water slowly and deeply. Apply mulch 3 in. deep starting 3 in. from the trunk.

Growing Tips

The first year, unless there's a soaking rain, in spring and fall slowly and gently pour two to three bucketsful of water around the roots every two weeks; in summer every week or ten days. Maintain the mulch.

Care

Apply a slow-release, organic fertilizer in early spring, at half the recommended rate, from the drip line to a distance $1^1/2$ times the tree's height. Water it in. Replenish the mulch. The flowers appear on new growth, so you can cut the plant back in late winter or early spring to keep it small, and to encourage greater flowering.

Companion Planting and Design

Smoke tree is a lovely addition to any shrub grouping, and makes a beautiful hedge.

Our Personal Recommendations

We like several of the colorful named varieties: 'Royal Purple' unfolds from a rich maroon red to a rich purple that doesn't fade; 'Velvet Cloak' is a luminous dark purple; 'Black Velvet' has dark purple foliage. 'Notcutts' Variety' is a strikingly rich, dark maroon purple. Where a larger plant can be used, the 20- to 30-ft. native American smoke tree, *C. obovatus* (Zone 3), would be our choice because the color is more spectacular. Michael Dirr says, "It may be the best of all American shrub trees for intensity of color."

A favorite of the Victorians, attractive in every season, the smoke tree can be counted on for beautiful foliage, romantic effect, and intense fall color. In June and early July tiny, inconspicuous, yellowish flowers appear, then in midsummer clouds of long, pink-gray fruiting panicles envelop the branches in misty halos that create a smoky effect. The source is thousands of tiny hairs attached to the developing fruit that dangles in clusters at the ends of the branches. Rounded, bluish purple or wine colored to dark green in summer, the leaves change in fall to yellow, red, and purple. The fall color is most pronounced in the hybrids. Medium to slow growing, as the tree matures the bark becomes corky and quite beautiful. Deer love it!

Other Names
Venetian Sumac, Wig Tree

Bloom Period and Seasonal Color
Smoky effect July and August; yellow, red, purple fall foliage.

Mature Height × Spread
10 to 15 ft. × 10 to 15 ft.

Zones
4 to 8

Dogwood
Cornus spp., cultivars, and hybrids

The dogwood is a graceful tree whose layered branches are covered in mid-spring with sparkling white, star-shaped flowers (actually bracts), followed in fall by bright red fruits that attract birds. Cold turns the foliage red-plum. The wild dogwood that blooms with the redbuds at the edges of our woodlands is the 20- to 30-ft. Cornus florida, *which now has problems with anthracnose and borers; many plant it anyway for its beauty. Dr. Elwin Orton of Rutgers University has crossed C. florida with the Chinese dogwood, C. kousa, and produced C. × rutgeriensis, and a group of hybrids resistant to anthracnose and borers; patented, they're marketed as the Stellar series. The other dogwood we recommend is the late-blooming, disease-resistant Chinese dogwood, C. kousa var.* chinensis, *whose flowers perch like butterflies on branches that droop a little. The bark exfoliates attractively as the plant matures.*

Bloom Period and Seasonal Color
Spring; white, pink, and pink-red; fall foliage colors red-plum and red fruits ripen.

Mature Height × Spread
20 to 30 ft. × 20 to 25 ft.

Zones
5 to 8

When, Where, and How to Plant
Plant a young, container-grown or balled-and-burlapped dogwood in early spring while it's still dormant. Handle the rootball with care. Dogwoods do best in partial or dappled light though they can handle full sun if the soil is humusy and moist. Ideal is a well-drained site with acid pH, 5.5 to 6.5, and about 40 percent humus. See Soil Preparation in the Introduction, and the planting instructions at the beginning of this chapter. Provide a planting hole three times the width of the rootball and twice as deep. Set the tree so the crown will be an inch or so above ground level. Staking might help the tree grow straighter, but remove it once the tree is established. Shape the earth around the crown into a wide saucer. Water slowly and deeply. Apply mulch 3 in. deep starting 3 in. from the trunk.

Growing Tips
The first year, unless there's a soaking rain, in spring and fall slowly and gently pour two to three bucketsful of water around the roots every two weeks; in summer every week or ten days. Maintain the mulch.

Care
Apply a slow-release, organic, acid fertilizer in early spring from the drip line to a distance $1^1/2$ times the tree's height. Water it in. Replenish the mulch.

Companion Planting and Design
Dogwoods are beautiful at the edge of a woodland, centering a lawn, or by a stone wall—almost anywhere.

Our Personal Recommendations
'Cloud 9' is one of the best large-flowering white cultivars of *C. florida;* 'Multibracteata' and 'Pluribracteata' have double white flowers; 'Rubra' has pinkish red flowers and the foliage colors well in the fall. The kousa dogwood 'Milky Way', a broad, bushy tree, produces quantities of white blooms; the bracts of the hybrid 'Summer Stars' stay beautiful for up to six weeks. Two other dogwood species with great appeal are 20- to 25-ft. *C. mas* (Zone 4), cornelian cherry, a yellow-flowered tree with showy, edible, acid-scarlet fruits that attract birds; there are varieties with yellow and variegated leaves.

When, Where, and How to Plant

Plant a balled-and-burlapped redbud in early spring—it can be difficult to transplant. Redbuds flower most fully growing in full sun but do well in open woodlands as long as they receive four to six hours of sun or all day dappled light. The cultivars can show winter die back, so choose a somewhat protected spot. Redbud succeeds in well-drained sites in either alkaline or acid soil, but not in a permanently wet location. See Soil Preparation in the Introduction, and the planting instructions at the beginning of this chapter. Provide a planting hole three times the width of the rootball and twice as deep. Set the tree so the crown will be an inch or so above ground level. The tree might grow straighter if it's staked, but remove the stake once the tree is established. Shape the earth around the crown into a wide saucer. Water slowly and deeply. Apply mulch 3 in. deep starting 3 in. from the trunk.

Growing Tips

The first year, unless there's a soaking rain, in spring and fall slowly and gently pour two to three bucketsful of water around the roots every two weeks; in summer every week or ten days. Maintain the mulch.

Care

Apply a slow-release, organic fertilizer in early spring from the drip line to a distance $1^1/2$ times the tree's height. Water it in. Replenish the mulch.

Companion Planting and Design

The redbud is small enough to use at the back of a shrub or a flower border; well grown, it will be large enough at maturity to be a specimen tree for a small yard. It is especially charming naturalized at the edge of an open woodland.

Our Personal Recommendations

'Royal White' is another beautiful white-flowered cultivar. The flowers of 'Wither's Pink Charm' are a clear pink. 'Forest Pansy' is a favorite of our Connecticut consultants, Judith and Pat Murphy. It's a strikingly colorful, purple-leaved redbud. 'Flame' is an attractive, double-flowered form.

When the wild dogwoods are just ready to bloom at the edge of the woodlands, the slim branches of little redbuds growing nearby are covered with showy, red-purple or magenta buds opening into rosy pink flowers. Usually after it blooms, but sometimes before, this multi-stemmed or low-branching native tree puts forth reddish purple leaves that change to dark, lustrous green, and often turn to gold in the fall. A mature redbud reaches 20 to 30 ft. in the wild but is likely to be half that size in cultivation. The fruit is a brown beanlike pod. Some lovely cultivated varieties are available but the excitement these days is generated by a beautiful white form, Cercis canadensis 'Alba'—not to be confused with a white subspecies of C. texensis.

Bloom Period and Seasonal Color
Early spring; red-purple, lavender-pink, magenta, white.

Mature Height × Spread
20 to 30 ft. × 25 to 35 ft.

Zones
4 to 8

European Hornbeam

Carpinus betulus 'Fastigiata'

The hornbeams are among the best medium to small trees for landscapes in urban areas. Fairly slow growers, they give good shade when mature. The European hornbeam withstands smoke, dust, and drought, and is considered one of the finest medium to small shade trees for city gardens. The papery fruits look like small lanterns. 'Fastigiata' is a handsome pyramidal form, and there are variegated and weeping cultivars. The American hornbeam, blue beech ironwood, Carpinus caroliniana, a small, handsome, slow-growing, 20- to 30-ft. tree that grows wild in woodlands all over the East, is hardier than the European hornbeam—to Zone 2. The bark is gray-blue and fluted, and perhaps for that reason it also is known as "blue beech." The foliage in autumn is orange to dark red. It makes an attractive street tree, but it is difficult to transplant.

Bloom Period and Seasonal Color
Spring; insignificant white florets.

Mature Height × Spread
30 to 40 ft. × 20 to 30 ft.

Zones
4 to 7

When, Where, and How to Plant
Plant a young container-grown or balled-and-burlapped tree in early spring while the plant is still dormant. The hornbeam is not easy to transplant, so handle the rootball with care. The European hornbeam does best in full sun but tolerates part shade. It can manage in soil that is either acid or alkaline. The American hornbeam does well in part or full shade, and in somewhat acid soil. See Soil Preparation in the Introduction, and the planting instructions at the beginning of this chapter. Provide a planting hole three times the width of the rootball and twice as deep. Set the tree so the crown will be an inch or so above ground level. Staking might help the tree grow straighter, but remove it once the tree is established. Shape the earth around the crown into a wide saucer. Water slowly and deeply. Apply mulch 3 in. deep starting 3 in. from the trunk.

Growing Tips
The first year, unless there's a soaking rain, in spring and fall slowly and gently pour two to three bucketsful of water around the roots every two weeks; in summer every week or ten days. Maintain the mulch.

Care
Apply a slow-release, organic fertilizer in early spring from the drip line to a distance $1^1/2$ times the tree's height. Water it in. Replenish the mulch.

Companion Planting and Design
The European hornbeam is a very shearable tree that in Europe is used in high hedges and to create allées of pleached trees (closely planted trees or shrubs sheared to create a high wall). Here you see it often in malls and commercial developments. The little American hornbeam is an excellent choice for naturalizing near streams and rivers, as it tolerates pollution, wet soil, and periodic flooding.

Our Personal Recommendations
Two varieties that lend character to a landscape are 'Columnaris', a narrow form of European hornbeam, and 'Pendula', a weeping tree.

Flowering Cherry
Prunus spp. and hybrids

When, Where, and How to Plant
Transplant a balled-and-burlapped tree in early spring. Flowering fruit trees bloom best in full sun. The ideal soil is well-drained, sandy loam, pH 6.0 to 7.5. See Soil Preparation in the Introduction, and the planting instructions at the beginning of this chapter. Provide a planting hole three times the width of the rootball and twice as deep. Set the tree so the crown will be an inch or so above ground level. The tree might grow straighter if it's staked, but remove the stake once the tree is established. Shape the earth into a wide saucer. Water slowly and deeply. Apply mulch 3 in. deep starting 3 in. from the trunk.

Growing Tips
The first year, unless there's a soaking rain, in spring and fall slowly and gently pour two to three bucketsful of water around the roots every two weeks; in summer every week or ten days. Maintain the mulch.

Care
Apply a slow-release, organic fertilizer in early spring from the drip line to a distance 1¹/₂ times the tree's height. Water it in. Replenish the mulch. After the tree has bloomed, remove any sprigs that will become branches headed for the center of the tree or that will ultimately cross other branches. Roots are close to the surface, so weed by hand.

Companion Planting and Design
The Higan cherry is a specimen tree, and its best use is as a featured plant set where it can be seen at a distance. Cultivars of the sargent cherry, recommended below, are excellent street trees, and beautiful set out as specimens in lawns, large or small.

Our Personal Recommendations
A favorite of Connecticut consultant Judith Murphy is *P. subhirtella* 'Autumnalis' (Zone 6), a double-flowered pink cherry that blooms fully in early spring and repeats some in fall. The sargent cherry, *P. sargentii* (Zone 6), is one of the most useful cherries: the deep pink flowers are showy, it is big enough to provide shade for a small garden, has bronzy leaves that redden in fall, and the polished mahogany bark is handsome in winter.

Among the first flowering trees to burst into bloom after a New England winter are species and hybrids of the genus Prunus. *There are flowering plums, apricots, peaches, almonds, and nectarines but the most celebrated are the flowering cherries. Bred for their blooms, they produce rudimentary fruit appealing to birds. The Higan cherry, P. subhirtella 'Pendula', is one of the most beautiful, a classic weeping cherry. One of the earliest, it bears abundant single pink flowers hanging from graceful, drooping branches. The fruits are black and inconspicuous. 'Pendula Plena Rosea' (syn. 'Yae-Shidare-Higan'), double weeping cherry, is a pink double that blooms later. 'Snow Fountain' is a white form. In Zone 3 the little Amur cherry, P. maackii, is hardy—not showy, but still a flowering cherry, and a major asset is the glossy red-brown exfoliating bark striped with black and gray like the white birch. It bears 2- to 3-in. racemes of small white flowers, followed by black berries that attract birds.*

Bloom Period and Seasonal Color
April to May; pink flowers.

Mature Height × Spread
20 to 50 ft. × 20 to 50 ft.

Zones
5 to 8

Flowering Crabapple
Malus spp., cultivars, and hybrids

Apple trees thrive in New England, but the Malus found in most gardens is the flowering crabapple. These small, spreading trees are covered in spring with exquisite apple blossoms, fragrant in some hybrids, and the brilliant fall fruits are decorative and attract birds. Older varieties have problems, but there are new and beautiful disease-resistant hybrids. One of the best is 'Donald Wyman', a showy crab with soft pink buds opening to white. The magnificent 18-ft. Japanese crabapple, M. floribunda, has much to recommend it: a branch spread of 25 ft., a lovely silhouette in winter, buds that are deep pink opening to white, fragrant flowers, and yellow-red fruits. If you want to attract herds of deer to your property, grow "real" apples (or pears)—but be prepared to share the rest of your garden with them as well.

Other Name
Flowering Crab

Bloom Period and Seasonal Color
Mid-spring; pink or carmine buds opening to white; colorful fruits follow.

Mature Height × Spread
10 to 25 ft. × 10 to 25 ft.

Zones
4 to 7

When, Where, and How to Plant
A young container-grown or balled-and-burlapped crabapple transplants readily in early spring or fall. The best light is full sun. Don't plant within 500 ft. of a red cedar, which can lead to rust fungus diseases. Crabs adapt and flourish in well-drained, heavy, loamy soil on the acid side, pH 5.0 to 6.5. See Soil Preparation in the Introduction, and the planting instructions at the beginning of this chapter. Provide a planting hole three times the width of the rootball and twice as deep. Set the tree so the crown will be an inch or so above ground level. Staking might help the tree grow straighter, but remove it once the tree is established. Shape the earth around the crown into a wide saucer. Water slowly and deeply. Apply mulch 3 in. deep starting 3 in. from the stem.

Growing Tips
The first year, unless there's a soaking rain, in spring and fall slowly and gently pour two to three bucketsful of water around the roots every two weeks; in summer every week or ten days. Maintain the mulch.

Care
Apply a slow-release, organic fertilizer for acid-loving plants in early spring from the drip line to a distance 1 1/2 times the tree's height. Water it in. Replenish the mulch. Remove branches heading to the center of the tree, or crossing others. Prune after the tree has bloomed, or in summer; orchardists are now pruning dwarf fruit trees in summer.

Companion Planting and Design
A flowering crabapple should be set out as a featured specimen.

Our Personal Recommendations
Connecticut consultant Judith Murphy's favorite large crab is *M. floribunda* 'Snowdrift'. Her favorite small crab is *M. sargentii*, the dwarf sargent crab, which is just 5 to 8 ft. high and twice as wide. Other exceptional crabapples are 'Narragansett', a resistant introduction of the U.S. National Arboretum, recommended for small gardens; the Brooklyn Botanic Garden's striking introduction, weeping 'Red Jade', whose fruits are a glossy red; and 'Sugar Tyme' and 'White Cascade', graceful, drooping crabapples with white flowers.

Franklin Tree
Franklinia alatamaha

When, Where, and How to Plant

The Franklin tree is not always easy to transplant, so if you can, purchase a young container-grown or balled-and-burlapped tree from a reliable nursery. Set the tree out in early spring while it's still dormant. The flowers and fall color are most remarkable when the tree is growing in full sun. Even in Zone 5, it needs a site protected from cold north winds. The Franklin tree thrives in well-drained soil that is fertile, loose, humusy enough to hold moisture, and in the acid range, pH 5.0 to 6.0, although it adapts to mildly alkaline soils. See Soil Preparation in the Introduction, and the planting instructions at the beginning of this chapter. Make the planting hole three times the width of the rootball and twice as deep. Set the tree so the crown will be an inch or so above ground level. Staking might help the tree grow straighter, but remove it once the tree is established. Shape the earth around the crown into a wide saucer. Water slowly and deeply. Apply mulch 3 in. deep starting 3 in. from the stem.

Growing Tips

The first year, unless there's a soaking rain, in spring and fall slowly and gently pour two to three bucketsful of water around the roots every two weeks; in summer every week or ten days. Maintain the mulch.

Care

Apply a slow-release, organic fertilizer for acid-loving plants in early spring from the drip line to a distance 1^1/2 times the tree's height. Water it in. Replenish the mulch.

Companion Planting and Design

The Franklin tree is an exceptionally lovely plant that belongs out in the open where its flowers and fall color can be appreciated.

Our Personal Recommendation

Plant the species.

The Franklin tree, a lovely little flowering tree with a romantic history, bears fragrant 3-in., white flowers from late summer with some bloom in fall. New growth at the tips of the upright spreading branches gives the plant an airy, open look. The long, lustrous leaves appear late in the spring; in summer they turn bright green; then in fall they color bronze, orange, and red. The bark is interestingly ridged. The tree is native to North America but no longer found in the wild. In 1765 John Bartram discovered it growing near Fort Barrington along Georgia's Altamaha River, and he collected seeds. Bartram planted his seeds and grew the first cultivated trees at his home near Philadelphia. He named it for Benjamin Franklin.

Other Name
Ben Franklin Tree

Bloom Period and Seasonal Color
Late summer into fall; white with showy yellow stamens; fall foliage is bronze, orange, red.

Mature Height × Spread
15 to 20 ft. × 6 to 15 ft.

Zones
5 to 8

Ginkgo
Ginkgo biloba

A tall, stately tree ideal for city parks, the ginkgo has easily recognized, fan-shaped leaves and turns a truly luminous butter-yellow-gold in fall, and the color lasts. It forms a rounded crown near the top of the tall, straight trunk. Because it tolerates pollution and salt it has been used as a street tree but that isn't its best use. Though it bears these broad, triangular leaves, it is more closely related to conifers (cone bearing trees and shrubs). This ancient species is estimated to have been growing on the planet for 150 million years: a Korean ginkgo has been documented as 1,100 years old. The strain we have now comes from China, but at one time it grew wild on this continent.

Other Name
Maidenhair Tree

Bloom Period and Seasonal Color
March and April; gold fall foliage.

Mature Height × Spread
30 to 50 ft. × 30 to 50 ft.

Zones
4 to 9

When, Where, and How to Plant

Ginkgos transplant readily in spring while the plant is still dormant, and in fall before Indian summer. Chris Donnelly, Connecticut's D.E.P, Forestry Division, recommends plants grown from seed, which have better form than those developed from cuttings. The ginkgo requires full sun, at least six hours a day. It does well in almost any soil, but thrives in sandy, deeply dug, well-drained, moist soil with a pH 5.5 to 7.5. See Soil Preparation in the Introduction, and the planting instructions at the beginning of this chapter. Provide a planting hole three times the width of the rootball and twice as deep. Set the tree so the crown will be an inch or so above ground level. Staking might help the tree grow straighter, but remove it once the tree is established. Shape the earth around the crown into a wide saucer. Water slowly and deeply. Apply mulch 3 in. deep starting 3 in. from the stem.

Growing Tips

The first year, unless there's a soaking rain, in spring and fall slowly and gently pour two to three bucketsful of water around the roots every two weeks; in summer every week or ten days. Maintain the mulch.

Care

Apply a complete, slow-release, long lasting lawn fertilizer in early spring from the drip line to a distance $1^1/_2$ times the tree's height. Water it in. Replenish the mulch. Cut away any young branches that will grow into the center of the tree or rub against other branches.

Companion Planting and Design

A mature ginkgo is a tall, stately, handsome tree at its best growing in a large landscape or park setting. Its open form is not as attractive as a young tree, and it's too tall to look well in a small garden when it begins to mature.

Our Personal Recommendations

Ask for and make sure you get a male ginkgo. The female tree produces a messy, plum-like fruit that smells badly. One of the best-looking cultivars is a broad-headed male called 'Autumn Gold'. The male clone 'Princeton Sentry'® has a narrow, upright form.

Golden Weeping Willow

Salix × *sepulcralis* var. *chrysocoma*

When, Where, and How to Plant

Plant a container-grown or balled-and-burlapped willow in spring while it is still dormant. You can root whips of a willow if you cut them before the plant leafs out: stick a bunch of whips in a moist spot and chances are many will root. The willows are most beautiful growing in full sun. Keep willows far away from water pipes, which they regularly invade. To flourish they must have sustained moisture but they tolerate a range of soils, from pH 5.5 to 7.5. See Soil Preparation in the Introduction, and the planting instructions at the beginning of this chapter. Provide a planting hole three times the width of the rootball and twice as deep. Set the tree so the crown will be an inch or so above ground level. Staking might help the tree grow straighter, but remove it once the tree is established. Shape the earth around the crown into a wide saucer. Water slowly and deeply. Apply mulch 3 in. deep starting 3 in. from the trunk.

Growing Tips

The first year, unless there's a soaking rain, in spring and fall slowly and gently pour two to three bucketsful of water around the roots every two weeks; in summer every week or ten days. Maintain the moisture and the mulch.

Care

Apply a slow-release, organic fertilizer in early spring from the drip line to a distance 1¹/₂ times the tree's height. Water it in. Replenish the mulch. If pruning is needed, summer and fall are the best times.

Companion Planting and Design

Fast growing, you can naturalize weeping willows along stream banks to hold the soil, and in suburban yards to create airy screening. Place the tree where wind will sweep through the branches.

Our Personal Recommendation

Another beautiful weeping willow tree is the 30- to 40-ft. Babylon weeping willow, *S. babylonica*, whose branches sweep the ground; but it is hardy only to Zone 6, and the true species can be hard to find.

Fast growing, easily rooted, upright, and graceful, willows mark the streams and rivers in milder parts of New England. They are among the first trees to leaf out in early spring and the foliage of many species turns to gold in fall and stays until the last days of autumn. For gardeners the most appealing willow is the 50- to 70-ft. weeping tree known as Salix × sepulcralis var. chrysocoma (a cross between the Babylon weeping willow, S. babylonica, and the white willow, S. alba 'Tristis'). The most graceful of all weeping trees, exquisite in motion, ideal for planting near ponds and lakes, it develops a rounded outline with age. The males present the elongated clusters, or catkins, that in shrubby species are called "pussy willows." The florist's pussy willow is the goat willow, S. caprea (Zone 4), which bears velvety, silvery-gray catkins. S. gracilistyla var. melanostachys is an interesting new shrubby pussy willow cultivar whose catkins appear almost black.

Bloom Period and Seasonal Color
Early spring; golden.

Mature Height × Spread
30 to 70 ft. × 30 to 70 ft.

Zones
4 to 7

Japanese Maple
Acer palmatum

The most elegant foliage tree used in landscaping is the Japanese maple, Acer palmatum. It comes in various sizes, shapes, and colors—weeping, upright, tall shrub, or small tree, and the foliage may be green, pink, red, or black-red. The best upright deep red variety is probably A. palmatum 'Bloodgood', which is about 8 to 10 ft. tall. The leaves hold their brilliant spring red well, then change to green and in fall become a rich scarlet. The most elegant of the smaller forms is the threadleaf Japanese maple, A. palmatum 'Dissectum Atropurpureum', which is 6- to 8-ft. tall, and has exquisite, deeply cut leaves and a picturesque weeping form. The ferny foliage is a rich purple-red in spring, fades toward green-plum in summer, then turns a spectacular orange in the fall.

Bloom Period and Seasonal Color
Spring foliage is red, fading toward green in summer, and fiery shades in the fall.

Mature Height × Spread
6 to 20 ft. × 6 to 20 ft.

Zones
5 to 9

When, Where, and How to Plant
Japanese maples benefit from special care in transplanting. In early spring set out a container-grown plant, or a young balled-and-burlapped specimen. The Japanese maple needs four to seven hours of sun to color well, but in warmer areas it may burn if it is without some protection from the noon sun and from hot afternoon sun. It does best in a well-drained site and humusy, rich, moist, slightly acid soil, but it is fairly adaptable. See Soil Preparation in the Introduction, and the planting instructions at the beginning of this chapter. Provide a planting hole three times the width of the rootball and twice as deep. Set the shrub so the crown will be an inch or two above ground level. The taller Japanese maples may grow straighter if staked for the first year—don't leave a stake on after the tree is growing strongly. Shape the soil around the crown into a wide saucer. Water slowly and deeply. Apply mulch 3 in. deep starting 3 in. from the crown.

Growing Tips
The first year, unless there's a soaking rain, in spring and fall slowly and gently pour two to three bucketsful of water around the roots every two weeks; in summer every week or ten days. Maintain the mulch.

Care
In droughts, water a Japanese maple slowly and deeply every two weeks. Japanese maples rarely require pruning to develop a beautiful form. Fertilize in early spring.

Companion Planting and Design
We have used vinca and ajuga as ground covers under a Japanese maple; if the shade cast is dense, you can thin a few branches.

Our Personal Recommendations
'Bloodgood' and the threadleaf Japanese maple are our recommendations. Another beauty is the full moon Japanese maple, *A. japonicum* 'Aureum', a 10- to 20-ft. tree whose foliage in spring is a soft glowing yellow green and in fall turns to luminous crimson tinged with purple.

Japanese Pagoda Tree
Sophora japonica

When, Where, and How to Plant

Plant a *young* balled-and-burlapped or container-grown tree in spring while it is still dormant. The Japanese pagoda tree is somewhat tender to cold when young, but when it is established and growing well it will withstand more cold. It flowers most fully when growing in full sun. Ideal is a well-drained site with space all around. The Japanese pagoda tree adapts to a wide range of soils, and tolerates poor soil, pollution, and, once mature, drought. See Soil Preparation in the Introduction, and the planting instructions at the beginning of this chapter. Provide a planting hole three times the width of the rootball and twice as deep. Set the tree so the crown will be an inch or so above ground level. Staking might help the tree grow straighter, but remove it once the tree is established. Shape the earth around the crown into a wide saucer. Water slowly and deeply. Apply mulch 3 in. deep starting 3 in. from the stem.

Growing Tips

The first year, unless there's a soaking rain, in spring and fall slowly and gently pour two to three bucketsful of water around the roots every two weeks; in summer every week or ten days. Maintain the mulch.

Care

Apply a complete, slow-release, long lasting, organic fertilizer in spring before growth begins, to just beyond the drip line at half the recommended rate, and water it in. Replenish the mulch. Repeat in November. In the fall after the leaves go, prune to create a strong central leader.

Companion Planting and Design

The tree is lovely underplanted with a living mulch of any one of the drought-tolerant ground covers, such as periwinkle or ajuga. Hostas, liriope, and small spring-flowering bulbs such as wood hyacinths are also acceptable ground covers.

Our Personal Recommendation

Princeton Nurseries has introduced a cultivar, 'Regent', that has a large oval crown of glossy, dark green leaves; it is said to come into bloom at six to eight years of age.

An airy, exceptionally beautiful tree for parks, the Japanese pagoda tree bears showy panicles of creamy white, somewhat fragrant, pea-like flowers for several weeks during the summer. The flowers are followed by drooping clusters of fruits—showers of pale-green, winged pods that look like beads and are persistent, and just as beautiful as the flowers. Gardeners who have planted the species often are disappointed to discover that the flowers don't begin to appear until the tree is ten to fourteen years old—but the display is worth waiting for. The bark is pale gray and the foliage handsome. A rapid grower, the Japanese pagoda tree tolerates drought and difficult city conditions; it's a good specimen plant for large lawns, parks, and golf courses.

Other Name
Chinese Scholar-Tree

Bloom Period and Seasonal Color
July through mid-August; panicles of creamy white flowers followed by drooping clusters of pale-green, winged pods.

Mature Height × Spread
40 to 50 ft. × 30 to 40 ft.

Zones
4 to 7

Japanese Stewartia

Stewartia pseudocamellia

The stewartias are small trees and tall shrubs that bear 2¹/₂- to 3¹/₂-in. camellia-like flowers in mid- to late summer when little else blooms. Japanese stewartia is a beautiful small tree with many assets—exquisite flowers, colorful foliage, and peeling bark that shows cinnamon red, gray, and shades of orange. The blossoms are small, cup shaped, and the color is a beautiful creamy white set off by a prominent mass of orange anthers at the center. When the leaves emerge in early spring they are purple-bronze. In summer they turn green, and with cold weather they change to yellow, purple-orange, and bronze-red. As the plant matures, the bark sheds in striking patterns of cinnamon red-gray and orange. It needs some protection in Zones 4 and 5.

Bloom Period and Seasonal Color
Mid- to late summer; white petals with orange anthers; fall foliage is yellow, purple-orange, and bronze-red; mature trees have colorful exfoliating bark.

Mature Height × Spread
30 to 40 ft. × 20 to 30 ft.

Zones
4 to 8

When, Where, and How to Plant
Plant a small, young, container-grown or balled-and-burlapped tree in early spring while it's still dormant. The flowers and fall color are most remarkable when the tree is growing in full sun. It thrives in soil that is fertile, moist, contains a third to a half leaf mold or peat moss, and is in the acid range, pH 4.5 to 5.5. See Soil Preparation in the Introduction, and the planting instructions at the beginning of this chapter. Provide a planting hole three times the width of the rootball and twice as deep. Set the tree so the crown will be an inch above ground level. Staking might help the tree grow straighter, but remove it once the tree is established. Shape the earth around the crown into a wide saucer. Water slowly and deeply. Apply mulch 3 in. deep starting 3 in. from the stem.

Growing Tips
The first year, unless there's a soaking rain, in spring and fall slowly and gently pour two to three bucketsful of water around the roots every two weeks; in summer every week or ten days. Maintain the mulch.

Care
Apply a slow-release, organic fertilizer for acid-loving plants in early spring from the drip line to a distance 1¹/₂ times the tree's height. Water it in. Replenish the mulch.

Companion Planting and Design
Stewartia is beautiful as a lawn specimen, grouped in a shrub border with low-growing azaleas, and at the edge of an open woodland.

Our Personal Recommendations
Our favorite is Japanese stewartia, but for small gardens the very similar Korean stewartia, *S. koreana*, may be a better fit. The flowers are larger and flatter than those of the species above, and tend to appear over a longer period. The leaves turn to red and purple in the fall, and the bark flakes to show gorgeous patches of soft silvery-buff streaked with cinnamon and orange-brown. Chinese stewartia, *S. sinensis*, is smaller still in every way; the flowers are scented but the foliage does not take on the rich autumn hues of the other species.

Maple

Acer spp. and cultivars

When, Where, and How to Plant

Choose a container-grown or balled-and-burlapped tree and plant it in fall before Indian summer, or in early spring while the tree is still dormant. Most maples do best in slightly acid soil and full sun, but almost any well-drained, rich, moist soil will do. Very young saplings of the swamp maple and its cultivars transplant readily bare root. See Soil Preparation in the Introduction, and the planting instructions at the beginning of this chapter. For all maples provide a planting hole three times the width of the rootball and twice as deep. Set the tree so the crown will be an inch or so above ground level. Staking might help the tree grow straighter, but remove it once the tree is established. Shape the earth around the crown into a wide saucer. Water slowly and deeply. Apply mulch 3 in. deep starting 3 in. from the stem.

Growing Tips

The first year, unless there's a soaking rain, in spring and fall slowly and gently pour two to three bucketsful of water around the roots every two weeks; in summer every week or ten days. Maintain the mulch.

Care

Do not let the soil around a young maple go dry at any time; in dry spells, water even mature maples deeply, since they have a shallow root system. In spring before growth begins, apply a complete, slow-release, long-lasting, organic lawn fertilizer from the drip line to a distance 1 1/2 times the tree's height and water it in. Replenish the mulch.

Companion Planting and Design

Most large maples are better in large landscapes, and as park trees rather than street trees unless watered in droughts. The roots of a vigorous maple will buckle cement sidewalks and patios.

Our Personal Recommendations

The sugar maple cultivar 'Green Mountain' is very hardy—to -40 degrees Fahrenheit—and can handle more drought than some others; 'Bonfire' may grow faster than the species and has more reliable fall color. An outstanding red maple cultivar is 40-foot 'Red Sunset', which has exceptional orange-red fall color.

For the New England home garden perhaps the most valuable shade tree is the majestic maple. In spring, it covers itself with colorful buds, and in fall the leaves turn to yellow, orange, and bright red. The species renowned for fall color is the big, beautiful, slow-growing sugar maple, Acer saccharum, the source of maple syrup. A mature sugar maple has a pyramidal shape, great strength and character, and wide branches that provide dappled shade. In the wild, it reaches 100 ft. and more. Though smaller in cultivation, it's a magnificent tree for parks and large landscapes. For smaller gardens the faster-growing swamp or red maple, A. rubrum, is used. Its fall color is often a more intense red, but it has more root problems than the sugar maple. The maples withstand some pollution.

Bloom Period and Seasonal Color
Spring; greenish yellow to red buds in the sugar maple and garnet red buds in the swamp maple and its cultivars; foliage turns in fall to yellow, orange, and bright red.

Mature Height × Spread
60 to 75 ft. × 40 ft.

Zones
3 to 9

Oak

Quercus spp.

The oaks are magnificent spreading shade trees suited to parks, large landscapes, and city streets—long-lived, symmetrical, and handsome. The finest of the oaks for fall color is the red oak, Quercus rubra (syn. Q. borealis), a quick-growing, clean tree 60, 75, to 95 ft. tall. The new leaves are red in spring and turn russet to wine red in fall. It withstands urban pollution and is a good tree for lawns, parks, and golf courses. For a large landscape we recommend the white oak, Q. alba (Zone 5), which is the state tree of Connecticut. The finest native oak, it has an arresting silhouette, and slowly attains heights of 80 to 90 ft. The foliage tends toward blue-green in summer, and in fall changes to wine red and persists. Production difficulties and slow growth make it hard to find.

Bloom Period and Seasonal Color
Fall foliage turns yellow or nut brown, or various shades of red and russet.

Mature Height × Spread
40 to 95 ft. × 40 to 60 ft.

Zones
4 to 8

When, Where, and How to Plant

Plant an oak while it is still dormant in early spring. Buy a young container-grown or balled-and-burlapped tree and handle it with TLC: most oak species have taproots that can be damaged. Generally, the species does best growing in full sun and prefers moist, fertile, somewhat acid, well-drained, sandy loam. See Soil Preparation in the Introduction, and the planting instructions at the beginning of this chapter. Provide a planting hole three times the width of the rootball and twice as deep. Set the tree so the crown will be an inch or so above ground level. Staking can help the tree grow straighter, but remove it once the tree is established. Shape the earth around the crown into a wide saucer. Water slowly and deeply. Apply mulch 3 in. deep starting 3 in. from the trunk.

Growing Tips

The first year, unless there's a soaking rain, in spring and fall slowly and gently pour two to three bucketsful of water around the roots every two weeks; in summer every week or ten days. Maintain the mulch.

Care

Apply a complete, slow-release, long-lasting, organic lawn fertilizer in early spring from the drip line to a distance $1^1/_2$ times the tree's height. Water it in. Replenish the mulch. Water deeply during droughts until the plant is growing well. In late winter, prune to develop a strong central leader.

Companion Planting and Design

Red oaks are the best choice for quick growth and a small urban landscape.

Our Personal Recommendations

We like the red oak. A really hardy oak is *Q. macrocarpa*, the bur or mossycup oak, which withstands winters in Zone 2. A big, impressive, inspiring tree 70 to 80 ft. tall, it has corky branches and a picturesque appearance. Difficult to transplant but very adaptable—thriving in alkaline soil, dry or wet. It tolerates urban conditions better than most oaks and is used in parks and large landscapes.

Red Horse Chestnut
Aesculus × carnea 'Briotii'

When, Where, and How to Plant
Transplant container-grown or balled-and-burlapped horse chestnut trees in early spring. The horse chestnuts thrive in full sun, but they also do well in bright shade. The most successful plants are grown in moist, well-drained soil whose pH is around 6.5, but they are tolerant of other soils. See Soil Preparation in the Introduction, and the planting instructions at the beginning of this chapter. Provide a planting hole three times the width of the rootball and twice as deep. Set the tree so the crown will be an inch or so above ground level. Staking might help the tree grow straighter, but remove it once the tree is established. Shape the earth around the crown into a wide saucer. Water slowly and deeply. Apply mulch 3 in. deep starting 3 in. from the main stem.

Growing Tips
The first year, unless there's a soaking rain, in spring and fall slowly and gently pour two to three bucketsful of water around the roots every two weeks; in summer every week or ten days. Maintain the mulch.

Care
In early spring apply a complete, slow-release, long lasting, organic fertilizer from the drip line to a distance $1^1/_2$ times the tree's height. Water it in. Replenish the mulch. Even after the plant is established and growing well, water deeply during droughts. Prune out any young branches that will grow into the center of the tree or rub against other branches.

Companion Planting and Design
'Briotii' is an excellent choice for a large yard, and it is used extensively for shade in street plantings, in parks, golf courses, and on campuses.

Our Personal Recommendations
'Briotii' is our first choice for the home garden, but its big and beautiful cousin, *A. hippocastanum* 'Baumannii', whose flowers are white and double, is an inspired choice for the larger landscape and it is hardy in Zone 3.

The beautiful European and Asian horse chestnut trees are cousins to our native buckeyes. The horse chestnuts are admired for their showy spring flowers, but they are planted mainly for the wide branching and dense foliage that make these superior shade trees. The red horse chestnut is a hybrid resulting from crossing the North American native red buckeye, Aesculus pavia, with the European horse chestnut, A. hippocastanum. The cultivar 'Briotii' is a beautiful pyramidal tree that bears showy, upright panicles of flowers 8 to 10 in. long in rosy shades. The leaves have the shape of a hand and retain their rich dark green well into October. The fruit of the horse chestnut is of no interest as they are inedible and prickly.

Bloom Period and Seasonal Color
Early to mid-May; rose-red or salmon-red flowers.

Mature Height × Spread
45 to 60 ft. × 35 to 45 ft.

Zones
4 to 7

Russian Olive

Elaeagnus angustifolia

From freezing Zone 2 through mild Zone 7 the Russian olive is used north of our border, out west, and along the coast for erosion control and as a tall hedge and windbreak. A rugged, winter hardy tree with silvery foliage, it came to us from southern Europe and western Asia and has been here since colonial days. The plant has an open, rather picturesque structure, and the narrow willow-like leaves are gray-green above and covered with silvery white scales beneath. Though it looks somewhat like the olive trees of southern Europe, the fruit that develops from the small, fragrant, cream-yellow flowers that appear in spring are yellow or orange with silvery scales, sweetish, not a bit like an olive. The Russian olive tolerates poor soil, a lot of pruning, drought, neglect, as well as salt and wind. Russian olive is on the invasive plants list in several states, but it sometimes happens that one state's environmental threat is another state's bank holder.

Bloom Period and Seasonal Color
Spring; small, fragrant, cream-yellow flowers.

Mature Height × Spread
20 ft. × 15 to 20 ft.

Zones
2 to 7

When, Where, and How to Plant
Set out a container-grown or balled-and-burlapped Russian olive in the spring while the plant is still dormant. This tree will do best in full sun, but can succeed in part sun. Russian olive can handle a windy location and in fact will end up looking quite picturesque there. It thrives in a light sandy loam but it succeeds in almost any soil, including salty coastal soils. See Soil Preparation in the Introduction, and the planting instructions at the beginning of this chapter. Provide a planting hole three times the width of the rootball and twice as deep. Set the tree so the crown will be an inch or so above ground level. Staking might help the tree grow straighter, but remove it once the tree is established. Shape the earth around the crown into a wide saucer. Water slowly and deeply. Apply mulch 3 in. deep starting 3 in. from the stem.

Growing Tips
The first year, unless there's a soaking rain, in spring and fall slowly and gently pour two to three bucketsful of water around the roots every two weeks; in summer every week or ten days. Maintain the mulch.

Care
In early spring apply a complete, slow-release, long lasting, organic lawn fertilizer from the drip line to a distance $1^1/2$ times the tree's height. Water it in. Replenish the mulch.

Companion Planting and Design
Naturalized, or planted as a tall hedge and more or less neglected, the Russian olive usually stays to 12 to 15 ft. Provided with care and space to expand, the Russian olive can grow at a medium to fast rate reaching a height of 30 to 40 ft.

Our Personal Recommendation
Plant *E. angustifolia*, but be wary of other, potentially more invasive species, such as the autumn olive, *E. umbellata*.

Serviceberry
Amelanchier arborea

When, Where, and How to Plant

Plant a container-grown or balled-and-burlapped plant in early spring while the tree is still dormant, or in the fall before Indian summer. The serviceberry is at its very best and blooms well in full sun and in bright, all-day, filtered light. It grows in almost any soil, but thrives in moist, well-drained, acid soil, pH 5.0 to 6.5. See Soil Preparation in the Introduction, and the planting instructions at the beginning of this chapter. Provide a planting hole three times the width of the rootball and twice as deep. Set the tree so the crown will be an inch or so above ground level. The tree might grow straighter if it's staked, but remove the stake once the tree is established. Shape the earth around the crown into a wide saucer. Water slowly and deeply. Apply mulch 3 in. deep starting 3 in. from the trunk.

Growing Tips

The first year, unless there's a soaking rain, in spring and fall slowly and gently pour two to three bucketsful of water around the roots every two weeks; in summer every week or ten days. Maintain the mulch.

Care

Apply a slow-release, organic fertilizer in November and in early spring from the drip line to a distance 1 1/2 times the tree's height. Water it in. Replenish the mulch. Maintain soil moisture.

Companion Planting and Design

The serviceberries are most effective in groups at the edge of a woodland or as a backdrop for an island of shrubs where the fall color will be seen. They're excellent trees to plant near streams and lakes.

Our Personal Recommendations

There are some interesting and colorful cultivars of the naturally occurring hybrid *A.* × *grandiflora*, a cross between *A. arborea* and *A. laevis*, the Allegheny serviceberry: 'Robin Hill Pink' buds start out pink and fade to white; 'Autumn Brilliance' has a better red color in fall.

The serviceberries are airy little trees that grow in open woodlands and bear clusters of delicate ivory-white flowers in very early spring. The blossoms are followed by persistent, usually black, berry-like fruits that are rather sweet—and edible, something like a blueberry—and very attractive to birds. In fall, the leaves turn to yellow, orange, and eventually to dark red. Amelanchier arborea, the downy serviceberry or Juneberry, is a lovely little upright species that is one of the first trees to bloom in New England woods. Fall color is excellent and the attractive gray bark is streaked with red. The shadblow, A. canadensis, which is found in bogs and swamps from Maine to South Carolina, is an excellent tree for naturalizing in cooler areas—Zone 3—and for wet woodlands. It is an erect multi-stemmed little shrub or small tree 6 to 30 ft. tall.

Other Names
Shadblow, Shadbush, Juneberry, Downy Serviceberry

Bloom Period and Seasonal Color
Early spring; white flowers.

Mature Height × Spread
15 to 25 ft. × variable spread

Zones
4 to 9

Sour Gum
Nyssa sylvatica

In fall, this is one of the most beautiful of all our native trees—the leaves change to fluorescent yellow, orange, scarlet, and purple. The tree is pyramidal in form, with somewhat drooping branches. The usual height is 30 to 50 ft., but it grows taller in the wild, especially near water. Bees visit the small, nectar-rich, greenish white flowers that appear in spring, and an exceptionally flavorful honey is made from it. The flowers are followed by bluish fruits that are somewhat hidden by the leaves and are relished by bears and other wildlife. The bark is dark charcoal gray, broken into thick blocky ridges, giving the plant winter appeal. It tolerates pollution well enough to be used as a street tree in the suburbs.

Other Names
Black Gum, Black Tupelo

Bloom Period and Seasonal Color
Spring; small greenish white flowers; fall foliage is fluorescent yellow to orange to scarlet to purple.

Mature Height × Spread
30 to 50 ft. × 20 to 30 ft.

Zones
4 to 9

When, Where, and How to Plant
The sour gum has a taproot, which makes it very difficult to transplant successfully. Choose a thriving, *young*, container-grown plant, and set it out with the utmost of care. In cultivation it does best in full sun or bright, dappled shade. It requires moist, well-drained, acid soil, pH 5.5 to 6.5, and needs some protection from wind. See Soil Preparation in the Introduction, and planting instructions at the beginning of this chapter. Provide a planting hole three times the width of the rootball and twice as deep. Set the tree so the crown will be an inch or so above ground level. Staking might help the tree grow straighter, but remove it once the tree is established. Shape the earth around the crown into a wide saucer. Water slowly and deeply. Apply mulch 3 in. deep starting 3 in. from the stem.

Growing Tips
The first year, unless there's a soaking rain, in spring and fall slowly and gently pour two to three bucketsful of water around the roots every two weeks; in summer every week or ten days. Maintain the mulch.

Care
Apply a complete, slow-release, long-lasting, organic fertilizer for acid-loving plants before growth begins from the drip line to a distance 1¹/₂ times the tree's height. Water it in. Replenish the mulch. In late fall, cut away any branches that grow into the center of the tree or rub against other branches.

Companion Planting and Design
The sour gum looks its best featured at the edge of a lawn or near a stream or a pond where its autumn foliage will be seen. It is also successful at the shore.

Our Personal Recommendation
We recommend the species.

When, Where, and How to Plant

In early spring buy a *young*, still-dormant, container-grown plant from a reliable nursery, and handle the transplanting with great care. Sourwood does well in full sun, but it tolerates bright filtered light all day or partial bright shade. It requires a well-drained site, and acid soil, pH 5.5 to 6.5. See Soil Preparation in the Introduction, and the planting instructions at the beginning of this chapter. Provide a planting hole three times the width of the rootball and twice as deep. Set the tree so the crown will be an inch or so above ground level. Staking might help the tree grow straighter, but remove it once the tree is established. Shape the earth around the crown into a wide saucer. Water slowly and deeply. Apply mulch 3 in. deep starting 3 in. from the stem.

Growing Tips

The first year, unless there's a soaking rain, in spring and fall slowly and gently pour two to three bucketsful of water around the roots every two weeks; in summer every week or ten days. Maintain the mulch.

Care

Spread a compete, slow-release, long lasting, organic fertilizer for acid-loving plants in early spring before growth begins to a distance $1^1/_2$ times the tree's height. Water it in. Replenish the mulch.

Companion Planting and Design

Sourwood is known as the lily-of-the-valley tree—and considered second only to one other native flowering tree, the dogwood. We recommend that you make it a prominent feature of your landscape in a spot where it can be enjoyed all year long.

Our Personal Recommendation

Plant the species.

This lovely native tree of modest height veils itself in drooping racemes of fragrant, white, urn-shaped flowers in the summer. Then in the fall, its large, dark green leaves turn yellow, orange, red, and purple. Attractive seedpods follow the flowers and persist through fall. The tree has deeply furrowed bark, which is an attractive winter feature. Sourwood is a slow-growing tree that takes a dozen years to reach a height of 15 ft. or so. It is attractive to bees and is a source of a superb honey. Sourwood is a beautiful tree that naturalizes fairly easily and is well worth the effort needed to establish it in the home landscape. It does not transplant easily nor does it tolerate urban pollution.

Other Names
Lily-of-the-Valley Tree, Sorrel Tree

Bloom Period and Seasonal Color
Late June, early July; white flowers; yellow, orange, red, and purple foliage in fall.

Mature Height × Spread
25 to 30 ft. × 20 ft.

Zones
5 to 9

Star Magnolia
Magnolia stellata

There was a time when magnolias were a rarity in New England. Perhaps the winters are milder, or gardeners have become more daring. Today, here in our northwest Connecticut, many good-sized magnolias bloom in spring, so we know they have lived through decades of our winters. One of the loveliest hardy species is the star magnolia, Magnolia stellata, a leaf-losing magnolia whose flowers appear early, before the leaves—twelve to eighteen narrow, pure white, fragrant petals. A mature star magnolia in bloom is a glorious sight. The fragrant cultivar 'Waterlily' has fourteen to twenty-four petals, is pink in bud, opening to white. Another hardy magnolia is M. × loebneri, which blooms later and grows to 20 to 25 ft. much sooner. These flowers have as many as fifteen petals. 'Merrill' (Zone 3) bears masses of 3- to 3¹/2-in. flowers and has a beautiful branching habit.

Bloom Period and Seasonal Color
Spring; flowers are cream white.

Mature Height × Spread
15 to 20 ft. × 10 to 15 ft.

Zones
4 to 8

When, Where, and How to Plant
Transplant a young container-grown or balled-and-burlapped magnolia with care, before new growth begins in early spring. Full sun is best but four to six hours of sun, or all-day filtered light will do. Look for a site that is protected from the north wind but not particularly warm: these magnolias tend to have their too-early blossoms ruined by late frosts. Ideal soil is acid, pH 5.0 to 6.5, fertile, humusy, and well drained, but not dry. See Soil Preparation in the Introduction, and follow the planting instructions at the beginning of this chapter. Make the hole three times as wide and twice as deep as the rootball. Set the tree so the crown will be about 1 or 2 in. above ground level. Staking may keep the tree growing straight, but remove it once the tree is established. Shape the soil around the crown into a wide saucer. Water slowly and deeply. Apply mulch 3 in. deep starting 3 in. from the trunk.

Growing Tips
The first year, unless there's a soaking rain, in spring and fall slowly and gently pour two to three bucketsful of water around the roots every two weeks; in summer every week or ten days. Maintain the mulch.

Care
Apply a slow-release, organic fertilizer for acid-loving plants in early spring from the drip line to a distance $1^1/2$ times the tree's height. Water it in. Replenish the mulch. Magnolias are most beautiful allowed to develop without pruning; any pruning should be done after the tree has bloomed.

Companion Planting and Design
These magnolias are star performers and need space all around to develop well. They're excellent as tall foundation plants for grounds around large buildings.

Our Personal Recommendations
Our two favorites are 'Waterlily' and 'Merrill'. But M. × loebneri 'Leonard Messel' is popular, a beautiful little multi-stemmed magnolia whose buds are flushed purple-pink on the outside and open to white.

Sweet Gum
Liquidambar styraciflua

When, Where, and How to Plant

Plant a young container-grown or balled-and-burlapped tree in early spring while the tree is still dormant. Handle the rootball with care: under the best of circumstances it takes a while to recover from the move. Sweet gum requires full sun, tolerates part shade, but not pollution. Set the tree where there will be lots of space all around for the development of its root system. It does best in well-drained, moist, acid soil, pH 5.5 to 6.5. See Soil Preparation in the Introduction, and planting instructions at the beginning of this chapter. Provide a planting hole three times the width of the rootball and twice as deep. Set the tree so the crown will be an inch or so above ground level. Staking might help the tree grow straighter, but remove it once the tree is established. Shape the earth around the crown into a wide saucer. Water slowly and deeply. Apply mulch 3 in. deep starting 3 in. from the stem, and extending as far out as the seedpods will drop.

Growing Tips

The first year, unless there's a soaking rain, in spring and fall slowly and gently pour two to three bucketsful of water around the roots every two weeks; in summer every week or ten days. Maintain the mulch.

Care

Apply a complete, slow-release, long lasting, organic lawn fertilizer in early spring before growth begins to a distance 1 1/2 times the tree's height. Water it in. Replenish the mulch. Repeat in November. If any pruning is required, do it in late winter before the buds swell.

Companion Planting and Design

Sweet gum is an excellent choice for a large, open landscape that was previously forested wetland, for example. It's a superb lawn tree, but its prickly fruit must be removed before mowing near it.

Our Personal Recommendations

'Rotundiloba' does not produce the prickly balls that are such a nuisance. 'Burgundy' has dark red to maroon fall color and holds its color late. The hardiest is 'Moraine', which grows faster than the species and turns a rich red, but has the gumball seedpods.

The American sweet gum is a tall, handsome shade tree with large, five-pointed leaves that in fall turn to true yellow, red, and purple—a spectacular show most years. In summer, the leaves are a deep, attractive, glossy green. The bark is grayish brown and interestingly corky. A big tree, in moist soil it grows rather quickly, 2 to 3 ft. a year. In dry soil, the growth is a little slower. The common name refers to the sap, which is rather sweet and gummy. Male and female flowers are produced in dense clusters and mature into prickly, woody seedpods that litter. It makes a superb lawn tree as long as the means exist to remove the prickly fruit before mowing.

Other Name
American Sweet Gum

Bloom Period and Seasonal Color
April to May; flowers are inconspicuous; fall foliage is true yellow, red, and purple.

Mature Height × Spread
50 to 60 ft. × 35 to 45 ft.

Zones
5 to 8

Thornless Honeylocust
Gleditsia triacanthos var. *inermis* 'Shade Master'

The honeylocusts are large, broadheaded trees with fine textured, feathery foliage that often turns a spectacular clear yellow to yellow-green when cold weather comes. They withstand urban conditions and have become popular lawn and street trees. The species, Gleditsia triacanthos, commonly called the honeylocust, is native to North America. It is famous for its armor—4-inch thorns. The variety 'Shade Master' is fast-growing with a short trunk, an open crown, and, best of all, it is thornless so you can plant it where children will play. Though the bright green summer foliage is dense, it casts a light dappled shade, which allows grass to grow close to the trunk. And when the fine leaves fall, they more or less blow themselves away—no raking. The slightly fragrant spring flowers are followed in most honeylocusts by long, curving seedpods that can be messy: but 'Shade Master' is essentially pod-less.

Bloom Period and Seasonal Color
Spring; yellow flowers; in fall, golden foliage.

Mature Height × Spread
70 ft. × 50 ft.

Zones
4 to 9

When, Where, and How to Plant
Plant a container-grown or balled-and-burlapped honeylocust at almost any season. It needs full sun in order to thrive. It will do best in rich, moist soil with a high pH, but is tolerant of other situations, and once established handles drought and even tolerates salt—a consideration where roads are salted. See Soil Preparation in the Introduction, and planting instructions at the beginning of this chapter. Provide a planting hole three times the width of the rootball and twice as deep. Set the tree so the crown will be an inch or so above ground level. Staking might help the tree grow straighter, but remove it once the tree is established. Shape the earth around the crown into a wide saucer. Water slowly and deeply. Apply mulch 3 in. deep starting 3 in. from the stem.

Growing Tips
The first year, unless there's a soaking rain, in spring and fall slowly and gently pour two to three bucketsful of water around the roots every two weeks; in summer every week or ten days. Maintain soil moisture and the mulch.

Care
Apply a complete, slow-release, long lasting, organic lawn fertilizer in early spring before growth begins to a distance $1^1/2$ times the tree's height. Water it in. Replenish the mulch. Repeat in November.

Companion Planting and Design
An excellent lawn and street tree.

Our Personal Recommendations
'Shade Master' is our choice. But there are some other interesting cultivars. The new leaves of 'Sunburst' are yellow, turning to bright green—this cultivar grows relatively slowly to 30 or 35 ft. 'Moraine' is a tall pod-less variety that resists the webworm that plagues some other varieties.

Tuliptree

Liriodendron tulipifera

When, Where, and How to Plant

The tuliptree requires care in transplanting. Plant a young, container-grown or balled-and-burlapped tree in early spring while it is still dormant. The tuliptree requires full sun. It does well in almost any soil, but thrives in sandy, deeply dug, well-drained, moist soil that is slightly acid, pH 5.5 to 6.5. See Soil Preparation in the Introduction, and planting instructions at the beginning of this chapter. Provide a planting hole three times the width of the rootball and twice as deep. Set the tree so the crown will be an inch or so above ground level. Staking might help the tree grow straighter, but remove it once the tree is established. Shape the earth around the crown into a wide saucer. Water slowly and deeply. Apply mulch 3 in. deep starting 3 in. from the stem.

Growing Tips

The first year, unless there's a soaking rain, in spring and fall slowly and gently pour two to three bucketsful of water around the roots every two weeks; in summer every week or ten days. Maintain the mulch.

Care

Spread a complete, slow-release, long lasting, organic lawn fertilizer in early spring from the drip line to a distance 1 1/2 times the tree's height. Water it in. Replenish the mulch. In periods of drought water even well-established trees deeply every week. Any pruning should be done in winter; remove young branches that will grow into the center of the tree or rub against other branches.

Companion Planting and Design

This majestic, long-lived native tree is suited to large parks and landscapes and should be allowed enough space all around to be seen. If seeing the flowers is part of the purpose of planting the tree, you will have to place it near an observation point looking toward or down onto the top of the tree. The tuliptree can tolerate city conditions and is handsome in a park, but can be too big for street planting.

Our Personal Recommendations

Plant the species. A variegated form, 'Aureo-marginatum', has leaves edged with yellow.

The tulip poplar is a tall, majestic native shade tree that is probably the tallest and straightest hardwood in America. The tuliptree grows wild from Massachusetts to Florida, and westward to Wisconsin and Mississippi. It is named for the greenish yellow, tulip-like flowers that appear late in the spring or early summer. Unfortunately, they're borne high in the branches, and therefore aren't readily visible from below. The seeds in the cone-like fruits, which resemble those of the large magnolias, to which it is related, attract finches and cardinals. The leaves are quite distinctive—blue-green and rather like a maple leaf with its end squared off. In fall, the leaves turn a rich, handsome canary yellow that makes a very nice show.

Other Name
Tulip Poplar

Bloom Period and Seasonal Color
Late May or early June; chartreuse blossoms touched at the base with bright orange; leaves are canary yellow in fall.

Mature Height × Spread
70 to 90 ft. × 35 to 50 ft.

Zones
4 to 9

217

White Fringe Tree
Chionanthus virginicus

In mid-spring, just as the leaves are filling in, this lovely little tree is wrapped in a mist of delicate, 6- to 8-in. long, lightly scented, greenish white flowers that consist of drooping, fringe-like petals. With the first real cold in autumn, the fringe tree's leaves turn a luminous yellow-gold and hang on as long as the weather stays fairly moderate. The female plants bear bloomy, purple fruit the birds relish. The petals of the flowers on male trees are larger and showier, but the fruit is smaller and somewhat hidden by the foliage. This is an American tree that grows wild in many areas of the Southeastern U.S. But it is cold hardy here, to at least -30 degrees Fahrenheit. The fringe tree is slow growing and tolerates urban pollution.

Other Names
Grancy Graybeard, Old Man's Beard

Bloom Period and Seasonal Color
Mid-spring; white; foliage turns pure yellow in fall.

Mature Height × Spread
15 to 25 ft. × 15 to 25 ft.

Zones
3 or 4 to 9

When, Where, and How to Plant
Set out a young container-grown or a balled-and-burlapped tree in early spring while the tree is still dormant. Handle the rootball with care. The fringe tree flowers best in full sun but makes do with four to six hours of sun or bright, filtered light all day. The ideal site is near water in slightly acid soil, pH 5.5 to 6.5. See Soil Preparation in the Introduction, and the planting instructions at the beginning of this chapter. Provide a planting hole three times the width of the rootball and twice as deep. Set the tree so the crown will be an inch or so above ground level. Staking might help the tree grow straighter, but remove it once the tree is established. Shape the earth around the crown into a wide saucer. Water slowly and deeply. Apply mulch 3 in. deep starting 3 in. from the trunk.

Growing Tips
The first year, unless there's a soaking rain, in spring and fall slowly and gently pour two to three bucketsful of water around the roots every two weeks; in summer every week or ten days. Maintain the mulch.

Care
Apply a slow-release, organic fertilizer for acid-loving plants in early spring from the drip line to a distance $1^{1}/_{2}$ times the tree's height. Water it in. Replenish the mulch. The white fringe tree flowers on the previous season's growth; after flowering, cut out young branches that will grow into the center of the tree or rub against other branches.

Companion Planting and Design
Beautiful as a specimen where you'll see it at a slight distance—in the center of a lawn or by a pond. An underplanting of periwinkle, ajuga, and small, spring-flowering bulbs such as wood hyacinths sets the tree off nicely.

Our Personal Recommendation
For small gardens in Zone 5, the small, more formal little multi-stemmed Chinese fringe tree, *C. retusus*, is a better choice. It bears male and female flowers on the same plant. It blooms on the current season's new growth, so prune it in late winter before growth begins.

Winter King Hawthorn

Crataegus viridis 'Winter King'

When, Where, and How to Plant

Plant a balled-and-burlapped or a container-grown tree in early spring while the plant still is dormant. Hawthorns are at their very best when planted in full sun. They tolerate many soils, but thrive in well-drained soil that contains enough humus to sustain moisture, with pH 5.5 to 7.5. See Soil Preparation in the Introduction, and the planting instructions at the beginning of this chapter. Provide a planting hole three times the width of the rootball and twice as deep. Set the tree so the crown will be an inch or so above ground level. Staking might help the tree grow straighter, but remove it once the tree is established. Shape the earth around the crown into a wide saucer. Water slowly and deeply. Apply mulch 3 in. deep starting 3 in. from the trunk.

Growing Tips

The first year, unless there's a soaking rain, in spring and fall slowly and gently pour two to three bucketsful of water around the roots every two weeks; in summer every week or ten days. Maintain the moisture and the mulch.

Care

Apply a slow-release, organic fertilizer in early spring from the drip line to a distance 1 1/2 times the tree's height. Water it in. Replenish the mulch. If pruning is needed, the best seasons for pruning are winter and early spring.

Companion Planting and Design

Because of the thorns, hawthorns aren't suited to planting where children will be tempted to climb them. A hawthorn is especially "right" planted in a small meadow where birds can enjoy the fruits. It is especially picturesque in naturalized areas with ornamental grasses.

Our Personal Recommendations

We like 'Winter King'. The Lavalle hawthorn, *C. × lavallei* (Zone 4), which has minimal thorns, has white flowers and foliage that colors bronze or copper-red in fall. It is also particularly tolerant of urban conditions.

The hawthorns are small, thorny, picturesque flowering trees with wide-spreading branches that make charming shade trees for small gardens. They also are used as tall privacy hedges and to create screening. An outstanding cultivar is 'Winter King'. It has a graceful rounded form, silvery bark that sheds attractively as the tree matures, and gray-green foliage that turns gold-yellow, scarlet, and purple in fall. The thorns are about 1 in. long. In early spring it covers its branches with clusters of white flowers like little wild roses and follows them with colorful masses of showy, orange-red, berry-like fruits that persist long into winter. Birds relish the fruits and nest in the trees. While the hawthorn is an excellent tree for the garden, it sheds fruit messily, so don't plant it near a path or by the street.

Other Name

Green Hawthorn

Bloom Period and Seasonal Color

Spring; white flowers; gold, scarlet and purple foliage in fall.

Mature Height × Spread

20 to 30 ft. × 20 to 30 ft.

Zones

4 to 7

Vines *for New England*

Vines create lush vertical accents, invaluable when you want a real visual impact taking up little space in the ground. The leafy greens soften, beautify, transform, hide problems. You can create an (almost) instant shade garden by training a leafy vine—trumpet vine, for example— to cover a pergola or a trellis. A climbing rose romances a balcony. Ivy greens ugly stumps. Vines climbing wires between the railing and the roof of a porch make a privacy screen. A vine can frame an attractive view and draw your eye to it. You can clothe a barren slope with a waterfall of vines by planting several at the top of a slope and training the runners to grow down. Fragrant vines belong where you can enjoy the scent. Sweet autumn clematis is especially fragrant—it grows like a tidal wave all summer then covers itself with a foam of small, sweetly fragrant white flowers in fall.

Vines grow rapidly—up or down, or sideways, according to how you train the leading stems, and the supports you provide. When choosing a vine consider how you are going to prune it when it gets to the top. How a vine climbs dictates what it needs as support. Vines that climb by twining stems

require something narrow such as a wooden post, a pipe, wires, or strings. Vines that climb by twining tendrils or leaf petioles—clematis, for example—require a structure of wires, or wire mesh. Vines that climb by aerial rootlets that secrete an adhesive glue, like English ivy, need only a rugged surface, such as a brick or stucco wall, or a rough, unpainted fence. Vines that eventually will be very heavy— climbing hydrangea, and wisteria—need the support of heavy timbers, or a dead tree, to hold them up.

Vines hold moisture: make sure the lumber that will support a vine is pressure-treated. Don't set a vine to growing up a wooden wall, because its moisture can cause rot. Allow 3-in. or more air space between foliage and a house wall—vines need air circulation all the way around. Avoid planting vines that climb by tendrils near trees, large shrubs, windows, or shutters.

Honeysuckle 'Dropmore Scarlet'

Clematis

Where to Plant, and Care

Cultivated vines can be as invasive as any local weed vine—so plant a vine only where it won't escape into the wild. You plant a container-grown vine the same way you plant a shrub: see Soil Preparation and Improvement in the Introduction, and planting instructions in the Shrubs chapter. The first year, slowly and gently pour two to three bucketsful of water around the roots every week or ten days unless there's a soaking rain. Maintain the mulch throughout the summer. If the vine is sheltered from rain, hose it down now and then in summer—but don't hose it when it is coming into, or already in, bloom. In early spring before growth begins, broadcast an organic fertilizer around the plant and scratch it in. Replenish the mulch if necessary. Repeat in fall.

Pruning for Vines

We can't give instructions for pruning vines that will apply to all. Wisteria requires special handling, as do some others. But to keep all vines healthy and good looking, remove dead, extraneous, or weak wood. Prune large, fast-growing vines severely every year. When to prune depends on the plant itself. The rule of thumb is, before growth begins, prune flowering vines that bloom on wood that grows in the current year. Prune flowering vines that bloom in spring on wood produced the year before right after the flowers fade. Prune vines that do not flower in summer right after the major thrust of seasonal growth. Avoid pruning in the fall: wounds heal slowly then and pruning stimulates growth, which may come too late to harden off before the first frosts. It isn't necessary to paint, tar, or otherwise cover a pruning cut.

Other Options

If you want to try the effect of a vine without making it a permanent fixture in your landscape, plant one of the fast-growing annual climbers. Our favorites are: scented hyacinth bean, *Lablab purpureus* (also known as *Dolichos lablab*); and the white-flowered moonvine, *Ipomea alba* (formerly *Calonyction aculeatum*), and its cousin the morning glory, *Ipomea tricolor* 'Heavenly Blue'.

Clematis
Clematis spp., cultivars, and hybrids

The striking beauty of the flowers of the clematis hybrids has made this the most popular—and most hybridized—of all the climbers. In our cool summers, the flowers last well but not all the beautiful hybrids are hardy throughout New England. The Jackmanii hybrids, from Clematis × jackmanii, which bear big, beautiful blooms, are hardy all the way to northern Maine. Clematis vines have attractive dark green foliage, and climb by attaching leaf petioles (stalks) to the support provided. In time a clematis will sprawl over other vegetation, walls, trellises, posts, fences, and arbors. Most clematis hybrids bloom in spring or summer; some bloom twice, and others bloom in the fall. Clematis isn't a difficult plant, but pruning affects the way it blooms, and its timing is important. To help the plant do its best, before you buy a clematis, make sure you will be able to acquire the pruning information you need. The vines expand at a rate of 5 to 10 ft. in a single season.

Bloom Period and Seasonal Color
Spring, summer, or fall; white, and shades of blue, mauve, pink, red, lavender, purple, yellow, and bi-colors.

Mature Length
8 to 20 ft.

Zones
Jackmanii Group: 3 to 8

When, Where, and How to Plant
Set out container-grown plants in mid-spring in a protected, airy site where the vines will be in the sun, and the roots somewhat shaded: the roots need to be cool. Soils with a pH between 6.0 and 7.5 are recommended, but clematis tolerates somewhat acid soils. See Soil Preparation in the Introduction, and planting instructions in the Shrubs chapter. Provide a planting hole three times the width of the rootball and twice as deep. Set the vine so the crown is at ground level. Provide twine or wire for support, or to lead the vines to a wall, a fence, a tree, or other support. Make a saucer of earth around the plant. Apply and maintain a mulch 3 in. deep starting 3 in. from the stem.

Growing Tips
The first year, unless there's a soaking rain, in spring and fall pour a bucketful of water around the roots every two weeks; in summer every week or ten days. Check the vines often and prune to train them in the desired direction.

Care
Using a slow-release organic fertilizer, fertilize lightly in fall and again in spring. Prune clematis that blooms in spring on last year's wood lightly right after the vines finish blooming; prune clematis that blooms on new wood just as the leaf buds begin to swell, by cutting the flowering stems back to buds within 4 to 6 in. of the main branches.

Companion Planting and Design
The big-flowered hybrids are lovely paired with open-branched shrubs or roses.

Our Personal Recommendations
For spectacular flowers in summer, plant 'Nelly Moser', a large mauve pink with a deep pink bar; 'Duchess of Edinburgh', a scented, large, double white; and Jackmanii clematis 'Purpurea Superba', whose 5-in. blooms are a rich violet purple. For masses of small fragrant flowers in spring plant anemone clematis, *C. montana* var. *rubens*, which succeeds even north of Boston, and white 'Alba'. For fall fragrance, plant (and control) sweet autumn clematis, *C. terniflora* (formerly *C. maximowicziana* and *C. paniculata*) (Zone 4), a rampant vine that produces a froth of tiny, sweetly fragrant, whitish flowers in late summer.

Climbing Hydrangea

Hydrangea anomala var. *petiolaris*

When, Where, and How to Plant

Set out a container-grown plant in early spring, disturbing the rootball as little as possible. It will be slow to re-establish and show new growth. The climbing hydrangea flowers best in full sun, and does well in part shade, but won't flower as bountifully. It tolerates salt air and can be used by the sea but will need protection from direct salt spray. Provide deeply dug, rich, moist, loamy soil. See Soil Preparation in the Introduction, and planting instructions in the Shrubs chapter. Provide a planting hole three times the width of the rootball and twice as deep. Set the vine so the crown is at ground level. With soft twine, tie the vine to the structure that will support it. Shape the soil around the crown into a wide saucer. Water slowly and deeply. Apply mulch 3 in. deep starting 3 in. from the crown.

Growing Tips

The first year, unless there's a soaking rain, in spring and fall slowly and gently pour two to three bucketsful of water around the roots every two weeks; in summer every week or ten days.

Care

Using a slow-release organic fertilizer, fertilize in fall and again in spring. Replenish the mulch. Prune after flowering. Though it's slow growing, once a climbing hydrangea matures, it can become invasive and will need to be controlled.

Companion Planting and Design

Climbing hydrangea becomes a massive, many-layered, strong, structural landscape element that is ideal for enhancing a high brick or stone wall, as well as trees, arbors, and other free standing structures. The climbing hydrangea is slow growing, so it will take time to achieve any significant screening, but it's long lived, so that balances things out.

Our Personal Recommendation

Plant the species.

This slow-growing, climbing vine with its lustrous, dark-green leaves is probably the most beautiful, massive, and formal climber we have. A mature specimen is magnificent in late spring and early summer when it opens clusters of small, fragrant florets backed by showy white bracts. Clinging by means of root-like attachments, the branches extend 2 to 3 ft. outward, which gives the vine a full, rich silhouette. Though not evergreen, the leaves are a fine green, and they stay that color until late fall. In time, the central stem thickens and becomes woody, and the cinnamon-colored bark exfoliates in an attractive way. It will grow up brick, stucco, and stone walls, chimneys, arbors, and trees. It becomes massive and must have strong support. It is hardy on the coast of Maine and inland as far north as southern Maine.

Bloom Period and Seasonal Color
Spring and early summer; white bracts.

Mature Length
60 to 80 ft.

Zones
5 to 7

Goldflame Honeysuckle
Lonicera × heckrottii

The honeysuckles are fast-spreading, climbing, twining vines or tall shrubs. Many grow wild in New England, bearing sweetly scented flowers followed by bright, berry-like fruits attractive to birds that disperse the seeds. Uncontrolled, they will take over the property. Goldflame, or coral honeysuckle, is a cross between two native honeysuckle species and is considered the most beautiful of the twining, climbing types. It bears carmine buds that open to yellow and then change to pink, and it stays in bloom from late June to fall. The fruit is red and not borne as profusely as other species, nor is the vine as vigorous, which keeps it well behaved. That's the honeysuckle to plant for its flowers. L. × brownii 'Dropmore Scarlet' is hardy in cold Zone 3.

Other Name
Coral Honeysuckle

Bloom Period and Seasonal Color
Late spring to fall; carmine buds opening to yellow and changing to pink.

Mature Length
10 to 20 ft.

Zones
4 to 8

When, Where, and How to Plant
The best times for planting honeysuckle is in fall before Indian summer and in early spring while the plant is still dormant. Honeysuckle is most happy, and fragrant, growing in full sun—although, with four to six hours of sun, or all-day filtered light, goldflame performs well. It does best when its roots are shaded and cool, and the vine is in the sun. Honeysuckles thrive in moist, loamy soils in the neutral range, pH 6.0 to 7.5, but tolerate other soils. See Soil Preparation in the Introduction, and planting instructions in the Shrubs chapter. Provide a planting hole three times the width of the rootball and twice as deep. Set the vine so the crown is at ground level. Prune back to the main two or three stems and tie these to the structure that will support the vine. Shape the soil around the crown into a wide saucer. Water slowly and deeply. Apply mulch 3 in. deep starting 2 to 3 in. from the crown.

Growing Tips
The first year, unless there's a soaking rain, in spring and fall slowly and gently pour two to three bucketsful of water around the roots every two weeks; in summer every week or ten days.

Care
Using a slow-release organic fertilizer, fertilize lightly in fall and again in spring. Before growth begins in late winter cut out weak, crowded, or dead growth, and trim long shoots back to a pair of buds near the main stem.

Companion Planting and Design
Goldflame is perfect in a cottage garden, and shows well climbing archways, fences, arbors, mailboxes, and lampposts. Combined with a climbing rose and clematis, it makes a beautiful flowering pillar.

Our Personal Recommendations
Goldflame is our favorite for looks. For scent, we recommend the less showy but very fragrant winter honeysuckle shrub, *L. fragrantissima*, which blooms in the spring. Japanese honeysuckle, *L. japonica*, which blooms all summer, is extremely fragrant, but also very invasive, and on invasive species lists in several states. So be wary of planting both Japanese and winter honeysuckle if you live near a wild area. Both are hardy in Zones 4 to 8.

Japanese Wisteria
Wisteria floribunda

When, Where, and How to Plant

Set out a container-grown plant in early mid-spring while the vine is still dormant. Plant it in full sun. Wisteria thrives in soil with a high pH, but tolerates modest acidity. Provide soil that is deeply dug and well drained. See Soil Preparation in the Introduction, and planting instructions in the Shrubs chapter. Make the planting hole three times the width of the rootball and twice as deep. Set the vine so the crown is at ground level and prune it to one main stem, or more if you wish. With soft twine, tie the stem(s) to a strong support. Shape the soil around the crown into a wide saucer. Water slowly and deeply. Apply mulch 2 in. deep starting at the crown.

Growing Tips

The first year, unless there's a soaking rain, in spring and fall slowly and gently pour two to three bucketsful of water around the roots every two weeks; in summer every week or ten days.

Care

Fertilize with a slow-release organic fertilizer in early spring, 5 pounds per 100 sq. ft. Prune the vine back ruthlessly to the desired branching structure, and to make it bloom. When it reaches the desired height, prune the main stem(s), back so the laterals will develop, and tie the laterals to supports leading them in the direction you want them to grow. Japanese wisteria blooms on old wood and last season's growth; keep it blooming by cutting back all big, old shoots, leaving only three to four buds on each shoot.

Companion Planting and Design

You can underplant with drought-tolerant ground covers, like periwinkle or ajuga. Hostas, liriope, and small, spring-flowering bulbs like wood hyacinths, are also acceptable ground covers.

Our Personal Recommendations

We like 'Longissima Alba', which bears fragrant white flowers in clusters 15 to 24 in. long; 'Rosea', a lovely pale rose with 18-in. racemes; 'Issai', a blue-violet with 24- to 30-in. racemes; and 'Macrobotrys', whose violet to red violet flowers are borne in 18- to 36-in. racemes and have excellent fragrance.

Dreamy, romantic, seductive, irresistible, a wisteria in full bloom is everything a flowering vine can be! Picture long drooping clusters of lightly scented, pastel-colored, single or double blooms dripping from gnarly vines, and sprays of dainty new leaves. That said, wisteria should be approached with caution. You can plant it to climb pillars and arbors, as "green roofing" for porches, and to soften the harsh lines of stone walls. But do not plant where it can reach windows, doors, shutters, or gutters, or near a live tree. It can invade and damage attics, and it destroys trees. As it matures, the weight is considerable, so you must provide a strong support. The cultivars tend to be less invasive than the species. And there are native species with smaller flower clusters. But if you're a romantic at heart...

Bloom Period and Seasonal Color
April, May, or June; in pink, white, or lilac.

Mature Length
30 to 50 ft.

Zones
4 to 8

Trumpet Vine
Campsis radicans

The trumpet vines are woody, vigorous (read: rampant), indomitable, and fast growing deciduous climbing vines that will quickly provide you with a dense, leafy "green roof" for arbors and pergolas. The delightful bonus is a long-season crop of fresh, showy, trumpet-shaped flowers that appeal mightily to hummingbirds. You can also use a trumpet vine to cover fence posts and to soften bleak corners and bare stone and masonry walls. The vines climb by means of aerial rootlets, and grow at a run to 30 to 40 ft. As trumpet vine matures, it becomes woody and very heavy, so provide a strong support. You must be prepared to prune this vine often: although it is native to the United States, do not plant it where it can escape and invade wild areas.

Bloom Period and Seasonal Color
From spring through early fall; shades of orange, yellow, red.

Mature Length
10 to 25 ft.

Zones
4 to 9

When, Where, and How to Plant
Set out container-grown plants in early mid-spring, or in early fall. Trumpet vine grows almost anywhere in almost any soil and almost any light, but it flowers best growing against a warm wall and in full sun. See Soil Preparation in the Introduction, and planting instructions in the Shrubs chapter. Provide a planting hole three times the width of the rootball and twice as deep. Set the vine so the crown is at ground level. With soft twine, tie or lead the vine to the sturdy structure that will support it. Shape the soil around the crown into a wide saucer. Water slowly and deeply. Apply mulch 3 in. deep starting 1 to 2 in. from the crown.

Growing Tips
The first year, unless there's a soaking rain, in spring and fall slowly and gently pour two to three bucketsful of water around the roots every two weeks; in summer every week or ten days.

Care
Do not allow the roots to dry out in summer. In late winter, replenish the mulch. The colorful trumpets are produced on new growth, so early every spring prune the secondary stems back to a few buds—really, do it!—to encourage new flowering spurs. After the first year or two, when the vine is filling its space, in late fall or in early spring, prune leafy young shoots to within a few buds of old wood. Remove any out-of-control stems at any time during the growing season.

Companion Planting and Design
Trumpet vine really doesn't need companion plants. It grows into a floriferous, beautiful (heavy!) green roof for a pergola or a terrace; give it solid supports and you can also use it to soften corners, hide drainpipes, and to screen ugly structures.

Our Personal Recommendations
We love *C. radicans* 'Flava', which has been popular for more than a century, for its rich yellow, or yellow-orange, blossoms; and 'Crimson Trumpet' whose blossoms are a velvety red. 'Madame Galen', a form of *C. × tagliabuana*, is a superior plant that is hardy in Zone 6 and may survive winters with protection in Zone 5.

When, Where, and How to Plant

The best times for planting Virginia creeper are in fall before Indian summer, and in early spring while it is still dormant. But container-grown plants will succeed planted almost any time. Virginia creeper colors best growing in full sun, thrives in light shade, and grows moderately even in deep shade. It tolerates pollution, city life, and almost any soil. Dig a modest planting hole about 6 in. deeper and wider than the rootball, and wider still toward the top. Set the plant with the crown 1 in. above ground level. With soft twine tie the vine to the structure that will support it. Make a saucer of earth around the plant to hold water. Apply a mulch 3 in. deep starting 3 in. from the stem.

Growing Tips

After planting, pour a half bucketful of water around the crown every week unless there's a soaking rain. Pinch out branch tips to keep the plant growing in whatever directions you want it to go.

Care

Prune to direct growth in spring before growth begins and, once the plant is growing well, broadcast a little organic fertilizer over the planting area. Replenish the mulch at the base often.

Companion Planting and Design

Woodbine's assets are its vigorous growth and fabulous fall color. Plant it where it will cover unsightly objects or clothe a dull wall. It is an excellent ground cover for out-of-the-way slopes where the fact that it looses its leaves in fall won't spoil the view.

Our Personal Recommendations

Virginia creeper's less hardy (Zone 4) kissin' cousin Boston ivy, *P. tricuspidata*, is much like the Virginia creeper, but it has a more lustrous leaf. The foliage of 'Purpurea' is purplish during the growing season. The cultivar 'Lowii' has small leaves when young and is a good choice for a small area. 'Beverley Brooks' has large leaves that turn scarlet in the fall. A variegated form of Virginia creeper, *P. quinquefolia* 'Monham', called Star Showers®, is hardy in Zones 5 to 9.

The Virginia creeper is a handsome, fast-growing, hardy, and invasive vine ideal for covering blank walls, a tree, a rock pile, everything you want hidden. Its glory is its fall color: the leaves turn a blazing scarlet in the autumn. When it is grown on a wall, after the leaves fall the asymmetrical tracery of the branches remains attractive, and the dainty reddish new growth that appears in spring is quite lovely. The flowers are insignificant greenish clusters hidden under the foliage; the dark berries that follow are enjoyed by birds. Virginia creeper's only drawbacks are that it can damage masonry, and, if you decide to remove it, the traces are hard to wipe out. It clings by means of tendrils that end in adhesive-like tips and you can't easily get rid of them all.

Other Name
Woodbine

Bloom Period and Seasonal Color
Crimson red in fall.

Mature Length
30 to 70 ft.

Zones
3 to 9

Water Plants *for New England*

A water garden is a small, beautiful world, a microcosm of tumbling water, undulating fronds, perfumed flowers, butterflies and dragonflies, and shimmering goldfish. Each of the water garden's living components, plants and animals, has a role in the health of the pond. The fish eat mosquitoes and other insects, including their larvae, and their waste provides nutrients that help sustain the pond plants. The aquatic plants are ornamental and they also contribute to the clarity and health of the water by taking up nutrients that encourage undesirable algae.

This is the "magic formula" for keeping a pond in balance, developed by Charles Thomas, former President of Lilypons Water Gardens, Buckeystown, Maryland:

For every 1 to 2 square feet of pond surface provide:

1 bunch (6 stems) submerged/oxygenating plants

1 black Japanese snail

2 inches of fish, using fish that are up to 6 inches long

$^1/_{10}$ of a small, or medium-size, water lily

(that is, 1 lily per 10 to 20 square feet)

$^1/_3$ of a marginal or a small, floating-leaved plant

(that is, 1 bog or marginal plant or 1 small-leaved floater for every 3 to 6 square feet)

Taro

The Aquatic Plants

Like land plants, the aquatics need sun to bloom well, respond to fertilizing, have active and dormant seasons, and are or are not winter hardy. The small leafy *submerged*, or oxygenating, plants, contribute oxygen. The *large-leaved floating plants*, the water lilies and lotus, float round pads and blossoms like many-petaled stars over the surface of the water, and provide a cool refuge for the fish. The *small floating-leaved plants* spread delicate green patterns between the lily pads and the lotus and give a pond a natural look. The upright *narrow-leaved plants* (irises, for example) and *broad-leaved plants* (elephant's-ear), which are called *marginals* or *bog plants*, frame the water garden and create contrast with the horizontal planes of the floating aquatics.

All together, water garden plants should cover no more than 1/3 to 1/2 of a 20-by-40-foot pond, and 60 to 70 percent of one 10 by 10 feet. A small water lily covers 90 percent of a tub 2 feet square. The aquatics are grown in pans or pails without drainage. They rest on shelves or platforms (bricks, stones, cement blocks) on the bottom or shelves of the water garden.

Additions of plants and fish to naturally wet places are subject to environmental protection laws. So plan to install your garden in an excavation waterproofed by a man-made, pre-formed container or a plastic liner. For site, don't choose a dip or hollow that will flood in storms. For a garden under 14 feet long, consider a pre-formed fiberglass liner; for larger, or odd-shaped ponds, use a flexible rubber sheet for a liner—the best last up to twenty-five years.

Water Lily 'St. Louis'

Pumps and Filters

The sound and movement of a water garden is created by a pump that moves the water through a filter. It then returns the water to the pond through a fountain or along a stream bed or a waterfall, and that aerates the pond. You can assist the filtering system in keeping the water clear by pumping the pond water through a bog garden and returning it to the pond through a creek planted in bog plants. The farther the water has to be pushed, the more powerful and costly the pump will be to buy and to operate. Small floating fountains powered by the sun are suitable for small water gardens. In the sun, they turn themselves on and send up sprays or showers 8 to 24 inches high. The largest solar fountains can move 60 gallons an hour!

Winter Care

If you can, disconnect the pump and filter for the winter, clean them and ready them for next spring. If the pump is hard-wired, lift it from the water, rinse it, wrap it in plastic, and set it beside the pond. Our pond is shallow and freezes hard in winter, so when the leaves start to fill the pond we bring our fish, Mo, Jo, and Slo, indoors to a big tank in the kitchen for the winter. The snails, tadpoles, and frogs stay in the pond for a long winter nap.

Anacharis
Egeria densa

Anacharis is one of the submerged plants—or "oxygenating plants"—used to contribute oxygen and to use up nutrients that would encourage the algae that can make a water garden murky. A small, leafy perennial with fern-like fronds, it grows from a container at the bottom of the pond right up to the top of the water and bears tiny white flowers at the tips of thin stems. Each tiny three-petaled white flower is half the size of a shirt button and has a yellow dot in the middle. Moving gently with the rhythm of wind and water, anacharis adds grace and charm to the pond, and fish spawn among the fronds. Other plants that perform the same functions but can take winters in Zone 4 are wild celery, Vallisneria americana, *whose ribbon-like leaves sway with the movement of the water, and various species of* Myriophyllum, *whose stems are covered with delicate, hair-like leaves.*

Other Name
Elodea

Bloom Period and Seasonal Color
Summer; tiny white blossoms.

Mature Length
Indefinite spread.

Zones
5 to 10

When, Where, and How to Plant
For every 1 to 2 sq. ft. of pond surface, you should plant one bunch (six stems) of submerged/oxygenating plants: they can be placed in the pond as soon as it has been filled. Water garden plants are grown in containers called pans, which have no drainage holes. Anacharis, and other submerged plants, are sold in bunches of six stems secured by a rubber band. Each stem with foliage is about 6 in. long, and from $1/4$ to 1 in. across. The oxygenating plants are set out in pans 4 in. deep, one bunch of submerged plants for every 6 sq. in. of container surface. Fill the pans with clean sand to within 1 in. of the rim. Rinse the submerged plants. Cut the rubber bands and press each bunch 2 in. into the sand. Cover the sand with $1/2$ to $3/4$ in. of rinsed gravel and fill the containers with water. Distribute the containers of submerged plants evenly over the bottom of the pond with 1 or 2 ft. of water overhead. Choose locations where the containers will receive at least six hours of sun and avoid places that will be shaded later by floating-leaved plants such as water lilies. If the strands start to grow long and skinny, they need more sun.

Growing Tips
To multiply your holdings, during the growing season take 5- or 6-in. cuttings of submerged plants 8 in. or longer, press the ends into containers filled with wet sand, and place them in the pond.

Care
Do not add fertilizer.

Companion Planting and Design
In a water basin or barrel garden one pan of submerged plants would be enough. A large pond will need more, and will be more interesting if you use a variety of oxygenating plants. Nurseries in our part of New England sell water hyacinth, a beautiful but very invasive plant. Be aware that it is illegal to grow it anywhere it survives winters because it grows like the expanding universe, clogging waterways and invading the habitats of native plants.

Our Personal Recommendation
Plant the species.

Black Princess Taro
Colocasia affinis var. *jenningsii*

When, Where, and How to Plant

You can grow a colocasia in the water garden, and also out of the pond if you keep it very moist. You can buy a container-grown colocasia in mid-spring: it can go into the pond when the water is almost 70 degrees Fahrenheit. We have started the tubers ourselves indoors four to six weeks before planting time: they're slow to start, like caladiums, but grow quickly once they get going. Each tuber is at least 7 to 9 in. in diameter and should be planted 1 in. deep in a $3^1/2$-quart pan that is 5 in. across. The best soil for colocasia is heavy, slightly acid, and contains a little humus. If you are going to place the pan in the water, cover the soil with $^1/2$ to $^3/4$ in. of rinsed gravel and fill the container with water. Set it in part or full shade with up to 5 in. of water over the crowns, or set it near the water.

Growing Tips

A colocasia growing out of the water garden needs to be in soil that is constantly moist. A colocasia does not need much fertilizing.

Care

Throughout the growing season remove dead foliage. After the first few freezes some pond owners cut all the verticals down to clear the water at once of decaying vegetation. It's a healthy practice. But colocasia might grow on if you lift it in the fall, and store it in a sunny greenhouse.

Companion Planting and Design

We prefer colocasia tucked into a corner of the pond, but a potted colocasia is a striking foliage accent growing anywhere.

Our Personal Recommendation

For smaller water gardens we like *C. esculenta* 'Hilo Beauty', a slightly smaller taro with green leaves mottled with ivory. It is planted with 2 in. of water over the crown.

The colocasias are huge, frost-tender perennials we grow as annuals in New England. They produce 2-ft. long, heavily veined leaves shaped like an arrowhead or an elephant's ear. The way the leaf is held at a sharp angle at the top of its stalk, and its size and coloring, give it a tropical, exotic look. In summer small pale yellow flowers similar to calla lilies bloom among the leaves on short stems. Black princess taro is a bold, shade-loving variety that has dark green leaves overlaid with black. Taro, or dasheen, is another superb species, C. esculenta, whose velvety green leaves often display brilliant white veins; the leaves of a new variety, 'Black Magic' elephant's-ear, are wine-purple and reach to 5 ft. In Hawaii and the South Sea Islands taro root is pounded and cooked to make a starchy staple called "poi."

Other Names
Taro, Dasheen, Elephant's-Ear

Bloom Period and Seasonal Color
Summer; foliage is the ornamental feature.

Mature Height × Spread
2 to $3^1/2$ ft. × 2 to 3 ft.

Zones
9 to 11

Lotus
Nelumbo nucifera

Lotus is a breathtakingly big and beautiful, 2- to 6-ft.-tall relative of the water lily. It needs full sun to flower, but the foliage and its growth habit are so interesting we plant it even where there isn't enough sun to bring it into bloom. The lotus starts the season by floating leaves that look like 12-in. lily pads. Then when it puts up magnificent, wavy-edged aerial leaves, the floating leaves below come together, and the perfumed lotus flowers rise. As big as a man's head, for three days they open mornings and close at teatime. The seedpods that follow look like the spout of a watering can, and are handsome in dried arrange-ments. In Zone 6 lotus blooms in mid July—farther north, in late July.

Other Name
Sacred Lotus

Bloom Period and Seasonal Color
Late July to August; hues and combinations of white, pink, red, yellow, and cream.

Mature Spread
1^1/$_2$ to 12 sq. ft. or more

Zones
4 to 11

When, Where, and How to Plant
Lotus, together with all the other ornamentals, should cover no more than ^{1}/$_3$ to ^{1}/$_2$ of a 20-by-40-ft. pond or 60 to 70 percent of one 10 by 10 ft. A lotus is shipped, or sold, bare root in a plastic bag during the few weeks in spring when the root-stock is in tuber form. Plant it at once: when the rootstock puts out runners, the tuber atrophies and planting is impossible. For a tuber 6 to 18 in. long, provide a pan 16 to 24 in. in diameter and 9 to 10 in. deep. Fill the pan with heavy garden soil free of peat, manure, vermiculite, or commercial potting mixes. Best is pH of 6.5 to 7.5 but pH 6.0 to 8.0 is OK. Bury the tuber 2 in. deep with the top ^{1}/$_2$ in. above the soil. Push a 10-14-8 water lily fertilizer tablet into the soil, and cover with ^{1}/$_2$ to ^{3}/$_4$ in. of rinsed gravel. Soak the container and place it in the pond.

Growing Tips
Lotus needs six to eight hours of sun, and to have no more than 2 to 3 in. of water over the growing tip.

Care
Remove yellowing foliage and spent blossoms and fertilize with a water lily pellet twice a month from spring up to a month before frosts are expected. If the pond typically freezes to the bottom, winter a lotus indoors in a cold, frost-free place and keep the soil from drying out.

Companion Planting and Design
One large lotus takes up as much space as a large water lily, and that is all most home ponds can host.

Our Personal Recommendations
For a small water garden use the miniature tulip lotus, 'Shirokunshi' or 'Tulip'; and 'Momo Botan', a double rose dwarf with a golden center, which spreads when grown in a pond, but in tubs and pans stays at 12 in. For a large pond, our favorite is the large magnificent 'Mrs. Perry D. Slocum'.

Parrot's-Feather

Myriophyllum aquaticum

When, Where, and How to Plant

Parrot's-feather, and other floating-leaved plants, together should cover only ¹/₃ to ¹/₂ of a 20-by-40-ft. pond or 60 to 70 percent of one 10 by 10 ft. Parrot's-feather is sold for mid-spring planting, usually in bunches of six cuttings secured by a rubber band. Plant it in a 4-in. deep pan filled with clean sand to within 1 in. of the rim. Rinse the stems, cut the rubber bands, and press the bunch 2 in. into the sand. Fish love to swim through *Myriophyllum* and to lay eggs there. They're also known to eat it, so provide a protective screen if your water garden includes fish. Cover the sand with ¹/₂ to ³/₄ in. of rinsed gravel and fill the container with water. Set it in the pond a few feet from the water lilies on the pond shelf, in full or partial sun, with 3 to 12 in. of water over the crown.

Growing Tip

Parrot's-feather has an appetite for pond nutrients, so there is no need to fertilize the plant.

Care

Keep the growth of this rapidly spreading plant pruned back. Just pinch off a stem at any point and pull out and discard the growth beyond. Now and then the delicate, hair-like leaves that cover the stems need to be gently hosed clean. Do not dispose of it where it can reach local waterways.

Companion Planting and Design

A nice group for a basin or barrel is the small tropical water lily 'Dauben', with variegated sweet flag for vertical accent, and frills of parrot's-feather cascading over the edge. Among other attractive small-leaved floaters are the tiny water clover, *Marsilea mutica*. For flowers, plant water poppies, *Hydrocleys nymphoides*; floating-heart, *Nymphoides peltata*; and the white or yellow snowflakes, *Nymphoides cristata* and *N. geminata*.

Our Personal Recommendations

Plant parrot's-feather and other small-leaved floaters with caution: they expand rapidly and easily overwhelm a neglected water garden. Don't plant them where they can escape into local waterways.

Parrot's-feather is one of several fast-growing, small-leaved floaters planted in large water gardens along with the big water lilies and lotus for visual interest and contrast. Like other small floaters, it's not hardy in most of New England so it is treated as an annual. It is grown primarily for the trailing stems, which are lovely cascading over a waterfall or the edge of a tub garden. The way it grows is interesting: as the stems rise from their underwater container toward the surface they develop sparse hair-like leaves. Then, as the stems reach the air, the leaves begin to grow in dense whorls, and trailing silvery-blue or lime-green "feathers" stretch out over the water. The foliage opens and closes daily. The leaves are green and maroon with mottled margins, and three to four inches in diameter. Charming little bright yellow flowers, with a fringe all around, pop open in summer.

Other Name
Diamond Milfoil

Bloom Period and Seasonal Color
Summer; yellow-green blooms.

Mature Spread
6-in. trailing tips

Zones
6 to 10

Water Lily

Nymphaea spp. and hybrids

The water lilies are the pond's stars, its most colorful flowers, and the most important and best loved of the large floating-leaved plants. They come in almost every color including blue and their large, round pads provide the fish with privacy and relief from hot summer sun. There are both hardy and tropical water lilies. The hardy water lilies are perennial here, though they need two to three years to bloom profusely. You can bring tropical lilies into bloom if your climate provides three to four weeks of temperatures above 80 degrees Fahrenheit. To save tropicals for next year you'll have to lift and store them for winter, like any tender perennial—a nuisance, but fun to try. Hardy lilies open only during the day, while the tropical lilies include both day- and night-flowering varieties. The hardy water lilies and the day-blooming tropical lilies open shortly after breakfast and close toward late afternoon. The heavily scented night-blooming tropical lilies open as the stars come out—fabulous in moonlight—and stay open until late morning.

Bloom Period and Seasonal Color
June to September; all colors and shades.

Mature Spread
Covers 3 to 12 sq. ft.

Zones
Hardy Water Lilies: 4 to 11

When, Where, and How to Plant
Water garden plants should cover no more than $1/3$ to $1/2$ of a 20-by-40-ft. pond, and 60 to 70 percent of one 10 by 10 ft. A small water lily covers 90 percent of a tub 2 ft. sq. Planting time is spring when the water has reached at least 55 degrees Fahrenheit. Lilies usually are sold bare root, ready for planting in the pans, pails, and tubs sold for aquatics. Plant water lilies in heavy garden soil free of peat, manure, vermiculite, or commercial potting mixes. Aquatics tolerate soils ranging between pH 6.0 and 8.0, but optimum is soil and pond water between pH 6.5 and 7.5. Set the plants so the growing tips are just above the soil. Push a 10-14-8 fertilizer tablet for aquatics into the soil of each container. Cover the soil with $1/2$ to $3/4$ in. of rinsed gravel. Soak the containers and place them in the pond in full sun as soon as the pond is filled (chlorine in tap water is safe for plants). Arrange the containers several inches apart on the pond shelf and on platforms that raise the plants to where they will be covered by the depth of water recommended by the growers.

Growing Tip
If you can reach the plants, remove spent blooms and yellowing foliage.

Care
Fertilize the lilies monthly during the spring and the summer. When the water temperature is over 75 degrees Fahrenheit, increase that to twice monthly. For winter, move containers of tropical lilies to a cold, frost-free storage place and keep the soil from drying out.

Companion Planting and Design
If space allows, grow both day- and night-blooming water lilies for nearly twenty-four hours of flowers, with the added bonus of evening fragrance.

Our Personal Recommendations
Two easy hardy water lilies for beginners are 'Fabiola', a shell pink that blooms freely its first year, and 'Dauben', a small day-blooming, soft blue-violet tropical that blooms with as little as three to four hours of direct sunlight a day.

When, Where, and How to Plant

Water iris transplants easily and grows vigorously in or out of water, as long as there is plenty of moisture around the roots. Growing in moist garden soil, it will bloom consistently but the flowers will be smaller. Started in early autumn, water irises will bloom the following year; planted in early spring they're shy and won't likely flower until the next spring. Plant these, and other marginals, in sets of three of one type to a container: when you combine various species of marginal plant, one usually overwhelms the others. Irises thrive in full sun at water's edge in pans with up to 10 in. of water overhead. Set the rhizomes at a slant, with the bottom 2 in. deep and the growing tip just clearing soil that is heavy, humusy, and slightly acid. Plant three to a 9-in. container and, if the pan is to be underwater, cover the soil with 1/2 to 3/4 in. of rinsed gravel. Place hybrids and double-flowered varieties in full sun with only 4 in. of water over the crowns.

Growing Tip

Cut back flowers that have gone by.

Care

In September press a fertilizer pellet into the soil. Before frost, clear away damaged or rotting foliage and move the container to the bottom of the pond. Every three to five years divide yellow flag in mid- to late summer or early fall.

Companion Planting and Design

The most appealing marginal plantings combine narrow-leaved irises with broad-leaved verticals such as elephant's-ear, *Colocasia*. Cattails and ornamental grasses are a lovely addition to the mix, as are water cannas and dainty umbrella plant, *Cyperus alternifolius*, and arrow-shaped water arum, *Peltandra virginica*. You can extend the iris season by including our native blue flag and planting Siberian irises beside the pond.

Our Personal Recommendation

The beautiful double-flowered yellow flag variety called 'Flora Plena' is about 2 ft. tall; it is hardy in Zone 5.

These irises, like other upright, narrow-leaved bog plants, move with the wind, adding motion to the design of the water garden. They are winter hardy here, and the most colorful of the narrow-leaved marginal plants. The first iris to flower, the yellow flag, blooms in spring. The vivid yellow blossoms have brown or violet veins and the beautiful sword-like foliage remains handsome all season. It forms attractive clumps of 1- to 2-in. wide leaves that are parrot green. Hybrids range in color from white to dark yellow and they are a little smaller. There are double-flowered forms. A stately European species, yellow flag has naturalized beside ponds and quiet streams all over temperate North America. This plant is larger than the garden iris, and our native blue flag, Iris versicolor, the beautiful 2- to 3-ft. tall wild iris found in wetlands in Zone 3.

Other Name
Water Iris

Bloom Period and Seasonal Color
June and July; yellow, and colorful hybrids.

Mature Height × Spread
3 to 4 ft. × 3 to 5 ft.

Zones
4 to 8

More About Fertilizers and Plant Nutrition

Our all-purpose recipe for fertilizing, followed by an explanation of why and when we use which product:

Flower and Shrub Garden

For each 100 square feet of new garden space add:

	Sun Garden	Shade Garden
Plant-Tone®	5-10 lbs.	0
Holly-Tone®	0	4-7 lbs.
Rock Phosphate	5-10 lbs.	0
Super Phosphate	0	3-5 lbs.
Greensand	5-10 lbs.	5-10 lbs.
Gypsum (for clay soils)	5-10 lbs.	5-10 lbs.
Osmocote® (8 month)	2 lbs.	2 lbs.

Till all these amendments plus organic matter into the soil, rake smooth, and your bed is ready to be planted.

Know What's in Your Fertilizer

In our experience, plant health depends on more than just the three essential nutrients, nitrogen, phosphorous, potash, provided in an all-purpose chemical fertilizer. The Viette family has been growing plants for over eighty years using natural, organic, blended fertilizers made up of at least ten to fourteen ingredients. These are earth-friendly products that include the three essential nutrients, and, in addition, have beneficial effects on the environment and the soil.

Adding natural organics to the soil has a positive effect on soil microorganisms, the micro-fauna and micro-flora of the soil, and beneficial earthworms. The soil structure and aeration is improved. Natural organics don't dissolve quickly and do not easily run off into rivers and lakes. Their breakdown is dependent on three factors—soil moisture, temperature, and microbial activity. The nutrient microbial release is a slow, gradual process that makes nutrients available exactly when the plants need them and over an extended period of time. The result is overall plant health, and plants with luxuriant and robust foliage and superb flowers.

In the past, we mixed our own blends of organic fertilizers in the nursery garage. Today the market-place offers packaged fertilizers that are blends of natural organics. Bulb-Tone®, Holly-Tone®, Plant-Tone®, and Rose-Tone® are the most complete on the market at this writing. Here's what they contain:

Holly-Tone® 4-6-4
Ingredients: dehydrated manure, animal tankage, crab meal, cocoa meal, cotton seed meal, dried blood, sunflower meal, kelp, greensand, rock phosphate, sulfate of potash, ammonium sulfate, single super phosphate (1 pound = $2^2/3$ cups)
Application Amounts: New Bed—10 lbs. per 100 sq. ft., 100 lbs. per 1000 sq. ft.; Established Bed—5 lbs. per 100 sq. ft., 50 lbs. per 1000 sq. ft.

Plant-Tone® 5-3-3
Ingredients: dehydrated manure, animal tankage, crab meal, cocoa meal, bone meal, dried blood, sunflower meal, kelp, greensand, rock phosphate, sulfate of potash
Application Amounts: New Bed—10 lbs. per 100 sq. ft., 100 lbs. per 1000 sq. ft.; Established Bed—5 lbs. per 100 sq. ft., 50 lbs. per 1000 sq. ft.

Bulb-Tone® 4-10-6

Ingredients: bone meal, crab meal, dehydrated manure, animal tankage, cocoa meal, dried blood, sunflower meal, greensand, rock phosphate, ammonium sulfate, single super phosphate

Application Amounts: New Bed—10 lbs. per 100 sq. ft.; Established Bed—5 lbs. per 100 sq. ft.

Rose-Tone® 6-6-4

Ingredients: dehydrated manure, animal tankage, crab meal, cocoa meal, dried blood, cottonseed meal, sunflower meal, kelp, greensand, bode phosphate, sulfate of potash, ammonium sulfate, single super phosphate

Application Amounts: New Plant—4 cups per plant; Established Plant—2 cups per plant

Greensand

Greensand is a mined mineral-rich marine deposit, also known as glauconite. These ancient sea deposits are an all-natural source of potash. It is an iron potassium silicate in which the potassium is the important element in the potash. Thirty-two or more micro ingredients are contained in greensand. There is 0.01% soluble potash in what is a total of 6% total potash K20. Greensand is non-burning and helps to loosen heavy clay soil. It also binds sandy soil for a better structure. It increases the water holding capacity of soils and it considered an excellent soil conditioner. Greensand promotes plant vigor, disease resistance, and good color in fruit. Greensand contains nitrogen, phosphorus, potassium, calcium, magnesium, sulfur, chlorine, cobalt, copper, iron, manganese, molybdenum, sodium, and zinc. Greensand also contains silica, iron oxides, magnesia, and lime. Dr. J.C.F. Tedrew, Rutgers University Soil Specialist, mentions that glauconite may have a considerable capacity for gradual release of certain plant food elements, particularly the so-called trace elements (micronutrients). Once greensand is impregnated with micronutrients it will later release them at a very slow rate.

Gypsum

Gypsum is a hydrated calcium sulfate. The actual amounts of calcium and sulfur can vary, but 22% calcium and 17% sulfur occurs in some formulations. Gypsum replaces sodium in alkaline soils with calcium and improves the drainage and aeration. Gypsum is an effective ammonia-conserving agent when applied to manured soils or other rapidly decomposing organic matter. The escaping ammonia is changed to ammonium sulfate, which is stable. Gypsum is applied at the rate of 10 lbs. per 100 sq. ft. in heavy clay soil and 5 lbs. per 100 sq. ft. in moderately clay soil. Gypsum improves the structure of the heavier soils rather than the sandy soils.

Osmocote®, Scotts and Scotts-Sierra All-Purpose Fertilizers

All-purpose chemical fertilizers contain balanced proportions of the three essential plant nutrients—nitrogen (N), phosphorus (P), and potassium (K). The numbers on the packaging, 5-10-5 and 10-10-10 for example, refer to the proportions of each element present. When you apply a granular all-purpose chemical fertilizer to the soil, the nutrients last a short time—five or six weeks. To keep the plants nourished using only chemical fertilizers, you must repeat the applications. Because they dissolve easily in water, these elements can contribute to the pollution of nearby streams and rivers, and eventually harm bigger bodies of water like the Chesapeake Bay. Somewhat similar are the soluble chemical fertilizers you mix with water and apply in a hose-end sprayer or a watering can. We use these fertilizers when a plant shows symptoms of nutrient deficiency, as a quick pick-up, or as a starter fertilizer. But for a general liquid fertilization there are organic counterparts of the chemical fertilizers: for example, fish emulsion and liquid seaweed, manure teas made by steeping dehydrated manure, and the compost teas that are becoming popular today.

Scientists have packaged the chemical fertilizers so they act like tiny little time pills, releasing their nutrients over a specified period. Examples are Osmocote® controlled release fertilizers, which come in 3-4 month, 8-9 month, and 12-14 month formulations. A similar product is Scotts controlled-release Agriform™ fertilizer tablets, which can last up to two years.

More About Pruning Trees and Shrubs

Pruning is part of regular garden maintenance, not just a solution to things gone wrong. The thing to keep in mind when you prune is that it stimulates growth, and that dictates what you should prune, and when.

What to Prune

To keep trees and shrubs looking their best and growing well, regularly remove weak, crowded stems; branches that will eventually cross each other; suckers, which are shoots growing at the base of a tree or shrub; and water sprouts, which are vigorous upright shoots that develop along a branch, usually where it has been pruned. Pruning is sometimes needed to open up the canopy of a tree or a shrub to let in air and sun. Pruning also causes denser growth, and can be used to encourage height and to control size. For the most appealing results, when you prune, follow the lines of the plant's natural growth habit.

Thinning Before

When to Prune

Our plant pages suggest a best time for pruning each plant. The rule is that trees and shrubs that bloom on this year's growth—hydrangeas for example, rose-of-Sharon, chaste tree, butterfly bush—are pruned early in the year, before growth begins. The growth that pruning encourages provides more places for flowers. Plants that bloom on wood from the previous year—ornamental fruit trees and most spring flowering trees and shrubs such as azaleas—are pruned as soon as possible after they bloom. Shade and evergreen trees typically are pruned every three or four years.

Flowering and evergreen shrubs may need maintenance pruning every season. Young vigorous plants will need more pruning than mature plants. Winter and early spring pruning stimulates plants to produce more unwanted suckers than late spring or summer pruning. So if it's a plant's nature to sucker heavily, as with lilacs and crabapples, summer is a better time to prune. On the other hand, pruning in late summer or early fall can cause growth that won't have time to harden off before winter.

Thinning After

Pruning Large Trees

When a large limb is involved, pruning is best undertaken in spring just before growth begins, or after maximum leaf expansion in June. Pruned then, the tree will likely roll calluses over the external wound, and, internally, it will protect itself by walling off the damaged tissue. Painting a wound has fallen out of favor but the *Cornell Cooperative Extension Illustrated Guide to Pruning* says "certain materials such as orange shellac may provide a temporary barrier to certain pathogens until a tree's natural barrier zones form." The alcohol in shellac is a disinfectant.

Evergreen trees are usually allowed to develop naturally, but deciduous trees may need pruning to grow up to be all they can be. After planting a balled-and-burlapped, or a container-grown, deciduous tree, remove any weak and injured branches, and those that will eventually rub across each other. For bare-root trees, some experts recommend thinning out a quarter of the branches so the canopy will be in better balance with the reduced root system. The year after planting pruning to shape a deciduous tree begins, and that continues over the next three to five years. The first step is to identify the strongest terminal leader, unless the tree is naturally multi-stemmed: the leader will become the trunk. Then prune all but the main limbs—the "scaffold branches"—that will define the structure of the tree. Choose as scaffolding those branches whose crotch is at a wide angle to the trunk. The height of the lowest scaffold branches depends on the activities planned under the tree. You can leave them in place for the first few years to protect the bark from sunscald and to provide more leaves to nourish the root system. The scaffold branches at each level should be a fairly equal distance from each other: spaced evenly all around the trunk, they make for better balance. For each next level of scaffold branches, choose limbs developing between or offset from, not directly over, the branches of the level below. In the following years, watch the growth of the tree and trim back any side branches growing taller than the leader.

Limb Removal

Pruning and Rejuvenating Shrubs

At planting time prune out weak and injured branches, and any crossing each other. To keep the shrub airy, then and later, you may need to remove a few branches from the base and to head back others. "Heading back" means cutting an unwanted branchlet back to where there is an outward facing branchlet or bud on the main stem. Shearing shrubs, unless they are growing as a hedge, is discouraged because it stimulates dense growth at the tips of the branches and distorts the natural shape of the plant.

You can use pruning to rejuvenate older shrubs grown leggy or out of scale with their place in the garden. There are three ways to rejuvenate deciduous shrubs, all initiated before growth begins in early spring, The most drastic way is to cut the whole plant back to within 6 to 10 inches of the ground: by July it will be a mass of upright canes. Remove half or more of these, and head the others back to outward facing buds at half or less of the height you want the shrub to be. A slightly less drastic way is to cut half, or more, of the older branches, including any that cross, and all suckers, back to the ground: at midsummer, remove all new canes and head back branching that develops on the canes you kept. The least drastic method is to remove a third to a quarter of the older branches over three, or even four, years, each year removing unwanted suckers and heading back crowded branching. You can rejuvenate broadleaved evergreen shrubs that have grown out of scale—rhododendrons, mountain laurels, boxwoods for example—by cutting them back to within 2 to 4 feet of the ground in late winter or early spring before growth begins. Leave branch ends at various heights so re-growth will appear natural. Re-growth will take two to four years.

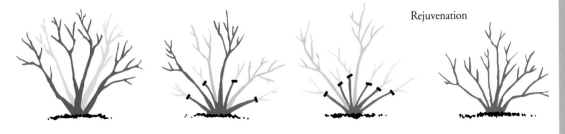

Rejuvenation

239

Gardening with Wildlife, Welcome and Otherwise

Birds:

Birds adopt gardens that provide food, water, and shelter. To attract birds, plant trees and shrubs that have berries and small fruits. Let stand the seedheads of ornamental grasses and various flowers for fall and early winter. Provide a water basin/bird bath near a shrub, preferably a dense evergreen, where birds can check for predators before flying in. Plant, or keep, tall trees for perching and nesting: pines and hemlocks provide nesting materials as well. Finally, if you have space, allow milkweed and other wild plants useful to birds to develop in a bramble away from house traffic.

To deter birds: our feathered friends are beautiful, lovable, inspiring, and useful in that they eat insects, some good and some bad. They also eat your berries and your garden and grass seeds. A mesh cover is almost the only way to protect berries. Remember when planting for birds that they drop seeds everywhere. Bears are eager for birdseed: if there are bears in your area, stocking a bird feeder may not be a good idea.

Hummingbirds:

Hummingbirds rely on sight, not scent, to locate their food. They are attracted by tubular, brightly colored flowers, and prefer single-petaled varieties to doubles. Like butterflies, hummingbirds require a continuous supply of nectar.

Bears, bees, and wasps love nectar, too: think twice before putting out sugared water.

Butterflies:

Ideal for a butterfly garden is the sun-warmed side of a south-facing fence, a wall, or a windbreak. Because this lovely thing is cold-blooded, it can fly only when warmed by the sun and in air that is 55 to 60 degrees Fahrenheit. On sunless days and at night butterflies roost in deeply fissured bark, or a butterfly hotel: a wooden box with perches and an entrance big enough for a butterfly with folded wings to slide through, a slot about 1/4 inch wide by about 3^1/$_2$ inches high. For basking, butterflies also need tall verticals that hold warmth—statuary, stones, standing logs. And a puddling place—a patch of damp sand or drying mud where male butterflies can gather and take up moisture and dissolved salts, which we believe are helpful for mating. The food for adult butterflies is the nectar in flowers. They are drawn to brightly colored flowers—purple, yellow, orange, and red. The caterpillars of most species need a specific host plant: *Peterson Field Guide to Eastern Butterflies* can tell you which. Learn to recognize the caterpillars of butterflies, and even many moths, so that you won't be tempted to eliminate them from the garden when you see them eating your plants.

Deer:

To attract Bambi and company, plant fruit trees. They relish apples and pears. They also adore hostas, rhododendrons, and other large, succulent leaves, and roses, raspberries, impatiens—anything that doesn't have itsy bitsy leaves or flowers. Provide a salt lick and water in a secluded spot, and for winter put out bales of hay.

To deter these oversize white-tailed rats: Every commercial deterrent we have tried so far has succeeded only until the deer decided it wasn't a sign of danger. Wrapping evergreens with burlap in late fall and winter works: for summer, use chicken wire—at a distance you won't see it. Or plant in small, fully enclosed spaces. To protect a large property, try fencing high enough for a tennis court, or double fences 4 to 5 feet apart. If you can't fence, you may be able to discourage them this way: at places where they enter your garden, hang tubes of crushed garlic, or predator urine, chunks of Irish Spring soap, or human hair damp with strongly scented lotions such as Avon's Skin So Soft. Hang them at the height of the deer's nose, a different scent at each entry point. Replace these scents with new different ones every four to six weeks of the gardening season.

Rabbits, Woodchucks, and Other Rodents:

To attract these sweet critters, develop a wilderness bramble with fallen logs far enough from the beaten path to let them feel safe. Provide a source of water. Time and nature will do the rest.

Chicken wire fencing that starts 24 inches underground keeps out most rodents: for woodchucks, make it 4 to 6 feet tall as well and leave it loose and floppy, not stiff enough to climb. Keeping raccoons out too requires enclosing your garden overhead as well.

Good Plants for Birds

Annuals, Perennials, and Grasses:

Ammophila breviligulata, American
  Beach Grass
Echinacea purpurea 'Magnus',
  Purple Coneflower
Echinops ritro, Globe Thistle

Helianthus annuus, Sunflower
Panicum virgatum, Switch Grass
Rudbeckia fulgida var. *sullivantii* 'Goldsturm',
  Black-Eyed Susan

Trees, Shrubs, and Vines:

Abies concolor, White Fir
Acer saccharum, Sugar Maple
Amelanchier arborea, Serviceberry
Arctostaphylos uva-ursi, Bearberry
Buxus spp., Boxwood
Cedrus libani ssp. *atlantica* 'Glauca',
  Blue Atlas Cedar
Cercis canadensis, Eastern Redbud
Chamaecyparis obtusa 'Nana Gracilis',
  Dwarf Hinoki Falsecypress
Chionanthus virginicus, White Fringe Tree
Cornus florida, Flowering Dogwood
Cotinus spp., Smoke Tree
Cotoneaster spp., Cotoneaster
Crataegus viridis, Hawthorn
× *Cupressocyparis leylandii*, Leyland Cypress
Euonymus alatus 'Compactus',
  Dwarf Burning Bush
Fagus grandifolia, American Beech
Juniperus spp., Juniper
Liquidambar styraciflua, Sweet Gum

Liriodendron tulipifera, Tuliptree
Lonicera × *heckrottii*, Goldflame Honeysuckle
Malus spp. and hybrids, Flowering Crabapple
Nyssa sylvatica, Sour Gum
Oxydendrum arboreum, Sourwood
Parthenocissus quinquefolia, Virginia Creeper
Picea pungens 'Glauca', Colorado Blue Spruce
Pinus strobus, Eastern White Pine
Prunus spp., Flowering Cherry
Pseudotsuga menziesii, Douglas Fir
Pyracantha coccinea, Firethorn
Pyrus calleryana, Callery Pear
Quercus spp., Oak
Rosa spp. and hybrids, Rose
Sciadopitys verticillata, Umbrella Pine
Spiraea spp., Spirea
Stewartia pseudocamellia, Japanese Stewartia
Taxus × *media*, Yew
Thuja occidentalis, Arborvitae
Tsuga canadensis, Canadian Hemlock

Good Plants for Hummingbirds

Annuals, Perennials, and Bulbs

Ageratum houstonianum, Ageratum
Ajuga spp., Bugleweed
Alcea ficifolia, Hollyhock
Allium spp., Flowering Onion
Antirrhinum majus, Snapdragon
Aquilegia spp., Columbine
Asclepias tuberosa, Butterfly Weed
Begonia grandis, Hardy Begonia
Chelone spp., Turtlehead
Crocosmia spp., Crocosmia
Dahlia spp. and hybrids, Dahlia
Delphinium spp., Larkspur
Dianthus spp., Pinks
Digitalis spp., Foxglove
Heuchera spp. and hybrids, Coral Bells
Hibiscus moscheutos, Marsh Rose Mallow
Hosta spp., Hosta
Impatiens walleriana, Impatiens
Kniphofia spp., Red Hot Poker

Lavandula angustifolia, Lavender
Lilium spp., Lily
Lobelia cardinalis, Cardinal Flower
Lobularia maritima, Sweet Alyssum
Mentha spicata, Mint
Monarda didyma, Monarda
Nepeta x faassenii, Catmint
Pelargonium spp. and hybrids, Geranium
Penstemon digitalis, Beardtongue
Petunia × *hybrida*, Petunia
Phlox paniculata, Phlox
Rosmarinus officinalis, Rosemary
Rudbeckia spp., Black-Eyed Susan
Salvia spp., Salvia and Sage
Scabiosa spp., Pincushion Flower
Stewartia pseudocamellia, Japanese Stewartia
Tropaeolum majus, Nasturtium
Verbena spp., Verbena
Zinnia elegans, Zinnia

Trees, Shrubs, and Vines:

Buddleja davidii, Butterfly Bush
Campsis radicans, Trumpet Vine
Caryopteris × *clandonensis*, Blue Spirea
Chaenomeles speciosa, Flowering Quince
Daphne × *burkwoodii* 'Carol Mackie', Daphne

Hibiscus syriacus, Rose-of-Sharon
Lonicera × *heckrottii*, Goldflame Honeysuckle
Sophora japonica, Japanese Pagoda Tree
Syringa vulgaris, Lilac
Wisteria floribunda, Japanese Wisteria

Good Plants for Butterflies

(Including plants for butterfly larvae, or caterpillars)

Achillea millefolium, Yarrow
Agastache spp., Anise Hyssop
Alcea spp., Hollyhock
Allium spp., Ornamental Onion
Alyssum saxatile, Alyssum
Aquilegia spp., Columbine
Aristolochia spp., Dutchman's Pipe
Arabis spp., Rockcress
Armeria maritima, Thrift
Asclepias tuberosa, Butterfly Weed
Asimina triloba, Paw Paw
Aster spp., Aster

Astilbe spp., Astilbe
Boltonia asteroides, Boltonia
Buddleja davidii, Butterfly Bush
Caryopteris × *clandonensis*, Blue Spirea
Centaurea spp., Bachelor's Buttons
Centranthus ruber, Jupiter's Beard
Ceratostigma plumbaginoides, Leadwort
Chelone spp., Turtlehead
Coreopsis spp., Tickseed
Crocosmia spp., Crocosmia
Delphinium spp., Larkspur
Dendranthema spp., Chrysanthemum, Daisy

Dianthus spp., Pinks
Echinacea purpurea, Purple Coneflower
Echinops ritro, Globe Thistle
Eryngium spp., Sea Holly
Eupatorium spp., Ageratum, Joe Pye Weed,
    White Snake Root
Filipendula rubra, Meadowsweet
Foeniculum vulgare, Fennel
Gaillardia spp., Indian Blanket
Helenium autumnale, Sneezeweed
Helianthus spp., Sunflower
Heliopsis helianthoides, Heliopsis
Hemerocallis spp., Daylily
Iberis spp., Candytuft
Iris pseudacorus, Yellow Flag
Kniphofia uvaria, Red Hot Poker
Lavandula angustifolia, Lavender
Liatris spicata, Blazing-Star
Lilium spp., Lily
Lindera benzoin, Spicebush
Lobelia spp., Cardinal Flower, Blue Lobelia
Monarda didyma, Monarda

Nepeta faassenii, Catmint
Origanum spp., Oregano
Passiflora spp., Passion Vine
Petroselinum crispum, Parsley
Phlox spp., Phlox
Physostegia virginiana, Obedient Plant
Primula spp., Primrose
Rosmarinus officinalis, Rosemary
Rudbeckia spp., Black-Eyed Susan
Ruta graveolens, Rue
Salvia spp., Salvia, Sage
Scabiosa spp., Pincushion Flower
Sedum spp., Stonecrop
Skimmia japonica, Skimmia
Solidago spp., Goldenrod
Spiraea japonica, Spirea
Stokesia laevis, Stokes' Aster
Vernonia noveboracensis, Ironweed
Verbena spp., Verbena
Veronica spp., Speedwell
Zinnia elegans, Zinnia

Starting Seeds Indoors

New England's growing season is unpredictable. We can have a heat wave in March, late frosts in May, just enough chill in early September to ruin the tomatoes, followed by a glorious lingering Indian summer. So we extend the growing season by starting seeds early indoors—in winter for spring planting, in summer for early fall planting. Seedlings of plants labeled "hardy" can be transplanted to the garden after the last frost. Others must wait until night temperatures reach 50 to 55 degrees Fahrenheit. But you can start seedlings outdoors early under a plastic cone called a "hot cap," an elegant, bell-shaped "cloche," strips of filmy tenting like Remay, or in a cold frame or a hot bed, projects beyond the scope of this book. The seed packet tells you whether you can start the plants indoors, and how much ahead of the outdoor planting season. For fast growers four to six weeks is usual; for slow-growers, ten to twelve weeks is typical. We recommend starting seeds in moistened STERILE commercial seed starter mix. We use the flats that have individual planting pockets and plastic covers. A humusy FERTILE planting mix is best for plants that will be indoors six weeks or more. Seed packets recommend planting depths. Use a pencil or a pointed stick to make planting holes: for medium-size seeds, 1/4 inch deep; for large seeds 1 inch deep is better. To sow very fine seeds, mix them half and half with builder's sand and broadcast them evenly over the planting mix from a saltshaker. The seed packet will tell you whether the seeds germinate best in the dark covered with soil, or uncovered so they get light.

Label the seeds—don't forget!—and cover the flat with its plastic top for the germination period. To speed germination, set it on a heat mat, or an old heating pad on "Low" and covered with plastic. Perennials tend to be slow to germinate, and require more attention than annuals. "Seed" leaves, called cotelydons, appear first. They contain starches and proteins the embryo draws on until the "true" leaves open and begin producing food. The cotyledons are present within the seed, along with an embryonic stem, a root, and all else necessary to create a new plant.

When all the seeds in the flat are sprouted, remove the cover and move the flat to good light. Seedlings that will go out to the garden in four or five weeks do well with the light on a sunny sill. They will eventually bend toward the sun: to keep them growing straight, rotate the container. Seedlings that will be indoors six weeks or more do best under grow lights, one cool and one warm white fluorescent bulb burned fourteen to sixteen hours a day. A fluorescent light garden is a worthwhile investment if you plan to start seeds indoors every year. Many gardeners keep their grow lights in the basement.

To keep the seedlings growing strongly during this period, maintain soil moisture. Water from the bottom, or mist the seedlings; pouring water over hair-thin stems flattens them. Add only as much water as the seedlings take up within an hour. Tip out any excess water. Air the room often if you can. The cotyledons are followed by the true leaves, which are more complex. Their unfolding indicates the plant has begun to grow. At that point, however tiny, the seedling can be transplanted successfully. As the seedlings become crowded, transplant each to an individual 4-inch pot filled with sterile potting mix. Fertilize seedlings that will be indoors six weeks or more every two weeks: we use a soluble houseplant fertilizer (20-20-20) at half strength.

Seedlings sulk in cold soil. Before moving them to the open garden, wait for daytime temperatures to reach 55 degrees Fahrenheit. Four or five days before transplanting to the garden, set the pots outdoors in a spot sheltered from direct sun and wind. The soil will dry more quickly outdoors, so check the pots often and water as needed.

New England Public Gardens

You can learn so much about plants and garden design by wandering the paths of public gardens! We love visiting gardens close to home where we know that the trees, shrubs, and perennials make it through our own winters. And we love seeing what the public gardens in other parts of New England can grow that we haven't dared try. The best time to visit is when the gardens are peaking—in most New England public gardens May and June are sure to offer lavish displays. The other best time to visit public gardens is when you can see what plants the pros use to keep color in the garden in fall and winter.

Connecticut

Barnhart Memorial Garden
Hayden Hill Rd. and Walkley Hill Rd.
Haddam, CT
203-345-2400
Small garden filled with many 1790-1820 period herbs, flowers, and vegetables. Open daily. Free.

Bartlett Arboretum,
University of Connecticut
151 Brookdale Road
Stamford, CT
203 322-6971

Caprilands Herb Farm
534 Silver St., Coventry, CT
860-742-7244
More than 30 theme gardens in a spectacular country estate setting. www.caprislands.com

Connecticut College Arboretum
270 Monhegan Ave., New London, CT
860-439-5020
Open daily. Guided tours available. Diverse plantings. www.arboretum.conncoll.edu

Cricket Hill Garden
670 Walnut Hill Rd.
Thomaston, CT
860-283-1042
More than 200 varieties of tree peonies.
www.treepeony.com

Dinosaur State Park Arboretum
400 West St.
Rocky Hill, CT
860-529-8423
Includes more than 250 species and cultivars of conifers, plus magnolias, katsuras, ginkgos, and other plants representative of the Dinosaur Age.
www.dinosaurstatepark.org

Elizabeth Park Rose Garden
150 Walbridge Rd.
West Hartford, CT
860-242-0017
Open daily, except holidays, dawn-dusk. Park designed by Olmsted & Son, gardens designed by Theodore Wirth. 800 rose varieties in the All-America Rose Selections test garden and Heritage Rose garden. Annual, herb, perennial, and rock gardens, 100-year-old Lord & Burnham greenhouses. www.elizabethpark.org

Gazebo Gardens
54 Hennequin Rd.
Columbia, CT
860-228-0244
Open May-July. Forty display gardens, with more than 1,000 species.

Glebe House Museum, Gertrude Jekyll Garden
Hollow Road
Woodbury, CT
203 263-2855

Marsh Botanical Gardens
Yale University
277 Mansfield St., Prospect St., and Hillside Terr.
Stratford, CT
These gardens were redesigned by Beatrix Farrand. Outdoor plots, greenhouses, and a display collection of native and exotic woody plants.

New Canaan Nature Center
144 Oenoke Ridge
New Canaan, CT
203-966-9577
40-acre property includes wildflowers, herbs, and perennial borders. Education building includes greenhouse. www.newcanaannature.org

Pardee Rose Garden
East Rock Park, 180 Park Rd.
Hamden, CT
203-946-8142
Open April-Oct., sunrise-sunset. All-America Rose
Selections with more than 50 varieties, perennials,
annuals, and herbs. www.newhavenparks.org

Sundial Herb Garden
59 Hidden Lake Road
Higganum, CT
860 345-4290

White Flower Farm
Rt. 63,
Litchfield, CT
860-567-8789
Unique specimens of trees and shrubs. Display
gardens of roses, perennials, bulbs, and annuals.
www.whiteflowerfarm.com

Massachusetts

Alexandra Botanic Garden, Hunnewell
Arboretum, Ferguson Greenhouses
Wellesley College
Wellesley, MA
617-283-1000
15 greenhouses feature desert plants, tropicals,
orchids, ferns, subtropical flora, temperate,
and aquatic. Hugely diverse arboretum.
www.wellesley.edu/Activities/homepage/web/
laboretum.html

Arnold Arboretum
125 Arborway
Jamaica Plain, MA
617-524-1718
North America's premiere collection of woody
plant material with more than 7,000 varieties of
trees. Free. www.arboretum.harvard.edu

Berkshire Botanical Gardens
5 West Stockbridge Rd.
Rte. 102 & 183
Stockbridge, MA
413-298-3926
www.berkshirebotanical.org

Case Estates of the Arnold Arboretum
135 Wellesley St.
Weston, MA
617-524-1718
This 75-acre former estate is a nursery and experimental station for the Arboretum. Ground covers,
rhodies, hostas, daylilies, iris, peonies, perennials
(emphasizing native-American plants).
www.msue.msu.edu/son/mod70/70000105.html

Codman House Gardens
Codman Rd.
Lincoln, MA
781-259-8843
15 acres of grounds feature Asian and European
shrubbery, a 20th century classical Italian
garden, and English cottage garden.
www.caperscatering.com/catering/venues/
venues/Codman%20House.htm

Cushing House Museum & Garden
98 High St.
Newburyport, MA
978-462-2681
Federal period mansion includes 19th-century
garden, herb garden, and fruit trees. Formal
boxwood garden with perennials and roses still
follow the original design. www.newburyhist.com

The Eleanor Cabot Bradley Reservation
2468B Washington St.
Canton, MA
781-821-2977
Lattice-walled Italianate garden includes perennials,
bulbs, and annuals, plus other plantings of rhododendrons, dogwoods, and azaleas.

Garden in the Woods
180 Hemenway Rd.
Framingham, MA
508-877-7630
New England's premiere wildflower showcase with
1,600 varieties of perennials, herbs, shrubs, and
trees. www.newfs.org

Glen Magna Farms
Ingersoll St.
Danvers, MA
978-774-9165
Estate with perennial, annual, shrubbery, and rose
gardens, statuary and garden pavilions. Open
9 a.m.-dark, Mon.-Fri.; 9 a.m.-noon Sat.-Sun.
www.glenmagnafarms.org

James P. Kelleher Rose Garden
Back Bay Fens, Park Dr.
Boston, MA
617-635-4505
Part of the Emerald Necklace designed by
Frederick Law Olmsted, this rose garden
includes hundreds of modern roses bordered
by yew hedges.

Mount Holyoke College Botanic Garden
Mount Holyoke College
50 College St.
South Hadley, MA
413-538-2116
Enjoy an arboretum, Victorian greenhouse, and
perennial gardens. ww.mtholyoke.edu/offices/botan

Naumkeag Gardens
Prospect Hill Rd.
Stockbridge, MA
413-298-3239
Famous formal landscaped gardens by Fletcher
Steele and Mabel Choate in magnificent
country setting. www.berkshireweb.com/
trustees/naumkeag.html

Nor'East Miniature Rose Inc.
58 Hammond St.
Rowley, MA
617-948-2408
Miniature rose garden—introduced varieties and
test cultivars. All-America Rose Selection (AARS)
demonstration garden includes test varieties of
both miniature and larger roses. Open daily, 8
a.m.-4 p.m. Closed on days when roses are
sprayed. Free. www.noreast-miniroses.com

Polly Hill Arboretum
809 State Rd., West Tisbury, MA
508-693-9426
This 60-acre arboretum features more than 2,000
varieties of woody plants and trees. About 80
plants are original cultivars, including rhododendrons, magnolias, stewartias, hollies, conifers, and
dogwoods. www.pollyhillarboretum.org

The Sedgwick Gardens at Long Hill
572 Essex St.
Beverly, MA
978-921-1944
114-acre estate with five acres of gardens, 400
species of plants, an apple orchard, and meadow.
Fee. www.thetrustees.org/ttor/ttorspaces.nsf/
ReservationLookup/Long+Hil

Stanley Park
400 Western Ave.
Westfield, MA
413-568-9312
Formal rose garden, perennial and herb gardens,
American Wildflower Society Display Garden,
rhododendron garden, All-America Rose
Selections garden, and five-acre arboretum.
Open seasonally. Fee. www.stanleypark.org

Tower Hill Botanic Garden
11 French Dr.
Boylston, MA
508-869-6111
One of New England's premiere public garden
facilities, the site features vast lawn garden and
intimate private gardens on 132 acres. Voted
favorite public garden by PPP. Fee. www.tower-
hillbg.org

Maine

Amen Farm Gardens
Naskeag Point Rd.
Brooklin, ME
207-359-8982
Arboretum featuring 150 uncommon trees.

Butterfly Gardens
Rt. 43, Farmington Rd.
Starks, ME
207-696-8165
Display gardens feature an array of perennials,
which are also offered for sale.

Coastal Maine Botanical Garden
Barter Island Rd.
Boothbay, ME
207-633-4333
Evolving 128-acre site with strong efforts to
eventually build a premiere garden.
www.mainegardens.org

Deering Oaks Rose Circle
Deering & Forest Ave.
Portland, ME
207-874-8300
Peak bloom of hybrid tea roses during July and
early August, with more than 600 species
exhibited. www.ci.portland.me.us/rec.htm

Fay Hyland Botanical Plantation
College Ave.
University of Maine
Orono, ME
207-581-2978
Botanic collection of exotic and hardy native plants.

Johnny's Selected Seeds Trial Gardens
Foss Hill Rd.
Albion, ME
207-437-9294
One of North America's largest vegetable and flower trial gardens in a Zone 4 rural setting

Lyle E. Littlefield Trial Garden
University of Maine
Orono, ME
207-581-2918
A premiere research facility for hardy plant material. www.ume.maine.edu/~nfa/lhc/little.htm

Pine Tree State Arboretum
153 Hospital Street
Augusta, ME
207-621-0031
Ornamental trees, extensive well-labeled hosta collection, forests. www.communityforest.org/page3.htm

Rogers Farm
Bennoch Rd.
Orono, ME
800-287-7396
All-America Selections display garden, rose hardiness trials, white garden, moon garden. www.umaine.edu/mafes/farms/rogers.htm

Thuya Garden/Asticou Terraces
Rt. 3
Northeast Harbor, ME
207-276-5130
Named for the area's abundant white cedars, *Thuya occidentalis*. Excellent reference library. Formal beds display a massive perennial collection. www.asticou.com/gardens.html

Wild Gardens of Acadia
Off Rte. 3
Acadia National Park, ME
207-288-3338
Twelve different plant habitats display Maine's native plants. www.acadiamagic.com/WildGardens.html

New Hampshire

The Balsams
Rte. 26, Dixville Notch, NH
603-255-3400
Vast resort gardens with 35,000 plants.

Celia Thaxter's Garden on Appledore Island
Maine/New Hampshire Coast
The Isles of Shoals Steamship Company provides ferry service from Portsmouth, NH. Make reservations through the Shoals Marine Laboratory,
607-254-2900
A recreation of the legendary island garden created by nineteenth century poet, Celia Thaxter. Visitors are welcome Wednesdays from mid-June through Labor Day.

Fuller Gardens
10 Willow Ave., North Hampton, NH
603-964-5414
Rose, perennial, and Japanese gardens, plus a conservatory. Open May-October. www.ohwy.com/nh/f/fullgard.htm

Pickity Place
Nutting Hill Rd.
Mason, NH
603-878-1151
This home was the model for the house in Little Red Riding Hood. Today, it offers a greenhouse with 270 varieties of herbs, heathers, scented geraniums, and unusual perennials, as well as outdoor public gardens. Nursery, gift shop, and restaurant. www.pickityplace.com

Rhododendron State Park
Rhododendron Rd., just off Rt. 119
Fitzwilliam, NH
603-532-8862
16 acres of wild rhododendrons bloom in early to mid-July. Wildflower trail, mountain laurel stand, and gardens at "The Old Patch Place." www.nhparks.state.nh.us/parkops/parks/rhododen.html

Sandy Point Discovery Center
89 Depot Rd.
Stratham, NH
603-778-0015
Native American vegetable garden, native plants gardens, freshwater wetlands, salt marshes, and forest. www.greatbay.org

Urban Forestry Center
45 Elwyn Rd.
Portsmouth, NH
603-431-6774
180 acres with gardens, arboretum, trails, and wildflowers. Open year-round. Free. www.nhdfl.com

Rhode Island

Blithewold Mansion
101 Ferry Rd., Rte. 114
Bristol, RI
401-253-2707
Colorful gardens and more than 1,500 native and exotic trees and shrubs grace Blithewold's landscape. www.blithewold.org

The Breakers
Ochre Point Ave.
Newport, RI
401-847-6543
Gardens at the former home of Cornelius Vanderbilt II. Parterre borders, greenhouses, and two-acre gardens. www.newportmansions.org

The Elms
Bellevue Ave.
Newport, RI
401-847-0478
French chateau-style house includes Classical Revival gardens with terraces, plus specimen trees, lower garden with marble tea houses, sunken garden, fountains, and more. www.newportmansions.org

Kinney Azalea Gardens
Rt. 108
South Kingston, RI
Azaleas and rhododendrons. www.gdeb.com/organizations/EBAC/garden_club/kinney.htm

Meadowbrook Herb Garden
93 Kingstown Rd.
Wyoming, RI
401-539-7603
Retail nursery with extensive herb display gardens.

Seahorse Grill and Gardens
364 Card's Pond Rd.
Matunuck, RI
401-789-3030
Seaside gardens with more than 300 varieties of perennials, grasses, shrubs, and climbing plants. www.theatrebythesea.com/about.html

Wilcox Park
High St.
Westerly, RI
401-596-2877
Open year-round. 18 acres of specimen trees, shrubs, display gardens, dwarf conifers, koi pond, fountain, and monuments. www.clan.lib.ri.us/wes/wilcoxparkl.html

Vermont

Cady's Falls Nursery
637 Duhamel Rd.
Morrisville, VT
802-888-5559
Known as the "Crown Jewel" of nurseries with lots of unusual and hard to find hardy plants.

Burlington Boathouse
College St.
Burlington, VT
802-865-3377
A waterfront park with numerous luxuriant display gardens. www.bpr.ci.burlington.vt.us/boathouse.html

Equinox Valley Nursery
Rt. 7A
Manchester, VT
802-362-2610
A retail nursery featuring a tropical conservatory and display gardens.

Evergreen Gardens of Vermont
Rt. 100
Waterbury Center, VT
802-244-8523
A large collection of hardy perennials.

Horticulture Research Center
Rt. 7
South Burlington, VT
802-658-9166
Associated with the University of Vermont, with plant clinics open to the public. pss.uvm.edu/dept/hort_farm

Little Siberia Perennials
966 Maston Hill Rd.
Granville, VT
802-767-3391
Featuring Zone 3-4 hardy perennials, heathers, shrubs, and roses in more than 20 gardens at this retail nursery. www.littlesiberia.com

Rocky Dale Gardens 806
Rocky Dale Rd.
Bristol, VT
802-453-2782
Retail nursery offering display gardens open to the public.

Shelburne Museum
Rt. 7
Shelburne, VT
802-985-3346
45-acre museum includes formal, perennial, heritage, and vegetable gardens, plus 30 varieties of lilacs. www.shelburnemuseum.org

Vermont Wildflower Farm
Peacham Pond Rd.
Marshfield, VT
802-426-3505
Self-guided tours from July to Sept., near Groton State Forest. www.americanmeadows.com/about.cfm

Some Outstanding New York Gardens

The New York Botanical Garden
Bronx River Parkway at Fordham Road
Bronx, New York 10458
718-817-8700

Buffalo and Erie County Botanical Gardens
South Park Avenue and McKinley Parkway
Buffalo, NY
716-828-1040

Cornell Plantations
One Plantations Road
Ithaca, NY
607-255-3020

Old Westbury Gardens
71 Old Westbury Road
Old Westbury
Long Island, NY
516-333-0048

Wave Hill
The Bronx
West 249th St. and Independence Ave.
New York, NY
718-549-3200

Plant Sources

The seeds and plants at nearby garden centers are often those most successful in our area, so we buy locally when the plants are available. When they're not, we buy from specialty nurseries that ship by mail. Most offer their catalogs are free. Many of the nurseries listed below have Internet sites that describe their products and sell them. You can find most by entering the nursery's name into a search engine such as Yahoo.com and Google.com.

New England Nurseries with a Broad Selection of Plants

Connecticut
Beardsley's Garden Center
Gay Street, Sharon, CT 06069
Phone: 960-364-0727

Country Flower Farms
320 Baileyville Road, Rt. 147
Middlefield, CT 06455
Phone: 860-349-3690
www.countryflowerfarms.com

Falls Village Flower Farm
27 Kellogg Road
Canaan, CT 06031
Phone: 860-824-0077

Gledhill Nursery
660 Mountain Road
West Hartford, CT 06117-1198
www.gledhillnursery.com

High Ridge Nursery Inc
1854 High Ridge Road
Stamford, CT 06903-4103
Phone: 203-329-9957

James S Hosking Nursery
114 Porter Street
Watertown, CT 06795-2239
Phone: 860-274-8889

John Scheepers, Inc.
23 Tulip Drive
Bantam, CT 06750

Kent Greenhouse
Route 7, Kent, CT
Phone: 860-927-3480

Lauray of Salisbury
493 Undermountain Road, RT 41
Salisbury, CT 06068
Phone: 860-435-2263

Litchfield Horticultural Center
258 Beach Street
Litchfield, CT 06759
Phone: 860-567-3707
www.litchfieldhorticulture.com

Nature Works 518 Forest Road
Northford, CT 06472
Phone: 203-484-2748
www.naturework.com

Old Farm Nursery
158 Lime Rock Road
Lakeville, CT 06039
Phone: 860-435-2272

Oliver Nurseries
1159 Bronson Road
Fairfield, CT 06430
Phone: 203-259-5609

Paley's Garden Center
Route 343, Sharon, CT 06069
PHone: 860-364-0674

Patrissi Nursery Center Inc
35 Ringgold Street
West Hartford, CT 06119-2155
Phone: 860-233-5578

Reynold's Farms Nurseries
23 Richards Avenue
Norwalk, CT 06854-2309
Phone: 203-866-5757

Salisbury Garden Center &
   Landscaping
167 Canaan Road
Salisbury, CT 06068-1602
Phone: 860-435-2439

Sam Bridge Nursery & Greenhouse
437 North Street
Greenwich, CT 06830
Phone: 203-869-3418
www.sambridge.com

Sunny Border Nursery
P. O. Box 483
Kensington, CT 06037
Phone: 800-732-1627
www.sunnyborder.com

Town & Country Farm & Garden
   Center Inc.
659 Danbury Road
Wilton, CT 06897-5002
Phone: 203-544-9266

White Flower Farm
Route 63
Litchfield, CT 067759-0050
Phone: 800-503-9624

Winterberry Gardens
2070 West Street
Southington, CT 06489
Phone: 860-378-0071

Young's Nurseries Inc
211 Danbury Road
Wilton, CT 06897-4005
Phone: 203-762-5511

Maine
Estabrook's Farm & Greenhouses
237 East Main Street
Yarmouth, ME 04096
Phone: 207-846-4398
www.estabrooksonline.com

Hoboken Garden
Route 1
Rockport, ME 04856-0309
Phone: 207-236-2891

Johnny's Selected Seeds
184 Foss Hill Road
Albion, MN 04910
Phone: 207-437-9294
ww.johnnyseeds.com

Longfellow's Greenhouses
81 Puddledock Road
Manchester, ME 04351
Phone: 207-622-5965

O'Donal's Nurseries, Inc.
6 County Road, RFD #4
Gorham, ME 04038
Phone: 207-839-4262
www.odonalsnurseries.com

Plainview Farm
529 Mountford Road North
Yarmouth, ME 04097
Phone: 207-829-5004
www.plainviewfarm.net

Plants Unlimited
US Route 1
Rockport, ME 04856
Phone: 207-594-7754

Provencher Landscape Nursery Inc
299 River Road
Lewiston, ME 04240-1030
Phone: 207-783-9777

Sprague's Nursery & Garden Center
1664 Union Street
Bangor, ME 04401-2205
Phone: 207-942-1394

Sunrise View Farm
2963 Main Street
Rangeley, ME
Phone: 207-864-2117

Massachusetts
Andrew Thomas & Sons Landscaping
1237 Randolph Avenue
Milton, MA 02186
Phone: 617-698-3348
www.athomasandsons.com

Attleboro Farms
491 Hickory Road
North Attleboro, MA 02760
Phone: 508-695-7200
www.attleborofarms.com

Cape Agricultural Supply Co Inc
Morrison's Home & Garden
Plymouth, MA 02362-1257
Phone: 508-746-0970

Corliss Bros. Garden Center &
    Nursery
31 Essex Road
Ipswitch, MA 01938
Phone: 978-356-5422
www.corlissbros.net

Farmer's Daughter, The
153 Millbury Street
Auburn, MA 01501
Phone: 508-832-2995
www.thefarmersdaughtergc.com

Great Brook Farms
356 Great Road
Bolton, MA 01740
Phone: 978-779-6680
www.greatbrookfarms.com

Groton Nursery & Garden Center
Route 225
West Groton MA 01472-0217
Phone: 978-448-5761

Kennedy's Country Gardens
85 Chief Justice Cushing Hwy.
Scituate, MA 02066-4409
Phone: 781-545-1266

Laughton Garden Center
165 Princeton Street
N. Chelmsford, MA
Phone: 800-633-0159
www.laughtonnursery.com

Mahoney's Garden Centers
242 Cambridge Street
Winchester, MA 01890
Phone: 781-729-5900
www.mahoneysgarden.com

Mahoney's Garden Centers
880 Memorial Drive
Cambridge, MA 02139
Phone: 617-354-4145

New England Nurseries Inc
216 Concord Road
Bedford MA 01730-2049
Phone: 781-275-2525

Northeast Nursery
234 Newbury Street
Peabody, MA 01960
Phone: 978-35-6550
www.northeastnursery.com

Russell's Garden Center
397 Boston Post Road
Wayland, MA 01778
Phone: 508-358-2283
www.russellsgardencenter.com

Shrewsbury Nurseries
957 Boston Turnpike
Shrewsbury, MA 01545-3382
Phone: 508-842-2831

Sixteen Acres Garden Center Inc.
1359 Wilbraham Road
Springfield, MA 01119-2614
Phone: 413-783-5883

Ward's Garden Center
600 South Main St., Rt. 7
Great Barrington, MA
Phone: 413-528-0166

Weston Nurseries
93 East Main Street
Hopkinton, MA
Phone: 508-435-3414
www.westonnurseries.com

Windy Hill Farm Inc
686 Stockbridge Road
Great Barrington, MA 01230-1270
Phone: 413-298-3217

Wyman Garden Center Inc.
135 Spring Street
Hanson, MA 02341-1025
Phone: 781-447-5400

New Hampshire
Bedford Fields
331 Route 101
Bedford, NH 03110
Phone: 603-472-8880

Churchills Garden Center Inc
12 Hampton Road
Exeter,   NH 03833
Phone: 603-772-2685

L. A. Brochu Inc.
121 Commercial Street
Concord, NH 03301-5025
Phone: 603-224-4350

Lake Street Garden Center
37 Lake Street
Salem, NH 03079-2243
Phone: 603-893-5858

Longacre Landscaping Inc
220 Mechanic St., RR 4
Lebanon, NH 03766-1516
Phone: 603-448-6110

Rolling Green Nursery
64 Breakfast Hill Road
Greenland, NH 03840
Phone: 603-436-2732

Spider Web Gardens
252 Middle Road
Center Tuftonbor, NH 03816-9708
Phone: 603-569-5056

Rhode Island

Clark Farms Garden Center
711 Kingstown Road
Wakefield, RI 02879
Phone: 401-783-8844
www.clarkfarms.com

Clark Farms Inc
711 Kingstown Road
Wakefield, RI 02879-3015
Phone: 401-783-8844

Forest Hills Nurseries Inc
310 Knollwood Avenue
Cranston, RI 02910-5131
Phone: 401-944-8282

Greenwood Nurseries Inc.
2826 Post Road
Warwick, RI 02886-3169
Phone: 401-737-4380

Island Garden Shop
54 Bristol Ferry Road
Portsmouth, RI 02871
Phone: 401-683-2231
www.igsinc.com

Warwick Nurseries Inc.
261 Warwick Avenue
Cranston, RI 02905-2515
Phone: 401-781-3700

Wood River Evergreens
101 Woodville Road
Hope Valley, RI 02832
Phone: 401-364-3387

Vermont

E. C. Browns' Nursery
Route 113
Thetford Center, VT 05075-0237
Phone: 802-785-2167

Four Seasons Garden Center
323 Industrial Avenue
Williston, VT 05495-9788
Phone: 802-658-2433

Gardener's Supply Company
128 Intervale Road
Burlington, VT 05401-2804
Phone: 802-660-3500

Homestead Landscaping &
  Garden Center Ltd.
Route 30
Bondville, VT 05340-0450
Phone: 802-297-1107

Horsfords Garden & Nursery
2111 Greenbush Road
Charlotte, VT 05445-9648
Phone: 802-425-2811

Lang Farm Nursery
51 Upper Main Street
Essex Junction, VT 05452-3102
Phone: 802-878-5720

Mettowee Mill Nursery
RR 30
Dorset,   VT 05251-0264
Phone: 802-325-3007

Skyline Nursery & Garden Center
1541 Skitchewaug Trail
Springfield, VT 05156-8807
Phone: 802-885-4090

Mail Order Nurseries with a Wide Selection of Plants

André Viette Farm & Nursery
994 Long Meadow Road
P. O. Box 1109
Fishersville, VA 22939
Perennials, daylilies, grasses

Arborvillage Farm Nursery
P.O. Box 227
Holt, MO 64048
Trees and shrubs

Arrowhead Alpines
P.O. Box 857
Fowlerville, MI 48836
Alpine plants

B & D Lilies
P.O. Box 2007
Port Townsend,WA 98368
Lilies

Bluestone Perennials, Inc.
7211 Middle Ridge Road
Madison, OH 44057-3096
Perennials, shrubs

Borbeleta Gardens
15974 Canby Avenue
Faribault, MN 55021
Phone: 507-334-2807
Perennials, etc.

Brent and Becky's Bulbs
7463 Heath Trail
Gloucester, VA 23601
Specialists in bulbs

Carroll Gardens
444 E. Main Street
Westminster, MD 21157
Perennials, roses, shrubs, trees

Chiltern Seeds
Bortree Stile
Ulverston
Cumbria LA12 7PB, England
Seeds

Crownsville Nursery
P.O. Box 797
Crownsville, MD 21032
Perennials, grasses

Eastern Plant Specialties
P.O. Box 226W
Georgetown, ME 04548
Trees, shrubs, perennials, wildflowers

Ferry-Morse Seeds
P.O. Box 1620
Fulton, KY 42041-0488
Seeds, plants, bulbs

Forestfarm
990 Temerow Road
Williams, OR 97544-9599
Trees, shrubs, perennials

George W. Park Seed Co.
1 Parkton Avenue
Greenwood, SC 29647-0001
Seeds, bulbs, plants

Heronswood Nursery
7530 NE 288th Street
Kingston, WA 98346
Perennials, trees, shrubs

High Country Gardens
2902 Rufina Street
Santa Fe, NM 87505
Perennials, roses, grasses

Jackson & Perkins
1 Rose Lane
Medford, OR 97501-0702
Roses, perennials, bulbs

Johnny's Selected Seeds
184 Foss Hill Road
Albion, MN 04910
Vegetables, herbs and flowers

John Scheepers, Inc.
23 Tulip Drive
Bantam, CT 06750
Bulbs, kitchen garden seeds

Klehm's Song Sparrow Perennial Farm
13101 E. Rye Road
Avalon, WI 53505
Peonies, Perennials, shrubs, trees, roses

Kurt Bluemel Inc.
22740 Greene Lane
Baldwin, MD 21013
Grasses, perennials

Oikos Tree Crops
P. O. Box 19425
Kalamazoo, MI 49019-0425
Trees, shrubs

Old House Gardens
536 Third Street
Ann Arbor, MI 48103
Heirloom bulbs

Plant Delights Nursery, Inc.
9241 Sauls Road, Raleigh, NC 27603
Perennials, grasses

Prairie Nursery, Inc.
P.O. Box 306
Westfield, WI 53964
Native wildflowers, native grasses

Roslyn Nursery
211 Burrs Lane
Dix Hills, NY 11746
Trees, shrubs, perennials

Seed Savers Exchange
3076 North Winn Road
Decorah, IA 52101
Vegetable and flower seeds

Seeds of Change
Fnesland, WI 53935
Organically grown vegetable and
    flower seeds

Select Seeds
180 Srickney Road
Union, CT 06076-4617
Heirloom flower seeds, annuals,
    perennials

Shepherd's Garden Seeds
30 Irene Street
Torrington, CT 06790
Tel: 800-482 3638

Siskiyou Rare Plant Nursery
2825 Cummings Road
Medford, OR 97501
Perennials, trees, shrubs, grasses

Stokes Seeds Inc.
P. O. Box 548
Buffalo, NY 14240
Perennials

Thompson & Morgan Inc.
P. O. Box 1308
Jackson, NJ 08527
Wide selection of seeds

Thompson & Morgan Inc.
P.O. Box 1308
Jackson, NJ 08527-0308
Seeds, plants, bulbs

W. Atlee Burpee & Co.
300 Park Avenue
Warminster, PA 18991
Wide selection

Wavecrest Nursery
2509 Lakeshore Drive
Fennville, MI 49408
Trees, shrubs, perennials

Wayside Gardens
1 Garden Lane
Hodges, SC 29695-0001
Everything—Perennials, shrubs,
    roses, bulbs

We-Du Nurseries
Route 5, Box 724
Marion, NC 28752-9338
Perennials, wildflowers

White Flower Farm
P. O. Box 50
Litchfield, CT 06759-0050
Perennials, shrubs, roses, bulbs

Wildseed Farms
P. O. Box 3000
Fredericksburg, TX 78624
Wildflower seeds

Mail Order Nurseries (Tender Perennials, Annuals, Tropical, House Plants, Bromeliads, Bougainvilleas, Cactus, Orchids, Pineapples, Begonia, Gesneriads, and African Violets)

Banana Tree, Inc.
715 Northampton Street
Easton, PA 18042

Davidson-Wilson Greenhouse, Inc.
RR2, Box 168
Crawfordsville, IN 47933

Glasshouse Works
Church Street
Stewart, OH 45778

Going Bananas
24401 SW 197 Avenue
Homestead, FL 33031

Good Scents
RR2, P. O. Box 168
Crawfordsville, IN 47933
Kartuz Greenhouse
P. O. Box 790
Vista, CA 92085

Lauray of Salisbury
493 Undermountain Road, RT 41
Salisbury, CT 06068

Logee's Greenhouse, Ltd
141 North Street
Danielson, CT 06239

Lyndon Lyon Greenhouse, Inc.
P. O. Box 249
Dolgeville, NY 13329

Stokes Tropicals
P. O. Box 9868
New Iberia, LA 70562
Sunshine State Tropcials
6329 Alaska Avenue
New Port Richey, FL 34653

Mail Order Nurseries for Roses

Chamblee's Rose Nursery
10926 US Highway 69 North
Tyler, TX 75706-8742
Phone: 800-256-7673

David Austin Roses Limited
15059 Highway 64 West
Tyler, TX 75704
Phone: 800-328-8893

Edmund's Roses
6235 SW Kahle Road
Wilsonville, OR 97070-9727
Phone: 888-481-7673

Hardy Roses for the North
Box 2048
Grand Forks, BC Canada VOH 1HO
Phone: 604-442-8442

Heirloom Old Garden roses
24062 NE Riverside drive
St Paul, OR 97137
Phone: 503-538-1576

High Country Roses
P. O. Box 148
Jensen, UT 84035-0148
Phone: 800 552-2082

Historical Roses
1657 W Jackson Street
Painesville, OH 44077
Phone: 216-357-7270

Jackson & Perkins Co.
1 Rose Lane
Medford, OR 97501-0702
Phone: 800-292-4769

Lowe's Own-Root Roses
6 Sheffield Road
Nashua, NH 03062
Phone: 603-888-2214

Meilland Star Roses
P O Box 249
Cutler, CA 93615
Phone: 800-457-1859

Nor'East Miniature Roses, Inc.
P. O. Box 307
Rowley, MA 01969-0607
Phone: 800-426-6485

The Antique Roses Emporium
9300 Lueckemeyer Road
Brenham, TX 77833
Phone: 800-441-0002

Mail Order Nurseries for Water Plants, Ponds, and Pools

Gilberg Farms
2172 Highway O
Robertsville, MO 63072
Phone: 636-451-2530

Lilypons Water Gardens
6800 Lilypons Road
Buckeystown, MD 21717
Phone: 800-999-5459

Springdale Water Gardens
P. O. Box 546
Greenville, VA 24440-0546
Phone: 800-420-5459

Glossary

Acid soil: soil whose pH is less than 7.0. A pH of 6.0 to 7.0 is mildly acid. The pH in which the widest range of flowers thrive is slightly acid, in the pH 5.5 to 6.5 range. Except for areas where limestone is prevalent, most garden soil in America is in this range. This pH is also suited to most plants described as acid loving.

Alkaline soil: soil whose pH is greater than 7.0. It lacks acidity, often because it has limestone in it. Mid-Atlantic soils tend to be alkaline.

All-purpose fertilizer: is available in three forms: powdered, liquid, or granular. It contains balanced proportions of the three important nutrients—nitrogen (N), phosphorus (P), and potassium (K). It is suitable for most plants.

Annual: a plant that lives its entire life in one season. It germinates, produces flowers, sets seed, and dies the same year.

Balled and burlapped: a tree or shrub grown in the field and dug, whose soil- and rootball is wrapped with protective burlap and tied with twine.

Bare root: describes plants without any soil around their roots, often packaged by mail order suppliers. The rule of thumb is to soak the roots ten to twelve hours before planting.

Bedding plant: usually annuals that are massed (planted in large groups) in a bed for maximum show.

Beneficial insect: insects and their larvae that prey on pest organisms and their eggs. Some that are well known include the ladybug and praying mantis.

Botanical name: plant names given in Latin accurately identifying the genus, species, subspecies, variety, and form. Here's an example: *Picea abies* forma *pendula* is the 1) genus, 2) species, and 3) form (*pendula*, meaning "pendulous" or "weeping") that is the botanical name for weeping Norway spruce. *Picea abies* 'Nidiformis' is the 1) genus, 2) species, and 3) variety. When the varietal name is between single quotation marks, it's what is called a "cultivar"—a cultivated variety, or a variety that has been cultivated and given a name of its own.

Bract: a modified leaf structure resembling a petal that appears close behind the flower or head of flowers. In some flowers, that of flowering dogwoods for example, the bract may be more colorful than the flowers themselves.

Bud union: a thickened area above the crown on the main stem of a woody plant. This is the point at which a desirable plant has been grafted, or budded, onto the rootstock of a plant that is strong but less ornamental.

Canopy: the overhead branching area of a tree, including its foliage.

Cold hardiness: the ability of a plant to survive the winter cold in a particular area or zone.

Common name: there is no such thing as an accurate "common name" for a plant. Names commonly used for plants are rarely common the world over, or even in a single country or state. Because they can vary from region to region, they are not as much help in locating plants as the scientific botanical names. Many are British "antiques" which continue to be used for their charm—for example, love-in-a-mist, fleabane, and lady's mantle. Botanical names find their way into common gardener language. Examples are: impatiens, begonia, petunia, salvia, zinnia, aster, astilbe, phlox, iris. In time, you will find yourself remembering many of the botanical names of the plants that interest you most.

Compost: organic matter, such as leaves, weeds, grass clippings, and seaweed, that has undergone progressive decomposition until it is reduced to a soft, fluffy texture. Soil that has been amended with compost holds air and water better and also has improved drainage.

Corm: an energy-storing structure, similar to a bulb, but actually a specialized stem, found at the base of a plant, such as crocosmia and crocus.

Crown: the base of a plant where the roots meet the stems.

Cultivar: the word stands for "cultivated variety." Cultivars are varieties named by gardeners and gardening professionals. They are developed, or selected, variations of species and hybrids.

Deadhead: the process of removing faded flower heads from plants in order to improve their appearance, stop unwanted seed production, and most often to encourage more flowering.

Deciduous: refers to trees and shrubs that loose their leaves in fall, a sign that the plant is going into dormancy for the period of weather ahead.

Division: the splitting apart of perennial plants in order to create several smaller plants. Division is a way to control the size of a plant, multiply your holdings, and also to renovate crowded plants that are losing their vitality.

Dormancy: the period, usually the winter, when plants temporarily cease active growth and rest. However, heat and drought can throw plants into summer dormancy. Certain plants, for example oriental poppies, spring-blooming wildflowers, and certain bulbs, can have their natural dormancy period in summer.

Established: the point at which a new planting begins to show new growth and is well rooted in the soil, indicating the plants have recovered from transplant shock.

Evergreen: plants that do not lose all their foliage annually with the onset of winter.

Exfoliating: to peel away in thin layers, as with bark.

Fertility/fertile: refers to the soil's content of the nutrients needed for sturdy plant growth. Nutrient availability is affected by pH levels.

Floret: a tiny flower, usually one of many forming a cluster, comprising a single flower head.

Foliar: refers to the practice of making applications to just the plant's foliage of dissolved fertilizer and some insecticides. Leaf tissue absorbs liquid quickly.

Germinate/germination: refers to the sprouting of a seed, the plant's first stage of development.

Graft/union: the point on the stem of a strong, woody plant where a stem (scion) from another plant (usually one that is more ornamental) has been inserted into understock so that they will join together into one plant.

Hardscape: the permanent, structural, non-plant part of a landscape, such as walls, sheds, pools, patios, arbors, and walkways.

Herbaceous: plants with soft stems, as opposed to the woody stem tissue of trees and shrubs.

Humus: almost completely decomposed organic materials such as leaves, plant matter, and manures.

Hybrid: a plant that is the product of deliberate or natural cross-pollination between two or more plants of the same species or genus.

Leader: the main stem of a tree.

Loam: a mix of sand and clay. When humus is added, loam is the best soil for gardening.

Low water demand: describes plants that tolerate dry soil for varying periods of time. They are often succulent and or have taproots.

Microclimate: pockets on a property that are warmer or cooler than the listed climatic zone. Hilly spots, valleys, nearness to reflective surfaces or windbreaks, proximity to large bodies of water can all contribute to altering the surrounding temperature.

Mulch: a layer of material (natural or man-made) used to cover soil to protect it from water or wind erosion, and to help maintain the soil temperature and moisture. Mulches also discourage weeds.

Naturalized: a plant that adapts and spreads in a landscape habitat. Some plants we think of as "native" are imports that have "naturalized", for example, *Phlox drummondii*, the annual phlox, self-sows and has naturalized in sand in the Outer Banks of North Carolina.

Nectar: the sweet fluid produced by glands on flowers that attract pollinators such as bees, butterflies, and hummingbirds.

Organic fertilizer: a fertilizer that is derived from anything that was living, such as bone meal, fish emulsion, manure, plants.

Organic material/organic matter: any substance that is derived from plants.

Peat moss: acid organic matter from peat sedges (United States) or sphagnum mosses (Canada) often mixed into soil to raise its organic content and sometimes as a mild acidifier.

Perennial: a flowering plant that lives for more than one season; the foliage often dies back with frost, but their roots survive the winter and generate new growth in the spring.

Perennialize: sometimes confused with "naturalize." The two words are not synonymous. Tulips many perennialize, that is come back for four years or more, but they don't become wild plants. "Naturalize" applies to a garden plant that becomes a wildflower of a region that is not its native habitat. It could be a native plant or an exotic plant.

pH: pH stands for potential of hydrogen. A measurement of the relative acidity (low pH) or alkalinity (high pH) of soil or water. Based on a scale of 1 to 14, pH 7.0 being neutral.

Pinch: to remove tender stems and/or leaves by pressing them between thumb and forefinger. The purpose is usually to deadhead, or to encourage branching and compactness. Hand shearing achieves the same purpose on plants whose blooms are too small to pinch out one at a time, pinks for example.

Planting season: refers to the best time to set out certain plants. The most vigorous growth occurs in spring. Early spring is the preferred planting time in cold zones, particularly for woody plants and for species that react poorly to transplanting. Early fall, after summer's heat has gone by and before cold comes, is an excellent time for planting in the Mid-Atlantic, provided the climate allows the roots two months or so to tie into the soil before cold shuts the plants down. Traditional planting seasons are spring and fall: availability of plants in containers/pots has added a new and valuable season to plant—the summer.

Pollen: the yellow, powdery grains in the center of a flower which are the plant's male sex cells. Pollen is transferred by wind and insects, and to a lesser extent by animals, to the female plants, whence fertilization occurs.

Raceme: describes a flower stalk where the blossoms are an arrangement of single-stalked florets along a tall stem; similar to a spike.

Rhizome: an energy-storing structure, actually a specialized stem, similar to a bulb, sometimes planted horizontally near the soil surface (iris), or beneath the soil surface (trillium). The roots emerge from the bottom and leaves and flowers grow from the upper portion of the rhizome.

Rootbound/potbound: the condition of a plant that has been confined in a container too long. Without space for expansion, the roots wrap around the rootball or mat at the bottom of the container.

Root division/rooted divisions: sections of the crown of a plant, usually of a perennial, that has been divided. This is most often the source of containerized perennial plants. A root division will perform exactly like the parent plant.

Rooted cuttings: cuttings taken from foliage growth perennials, usually, or from woody plants, that have been handled so as to grow roots. Rooted cuttings will perform exactly like the parent plant.

Seedling: plantlets started from seed. Flats and containers of annuals are usually seedlings. Seedlings of perennials, and especially of hybrids, may perform exactly as the parent did, but can't be counted on to do so. Which is why perennial growers of quality plants sell root divisions or rooted cuttings rather than seedlings.

Self-sow: some plants mature seeds, sow them freely, and the offspring appear as volunteers the following season.

Semi-evergreen: tending to be evergreen in a mild climate but deciduous in a colder climate.

Shearing: the pruning technique where plant stems and branches are cut uniformly with long-bladed pruning shears or hedge trimmers. Shearing is also a fast and easy way to deadhead plants with many tiny blooms, pinks for example.

Slow-release fertilizer: fertilizer that does not dissolve in water and therefore releases its nutrients gradually. It is often granular and can be either organic or synthetic.

Soil amendment: anything added to change the composition of the soil. Most often the element called for is humus—compost.

Succulent growth: the production of (often unwanted) soft, fleshy leaves or stems. Can be a result of over-fertilization.

Suckers: shoots that form new stems which can be useful, or not, depending on the plant. Removing lilac suckers keeps the parent plant strong and attractive.

Summer dormancy: in excessive heat some plants, including roses, slow or stop productivity. Fertilizing or pruning a partially dormant plant will stimulate it into growth.

Tuber: similar to a bulb, a tuber is a specialized stem, branch, or root structure used for food storage. It generates roots on the lower surface while the upper portion puts up stems, leaves, and flowers. Dahlia and caladium are examples.

Variegated: foliage that is streaked, edged, or blotched with various colors—often green leaves with yellow, cream, or white markings.

Variety: the only accurate names for plants are the scientific botanical names and these are given in Latin—genus, species, subspecies, variety, and form. In botany, "variety" is reserved for a variant of a species that occurs in the wild or natural habitat. It should not be used instead of, or confused with "cultivated variety," which has been shortened to "cultivar."

Wings: the tissue that forms edges along the twigs of some woody plants such as winged euonymus; or the flat, dried extension on some seeds, such as maple, that catch the wind and enable the seeds to fly away to land and grow in another place.

Bibliography

Aden, Paul. *The Hosta Book: Second Edition.* Timber Press, 1992.

American Horticultural Society A-Z Encyclopedia of Garden Plants, The. Christopher Bricknell and Judith D. Zuk, eds. DK Publishing, 1997.

André Viette Gardening Guide. Viette Staff.

Annuals: 1001 Gardening Questions Answered. Editors of Garden Way Publishing. Storey Books, 1989.

Armitage, Allan M. *Herbaceous Perennial Plants: Second Edition.* Stipes Publishing Co., 1997.

Armitage, Allan M., Asha Kays, Chris Johnson. *Armitage's Manuel of Annuals, Biennials, and Half-Hardy Perennials.* Timber Press, 2001.

A-Z Horticulture: Annuals for the Connoisseur.

A-Z of Annuals, Biennials & Bulbs (Successful Gardening). Reader's Digest, 1997.

Bales, Suzanne Fruitig. *The Burpee American Gardening Series: Annuals, Reissue Edition.* Hungry Minds, Inc., 1993.

Ball, Liz. *Pennsylvania Gardener's Guide.* Cool Springs Press, 2002.

Barash, Cathy Wilkinson. *Edible Flowers: From Garden to Palette.* Fulcrum Publishing, 1993.

Bar-Zvi, David, Kathy Sammis, Chani Yammer, Albert Squillance. *American Garden Guides:Tropical Gardening, Fairchild Tropical Garden.* Pantheon Books, 1996.

Bath, Trevor and Joy Jones. *The Gardener's Guide to Growing Hardy Geraniums.* Timber Press, 1994.

Bloom, Adrian. *Conifers for your Garden.* John Markham & Associates, 1987.

Boland, Tim, Laura Coit, Marty Hair. *Michigan Gardener's Guide: Revised Edition.* Cool Springs Press, 2002.

Bost, Toby. *North Carolina Gardener's Guide: Revised Edition.* Cool Springs Press, 2002.

Bradley, Fern and Barbara Ellis. *Rodale's All-New Encyclopedia of Organic Gardening.* Rodale Press, 1992.

Bridwell, Ferrell M. *Landscape Plants, Their Identification, Culture and Use: Second Edition.* Delmar Learning, 2002.

Brown, Deni. *The Herb Society of America Encyclopedia of Herbs and Their Uses.* DK Publishing, 2001.

Brown, George E. *The Pruning of Trees, Shrubs and Conifers.* Timber Press, 1995.

Bush-Brown, Louise, James Bush-Brown, Howard Erwin, Brooklyn Botanic Garden. *America's Garden Book: Revised Edition.* MacMillan, 1996.

Clarkson, Rosetta E. *Herbs, Their Culture and Uses.* MacMillan Publishing Co., 1949.

Clausen, Ruth Rogers and Nicolas Ekstrom. *Perennials for American Gardens.* Random House, 1989.

Colborn, Nigel. *Annuals and Bedding Plants.* Trafalgar Square Publishing

Cooke, Ian. *The Plant Finders Guide to Tender Perennials.* David & Charles Publishers, 2001.

Coombes, Allen J. *Dictionary of Plant Names.* Timber Press, 1985.

Courtright, Gordon. *Tropicals.* Timber Press, 1995.

Darke, Rick. *Ornamental Grasses for Your Garden.* Little Brown and Co., 1994.

Davis, Brian. *The Gardener's Illustrated Encyclopedia of Trees and Shrubs.* Rodale Press, 1987.

Den Ouden, P. and B.K. Boom. *Manuel of Cultivated Conifers.* Martinus Nijhoff, 1982.

Dictionary of Horticulture, National Gardening Association: Reprint Edition. Penguin USA, 1996.

Dirr, Michael A. *Manuel of Woody Landscape Plants: Fifth Edition.* Stipes Publishing Co., 1998.

DiSabato-Aust, Tracy. *The Well-Tended Perennial Garden.* Timber Press, 1998.

Edinger, Philip, Janet H. Sanchez, Sunset Books. *Annuals and Perennials.* Sunset Publishing Company, 2002.

Everett, Thomas H. *The New York Botanical Garden Illustrated Encyclopedia of Horticulture.* Garland Publishing, 1980.

Field Guide to North American Trees: Revised Edition. (Grolier)

Foster, Gordon.*Ferns to Know and Grow: Third Edition.* Timber Press, 1993.

Good Housekeeping Illustrated Encyclopedia of Gardening, The. William Morrow Hearst and Company, 1972.

Grey-Wilson, Christopher. *Poppies.* Timber Press, 2001.

Grey-Wilson, Christopher and Victoria Matthews. *Gardening with Climbers.* Timber Press, 1997.

Griffiths, Mark. *Index of Common Garden Plants: The New Royal Horticultural Society Dictionary.* MacMillan Press, 1994.

Grissel, Eric. *Thyme on My Hands: Reprint Edition.* Timber Press, 1995.

Halfacre, R. Gordon and Anne R. Shawcroft. *Landscape Plants of the Southeast: Fifth Edition.* Sparks Press, 1989.

Halpin, Anne. *Morning Glories and Moonflowers.* Simon & Schuster, 1996.

Harper, Pamela J. *Designing with Perennials.* Lark Books, 2001.

Hearst Garden Guides: Annuals. Ted Marston, ed. Hearst Books, 1993.

Hériteau, Jacqueline. *Glorious Gardens.* Stewart Tabori & Chang, 1998.

Hériteau, Jacqueline. *Virginia Gardener's Guide.* Cool Springs Press, 1997.

Hériteau, Jacqueline, H.M. Cathey, Staff of the National Arboretum. *The National Arboretum Book of Outstanding Garden Plants.* Simon & Schuster, 1990.

Hériteau, Jacqueline and Charles Thomas. *Water Gardens.* Houghton Mifflin Co., 1996.

Hériteau, Jacqueline and André Viette. *The American Horticultural Society Flower Finder.* Simon & Schuster, 1992.

Hortus Third. Staff of L. H. Bailey Hortorium, Cornell University. John Wiley & Sons, 1976.

Hoshizaki, Barbara. *Fern Growers Manual.* Random House, 1975.

Hudak, Joseph. *Gardening with Perennials Month by Month: Second Edition.* Timber Press, 1993.

Irwin, Howard S. *America's Garden Book.* Brooklyn Botanic Garden. John Wiley & Sons, 1996.

Iverson, Richard R. *The Exotic Garden, Designing with Tropical Plants in Almost Any Climate.* Taunton Press, 1999.

King, Michael and Piet Oudolf. *Gardening with Grasses.* Timber Press, 1998.

Leach, David G. *Rhododendrons of the World.* Scribner, 1961.

Loewer, Peter. *Growing and Decorating with Grasses.* Walker & Co., 1977.

Lowe, Judy. *Tennessee Gardener's Guide: Third Edition.* Cool Springs Press, 2002.

Massey, A.B. *Virginia Ferns and Fern Allies.*

Mazeo, Peter F. *Ferns and Fern Allies of Shenandoah National Park.*

McEwen, Currier. *Japanese Iris.* University Press of New England, 1990.

McEwen, Currier. *Siberian Iris.* Timber Press, 1996.

McVicar, Jekka. *Jekka's Culinary Herbs.* William Morrow Hearst and Co., 1997.

Moskowitz, Mark, Thomas Reinhardt, Martina Reinhardt. *Ornamental Grass Gardening.* Mark Moskowitz, 1994.

Naamlijist Van Vaste Planten. Van der Laar, Fortgens, Hoffman and Jong

Opler, Paul A. and Roger Tory Peterson. *A Field Guide to Eastern Butterflies (Peterson Field Guides).* Houghton Mifflin Co., 1998.

Ottesen, Carol. *Ornamental Grasses: Second Edition.* McGraw-Hill, 1995.

Poor, Janet M. and Nancy Brewster. *Plants That Merit Attention: Volume 1, Trees.* Timber Press, 1984.

Rice, Graham. *Discovering Annuals.* Timber Press, 1999.

Rice, Graham and Elizabeth Strangman. *The Gardener's Guide to Growing Hellebores.* Timber Press, 1993.

Rodale, J.I. and Staff. *Encyclopedia of Organic Gardening.* Rodale Press, 2000.

Rogers, Allan. *Peonies.* Timber Press, 1995.

Rohde, Eleanor Sinclair. *A Garden of Herbs.*

Shaver, Jesse M. *Ferns of the Eastern Central States.* Dover Publications, 1970.

Snodsmith, Ralph. *The Tri-State Gardener's Guide.* Cool Springs Press, 2001.

Southern Living Garden Guide: Annuals and Perennials. Lois Trigg Chaplin, ed. Oxmoor House, 1996.

Thomas, Graham Stuart. *Perennial Garden Plants, or, the Modern Florilegium: Third Edition.* Saga Press, 1990.

Trehane, Piers. *Index Hortensis: Volume 1, Perennials.* Timber Press, 1990.

Tripp, Kim and J.C. Raulston. *The Year in Trees.* Timber Press, 2001.

Van Gelderen, D.M. and J.R.P. van Hoey Smith. *Conifers: The Illustrated Encyclopedia.* Timber Press, 1996.

Viette, André and Stephen Still. *The Time Life Complete Gardener: Perennials.* Time Life.

Wyman, Donald. *Easy Care Ground Covers.*

Wyman, Donald. *Shrubs and Vines for American Gardens: Revised Edition.* Hungry Minds, 1996.

Wyman, Donald. *Wyman's Gardening Encyclopedia: Second Edition.* Simon and Schuster, 1987.

Yeo, Peter F. *Hardy Geraniums: Second Edition.* Timber Press, 2002.

Photography Credits

Thomas Eltzroth: pages 22, 23, 25, 27, 30, 31, 32, 33, 34, 35, 37, 38, 39, 40, 41, 44, 50, 53, 57, 60, 61, 62, 63, 64, 65, 66, 67, 69, 70, 71, 72, 73, 74, 75, 76, 77, 78, 81, 83, 85, 89, 90, 93, 94, 95, 96, 97, 100, 101, 102, 103, 104, 105, 106, 107, 111, 112, 114, 123, 124, 127, 130, 133, 137, 138, 143, 145, 148, 152, 153, 154, 155, 156, 157, 158, 159, 162, 164, 167, 172, 175, 176, 177, 178, 195, 200, 203, 205, 209, 214, 215, 216, 217, 227, 228, 229, 231, 234, back cover (first and second photos)

Liz Ball and Rick Ray: pages 26, 36, 45, 52, 55, 58, 59, 79, 80, 86, 87, 98, 99, 118, 122, 125, 128, 131, 144, 168, 179, 180, 181, 184, 186, 191, 192, 193, 194, 196, 198, 199, 202, 204, 206, 207, 210, 211, 212, 219, 223, 225, 230, 232, 233

Jerry Pavia: pages 16, 19, 24, 28, 29, 48, 54, 56, 68, 82, 84, 88, 91, 108, 113, 116, 117, 120, 126, 134, 135, 142, 146, 147, 149, 150, 160, 161, 166, 171, 173, 182, 183, 185, 187, 188, 189, 197, 201, 213, 220, 224, 226, 235, back cover (third photo)

André Viette: pages 46, 51, 109, 121, 129, 132, 139, 140, 141, 151, 170, 218, 221, 222, back cover (fourth photo)

Karen Bussolini: pages 8, 10, 13, 14, 17, 42, 43

Pamela Harper: pages 110, 165, 208

William Adams: page 115

Tim Boland and Laura Coit: page 169

Charles Mann: pages 92

Ralph Snodsmith: page 174

Mark Turner: page 136

Trademarked Product Credits

The following products, either trademarked or registered, appear in this book.

Bitrex® (Macfarlan Smith Ltd.)

Bulb-Tone®, Holly-Tone®, Plant-Tone®, and Rose-Tone® (Espoma Company)

First Choice® Sluggo Snail and Slug Bait (Western Farm Service, Inc.)

Icicle™ Pansies (Fernlea Flowers)

Osmocote® and Agriform™ (Scotts-Sierra Horticultural Products Company)

PermaTill® and VoleBloc™ (Carolina Stalite Company)

Princeton Sentry® Ginkgo (Princeton Nurseries)

Soil Moist™ (JRM Chemical, Inc.)

Stained Glassworks™ Coleus (The Flower Fields)

Star Showers® Virginia Creeper, *Parthenocissus quinquefolia* 'Monham' (Monrovia Nursery Company)

Supertunia™ Petunias (Proven Winners)

Surfinia® and Million Bells® Petunias (Jackson & Perkins Wholesale, Inc.)

Wave® and Tidal Wave® Petunias; Super Elfin® Impatiens (Pan American Seed Company)

Plant Index

Featured plant selections are indicated in **boldface**.

Meet the Authors

Jacqueline Hériteau and Holly Hunter Stonehill

Jacqueline (Jacqui) Hériteau and her daughter Holly Hunter Stonehill have gardened in many regions of New England—on a small farm in chilly northern Vermont; a warm sandy quarter acre in Chatham, Cape Cod; a development yard in urban Westport, Connecticut; a rooftop in Manhattan.

Holly's growing up years were divided between Manhattan and northwestern Connecticut, the foothill region of the Berkshire mountains where both authors and their families presently live. Holly is a graduate of the Professional Children's School in New York, and has crewed professionally on sailboats. With Jacqui, she has co-authored two cookbooks and originated the popular "Herbs & Spices" grow-and-cook recipe calendars. Cooking is their second passion.

Jacqui, whose background is in journalism, is known for her many books featuring environmentally sound plants and gardening methods. "It's my way to escape the heartbreak of failed plants and the tedious job of trying to figure out what went wrong and fix it."

Jacqui's first book, *The How To Grow and Cook It Book*, was a book club selection, as have been many of her books. She was General Editor for the authoritative *Good Housekeeping Illustrated Encyclopedia of Gardening*. In 1990 her *National Arboretum Book of Outstanding Garden Plants*, a Book-of-the-Month Club selection, brought her the American Nursery and Landscape Association's Communicator of the Year Award. In 1999 she was made a Fellow of the Garden Writers Association (GWA). She is the National Director of the Plant A Row for the Hungry campaign, an initiative of the Garden Writers Association.

Jacqui is the wife of artist Earl Hubbard. Holly is married to Robert J. Stonehill, Jr. Their joint family kitchen garden, which Holly designed, was featured in *Country Gardens Magazine*.